AutoCAD® 2022
Advanced

Learning Guide
Mixed Units - 1st Edition

AUTODESK.
Authorized Publisher

ASCENT - Center for Technical Knowledge®
AutoCAD® 2022
Advanced
Mixed Units - 1st Edition

Prepared and produced by:

ASCENT Center for Technical Knowledge
630 Peter Jefferson Parkway, Suite 175
Charlottesville, VA 22911

866-527-2368
www.ASCENTed.com

Lead Contributor: Renu Muthoo

Contents

© 2021, ASCENT - Center for Technical Knowledge®

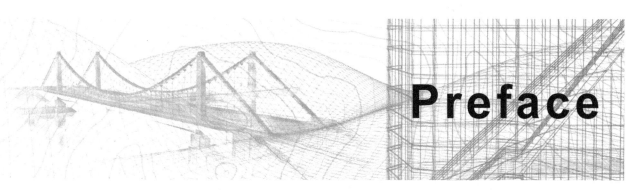

Preface

The *AutoCAD® 2022: Advanced* guide is designed for those using AutoCAD® 2022 with a Windows operating system. This guide is not designed for the AutoCAD for Mac software.

The *AutoCAD 2022: Advanced* guide introduces advanced techniques and teaches you to be proficient in your use of the AutoCAD software. This is done by teaching you how to recognize the best tool for the task, the best way to use that tool, and how to create new tools to accomplish tasks more efficiently.

Topics Covered

- Advanced text objects
- Working with tables
- Defining dynamic blocks and attributes
- Outputting and publishing files for review
- Collaboration and automation tools
- Creating, publishing, and customizing sheet sets
- Managing layers
- CAD management and system setup
- Enhancing productivity by customizing the AutoCAD interface
- Using macros and custom routines

Prerequisites

- Access to the 2022.0 version of the software, to ensure compatibility with this guide. Future software updates that are released by Autodesk may include changes that are not reflected in this guide. The practices and files included with this guide might not be compatible with prior versions (e.g., 2021).

- Completion of the *AutoCAD® 2022: Fundamentals* guide, or equivalent experience using the AutoCAD software.

Note on Software Setup

This guide assumes a standard installation of the software using the default preferences during installation. Lectures and practices use the standard software templates and default options for the Content Libraries.

Students and Educators Can Access Free Autodesk Software and Resources

Autodesk challenges you to get started with free educational licenses for professional software and creativity apps used by millions of architects, engineers, designers, and hobbyists today. Bring Autodesk software into your classroom, studio, or workshop to learn, teach, and explore real-world design challenges the way professionals do.

Get started today - register at the Autodesk Education Community and download one of the many Autodesk software applications available.

Visit www.autodesk.com/education/home/

Note: Free products are subject to the terms and conditions of the end-user license and services agreement that accompanies the software. The software is for personal use for education purposes and is not intended for classroom or lab use.

Lead Contributor: Renu Muthoo

Renu uses her instructional design training to develop courseware for AutoCAD and AutoCAD vertical products, Autodesk 3ds Max, Autodesk Showcase and various other Autodesk software products. She has worked with Autodesk products for the past 20 years with a main focus on design visualization software.

Renu holds a bachelor's degree in Computer Engineering and started her career as a Instructional Designer/Author where she co-authored a number of Autodesk 3ds Max and AutoCAD books, some of which were translated into other languages for a wide audience reach. In her next role as a Technical Specialist at a 3D visualization company, Renu used 3ds Max in real-world scenarios on a daily basis. There, she developed customized 3D web planner solutions to create specialized 3D models with photorealistic texturing and lighting to produce high quality renderings.

Renu Muthoo has been a Lead Contributor for *AutoCAD: Advanced* since 2016.

In This Guide

The following highlights the key features of this guide.

Feature	Description
Practice Files	The Practice Files page includes a link to the practice files and instructions on how to download and install them. The practice files are required to complete the practices in this guide.
Chapters	A chapter consists of the following - Learning Objectives, Instructional Content, Practices, Chapter Review Questions, and Command Summary. • **Learning Objectives** define the skills you can acquire by learning the content provided in the chapter. • **Instructional Content**, which begins right after Learning Objectives, refers to the descriptive and procedural information related to various topics. Each main topic introduces a product feature, discusses various aspects of that feature, and provides step-by-step procedures on how to use that feature. Where relevant, examples, figures, helpful hints, and notes are provided. • **Practice** for a topic follows the instructional content. Practices enable you to use the software to perform a hands-on review of a topic. It is required that you download the practice files (using the link found on the Practice Files page) prior to starting the first practice. • **Chapter Review Questions**, located close to the end of a chapter, enable you to test your knowledge of the key concepts discussed in the chapter. • **Command Summary** concludes a chapter. It contains a list of the software commands that are used throughout the chapter and provides information on where the command can be found in the software.
Appendices	Appendices provide additional information to the main course content. It could be in the form of instructional content, practices, tables, projects, or skills assessment.

Practice Files

To download the practice files for this guide, use the following steps:

1. Type the URL **exactly as shown below** into the address bar of your Internet browser, to access the Course File Download page.

   Note: If you are using the ebook, you do not have to type the URL. Instead, you can access the page simply by clicking the URL below.

   ## https://www.ascented.com/getfile/id/paracheiroPF

2. On the Course File Download page, click the **DOWNLOAD NOW** button, as shown below, to download the .ZIP file that contains the practice files.

3. Once the download is complete, unzip the file and extract its contents.

   The recommended practice files folder location is:
   C:\AutoCAD 2022 Advanced Practice Files

   Note: It is recommended that you do not change the location of the practice files folder. Doing so may cause errors when completing the practices.

Stay Informed!

To receive information about upcoming events, promotional offers, and complimentary webcasts, visit:

www.ASCENTed.com/updates

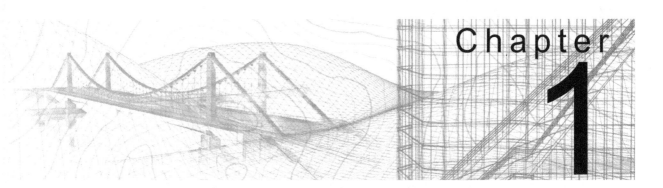

Introduction

Learn how to use the AutoCAD® software by completing a practice that will help you familiarize yourself with the structure of the practices available in this training guide, and learn the concepts that you are expected to know.

Learning Objective in This Chapter

- Review the use of the AutoCAD software by drawing, editing, and dimensioning a cross-section.

Practice 1a

Introduction

Practice Objective

- Review the use of the AutoCAD software by drawing, editing, and dimensioning a cross-section.

In this practice, you will draw, edit, and dimension a simple cross-section using a variety of tools (such as drawing aids and shortcut menu options), as shown in Figure 1–1. The purpose of this practice is to familiarize you with the style of the practices in this training guide and to review how to use the AutoCAD software.

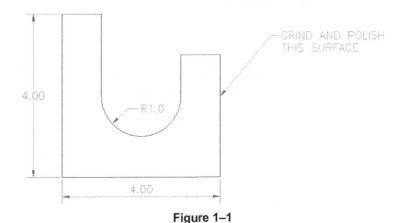

Figure 1–1

1. Open **Cross Section-I.dwg** from the practice files folder.

If *Object Snap is not displayed in the Status Bar, expand*

≡ *(Customization) and select 2D Object Snap.*

2. In the Status Bar, expand (Object Snap) and select only **Endpoint** and toggle **Object Snap On**.

3. Start the **Polyline** command. Use the **Endpoint** object snap to pick the left endpoint of the top right horizontal line.

4. Toggle (Polar Tracking) on if it is not already done.

5. Move the cursor straight down, type **1**, and press <Enter>.

6. Right-click in the drawing window and select **Arc**. Move the crosshair horizontally to the left, type **2**, and press <Enter> to select a point two units to the left.

7. Right-click in the drawing window and select **Line**. Draw a polyline segment straight up and pick the right endpoint of the top left horizontal line.

8. Right-click and select **Enter** to end the command.

9. Without starting another command, select the new polyline object that you just created to display the grips.

10. Right-click, expand **Polyline**, and select **Edit Polyline**. Select the **Join** option. Select all of the other lines in the drawing and press <Enter>. Press <Enter> again or press <Esc> to end the command. Note that the polyline and all the other lines are converted into a single object.

11. Select the polyline object (single object), the leader, and the Mtext note. Right-click and select **Move**. Move the objects **3 units** to the right.

12. In the ribbon, in the *Annotate* tab>Dimensions panel, expand the Layer Control and select the layer **Dimensions**.

13. Create a linear dimension on the bottom of the object and a radius dimension on the arc, as shown in Figure 1–1. When you are done dimensioning, press <Esc> to end the dimension command.

14. Select only the linear dimension, hover the cursor over the dimension grip for the dimension text and select **Above Dim Line** from the multifunctional grip list. The text moves above the line. Press <Esc> to exit the dimension.

15. Select the radius dimension, right-click and change the *Precision* to **0.0**. The text changes to **R1.0**.

16. Add a linear dimension to the left vertical line.

17. Double-click on the magenta text and modify it to say **GRIND AND POLISH THIS SURFACE**.

18. Open the Layer Properties Manager. Select the layer **Object** and set it to be active if it is not already active.

19. Right-click in the Layer Properties Manager and select **Select All but Current**. Freeze the selected layers and close the Layer Properties Manager. Only the PLine object displays in the drawing window without any dimensions or text.

20. Save and close the drawing.

Advanced Text Objects

When annotating a drawing, there are a number of different tools that can be used to accurately and efficiently communicate the information in a drawing. These include the annotation scale features to efficiently reuse and annotate objects and views. In addition, you learn how to use fields and control the drawing order of text and other objects.

Learning Objectives in This Chapter

- Create annotative styles for dimensions, multileaders, text, etc.
- Add annotative objects at different scales.
- Add fields to automate textual information in blocks and attributes.
- Control the display of objects and annotations in relation to items around them.

2.1 Annotation Scale Overview

The Annotation Scale features enable you to avoid creating multiple copies of the same annotation objects at different scales. This makes it easier to quickly dimension drawings that contain views at different scales. Using Annotation Scale, you can control which dimensions, text, etc., display in each scaled detail viewport, as shown in Figure 2–1.

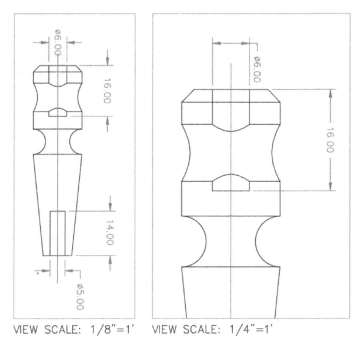

VIEW SCALE: 1/8"=1'   VIEW SCALE: 1/4"=1'

Figure 2–1

- Annotation objects include Single Line Text, Multiline Text, Text Styles, Dimensions, Dimension Styles, Multileaders, Multileader Styles, Geometric Tolerances, Blocks, Attributes, and Hatches.

Hint: Linetypes and Annotation Scale

Linetype spacing is controlled by the Annotation Scale through the **msltscale** system variable. This variable is set per drawing using templates.

- When set to **1** (the default in the template files supplied with the AutoCAD® software), linetypes are automatically scaled to the annotation scale.

- When set to **0**, they are not scaled to the annotation scale.

Working with Annotative Styles

*The **Annotative** option is also available in the Hatch Editor contextual tab and the Properties palette for various objects, such as Tolerance.*

Annotative styles are set by selecting the **Annotative** option in the Dimension Style, Multileader Style, Block Definition, Attribute Definition, and Text Style dialog boxes, as shown in Figure 2–2.

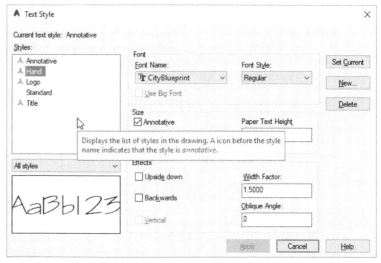

Figure 2–2

When set, you can identify an annotative style in one of the following ways:

- ⅄ (Annotation) displays next to the style name in the Text Style dialog box and in the list of style names in the *Home* tab>Annotation panel, as shown in Figure 2–3.

The Text Style, Dimension Style, and Multileader Style are all set to be Annotative and display the Annotation icon.

Figure 2–3

- ⅄ (Annotation) also displays when you hover the cursor over an annotative object in the drawing window, as shown in Figure 2–4.

Figure 2–4

How To: Add Annotative Objects

1. In a layout, switch to Paper Space and set up the viewports as required.
2. Select a viewport by selecting its border.
3. In the Status Bar, click **Viewport Scale** and select a scale in the list, as shown in Figure 2–5. The Annotation Scale automatically updates to match. Changing the Annotation Scale also changes the Viewport Scale.

Figure 2–5

4. (Optional) Click 🔒 (Lock/Unlock Viewport) to lock the viewport so that the scale and location cannot change.

- You can quickly lock or unlock viewports using 🔒 (Lock/Unlock Viewport) in the Status Bar, as shown in Figure 2–6.

Viewport unlocked

Viewport locked

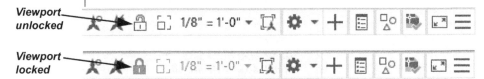

Figure 2–6

5. When you are ready to start adding annotative objects, activate one of the viewports.
6. Use annotative styles when creating the various annotation objects. They can be scaled to suit each viewport and do not display in viewports to which other annotation scales have been assigned.

- The annotative scale can also be set in the Properties of specific objects, such as text or dimensions, as shown in Figure 2–7.

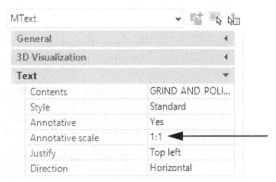

Figure 2–7

Hint: Changing Scale of Annotative Objects

In a viewport, when **Zoom** commands are used or the scale changes in the Viewports toolbar, the scale of the annotative objects is not modified. You must modify the Viewport Scale in the Status Bar for the annotative objects to change scale.

Viewing Annotative Objects at Different Scales

Annotation Scale is linked to the Viewport Scale, therefore, annotative objects (such as dimensions and text) display in layout viewports that have the same scale. If the Viewport Scale is changed, the annotative objects are not displayed. To ensure they remain displayed, add annotation scales to objects enabling them to be displayed in viewports of different scales. For example, you might want the room names to display in each view while the dimensions display in specific viewports, as shown in Figure 2–8.

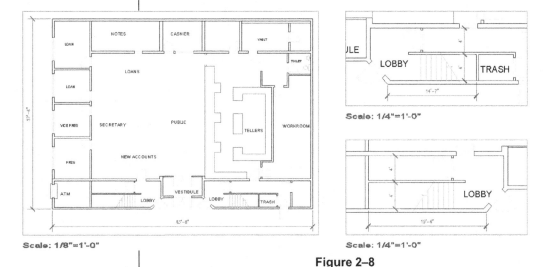

Scale: 1/4"=1'-0"

Scale: 1/8"=1'-0"

Scale: 1/4"=1'-0"

Figure 2–8

When a viewport's Viewport Scale is changed, the annotation objects displayed within it change as well. How the objects behave depends on how you set the annotation visibility and whether or not the scale is automatically added to the object.

	Annotation Visibility (Show annotation objects - At current scale): When toggled **Off**, only annotative objects with the current scale display. It is recommended that you use this option by default. It displays objects that are to be plotted.
	Annotation Visibility (Show annotation objects - Always): When toggled **On**, annotative objects for all of the scales display. Use when you need to add or remove an annotative object to the current scale.
	Add scales to annotative objects when the annotation scale changes: When toggled **Off**, annotation scales are not automatically added to objects in the viewport.
	Add scales to annotative objects when the annotation scale changes: When toggled **On**, any annotation objects in the drawing are updated to match the new annotation scale.

- When you add a scale to an object, a scale representation of that object is created.

- When you select an annotative object that has more than one scale, all of its scale representations display, as shown on the right in Figure 2–9. There is no limit to the number of scales that can be added to an object. However, too many scales can be confusing when you use grips to edit the object.

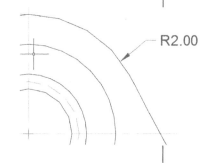

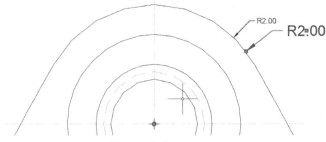

Figure 2–9

- If you modify the information contained in the annotation, all of the scale representations are updated.

- You can use grips to edit each scale representation separately in its associated viewport to suit the location.

Annotation Scale and Model Space

You can annotate objects in Model Space by setting the Annotation Scale in the Status Bar. It is linked to the Viewport Scale and displays in viewports that use the same Annotation Scale, as shown in Figure 2–10.

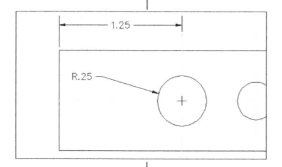
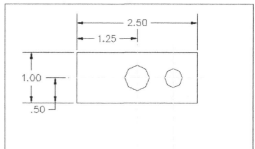

Figure 2–10

Modifying Annotative Object Scales

When you add annotative objects to a viewport, they automatically use the scale of the viewport. If you need to change the scale or move annotative objects out of a viewport, you can modify the scales associated with the objects or with the viewport.

- These tools are available in the *Annotate* tab>Annotation Scaling panel, or when you right-click on an annotative object, as shown in Figure 2–11.

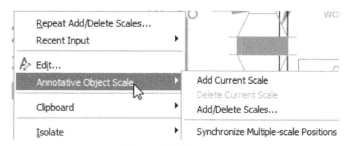

Figure 2–11

- If you want to display an annotative object that is not displayed in the current viewport scale, toggle on ![icon] (Show annotation objects - Always) in the Status Bar to display all of the scale representations of the objects. Right-click on the object that you want to include in your scale, expand **Annotative Object Scale** and select **Add Current Scale**.

- To display an annotative object in several viewports that use different scales, right-click on an annotative object, select

  Add/Delete Scales or click 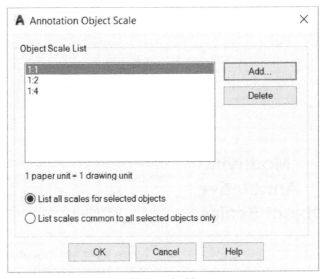 (Add/Delete Scale), and then select an annotative object. This opens the Annotation Object Scale dialog box (shown in Figure 2–12), where you can click **Add** to set the annotative scales that are used in each viewport.

Figure 2–12

- You can change the locations of individual scale representations. If you need to return them to one position, right-click, expand **Annotative Object Scale**, and select **Synchronize Multiple-scale Positions** or in the Annotation

  Scaling panel, click (Sync Scale Positions) to move all of the related representations to the same location as the selected object.

- If you do not want an annotative object to display in the current viewport, but want it to be visible in another viewport

  at a different scale, click (Delete) to delete the current scale.

Hint: Editing the Scale List

The Scale List is stored in each drawing file and is accessed using the Edit Drawing Scales dialog box, as shown in Figure 2–13. The list can vary from drawing to drawing. Therefore, if you want to use a standard scale list in each drawing you should create it in a template drawing.

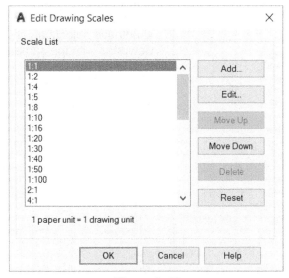

Figure 2–13

- To edit the Scale List, click **Viewport Scale** in the Status Bar and select **Custom...** at the bottom of the list.

- You can also click ⚎ (Scale List) in the *Annotate* tab> Annotation Scaling panel, as shown in Figure 2–14.

Figure 2–14

Practice 2a | Annotation Scale

Practice Objective

- Add annotative objects that are to be displayed in viewports that are set at a specific scale.

In this practice, you will specify the annotative styles for text, dimensions, multileaders, and hatches. You will then add annotative objects at different scales to only be displayed in viewports with the same scale setting, as shown in Figure 2–15.

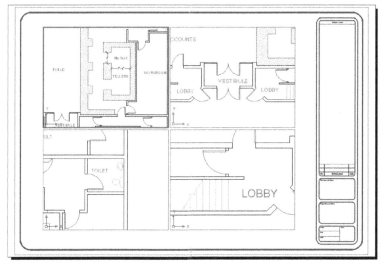

Figure 2–15

Task 1 - Annotative text and dimensions.

1. Open **Branch Bank-A.dwg** from the practice files folder.

2. In the *Home* tab>expanded Annotation panel, set the *Text, Dimension*, and *Multileader Style(s)* to **Annotative**, as shown in Figure 2–16.

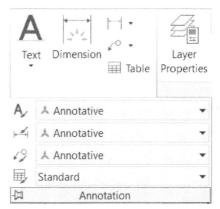

Figure 2–16

3. Switch to the **D-Sized** layout.

4. In Paper Space, select the border of the *Tellers* (top left viewport that displays the *Tellers* area) viewport. In the Status Bar, the Viewport Scale displays **1/4" = 1'-0"**. Press <Esc> to release the selected viewport.

5. Repeat the last step to verify that each viewport is displaying the correct Viewport Scale. The scales should be:

   • *Vestibule viewport:* **3/8"=1'-0"**

   • *Restroom viewport:* **1/2"=1'-0"**

   • *Lobby viewport:* **3/4"=1'-0"**

6. Select all four viewports. In the Status Bar, click

   🔒 (Lock/Unlock Viewport) to lock the viewports. Press <Esc> to release all selected viewports.

You can display the Layer Control in the Quick Access Toolbar for easy access.

7. Set the layer **Dimensions** to be current. Double-click inside the *Tellers* viewport to make it active. Add the text and dimensions, as shown in Figure 2–17. Note that these only display in the current viewport.

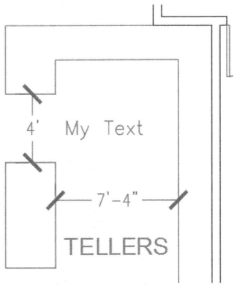

Figure 2–17

Task 2 - Set the annotative hatching.

---

1. Verify that the *Tellers* viewport is still active (or activate it) and set the layer **Hatching** to be current.

2. Verify that both Annotative options (and) are toggled off in the Status Bar.

3. Start the **Hatch** command.

4. In the *Hatch Creation* contextual tab>Options panel, click

   (Annotative) (highlighted).

5. In the Pattern panel, select **ANSI31**.

6. In the Properties panel, set the *Scale* to **1**.

7. Add hatching to the three counter areas inside the Tellers viewport.

8. In the Close panel, click (Close Hatch Creation).

9. In the *Vestibule* viewport, note that the counter area (top right corner) does not display the hatching. Since the hatching is annotative with a different annotative scale, it is only displayed in the *Tellers* viewport.

Task 3 - Add/delete scales.

1. Select the hatch object that you just created.

2. Right-click on the selected hatching, expand Annotative Object Scale and select **Add/Delete Scales**. The Annotation Object Scale dialog box opens. Note that only the **1/4"=1'-0"** annotation scale displays.

3. Click **Add** to add a scale. The Add Scales to Object dialog box opens.

4. Select **3/8"=1'-0"**, which is the scale of the *Vestibule* viewport.

5. Click **OK**. The scale is listed in the Annotation Object Scale dialog box.

6. Click **OK**. The hatching now displays in the *Vestibule* viewport because it matches the scale of the vestibule.

Task 4 - Set the annotation object display.

1. Switch to the *Model* tab and note how the annotative objects (i.e., the hatch, text, and dimensions) display.

2. In the Status Bar, note that [icon] (Show annotation objects - Always) is toggled on. Click on it to toggle it to display

   [icon] (Show annotation objects - At current scale). Note how the annotation objects disappear.

3. Save and close the drawing.

2.2 Using Fields

Fields are text objects that are designed to hold information that updates in a drawing when the base information changes, as shown in Figure 2–18. Fields can contain information, such as Date, Filename, Sheet Number, or Login name. They can be used in standard multiline text objects and in attributes and tables.

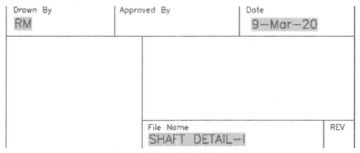

Figure 2–18

- Fields can be based on standard data or any property of an AutoCAD object, any AutoCAD system variable, and various other data information.

The Field dialog box can be opened in the following ways:

- In the ribbon, *Insert* tab>Data panel, click ⊞Ａ (Field)

- *Text Editor* contextual tab>Insert panel in the Multiline Text Editor

- The shortcut menu in a Table cell

- The Attribute Definition dialog box

- The Enhanced Attribute Editor

How To: Insert Fields

1. In the ribbon, *Insert* tab>Data panel, click 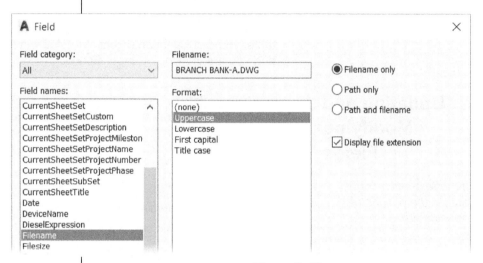 (Field).
2. In the Field dialog box, select the field that you want to include, as shown in Figure 2–19.

Figure 2–19

3. Select the required format and other options for the field.
4. Click **OK** to place the field in the drawing.

• When you select a field in the *Field names* area, the list of options changes in the *Format* area. For example, for the *Filename* field, you can specify the case for the text and whether or not to include the path; for the *Date* field, you can specify the date format, such as **9 March 2020** or **09/03/2020**, as shown in Figure 2–20.

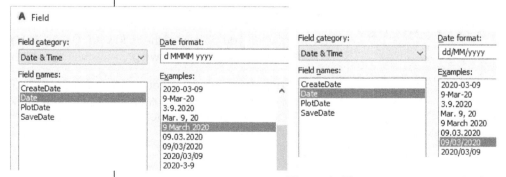

Figure 2–20

- You can select a *Field category* in the Field dialog box to filter the list of fields and narrow the options.

- The field displays with the current value highlighted in gray (the gray background does not plot). You can toggle it off in the Options dialog box in the *User Preferences* tab>*Fields* area by clearing the **Display background of fields** option.

- When you are working with *Object* fields in a text object or table, you can select an object even if it is in Model Space and you are working in Paper Space.

Updating and Modifying Fields

If the text editor is not active, the options are not available.

To manually update or modify a field, double-click on the text to open it in the text editor. Then right-click in the field and select the appropriate option from the shortcut menu, as shown in Figure 2–21.

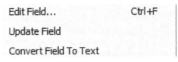

Edit Field...	Ctrl+F
Update Field	
Convert Field To Text	

Figure 2–21

Edit Field...	Opens the Field dialog box in which you can change the format, etc.
Update Field	Forces an update of the field, regardless of the automatic update settings.
Convert Field to Text	The field background is removed and the object becomes plain text.

- Fields that do not have a current value assigned, display as four dashes (----).

Field Settings

By default, the current values for fields update automatically in a drawing when you do any of the following: **Open**, **Save**, **Plot**, **eTransmit**, or **Regen** the drawing.

- To control which actions cause an update, use the Field Update Settings dialog box, as shown in Figure 2–22. Put a check in the options to automatically update fields.

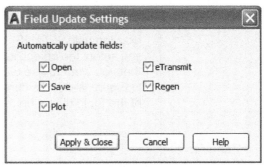

Figure 2–22

- To access the Field Update Settings dialog box, in the Options dialog box>*User Preferences* tab, click **Field Update Settings**, as shown in Figure 2–23.

Figure 2–23

Object Fields

Any property of an AutoCAD object can be used as a field. In the example shown in Figure 2–24, the fields display the area of several boundary polylines. When the boundaries are changed, the fields update to display the new area values of the polylines.

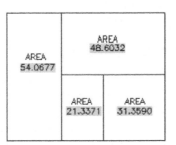
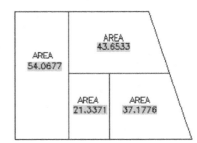

Figure 2–24

The *Object* field requires you to select a specific object in the drawing using 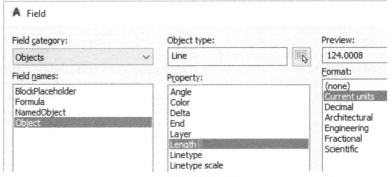 (Select Objects) in the Field dialog box. After you select the object, its properties are listed. Select the property that you want to use (such as *Length* in the case of a line shown in Figure 2–25). Its current value displays in the top right corner of the Field dialog box.

Figure 2–25

Fields in Blocks

Most fields can be included in a block definition and update within the block. For instance, the *Filename* field in a block updates with the name of the drawing file in which the block is inserted.

- Fields that do not update in blocks include those in the *Plot* category (*PaperSize*, *PlotScale*, etc.) and in the *Sheet Set* category. The value of these fields depends on the layout in which they have been placed or their location in Model/Paper Space.

- You can update the block information in the Properties dialog box. In the Application Menu, expand Drawing Utilities and select **Drawing Properties**. In the Properties dialog box, in the *Summary* tab, fill in the information. Save the drawing to update the information.

- Similar to block insertions, fields in XREFs use values from the host file (such as the filename).

Fields in Attributes

Fields can also be added to blocks by using a field to define the value of an attribute. For example, data in a title block, such as Filename or Title, would typically be created as attributes. If you use fields, these attributes automatically obtain their values from the drawing's properties. Having the field as an attribute value makes it easier to edit the value in the block as required.

- You can set the attribute value of a field in the Attribute Definition dialog box when you create the attribute or by editing it later.

- In the Attribute Definition dialog box, click (Insert Field) next to the *Default* field, as shown in Figure 2–26.

Figure 2–26

- For an existing attribute, double-click on the block to open it in the Block Editor and then double-click on the attribute to open the Enhanced Attribute Editor. You can assign a field to an attribute by right-clicking in the value field and selecting **Insert Field**.

- Alternatively, in the *Home* tab>Block panel or in the *Insert* tab>Block panel, expand

  the Edit Attribute flyout and click (Single). Select the block to open the Enhanced Attribute Editor.

Practice 2b | Fields

Practice Objectives

- Automate information in a title block by adding fields.
- Update fields from blocks.

In this practice, you will add fields to automate some of the information in a title block, as shown in Figure 2–27.

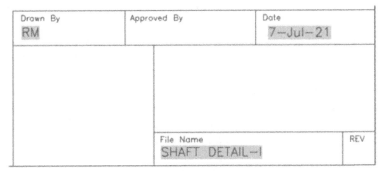

| Drawn By | Approved By | Date |
| RM | | 7–Jul–21 |

File Name
SHAFT DETAIL–1
REV

Figure 2–27

Task 1 - Add fields and automate the information.

1. Open **TBLK-A Landscape.dwg** from the practice files folder.

2. Zoom in on the title block information in the lower right corner.

3. In the *Insert* tab>Data panel, click 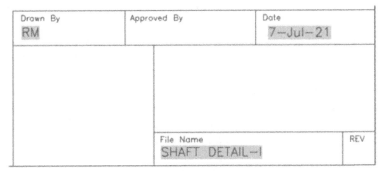 (Field).

4. In the Field dialog box, set the *Field category* to **Date & Time**. For *Field names,* select **SaveDate**, and in *Examples,* select the format that displays the current date in the form **d-MMM-yy** (For example, **7-Jul-21**). Click **OK** to close the dialog box.

5. In the *Date* area, pick a point to place the date in the title block. Note that the date when this file was last saved is displayed.

6. In the *Drawn By* area, double-click on **xxx** to edit this text. In the Text Editor, delete **xxx**. In the *Text Editor* contextual tab> Insert panel, click (Field).

7. In the Field dialog box, change the *Field category* to **Document**. For *Field names,* select **Author**, leave the *Format* as **(none)**, and click **OK** to close the dialog box.

8. Click ✔ (Close Text Editor). The field displays as ---- because a drawing author has not been specified in the file.

9. Repeat the process and edit the **xxx** in the *File Name* area. In the Text Editor, delete **xxx**. In the *Text Editor* contextual tab> Insert panel, click (Field).

10. In the Field dialog box, change the *Field category* to **Document**, if required. For *Field names*, select **Filename** and set the *Format* to **Uppercase**. Select **Filename only** and clear the **Display file extension** option. Click **OK** to close the Field dialog box and then close the Text Editor.

11. Save the drawing. Note that your date updates to the current date as the **Save** command automatically updates the values for fields. Close the drawing.

Task 2 - Update fields from blocks.

---

1. Open **Shaft Detail-I.dwg** from the practice files folder.

2. In the **A-Sized** layout, using the Blocks palette, insert the file **Titleblock-Shaft.dwg** (located in your practice files folder) as a block, with its insertion point as **0,0,0** in addition to the default scale and rotation. Close the Blocks palette.

3. Zoom in on the title block information.

4. In the Application Menu, expand Drawing Utilities, and select **Drawing Properties**. In the Properties dialog box, select the *Summary* tab. Enter your initials as the *Author* and click **OK**.

5. Save the drawing. The information in the fields updates with your initials in the *Drawn By* field, and the current date in the *Date* field.

6. Close the drawing.

Practice 2c | Object Fields

Practice Objective

- Display numerical values of closed polylines by adding text with fields.

In this practice, you will add text with fields that display the area of a polyline, as shown in Figure 2–28.

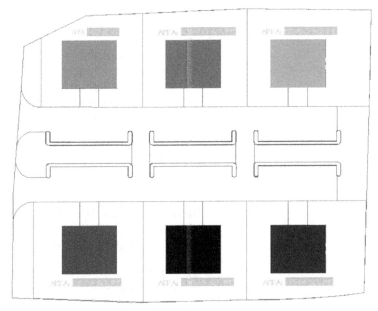

Figure 2–28

1. Open **Industrial Park-A.dwg** from the practice files folder.

2. Set the current layer to **Text**.

3. Start the **Multiline Text** command. Near the top of the top left lot, pick a point to place the text. Using the <Down Arrow>, select the **Height** option and set the *Height* to **5'**. Select the other corner for the text.

4. In the Text Editor, type **AREA:**. In the *Text Editor* contextual tab>Insert panel, click (Field).

5. In the Field dialog box, set the *Field* category to **Objects** and for *Field names*, select **Object**.

6. In the *Object type* area, click (Select object) and select the magenta polyline around the lot in which you are placing the text.

7. In the Field dialog box, set the following, as shown in Figure 2–29:
   - *Property*: **Area**
   - *Format*: **Architectural**
   - *Precision:* **0**

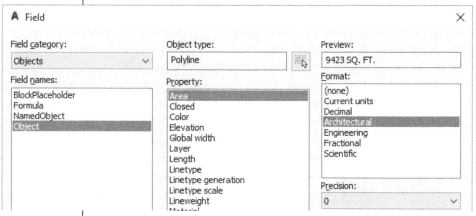

Figure 2–29

8. Click **OK** to close the Field dialog box.

Your font might be different than the font shown in Figure 2–28.

9. In the Text Editor, increase the width to display the information in a single line, as shown in Figure 2–30. Click (Close Text Editor) to end the **Multiline Text** command.

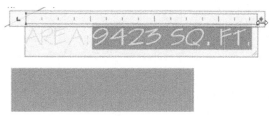

Figure 2–30

10. Repeat Steps 3 to 8 in several of the lots. (You cannot copy the text because you have to select a different polyline object corresponding to each plot.)

11. Use grips to stretch one of the boundary polylines to make it larger.

12. **Regen** the drawing to update the field. The area value changes based on the changes made to the polyline.

13. Save and close the drawing.

2.3 Controlling the Draw Order

As you are annotating a drawing, you might need to adjust the order of the overlapping objects. For example, you might have hatching on top of text but actually need to have the text on top of the hatching, as shown in Figure 2–31. You might also need to have a boundary around the text so that it stands out more prominently.

Figure 2–31

You can use several tools to make these adjustments, three of which include the following:

Draw Order

You can also select a draw order by right-clicking on an object and selecting Draw Order.

When you create new objects, they are created on top of existing objects in the drawing by default. Some objects, such as a wide polyline or hatch, can cover objects that were drawn earlier.

- You can select the **Draw Order** tool in the *Home* tab> expanded Modify panel.

- The various Draw Order options are listed as shown in Figure 2–32. You can change the objects to a different draw order by selecting the required option in the drop-down list.

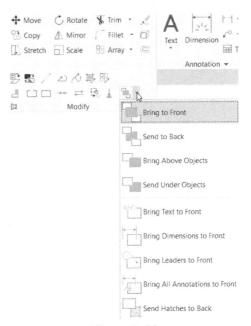

Figure 2–32

A few of the most commonly used options include:

(Bring to Front)	Puts the object at the top of the drawing order (in front of all of the other objects).
Send to Back)	Puts the object at the bottom of the drawing order (behind all of the other objects).
(Bring All Annotations to Front)	Puts all of the text, leader, and dimension objects at the top of the drawing order (in front of all of the other objects).
(Send Hatches to Back)	Puts hatches at the bottom of the drawing order (behind all of the other objects).

- When you assign a Draw Order to an object it maintains its position even after editing.

- A copied object inherits the Draw Order status of the original object.

Draw Order of Hatching

You can set the draw order of hatches while creating them by selecting an option in the *Hatch Creation* contextual tab> expanded Options panel. The **Send Behind Boundary** option makes it easier to select the hatch boundary after the hatching has been applied. The other options are shown in Figure 2–33.

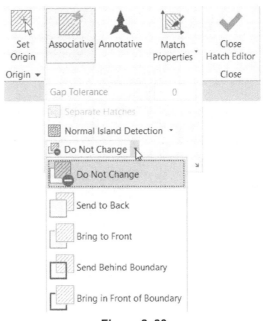

Figure 2–33

Masking Annotation Objects

You can mask objects behind text and dimension text. This is useful when you need to place text in front of other objects but do not want to trim the objects where they overlap, as shown in Figure 2–34.

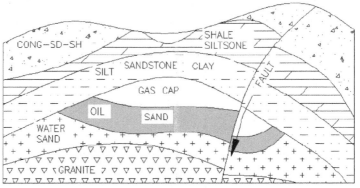

Figure 2–34

- You can select **A** (Background Mask) in the *Text Editor* contextual tab>Style panel.

- In the *Multiline Text* field, right-click in the Edit window and select **Background Mask**. The Background Mask dialog box opens, as shown in Figure 2–35.

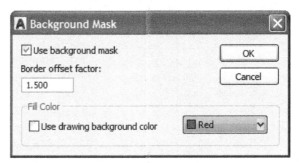

Figure 2–35

- You can select **Use background mask** and then set the **Border offset factor** (the space around the text) and the **Fill color**. You can use the background of the drawing or any other color as the fill color.

- The *Border offset factor* also sets the location of the text frame which can be toggled on using the Properties palette, as shown in Figure 2–36.

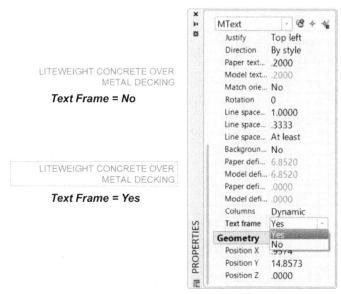

Figure 2–36

- You can add a mask to existing text or modify an existing mask. Open the text in the Text Editor again and right-click to open the Background Mask dialog box.

- Dimension text can be assigned a background mask in the dimension style. Set the *Fill color* in the *Text* tab in the Dimension Style dialog box to use the required mask, as shown in Figure 2–37.

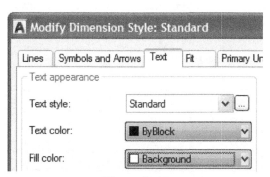

Figure 2–37

In the Home tab>
expanded Modify panel,
in the Draw Order
drop-down list, you can
use ABC (Bring Text to

Front) and (Bring
Dimensions to Front).

- Text and dimension text objects need to be in front in the Draw Order for the text mask to be visible. You can move all of the text and dimensions to the front by typing **texttofront** in the Command Line. You can bring **Text**, **Dimensions**, **Leaders**, or **All**, to the front, as shown in Figure 2–38.

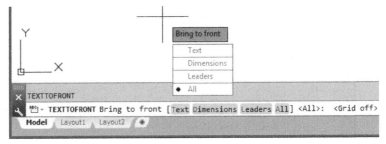

Figure 2–38

Adding a Wipeout

Another useful tool for overlapping objects, hatches, or other images is **Wipeout**. A wipeout puts a blank image on top of objects in an area that you want to mask or hide. For example, you could use a wipeout to mask objects behind text (as shown in Figure 2–39) or to break a dimension line where another one passes over it.

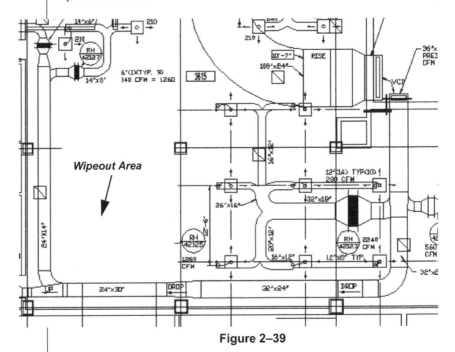

Figure 2–39

- A wipeout can be defined in two ways: using a polyline as the outline for the wipeout or picking points.

How To: Create a Wipeout

1. In the ribbon, *Home* tab>expanded Draw panel, or in the *Annotate* tab>Markup panel, click (Wipeout).
2. Pick points to define the boundary of the wipeout or press <Enter> to select a polyline.
3. If you select a polyline, you are prompted to erase it.
4. Press <Enter> to finish selecting points and create the wipeout.
5. Use the **Draw Order** command to move objects above or below the wipeout.
6. In the **Wipeout** command, use the **Frames** option to toggle off the frames around the wipeouts when you are finished, as shown in Figure 2–40.

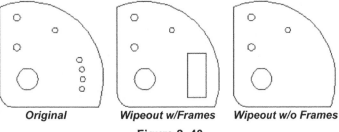

Original *Wipeout w/Frames* *Wipeout w/o Frames*

Figure 2–40

Options

First Point	Enables you to pick points to define the area to mask.
Polyline	Enables you to use an existing polyline to mask the area. The polyline must be closed, must be made of straight line segments, and cannot have a width. Only keep the polyline if you need to use it for plotting purposes.
Frames	Toggles the frames around all of the wipeouts in the drawing on, off, or to be displayed in the drawing window without being printed on the drawing sheets. If you need to select wipeout objects, toggle the frames **On** or **Visible**.

Practice 2d

Controlling the Draw Order

Practice Objective

- Control the display of objects by changing their overlapping order, adding a background mask to text, and covering part of the drawing with a Wipeout object.

In this practice, you will use the **Draw Order** command to control the display of an object, add a background mask to text, and add a Wipeout to cover part of a drawing, as shown in Figure 2–41.

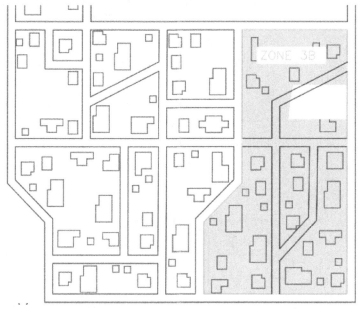

Figure 2–41

1. Open **Subdivision-F.dwg** from the practice files folder.

2. Note a solid yellow hatch in the right side of the plan. In the *Home* tab>expanded Modify panel, expand the Draw Order flyout and click (Send Hatches to Back). The buildings and roads that were hidden behind the hatch are now displayed, because the hatch is now behind them.

3. In the *Home* tab>expanded Modify panel, expand the Draw Order flyout and click (Send to Back) and select various buildings in Zone 3B (the yellow hatched area). Press <Enter> to exit the command. The selected buildings disappear as they are now hidden behind the hatch.

*Alternatively, right-click inside the Text Editor and select **Background Mask**.*

4. Zoom in on the **ZONE 3B** text in the upper part of the yellow hatch area. The lines of the buildings make the text difficult to read.

5. Double-click on the text to open the Text Editor. In the *Text Editor* contextual tab>Style panel, select A (Background Mask).

6. In the Background Mask dialog box, select **Use background mask** and **Use drawing background color** for the *Fill Color*. Click **OK** to apply the settings. Close the *Text Editor* contextual tab. Note a background rectangular mask for the text.

7. Draw a closed polyline around one of the blocks of buildings and some portion of the street in Zone 3B, as shown in Figure 2–42.

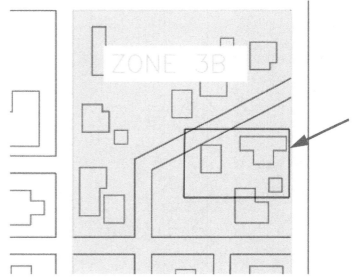

Figure 2–42

8. In the *Home* tab>expanded Draw panel, click (Wipeout).

9. Press <Enter> for the **Polyline** option and select the polyline that you just drew. Select **Yes** at the prompt to erase the polyline. The wipeout masks all of the objects enclosed in the polyline because it is drawn on top of them.

10. Start the **Wipeout** command again. Type **F** and press
    <Enter> to use the **Frames** option. Select **OFF** to toggle off
    the frame.

11. In the *Home* tab>expanded Modify panel, expand the Draw
    Order drop-down list and click (Bring to Front). Select
    anywhere on the street that is covered by the wipeout. Press
    <Enter>. Note that the street becomes visible over the
    wipeout.

12. Save and close the drawing.

Chapter Review Questions

1. What are the annotation scales linked to such that the annotative objects (e.g., dimensions and texts) display in the layout viewports that have the same scale?

    a. Dimension Style

    b. Text Style

    c. Linetype scale factor

    d. Viewport Scale

2. What is the purpose of a field in the AutoCAD software?

    a. Displays text that updates when the base information changes, such as a date or filename.

    b. Enables you to group objects in a selection set.

    c. Masks or hides a specified area of the drawing.

    d. Applies a pattern or color to a selected region.

3. By default, which actions can cause the values of fields to update automatically?

    a. Open, Update, Regen

    b. Open, Plot, eTransmit

    c. Save, Plot, Scale

    d. eTransmit, Save, Update

4. Which tool can be used to mask or hide a portion of a drawing by placing a blank image on top?

    a. **Block**

    b. **Image**

    c. **Field**

    d. **Wipeout**

5. To which object type does the **Background Mask** tool apply?

    a. Multiline text

    b. Multileaders

    c. Blocks

    d. Layers

6. You can only use polylines to define a wipeout area.

   a. True

   b. False

Command Summary

Button	Command	Location
	Annotation Visibility	• **Status Bar**
	Add scales to annotative objects when the annotation scale changes	• **Status Bar**
A	**Background Mask**	• **Ribbon:** *Text Editor* contextual tab> Style panel • **Shortcut Menu:** (*right-click in Multiline Text field*)>Background Mask
	Draw Order: Bring Above Objects	• **Ribbon:** *Home* tab>expanded Modify panel • **Shortcut Menu:** Draw Order>Bring Above Object
	Draw Order: Bring All Annotations to Front	• **Ribbon:** *Home* tab>expanded Modify panel
	Draw Order: Bring Dimensions to Front	• **Ribbon:** *Home* tab>expanded Modify panel
	Draw Order: Bring Leaders to Front	• **Ribbon:** *Home* tab>expanded Modify panel
	Draw Order: Bring Text to Front	• **Ribbon:** *Home* tab>expanded Modify panel
	Draw Order: Bring to Front	• **Ribbon:** *Home* tab>expanded Modify panel • **Shortcut Menu:** Draw Order>Bring to Front
	Draw Order: Send Hatches to Back	• **Ribbon:** *Home* tab>expanded Modify panel
	Draw Order: Send to Back	• **Ribbon:** *Home* tab>expanded Modify panel • **Shortcut Menu:** Draw Order>Send to Back

	Draw Order: Send Under Objects	• **Ribbon:** *Home* tab>expanded Modify panel • **Shortcut Menu:** Draw Order>Send Under Object
	Edit Attribute (Single)	• **Ribbon:** *Insert* tab>Block panel • **Ribbon:** *Home* tab>Block panel
	Field	• **Ribbon:** *Insert* tab>Data panel or *Text Editor* contextual tab>Insert panel
	Wipeout	• **Ribbon:** *Home* tab>expanded Draw panel

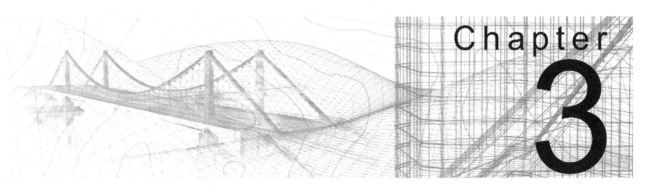

Working with Tables

Learn the various ways to store information by using the AutoCAD® software to link tables to an Excel spreadsheet, extract object data to a table, and create different table styles.

Learning Objectives in This Chapter

- Create a table linked to an Excel spreadsheet.
- Update data in a linked table.
- Set the properties for table cells, text, borders, and more by creating table styles.

3.1 Working with Linked Tables

Many companies store information in spreadsheets that can be used in a drawing set. Instead of creating a table in the AutoCAD software and filling it in from scratch, you can create a table linked to an Excel spreadsheet. This can be done using the **Copy** and **Paste Special** from clipboard method or by linking to the table using the **Table** command. Figure 3–1 shows an Excel table that has been copied into the AutoCAD software.

Door Schedule						
Code	Quantity	Level	Paint Colour	Description	Material	Interior/Exterior
A	5	1	White	Fire	Steel	Interior
B	1	1	White	Fire	Steel	Interior
C	6	1	Green	Garage	Steel	Exterior
D	5	1	White	Louvered	Wood	Interior
E	7	1	Green	French	Steel	Exterior
F	4	1	White	Panel	Wood	Interior
G	6	2	White	Insulated	Wood	Interior
H	4	2	White	Pocket	Wood	Interior
I	1	2	White	Fire	Steel	Interior
J	2	2	Green	Fire	Steel	Exterior
K	6	2	White	Panel	Wood	Interior
L	3	2	White	Panel	Wood	Interior
Window Schedule						
Code	Quantity	Level	Paint Colour	Description	Material	Interior/Exterior
A	2	1	White	Stained Glass	Wood	Exterior
B	3	1	White	Frosted Glass	Wood	Exterior
C	2	2	White	Safety Glass	Wood	Exterior

AutoCAD table

	A	B	C	D	E	F	G
1	**Door Schedule**						
2	**Code**	**Quantity**	**Level**	**Paint Colour**	**Description**	**Material**	**Interior/Exterior**
3	A	5	1	White	Fire	Steel	Interior
4	B	1	1	White	Fire	Steel	Interior
5	C	6	1	Green	Garage	Steel	Exterior
6	D	5	1	White	Louvered	Wood	Interior
7	E	7	1	Green	French	Steel	Exterior
8	F	4	1	White	Panel	Wood	Interior
9	G	6	2	White	Insulated	Wood	Interior
10	H	4	2	White	Pocket	Wood	Interior
11	I	1	2	White	Fire	Steel	Interior
12	J	2	2	Green	Fire	Steel	Exterior
13	K	6	2	White	Panel	Wood	Interior
14	L	3	2	White	Panel	Wood	Interior
15							
16	**Window Schedule**						
17	**Code**	**Quantity**	**Level**	**Paint Colour**	**Description**	**Material**	**Interior/Exterior**
18	A	2	1	White	Stained Glass	Wood	Exterior
19	B	3	1	White	Frosted Glass	Wood	Exterior
20	C	2	2	White	Safety Glass	Wood	Exterior
21							
22							
23							
24							
25							
26							
27							

Sheet1 / Sheet2 / Sheet3

Excel table

Figure 3–1

- The imported table uses the formatting from the Excel file.
- Any changes that you make to the linked Excel file can be updated in the AutoCAD table. You can also make changes in the AutoCAD table and save them back to the Excel file.

How To: Copy and Link a Spreadsheet to a Table

1. In Excel, select the cells that you want to include in the AutoCAD drawing and copy them to the clipboard.
2. In the AutoCAD software, in the *Home* tab>Clipboard panel, expand (Paste) and click (Paste Special).
3. In the Paste Special dialog box, select **Paste Link** and **AutoCAD Entities** as shown in Figure 3–2.

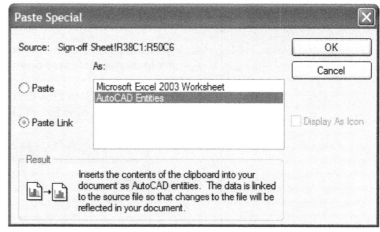

Figure 3–2

4. Click **OK**.
5. In the AutoCAD drawing, pick an insertion point for the table.

- If you use the **Paste** command rather than **Paste Special**, the table can still be updated in Excel but is not linked to the original file.

Table from a Data Link

The simplest way to link a table to an external file is to use **Cut** and **Paste**. Alternatively, you can use the **Table** command. The table can be linked to an entire Excel spreadsheet, a single cell, or a range of cells.

- You can have multiple data links in a drawing, all of which can be modified using the Data Link Manager.

How To: Create a Table from a Data Link

1. In the *Home* tab>Annotation panel or *Annotate* tab>Tables panel, click ⊞ (Table) to start the **Table** command.
2. In the Insert Table dialog box, select the **From a data link** option, as shown in Figure 3–3.

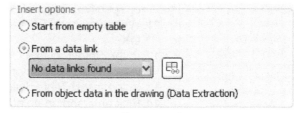

Figure 3–3

3. If you have an existing link, select it in the list and skip to Step 12.

4. If you want to create a new link, click 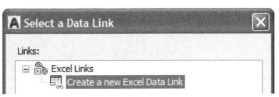 (Launch the Data Link Manager dialog) to open the Select a Data Link dialog box.

5. In the Select a Data Link dialog box shown in Figure 3–4, select **Create a new Excel Data Link**.

Figure 3–4

6. In the Enter Data Link Name dialog box, type a name for the link and click **OK**.

7. In the New Excel Data Link dialog box, you can select a file in the list or click ⬚ (Browse) to browse for a file.

8. In the Save As dialog box, select a file and click **Open**.

9. In the New Excel Data Link dialog box, specify the Link options, as shown in Figure 3–5.

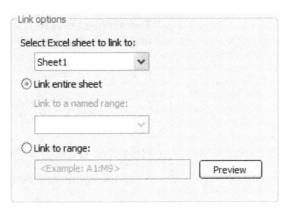

Figure 3–5

10. You can select a sheet (if there are several in the spreadsheet) and then link the entire sheet, a named range, or specify a range of cells.

11. When you have finished adding information to the table, click **OK**.

12. In the Select a Data Link dialog box, verify that the link you want to use is selected and click **OK**.

13. In the Insert Table dialog box, click **OK**.

14. Pick an insertion point on the sheet.

- If you are specifying a range of cells and do not use the correct form, the Invalid Range alert box opens, as shown in Figure 3–6.

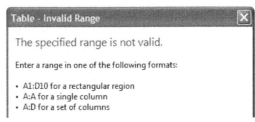

Figure 3–6

- Numbered ranges are functions in Excel that enable you to select a cell or range of cells and assign them a name. This name can be used in formulas and anywhere you would type a cell identifier or range of cells. It is a labeled shortcut to a set of data. By labeling a range of cells with a descriptive name, you can quickly identify the function or origin of the data contained in them.

 Link Cell: Displayed in the *Table Cell* contextual tab>Data panel when at least one cell is selected. Can be used to link individual cells or groups of cells to a cell(s) in a spreadsheet.

Using the Data Link Manager

If you know that you are going to link several files in your drawing, you can set them up in the Data Link Manager before you start the **Table** command. You can then select the link from a list in the Insert Table dialog box, as shown in Figure 3–7. You can open the Data Link Manager using ⬛ (Link Data), which is located in:

- The *Annotate* tab>Tables panel, and
- The *Insert* tab>Linking & Extraction panel.

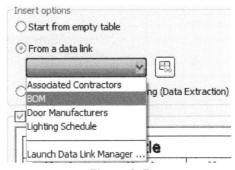

Figure 3–7

- To create a new Excel data link, in the Data Link Manager dialog box, select **Create a new Excel Data Link**, as shown in Figure 3–8.

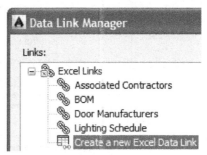

Figure 3–8

- Clear the **Preview** option to save time when working in the Data Link Manager.

- Expand the New or Modify Excel Data Link dialog box to display the extra options for modifying and creating data links, including cell content and formatting, as shown in Figure 3–9.

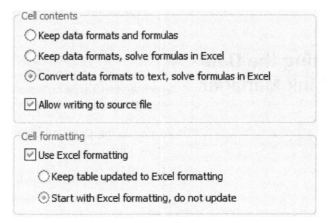

Figure 3–9

- Select **Allow writing to source file** to write modified data from the AutoCAD file to the source file.

Updating Table Links

You can update table data in two directions in a linked table, in the current drawing.

- In the shortcut menu, use the **Update Table Data Links** option (shown in Figure 3–10) to update the AutoCAD table from the source. Use **Write Data Links to External Source** to write the AutoCAD data to the source (this only works if **Allow writing to source file** is selected in the *Cell contents* area, in the New or Modify Excel Data Link dialog box).

- In the *Annotate* tab>Tables panel or *Insert* tab>Linking & Extraction panel, you can also use  (Download from Source) to update the linked table data from the external source file and (Upload to Source) to update the linked data in the external source file from the current AutoCAD table, as shown in Figure 3–11.

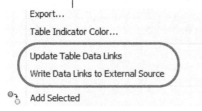

Figure 3–10

Figure 3–11

- The **Data Link Has Changed** bubble displays when the AutoCAD software detects that a linked file has been modified, as shown in Figure 3–12.

Figure 3–12

- In the Status Bar, right-click on  (Data Link) as shown in Figure 3–13, and either open the Data Links dialog box or update all data links.

Figure 3–13

- Linked and locked tables display icons when they are selected and you move the cursor over them. If you hover the cursor, it displays information about the data link, as shown in Figure 3–14.

	A	B	C	D	E	F
1	ITEM	TAG	QTY	CATALOG	MFG	DESCRIPTION
2	1	LT151	2	800T-P16H	AB	GREEN PILOT LIGHT-STANDARD
3	2	PB167	1	800H-BR6D1	AB	PUSH BUTTON MOMENTARY
4	3	LT161	1	800T-P16J		
5	4	PB201	2	800H-BR6D2		
6	5	PB159	3	800T-D6DT		
7	6	LT151	3	800T-W100A		
8	7	CB101	1	EGB3100FFG		
9	8	CB103	2	EGB3070FFG		
10	9	CB121	1	EGB2030FFG		
11	10	CB152	1	EGB101FFFG	EATON	CIRCUIT BREAKER 1 POLE

Data Link
Bulbs and Wires
C:\AutoCAD 2020 Advanced Practice Files\Electrical BOM.xls
Link details: Entire sheet: Sheet1
Last update: 3/29/2019 11:35:26 AM
Update status: Succeeded
Update type: Updated from source
Lock state: Content locked

Figure 3–14

- Linked cells are locked by default to protect them from accidental modification. Green corner brackets display when the table is selected, indicating their status. To edit a cell, select it, right-click, expand Locking and select **Unlocked**. When a cell is unlocked, it can be modified.

- You can add columns and rows to a linked AutoCAD table. They are not removed when the data is updated from the source file.

 Download from source: Available in the *Table Cell* contextual tab>Data panel when at least one cell is selected. Can be used to update the information in a linked file.

3.2 Creating Table Styles

Table styles define properties for table cell styles, such as text style and height, border properties, table direction, and cell margins. The standard templates in the AutoCAD software include a single predefined style named Standard. You can create custom styles as required in the Table Style dialog box, as shown in Figure 3–15.

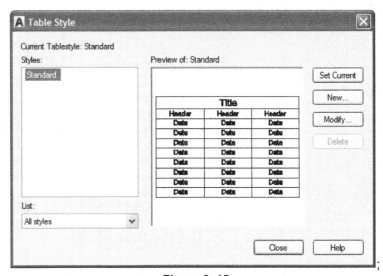

Figure 3–15

- The text style and size for each cell should be set in the table style, but you can also modify it in the *Text Editor* contextual tab as you enter the text.

- The number of rows and columns is specified when you insert the table. They are not defined in the style.

- Table styles do not include any values for the table cells.

How To: Create a Table Style

1. In the ribbon, *Home* tab>expanded Annotation panel click (Table Style) or in the *Annotate* tab>Tables panel, select the setting arrow.
2. Click **New**.

3. Type a name for the table style and select an existing style as the starting template, as shown in Figure 3–16.

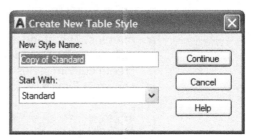

Figure 3–16

4. Click **Continue**.
5. In the New Table Style dialog box, you can select a table to use as a starting point in the *Starting table* area, and specify the table direction in the *General* area.
6. In the *Cell styles* area, select the cell style that you want to modify in the list or create a new style. The **Data**, **Header**, and **Title** options are included with the **Standard** style.
7. For each cell style, work through the tabs for *General*, *Text*, and *Borders*.
8. Click **OK** to return to the Table Style dialog box.
9. Select a style to be current and click **Set Current**.
10. Click **Close**.

Table Style Options

You can create a new table style and set the various options in the New Table Style dialog box, as shown in Figure 3–17.

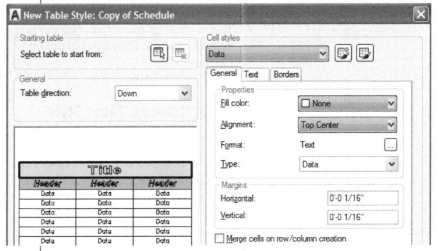

Figure 3–17

The preview displays the default table style. If you would rather display the table you are working on, you can set it as the preview in the *Starting table* area in the New Table Style dialog box.

 Select a table to use as the starting table for this table style: Sets the table you are working with to be displayed in the preview. Otherwise you can use the default style.

 Remove the starting table from this table style: Sets the preview to display the default style or enables you to select a different table. An alert box opens to verify that you want to do this.

In the *General* area, the *Table direction* can be set to either **Up** or **Down**, as shown in Figure 3–18.

- **Down** locates the Title and Header rows at the top of the table.
- **Up** locates them at the bottom of the table.

Figure 3–18

Cell Style Options

To modify the cell styles, you first select an existing cell style from the list, as shown in Figure 3–19. Then you work through the tabs to customize the cell style.

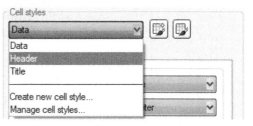

Figure 3–19

 Create a new Cell Style: Opens the Create New Cell Style dialog box in which you can specify a new cell style name and select a starting style.

 Manage Cell Styles dialog: Opens the Manage Cell Styles dialog box in which you can create new cell styles, and rename or delete existing ones.

General

In the *General* tab (shown in Figure 3–20), you can set properties, such as the *Fill color* and *Alignment* of objects in the cell. You can also specify the *Format* of the cell. The default is **General** but it can be set to **Decimal Number**, **Percentage**, **Text**, **Whole Number**, etc. The *Type* can be set to **Data** or **Label**. You can also set the **Margins** for the cell.

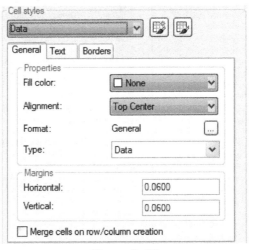

Figure 3–20

*   New cells can be merged together automatically as you create columns and rows using the same cell style. For example, you might want all of the cells using the **Title** cell style to be merged together. By default, the *Standard* Table Style has the **Title** cell style set to merge, while the **Header** and **Data** cell styles are not.

Text

In the *Text* tab (shown in Figure 3–21), you can set the *Text style*, *Text height*, *Text color*, and *Text angle*.

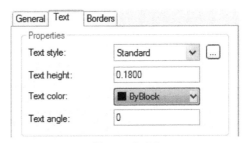

Figure 3–21

- The **Text angle** option forces the text to be at an angle. This rotates the text in the cell at the selected angle. In the example shown in Figure 3–22, the **Data** cell style is rotated at a 45 degree angle.

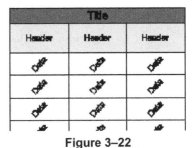

Figure 3–22

Borders

In the *Borders* tab (shown in Figure 3–23), you can control the visibility of the grid lines including **Lineweight**, **Linetype**, **Color**, and **Double line**, and where you want the borders to be placed around each cell of the style.

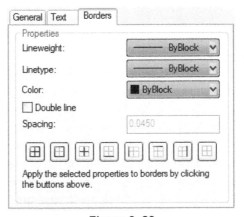

Figure 3–23

- When the **Double line** option is selected, you can enter a distance in the *Spacing* field to determine how far apart the double lines are going to be drawn.

Practice 3a | Working with Tables

Practice Objectives

- Add a table whose data is linked to an external spreadsheet file.
- Modify a table and update the data in the linked file.
- Create a new table style and apply it to an existing table.

In this practice, you will create and update a table from an external link. You will also create and apply a table style and apply a cell style to individual cells. In the first two tasks you will create a table from an external link and then update it from the source and to the source. The completed drawing is shown in Figure 3–24. In Task 3, you will create a table style and apply it to an existing table.

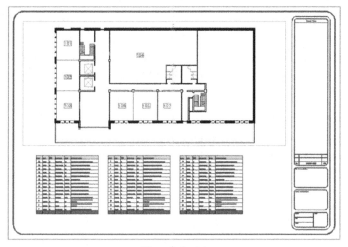

Figure 3–24

Task 1 - Create an externally linked table.

1. Open **Occupancy-Ad-A.dwg** from the practice files folder.

2. Switch to the **Electrical** layout.

3. In the *Home* tab>Annotation panel, click ▦ (Table) and set the *Table style* to **Electrical** in the Insert Table dialog box.

4. In the *Insert options* area, select **From a data link** to create a table from an external source.

5. Click 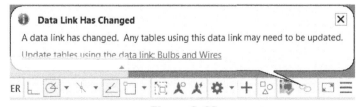 (Launch the Data Link Manager dialog) to open the Select a Data Link dialog box.

6. Select **Create a new Excel Data Link**. The Enter Data Link Name dialog box opens.

7. Type **Bulbs and Wires** and click **OK**. The New Excel Data Link dialog box opens.

8. Click (Browse) to browse for a source file. The Save As dialog box opens.

9. Select **Electrical BOM.xls** in the practice files folder and click **Open**. The New Excel Data Link dialog box now displays additional options.

10. In the *Link options* area, ensure that **Link entire sheet** is selected, and then click **OK**.

11. In the Select a Data Link dialog box, click **OK**.

12. In the Insert Table dialog box, click **OK** and pick an insertion point below the viewport to locate the table in the drawing.

13. The table is too long to fit on the page. Use grips to break it into three columns (under each red background empty row), similar to that shown in Figure 3–24.

14. Save the drawing.

Task 2 - Update the table and write data to the source.

To complete this part of the practice, you need to have a copy of Microsoft Excel on the workstation.

1. From Windows Explorer, open **Electrical BOM.xls** in Microsoft Excel from the practice files folder.

2. Change several of the *QTY* (quantity) numbers.

3. Save and close the Excel file.

4. Switch back to the AutoCAD software. An information bubble opens (as shown in Figure 3–25) indicating that the external source has been modified.

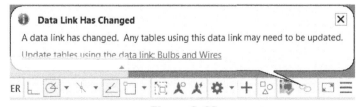

Figure 3–25

5. In the information bubble, select **Update tables using the data link** to update the data in the table with the modified data from the Excel file. Note that the *QTY* changes you made in the Excel file are displayed in the updated table.

6. Zoom in on the top of the AutoCAD table and select the cells E2 through E7. Right-click and select **Locking>Unlocked** (as shown in Figure 3–26) to unlock the cells.

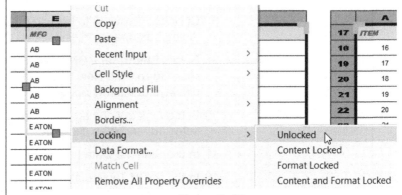

Figure 3–26

7. Change the *MFG name* in each of the cells to **SQD**.

8. In the *Insert* tab>Linking & Extraction panel, click (Upload to Source). Select the table and press <Enter>. All of the modifications in the AutoCAD table are written to the source file.

9. From Windows Explorer, open **Electrical BOM.xls** and note the changes to the cells.

10. Close the Excel file and save the drawing.

Task 3 - Create table styles.

In this task, you will create a table style with several cell styles and apply it to an existing table. You will also select individual cells and apply a cell style to them. The completed table is shown in Figure 3–27.

Occupancy Table			
First Floor			
Room #	Department	Area	Use
101	Marketing	452.0 SQ. FT.	Office
102	Marketing	463.2 SQ. FT.	Office
103	Sales	452.0 SQ. FT.	Office
104	Engineering	2712.8 SQ. FT.	Drafting Room
105	Engineering	463.9 SQ. FT.	Office
106	Engineering	466.9 SQ. FT.	Office
107	Engineering	463.9 SQ. FT.	Office
	Total Area:	5474.6876 SQ. FT.	

Figure 3–27

1. Switch to the Occupancy layout.

2. In the ribbon, in the *Home* tab>expanded Annotation panel, click ▦ (Table Style).

3. In the Table Style dialog box, click **New** to create a new table style.

4. Name the new style **Schedule**, verify that the **Standard** table style is selected from the Start With drop-down list (as shown in Figure 3–28), and click **Continue**.

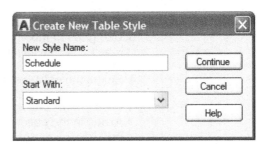

Figure 3–28

5. In the New Table Style dialog box, set the following:
   - In the Cell styles drop-down list, select **Title**.
   - In the *General* tab, set the *Fill color* to **Cyan**.
   - In the *Text* tab, set the *Text style* to **Title** and the *Text height* to **1/4"**.
   - In the *Borders* tab, set the *Lineweight* to **0.60mm** and click ▦ (Outside Borders).

6. Similarly, set the following:
   - In the Cell styles drop-down list, select **Header**.
   - In the *General* tab, set the *Fill color* to **Green**.
   - In the *Text* tab, set the *Text style* to **Logo**.

7. Similarly, set the following:
   - In the Cell styles drop-down list, select **Data**.
   - In the *Text* tab, set the T*ext height* to **1/8"**.

8. In the Cell styles drop down list, select **Create a new cell style** and name it **Areas**. Ensure that the *Start With* field is set to **Data**. Click **Continue**.

9. In Cell styles, select **Areas**, and then in the *General* tab, set the *Alignment* to **Middle Right**.

10. Click **OK**. In the Table Style dialog box, click **Close**.

11. In the *Occupancy* layout, select the table.

12. In the *Annotate* tab>Tables panel, select the new style **Schedule** (as shown in Figure 3–29) to apply it to the selected table.

Figure 3–29

13. Use grips to modify the rows and columns as required to match the new layout of the table.

14. Select the cells under *Area*.

15. In the *Table Cell* contextual tab>Cell Styles panel, select **Areas** in the gallery to apply it to the selected cells. Note that the values are right justified, as shown previously in Figure 3–27.

16. Save the drawing.

Chapter Review Questions

1. You can create an AutoCAD table that is linked to data in an Excel spreadsheet.

   a. True

   b. False

2. How do you update a linked AutoCAD table from an external source file?

   a. **Create Table**

   b. **Link Cell**

   c. **Download from Source**

   d. **Upload from Source**

3. When you create a table, you can use a Data Link. To which type of file does the Data Link connect?

   a. Excel spreadsheet

   b. Google docs

   c. Word document

   d. Access database

4. Select the properties for which you can define a Table Style. (Select all that apply.)

   a. Number of rows and columns

   b. Cell margins

   c. Table direction

   d. Border properties

5. In the New Table Style dialog box, in the *General* area, which *Table direction* option locates the Title and Header rows at the top of the table?

   a. Up

   b. Down

   c. Top

   d. Bottom

Command Summary

Button	Command	Location
	Download from Source	• **Ribbon:** *Annotate* tab>Tables panel or *Insert* tab>Linking & Extraction panel
	Link Data	• **Ribbon:** *Annotate* tab>Tables panel or *Insert* tab>Linking & Extraction panel • Command Prompt: datalink
	Table	• **Ribbon:** *Home* tab>Annotation panel or *Annotate* tab>Tables panel
	Table Style	• **Ribbon:** *Home* tab>expanded Annotation panel or *Annotate* tab>Tables panel settings arrow
	Upload to Source	• **Ribbon:** *Annotate* tab>Tables panel or *Insert* tab>Linking & Extraction panel

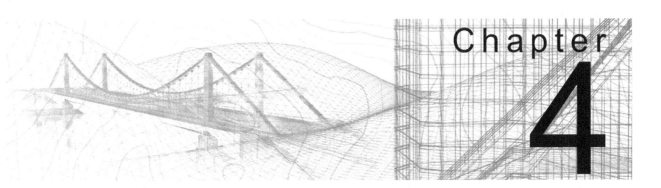

Projects - Advanced Annotation

This chapter contains a practice project that can be used to gain additional hands-on experience with the topics and commands covered so far in this training guide. This practice is intended to be self-guided and does not include step-by-step information.

Project Objective in This Chapter

- Annotate a floorplan drawing using fields and tables.

Practice 4a

Fields and Tables

Practice Objective

- Create fields in a table to display the floorplan areas of each space.

In this project, you will use fields to display the areas of the spaces in a floorplan and create a table for calculating the quantity of paint required to paint several rooms. The completed drawing is shown in Figure 4–1.

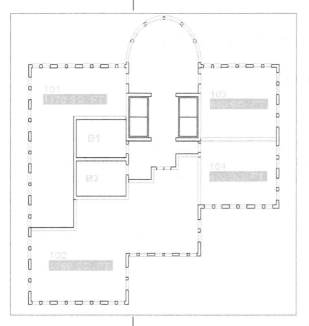

PAINT ESTIMATE—WALLS					
Room	Perimeter	Height	Wall Area	Doors	Windows
101	176	9	1584	1	18
102	224	9	2016	2	22
103	104	9	936	1	10
104	100	8	800	1	10
TOTALS:			5336	5	60

Door Area	100	
Window Area	900	
Wall Area:	4336	
Wall Paint (Gallons):	12.4	
Trim Paint (Gallons):	1.8	

Figure 4–1

1. Open **Tenants-A.dwg** from the practice files folder.

2. Toggle off the layer **Doors** and set the layer **Space** to be current.

3. Use the **Boundary** command, with *Island detection* **off**, to create a polyline (*Object type* - **Polyline**) in each numbered room. (Hint: The full boundary area must be visible on screen.)

⌐┼ *(Boundary) is available in the Home tab>Draw panel>Hatch flyout.*

4. Edit the room number text to include an *Object* field that displays the area of the room (**Architectural** with *Precision* **0**). Select the boundary polylines (green) as the object for the field (it can help to toggle off the layer **Walls**). Modify the text format and line length as required. The areas are shown in Figure 4–2.

*The color of the layer **Text** has been changed for printing clarity.*

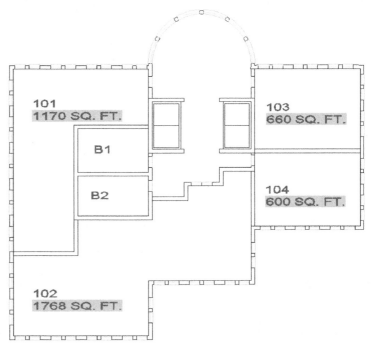

101
1170 SQ. FT.

103
660 SQ. FT.

B1

104
600 SQ. FT.

B2

102
1768 SQ. FT.

Figure 4–2

5. Switch to the **D-Sized** layout and make the layer **Text** the current layer.

6. Create a table that looks like the one shown in Figure 4–3. Use the **Standard** table style.

PAINT ESTIMATE–WALLS					
Room	Perimeter	Height	Wall Area	Doors	Windows
101	176	9		1	18
102	224	9		2	22
103	104	9		1	10
104	100	8		1	10
TOTALS:					
Door Area:					
Window Area:					
Wall Area:					
Wall Paint (Gallons):					
Trim Paint (Gallons):					

Figure 4–3

7. Add formulas in the appropriate cells for the following calculations. The required calculations are outlined for you and you need to decide how to create the formulas in the cells. Complete as many of the calculations as time permits.

Wall Areas:	Perimeter multiplied by the Height.
Total Wall Area:	Sum of all Wall Areas.
Total # Doors:	Sum of all Doors.
Total # Windows:	Sum of all Windows.
Door Area:	Number of Doors multiplied by 20.
Window Area:	Number of Windows multiplied by 15.
Paintable Wall Area:	Total Wall Area minus Door and Window Areas.
Wall Paint (Gallons):	Paint-able Wall Area divided by 350.
Trim Paint (Gallons):	Number of Doors multiplied by 20 plus Number of Windows multiplied by 7.5, all divided by 350.

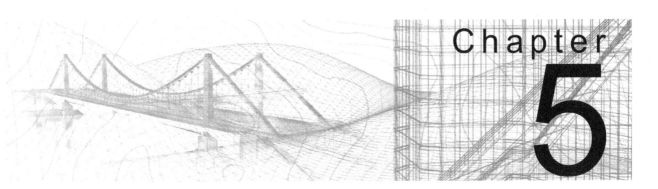

Dynamic Blocks

AutoCAD® blocks enable users to reuse groups of lines and curves representing one object in the model. Blocks, such as bolts or doors, are very similar except for their lengths or widths. Instead of using many separate blocks to represent each size or variation of an object, you can define a single dynamic block to manage all of the sizes and variations. In this chapter, you learn how to insert and modify dynamic blocks, create dynamic blocks, and use dynamic block authoring tools.

Learning Objectives in This Chapter

- Reduce the number of necessary blocks in a library by using dynamic blocks.
- Insert and modify the visibility of dynamic blocks.
- Create new or convert existing blocks into dynamic block definitions.
- Add parameters and actions to objects in a block to make it dynamic.
- Add geometric or dimensional constraints to a dynamic block to help it retain its correct shape.
- Create a block table that enables users to select from a list rather than using grips to adjust a dynamic block.
- Adjust the visibility options of objects in a dynamic block.

5.1 Working with Dynamic Blocks

With conventional AutoCAD blocks, an individual block cannot easily be modified. You need to redefine or explode the block. Dynamic blocks are designed to be easily resized or modified in a variety of other ways. For example, you can define a bolt block that stretches to fit any of the standard bolt lengths that you use, as shown in Figure 5–1. In an electrical diagram, one block of a switch can display its open or closed state, as shown in Figure 5–1.

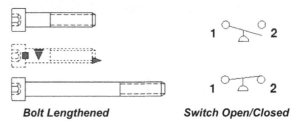

Bolt Lengthened   **Switch Open/Closed**

Figure 5–1

Using dynamic blocks can reduce the number of blocks in your block library.

- Not all dynamic blocks have the same modification features. The features depend on the modifications that are built into the block when it is defined.

- When a dynamic block is selected, special grips on it display the available types of modification. The arrow grip on the end of the bolt (shown in Figure 5–1) enables you to stretch the object. You can use grips to modify a block after it has been inserted.

- The AutoCAD software contains several sample dynamic blocks that display in the Tool Palettes. You can identify dynamic blocks by the lightning bolt that displays on the block icon, as shown in Figure 5–2.

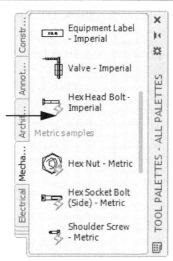

Figure 5–2

Inserting Dynamic Blocks

Inserting dynamic blocks follows the procedures that are used when inserting standard blocks. However, dynamic blocks can include special insertion options: insertion point cycling and automatic alignment.

*   Only blocks that are created with these features have this functionality.

*   Some dynamic blocks are annotative and are automatically scaled according to the Annotation Scale that is set in the Status Bar.

How To: Insert a Block with Multiple Insertion Points

You cannot drag-and-drop the block for insertion point cycling to work.

1. Click on the block in the tool palette.
2. Press <Ctrl> to step to the next insertion point.
3. Continue pressing <Ctrl> until you reach the insertion point that you want to use. You can press <Ctrl>+<Shift> to cycle back through the insertion points. A block with multiple insertion points is shown in Figure 5–3.

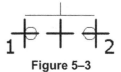

Figure 5–3

4. Pick a location in the drawing at which to place the block.

How To: Insert a Block Using Automatic Alignment

You cannot drag-and-drop the block for automatic alignment to work.

1. Click on the block in the tool palette. Move the cursor toward the object to which you want to align the block.
2. When the block is aligned correctly (as shown in Figure 5–4), click to place it.

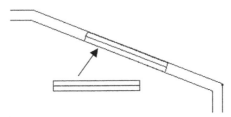

Figure 5–4

- Object snaps work with the **Alignment** option. To place the block anywhere along the line, you might need to toggle off the default object snaps or use the **Nearest** osnap.

Modifying Dynamic Blocks

Depending on the features built into the dynamic block, you can use a variety of methods or *actions* to modify it. All of the actions are rarely available in one block, but blocks can have more than one action. The special grips displayed on a selected block indicate the available actions, as shown in Figure 5–5.

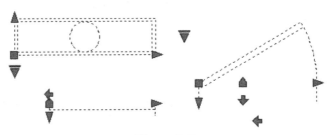

Figure 5–5

- Some of the special grips display a tooltip when you hover over them. The tooltip explains its use and indicates the action required, as shown in Figure 5–6.

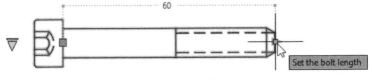

Figure 5–6

Typical Dynamic Block Grips

▶ Stretching, Arraying, and Scaling

The Lengthen/Shorten grip ▶ can scale, stretch, and in some cases array objects. In the example shown in Figure 5–7, you can add many different sized bolts by using the ▶ grip on the right side. The grip stretches the length to the various lengths.

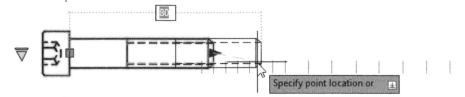

Figure 5–7

The line marks display preset increments for scaling/stretching. These can be set in the block definition for the required standard sizes (for example, standard bolt lengths or window lengths).

● ◀ Rotating and Flipping Objects

Use the Rotate grip ● to rotate the block or objects in the block. In the callout block shown in Figure 5–8, only the arrow rotates. The circle and text stay in place. As with the Stretch/Scale/Array grip, tick marks display any preset increments for rotating, if they have been defined in the block.

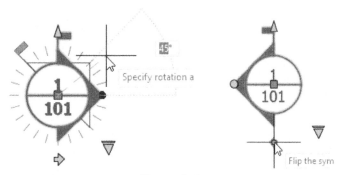

Figure 5–8

Click once on the Flip grip ◀ to flip the block or the objects in it. In the example shown in Figure 5–8, only the arrow flips, not the text.

🏠 Aligning Objects

Blocks using the Align feature can be aligned during insertion or you can use the Align grip 🏠 at any time. Select the grip and drag the block close to an object. The block automatically uses the rotation angle of that object, as shown in Figure 5–9. Therefore you do not need to determine the rotation angles.

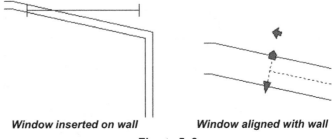

Window inserted on wall   *Window aligned with wall*

Figure 5–9

▼ Selecting from Lists

The List ▼ grip opens a list of options that are defined in the block. The options can be size parameters, the number of blocks arrayed, or even different views of a block to be displayed. In the example of the bolt block in Figure 5–10, it contains a list where you can select the standard sizes for the bolt.

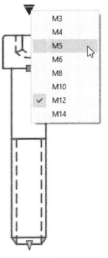

Figure 5–10

■ Inserting and Moving Objects

The Base point ■ grip indicates the insertion point of the block, and other points that might have been assigned in the block. It can move the entire block or just one entity within it. A block with multiple insertion points is shown in Figure 5–11.

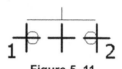

Figure 5–11

Practice 5a

Inserting and Modifying Dynamic Blocks

Practice Objective

- Add various dynamic blocks from the Tool Palette and adjust them dynamically using their grips.

Mechanical Practice

In this practice, you will insert a dynamic bolt and use grips to adjust its size, as shown in Figure 5–12.

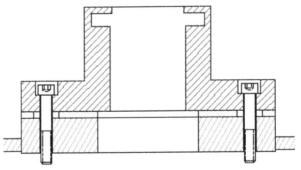

Figure 5–12

1. Open **Assembly-M.dwg** from the practice files folder.

2. Open the Tool Palettes if it is not already open.

3. In the *Mechanical* tab, locate the block **Hex Socket Bolt (Side) - Metric** and note that it is a dynamic block. Drag and drop the **Hex Socket** block anywhere in the drawing. Using the **Rotate** command, rotate it **–90** degrees, and place it to one side of the objects.

4. Zoom in on the **Hex Socket** block and select it to display the grips.

5. Select the ▼ grip to open the list of sizes. Try several different sizes and then select **M12**.

6. Use the square grip to move the bolt into one of the holes, as shown in Figure 5–13.

7. Verify that 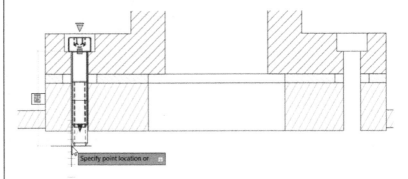 (Dynamic Input) is toggled on and select the arrow grip on the bottom end of the bolt shaft. Note the current length of the shaft (60mm) and the marks below the bottom end that display the preset increments. Stretch the shaft to the *length* of **75mm**.

Figure 5–13

8. Using <Ctrl> and the square grip, copy the bolt to the other hole.

9. Save and close the drawing.

Architectural Practice

In this practice, you will add titles, a section callout, a graphic scale, and a north arrow to a layout, as shown in Figure 5–14. In another layout you will insert and manipulate a detail layout grid.

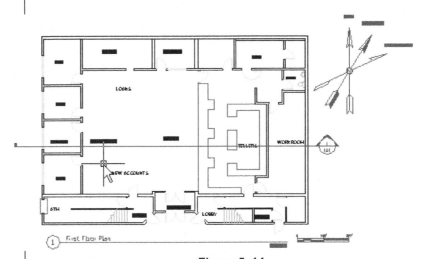

Figure 5–14

1. Open **Bank Layouts-A.dwg** from the practice files folder.

2. Switch to the **Plans and Sections** layout.

3. Open the Tool Palettes if it is not already open.

4. In the Tool Palettes>*Annotation* tab, add the block **Drawing Title - Imperial** under each of the viewports. Use the ▸ grip to stretch the title lines so that they extend to the full length of the viewports.

5. Add the block **Section Callout - Imperial** at the right side of the floor plan view. Use the grips to ● rotate and ▸ stretch it so that it cuts through the building, as shown in Figure 5–14.

6. Add the block **Graphic Scale - Imperial** to the floor plan view near the right side of the drawing title block (of the floor plan), as shown in Figure 5–14. Click the ▼ list grip to display the list and select one of the scales.

7. Add the block **North Arrow - Imperial** near top right side of the floor plan and modify the angle of the Geometrical arrow. Modify the angles of the other arrows and move their labeling along with them.

8. Switch to the **Details** layout.

9. Insert the block **Detail Layout Grid - Imperial** in the lower left corner.

10. Using the AutoCAD **Scale** command, scale the block by a *scale factor* of **8**.

11. Modify the block using the ▦ grip in the upper right corner, which enables you to create an array of six detail grids, as shown in Figure 5–15.

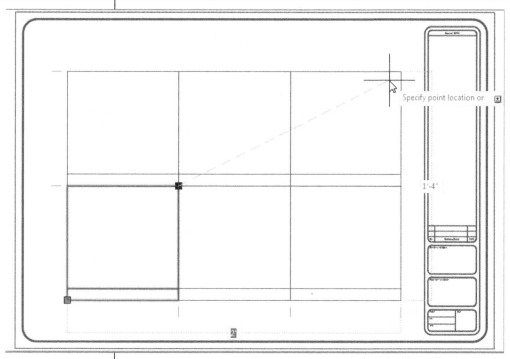

Figure 5–15

12. Move the array as required to center it in the sheet.

13. Save and close the drawing.

5.2 Creating Dynamic Block Definitions

The Block Editor enables you to create new dynamic block definitions from scratch or modify an existing block to make it a dynamic block. Additionally, you can add actions and parameters that turn a conventional block into a dynamic block.

- When you start the **Block Editor** command, the Edit Block Definition dialog box opens, as shown in Figure 5–16. Once you select a block or enter a new name and click **OK**, the Block Editor environment opens with a *Block Editor* contextual tab. If you right-click on an existing dynamic block in the drawing window and select **Block Editor** from the shortcut menu, it opens the block directly in the Block Editor environment with the *Block Editor* contextual tab.

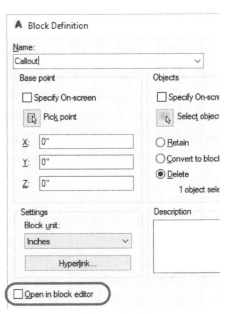

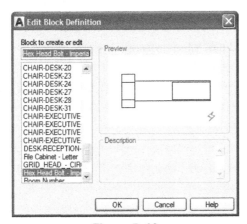

Figure 5–16   Figure 5–17

- Alternatively, if the objects have already been drawn, you can use the Block Definition dialog box (*Home* tab>Block panel or

  Insert tab>Block Definition panel, click ⬚ (Create Block)) to create a block and use the **Open in block editor** option, as shown above in Figure 5–17. This option opens the newly created block in the Block Editor environment, where you can add actions and parameters which converts the conventional block into a dynamic block.

How To: Create a Dynamic Block from Scratch

1. In the *Home* tab>Block panel or in the *Insert* tab>Block Definition panel, click [icon] (Block Editor).
2. In the Edit Block Definition dialog box, type a name for the new block.
3. Click **OK**. The *Block Editor* contextual tab opens without any objects.
4. Draw objects for the block using the regular drawing and editing tools.
5. Add parameters and actions as required.
6. Click [icon] (Close Block Editor) to create the block.

How To: Turning a Conventional Block into a Dynamic Block

1. Double-click on an existing block to open the Edit Block Definition dialog box.
2. Select the block that you want to edit from the list and click **OK**.
3. In the *Block Editor* contextual tab, add dynamic parameters and actions.

Hint: Locking the Block Editor

Double-clicking on a block opens the Edit Block Definition dialog box. However, if you do not have experience creating dynamic blocks, or are not authorized to modify them, you might want to change the default.

- Setting the system variable *blockeditlock* to **1** causes the Properties palette to open when double-clicking on a block rather than the Block Editor. You cannot open the Block Editor using any other methods, such as the ribbon or Command Line.

- Setting the system variable *blockeditlock* back to **0** enables you to open the Block Editor again.

5.3 Dynamic Block Authoring Tools

In the Block Editor, you can add *parameters* and *actions* to objects in the block to make it dynamic. Figure 5–18 shows the Block Editor environment, where the drawing window changes into a Block Editor window with a *Block Editor* contextual tab displayed in the ribbon and the opened Block Authoring Palettes.

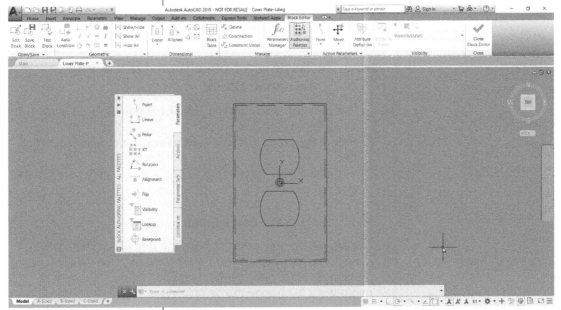

Figure 5–18

- By default, the Block Authoring Palettes for adding parameters and actions is open in the Block Editor.

- *Parameters* are similar to dimensions but they control the block geometry. For example, in a bolt block, you would add a linear parameter to define the length to be able to adjust the length of the bolt.

- *Actions* are added to parameters so that you can modify the parameter in the completed block. In the bolt example, the linear parameter specifies the dimension that you want to control. You can add a stretch action to that parameter so that you are able to stretch the bolt to the required length.

- At least one parameter must be specified in a dynamic block. In most cases it has both a parameter and an action associated with the parameter.

- You can also use regular drawing and editing tools in the Block Editor to modify the block geometry as required, including geometrical and dimensional constraints.

- Only one block can be open in the Block Editor at a time.

Block Editor Contextual Tab

The *Block Editor* contextual tab (shown in Figure 5–19) contains tools for creating and saving blocks, adding constraints, and adding various parameters and actions.

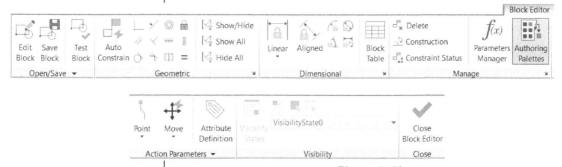

Figure 5–19

The panels in the *Block Editor* contextual tab perform the following functions:

- **Open/Save panel:** Includes commands to open a new or existing block, save the current block, or test the actions of the current block.

- **Geometric & Dimensional panels:** Include commands to apply geometrical or dimensional constraints to the current block (the same methods used in a standard drawing).

- **Manage panel:** Includes visibility commands for constraints, construction geometry, parameters in the Properties palette, and the Authoring Palette.

- **Action Parameters panel:** Enables you to add parameters and actions to the dynamic block.

- Other tools in the *Block Editor* contextual tab control the Visibility Parameters.

- Clicking the arrow in the bottom right corner of the Manage panel in the *Block Editor* contextual tab opens the Block Editor Settings dialog box shown in Figure 5–20. This enables to control all of the settings (including application of colors to objects) for the Block Editor environment.

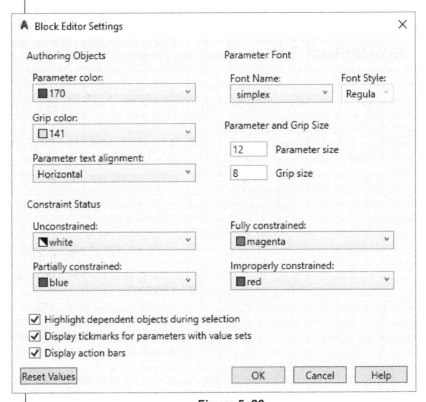

Figure 5–20

Parameters

Parameters are the first item that is added to dynamic blocks. They define any aspects of the geometry that you want to control with actions. The Parameters palette is shown in Figure 5–21.

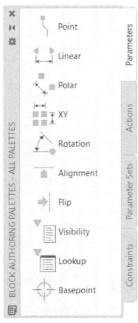

Figure 5–21

 (Point)	Displays an X,Y coordinate position in the drawing.
(Linear parameter)	Displays the distance between two points. Only the distance, not the angle, can be changed.
(Polar parameter)	Displays the distance between two points and an angle value. Both the distance and angle can be changed.
(XY parameter)	Displays a pair of horizontal and vertical dimensions from a specified base point.
(Rotation parameter)	Defines an **Angle** option.
(Alignment parameter)	Forces the entire block to rotate at an angle that is defined by another object in the drawing. This parameter does not need to have a specified action specified as well.

⚐ (Flip parameter)	Describes a line across which the block or selected objects can be mirrored. You need to associate a flip action with this parameter.
▱ (Visibility parameter)	Controls the visibility of objects in the block. Automatically creates a list of the visibility states that you define for the block. This parameter does not need to have a specified action.
▱ (Lookup parameter)	Creates a list of options that are stored in a table from which you can select. Typically this can hold various sizes that are related to other parameters and actions.
⊕ (Basepoint parameter)	Creates a base point that is relative to the block geometry. It can be included in an action selection set but cannot be associated with an action.

Actions

To use actions, you must associate them with a parameter. Typically, you select a key point of the parameter and the geometry that you want to include in the action. For example, if you want to stretch a dynamic block in one direction, you are required to associate the **Stretch** action with either a **Linear**, **Polar**, or **XY** parameter. The Actions palette is shown in Figure 5–22.

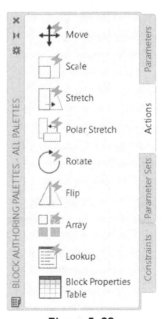

Figure 5–22

(Move Action)	Similar to the standard **Move** command. Works with **Point**, **Linear**, **Polar**, and **XY** parameters. Action is related to a specific grip in the dynamic block. Can be linked to the entire block contents or to individual objects in block.
(Scale Action)	Similar to the standard **Scale** command. Works with **Linear**, **Polar**, and **XY** parameters and can be linked to the entire block or individual objects in the block.
(Stretch Action)	Similar to the standard **Stretch** command. Works with **Linear**, **Polar**, and **XY** parameters. Can be linked to specific objects in block. Apply a stretch action to both ends of the parameters if action needs to work in both directions. **Stretch** only works in the direction of the parameter's arrow.
(Polar Stretch Action)	Similar to the standard **Stretch** command but includes an **Angle** option. Only works with **Polar** parameters.
(Rotate Action)	Similar to the standard **Rotate** command. Works with **Rotation** parameters and can be linked to entire block or to individual objects in block.
(Flip Action)	Mirrors objects around a reflection line. Works with **Flip** parameters.
(Array Action)	Similar to the standard rectangular **Array** command. Works with **Linear**, **Polar**, and **XY** parameters.
(Lookup Action)	Works with **Lookup** parameters. Creates a table in which you can assign data to the block based on the parameter information.
(Block Properties)	Defines the property sets for the block definition.

Parameter Sets

Parameter Sets create related parameters and associated actions at the same time. For example, if you want to flip objects in a block, you can apply a **Flip Set** and specify the reflection line. The Parameter Sets palette is shown in Figure 5–23.

Figure 5–23

How To: Place a Parameter from a Parameter Set

1. Select the Parameter Set that you want to use and follow the prompts to place the parameter.

2. (Action) displays an exclamation point in the icon, indicating that objects are not yet associated with the action.

3. Right-click on (Action) and select **Action Selection Set>New Selection Set**. Follow the prompts to select the objects.

- *Pair Sets* include two actions with the parameter (such as the Linear Stretch Pair Set, which includes a Stretch action at each end of the **Linear** parameter so that you can stretch either end).

- *Box Sets* include four actions with the parameter. With Pair and Box sets, you need to select the objects for each action separately.

Constraints

Constraints in a Dynamic Block help to retain the correct shape and geometry of the objects in the block, while the parameters and actions are applied to the objects. Constraints can be geometric or dimensional, and can be found in the *Block Editor* contextual tab, and in the Block Authoring Palettes, as shown in Figure 5–24.

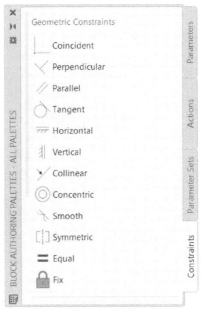

Figure 5–24

Figure 5–25 shows an example of a Dynamic Block with constraints.

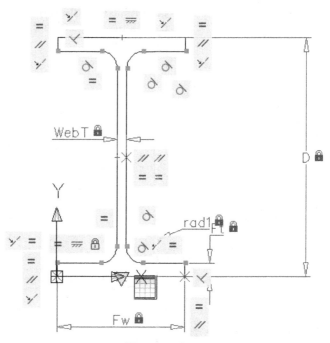

Figure 5–25

Labeling Parameters

If you want to label the grips in dynamic blocks you can select the related parameter and add a description in the *Property Labels* area in Properties, as shown in Figure 5–26.

- The *Distance name* contains the text that displays in the Dynamic Block Editor.

- *Parameter type* is the type of parameter that is being used.

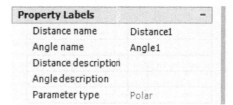

Property Labels	—
Distance name	Distance1
Angle name	Angle1
Distance description	
Angle description	
Parameter type	Polar

Figure 5–26

- The full name of the label and description varies according to the type of parameter selected.

Testing the Block

When you are working with a dynamic block that has constraints, testing the block helps to ensure that it works correctly. You can test the block without having to save it and without closing the Block Editor.

- In the *Block Editor* contextual tab>Open/Save panel, click (Test Block). It opens the block in a new test drawing named Test Block Window - [Block name].

- When you have finished testing the block, you can close the Text Block Window in the *File Name* tabs bar to return to the Block Editor Window.

Construction Geometry

When working with constraints, you might need to dimension an object (such as to the center line of a shelf), as shown in Figure 5–27. However, you might not want the center line to display when the block is in use. The center line can be changed to construction geometry, which does not display in the final block.

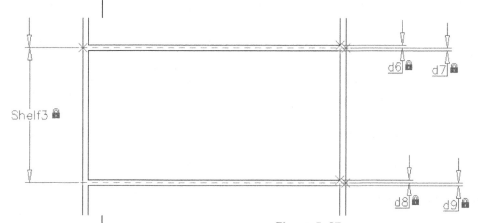

Figure 5–27

How To: Change Objects to Construction Geometry

1. In the *Block Editor* contextual tab>Manage panel, click (Construction).
2. Select the objects that you want to modify and press <Enter>.
3. Press <Enter> again to accept the default **Convert** option.

- You can use this command to show or hide all of the construction geometry, or to revert the geometry back to standard objects.

Applying Constraints in Dynamic Blocks

The methods of applying constraints in dynamic blocks are the same as when you use them in a standard drawing. First, use 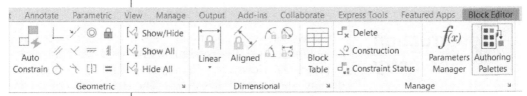 (Auto Constrain) to automatically place as many geometric constraints as possible and then add the dimensional constraints or additional geometric constraints. You can modify the parameters and add user parameters in the Parameters Manager.

All of these tools are located in the *Block Editor* contextual tab as shown in Figure 5–28.

Figure 5–28

Working with Parameters

The dimensional tools create constraint parameters that can be modified in the Parameters Manager. User parameters can also be added here, as shown in Figure 5–29. If attributes are added to the block, they also display in the Parameters Manager.

Do not use the tools in the Parametric tab when you are working in the Block Editor contextual tab. They do not display correctly in blocks.

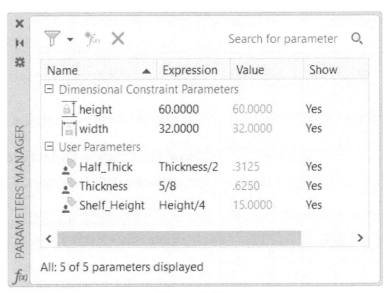

Figure 5–29

- When the block is inserted, the parameters displayed in the Parameters Manager are also displayed in the *Custom* area in Properties, as shown in Figure 5–30.

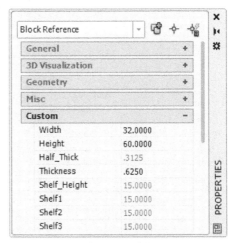

Figure 5–30

- If you do not want a constraint parameter to display, select it in the Block Editor. Then in Properties, change *Show Properties* to **No**, as shown in Figure 5–31.

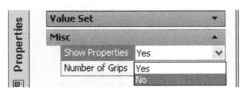

Figure 5–31

Fully Constrain a Dynamic Block

If you save the block before doing this step, an alert box opens. You can return to the block to finish constraining it, or save it and modify it later.

When constraints are created in a dynamic block, the block must be fully constrained to work correctly. Being fully constrained means that all relevant geometric and dimensional constraints have been applied. If this step is not done, the block might not work correctly.

- The block must have at least one fixed constraint. Click

  🔒 (Fix) in the Geometric panel and select a location for the constraint. This can be the same location as the base point.

- To determine whether objects have been constrained, click
  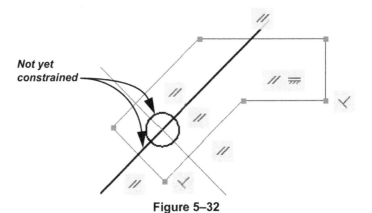 (Constraint Status) in the Manage panel. When it is toggled on, all of the objects that have constraints display in blue, as shown in Figure 5–32.

Not yet constrained

Figure 5–32

Creating a Block Table

In many cases, you want users of a dynamic block to select from a list of sizes rather than using grips to adjust the block. To do so, set up a Block Table using specific parameters that were created using constraints, as shown in Figure 5–33.

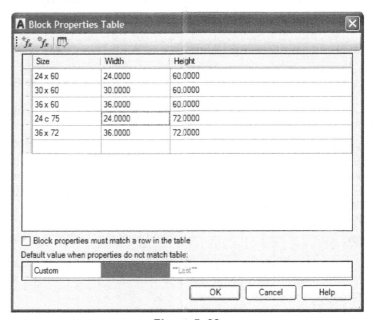

Block Properties Table

Size	Width	Height
24 x 60	24.0000	60.0000
30 x 60	30.0000	60.0000
36 x 60	36.0000	60.0000
24 c 75	24.0000	72.0000
36 x 72	36.0000	72.0000

☐ Block properties must match a row in the table

Default value when properties do not match table:

| Custom | | ""Last"" |

OK   Cancel   Help

Figure 5–33

- A dynamic block can only have one block table.

How To: Create a Block Table

1. Create the required parameters and name them in the Parameters Manager.

2. In the Dimensional panel, click ▦ (Block Table).

3. Specify a location for the block table in the drawing. At the prompt, accept one grip. The Block Properties Table dialog box opens.

4. In the Block Properties Table dialog box, click ⁺𝑓ₓ (Add properties...) to add an existing parameter to the table.

5. In the Add Parameter Properties dialog box, select one or more parameters to add to the table, as shown in Figure 5–34. Click **OK**.

This is where the List grip ▽ displays in the final block.

The available parameters can include attributes, parameters created with dimensional constraints, and user parameters.

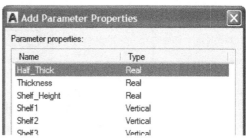

Figure 5–34

6. The table displays the selected parameters, as shown in Figure 5–35.

You can reorder the table columns by dragging and dropping the column name to a new location.

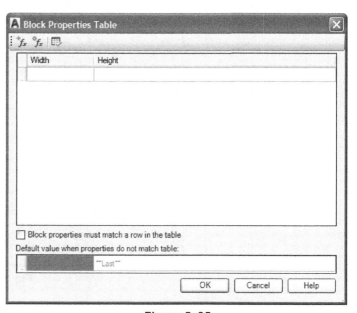

Figure 5–35

7. To add a parameter that does not exist in the drawing, click

   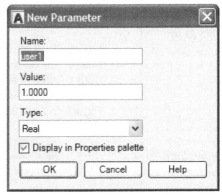 (Add parameters...). The New Parameter dialog box opens as shown in Figure 5–36. Specify a name, a default value, and the type of parameter (**Real**, **Distance**, **Area**, **Volume**, **Angle**, or **String**).

*If you want this parameter to display in Properties when the finished block is selected, select **Display in the Properties palette**.*

Figure 5–36

8. Click **OK**.
9. Fill out the table with the required information, as shown in the example in Figure 5–37.

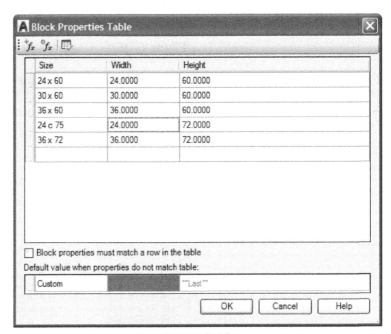

Figure 5–37

- If you select **Block properties must match a row in the table**, you can only select one of the sizes available in the table when using the block. If the option is not selected (as shown in Figure 5–38), you can create a custom size using the grips on the block.

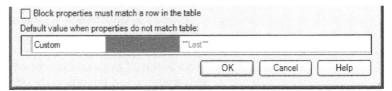

Figure 5–38

10. Click **OK** to close the Block Properties Table dialog box.

Auditing the Block Table

Before you try to close the Block Properties Table dialog box, verify that the parameters are working correctly. Click

(Audit) to audit the Block Properties Table. If there are any errors, an alert box opens explaining the problem as shown in Figure 5–39.

Follow the prompts in the alert box to correct the problem.

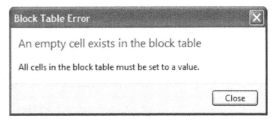

Figure 5–39

Practice 5b

Creating Dynamic Block Definitions

Practice Objectives

- Create a dynamic block with parameters and actions in it.
- Test its new dynamic properties.

This series of practices teaches you how to use a combination of parameters and actions in dynamic block definitions.

In this practice, you will create a dynamic block for a receptacle plate that can stretch to display one, two, or three sets of holes, as shown in Figure 5–40. You will apply a **Linear** parameter and Stretch and Array actions, and set an increment on the parameter.

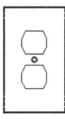 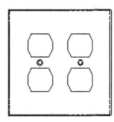 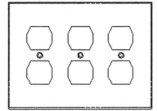

Figure 5–40

Task 1 - Create the block.

1. Open **Cover Plate-I.dwg** from the practice files folder.

2. In the *Home* tab>Block panel or *Insert* tab>Block Definition panel, click (Create Block).

3. In the Block Definition dialog box, name the block **Receptacle Cover**.

4. For the *Base point*, select the center of the screw hole. For *Objects*, select all of the objects.

5. Select **Open in block editor** and click **OK**.
   - The newly created block opens in the Block Editor environment with the *Block Editor* contextual tab and the Block Authoring Palettes displayed.

Task 2 - Add a linear parameter.

1. In the Block Authoring Palettes, in the *Parameters* tab, click

    (Linear).

Pick the top endpoints of the two outer vertical lines.

2. Select the two outer end points to display the full width across the top of the plate and place the dimension, as shown in Figure 5–41. The exclamation point indicates that an action has not yet been associated with the parameter.

Figure 5–41

Task 3 - Add stretch actions.

1. In the Block Authoring Palettes, in the *Actions* tab, click

   (Stretch).

2. Select the **Distance** parameter that you just created.

3. Select the right endpoint of the parameter to associate with the action.

4. Create a Crossing Window around the right vertical edge of the plate for the stretch frame, as shown in Figure 5–42.

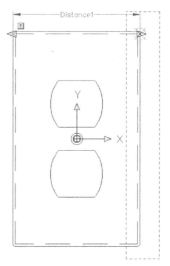

Figure 5–42

5. Create another crossing window around the same right vertical edge of the plate to select the objects. Do not select the holes, only the edge of the plate. Press <Enter> to complete the command.

6. Repeat the process to add another 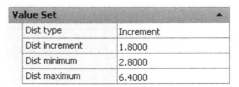 (Stretch) action to the other end of the **Linear** parameter.

Task 4 - Set up the increment values.

1. Select the **Distance** parameter and open the Properties palette.

2. In the Properties palette, set the *Value Set*, as shown in Figure 5–43 (*Dist type:* **Increment**; *Dist increment:* **1.8**; *Dist minimum:* **2.8**; *Dist maximum:* **6.4**).

Value Set	
Dist type	Increment
Dist increment	1.8000
Dist minimum	2.8000
Dist maximum	6.4000

Figure 5–43

3. Click ✔ to close the Block Editor and select **Save the changes to Receptacle Cover**.

4. In the drawing window, insert the block **Receptacle Cover** and test the Stretch Actions. The edge of the plate should stretch to two additional positions (**4.6000** and **6.4000**) on either side, as shown for the right side in Figure 5–44.

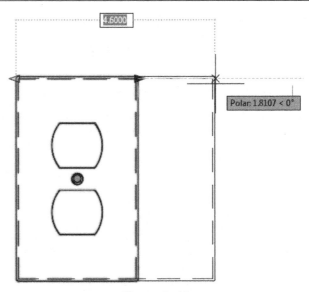

Figure 5–44

5. Right-click on the block **Receptacle Cover** and select **Reset Block** to restore it to its original size.

Task 5 - Create an array action.

---

1. Double-click on the block to open the Edit Block Definition dialog box and click **OK** to edit the block. You are in the *Block Editor* environment.

2. In the Block Authoring Palettes>*Actions* tab, click
   (Array).

3. Select the **Distance** parameter that you created earlier.

4. At the *Select objects:* prompt, select both the interior receptacle hole objects along with the screw hole. Press <Enter>.

5. For the distance between the columns, type **1.8** and press <Enter>.

6. Close the Block Editor and save the changes.

7. In the drawing window, test the block. You should be able to use the stretch grips to display 1, 2, and 3 sets of holes.

8. Save and close the drawing.

Practice 5c

Creating Dynamic Blocks with Constraints

Practice Objectives

- Add geometric and dimensional constraints to objects in a dynamic block to maintain its shape.
- Create user parameters to assign values and formulas to a dynamic block.
- Create a block table within a dynamic block to enable the block to be modified using a list.

In this practice, you will add geometric and dimensional constraints to objects in the Block Editor. You will modify dimension parameters and create user parameters, assigning values and formulas. You will test the block and flex the parameters to test how it works. Finally, you will create a Block Table with sizes so that the block can only be modified by size, as shown in Figure 5–45.

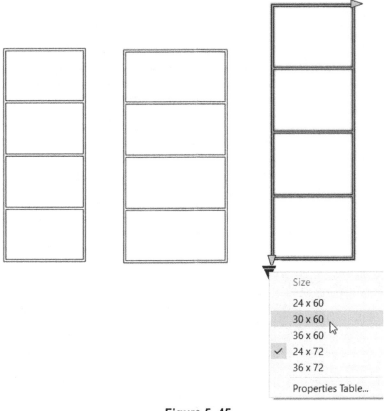

Figure 5–45

Task 1 - Create geometric constraints.

1. Open **Bookcase.dwg** from the practice files folder.

2. Double-click on the bookcase geometry to open the Edit Block Definition dialog box, which indicates that it is a block named **Bookcase-Elevation**.

3. In the Edit Block Definition dialog box, click **OK**. The **Bookcase-Elevation** block objects open in the Block Editor environment, with the *Block Editor* contextual tab and the Block Authoring Palettes displayed.

4. In the *Block Editor* contextual tab>Geometric panel, click the arrow to open the Constraint Settings dialog box. In the *Auto Constrain* tab of the dialog box, verify that all of the constraint types, except **Equal**, are set to **Apply**. Close the dialog box.

5. In the *Block Editor* contextual tab>Geometric panel, click

   (Auto Constrain).

6. Select all of the objects in the drawing and press <Enter>. The parameters display as shown in Figure 5–46.

Figure 5–46

7. Review the parameters that were placed. They include **Horizontal**, **Perpendicular**, **Parallel**, and **Colinear** constraints.

At least one Fix constraint must be in the drawing to fully constrain the block.

8. In the *Block Editor* contextual tab>Geometric panel, click 🔒 (Fix). Place the point in the lower left corner of the bookcase elevation.

9. In the *Block Editor* contextual tab>Geometric panel, click ⬚ (Hide All) to toggle off the geometric constraints display.

Task 2 - Add dimensional constraints.

1. In the *Block Editor* contextual tab>Dimensional panel, click ⬚ (Linear) and add two linear dimensions to the overall top and side, as shown in Figure 5–47. When adding the dimensions, select the top left outer corner first and then either the bottom left outer corner (for the side) or the top right outer corner (for the top). Press <Enter> to accept all of the defaults.

*Depending on the format selected in the Constraint Settings dialog box>Dimensional tab, your dimensions might display both the name and the value of the constraint. In Figure 5–47, only **Value** is set for the format.*

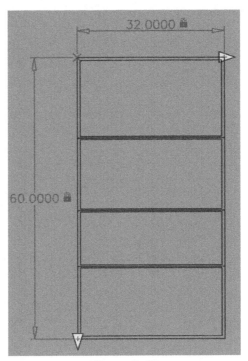

Figure 5–47

2. In the Open/Save panel, click (Test Block).

3. Use grips to resize the block. Only the outside rectangle moves. The inside objects are not yet connected.

4. Undo any changes.

5. Close the Test Block Window drawing by clicking **X** in the *File Tabs* bar. This returns you to the drawing in the Block Editor.

Task 3 - Create user parameters.

1. In the Manage panel, click $f_{(x)}$ (Parameters Manager) to open the Parameters Manager.

2. Change the name of the horizontal parameter to **width** and the vertical parameter to **height**.

3. In the Parameters Manager, click $^*\!f_x$ (Create a new user parameter) three times to add three user parameters with expressions.

   • After adding the three new user parameters, modify them by double-clicking in the three *Name* columns. Enter the names first for all three and then edit the values in the *Expression* column, as shown in Figure 5–48.

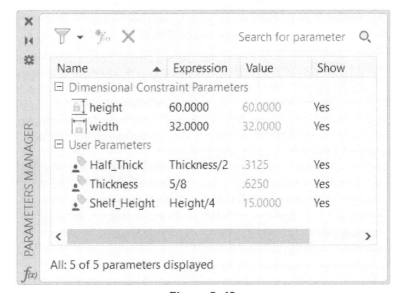

Figure 5–48

Task 4 - Continue constraining geometry.

1. In the Block Editor, zoom in to the top of the bookcase and the three shelves.

2. Add a Linear constraint between the top of the bookcase and the centerline of the first shelf, as shown in Figure 5–49. Press <Enter> to accept the default name and distance.

*In the Constraints Settings dialog box> Dimensional tab, use the **Name and Expression** format to display the name and the value of the constraint.*

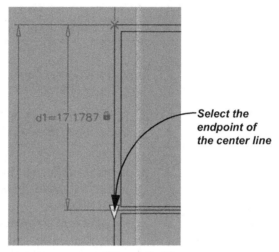

Select the endpoint of the center line

d1=17.1787

Figure 5–49

Select the endpoints of the center lines of the shelves. Ensure that you do not select the shelf geometry by mistake.

3. Add two more Linear constraints (d2 and d3) between the centerlines of the three bookshelves. Accept the default name and distance.

4. Add a Linear constraint between the centerline of the bottom shelf and the bottom end of the bookcase. Once you click to place the constraint, an alert box opens, as shown in Figure 5–50, prompting you that adding this constraint parameter would over-constrain the geometry. Click **Close**. The constraint is not placed.

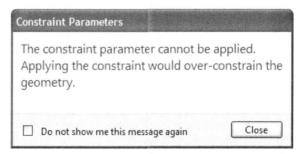

Constraint Parameters

The constraint parameter cannot be applied. Applying the constraint would over-constrain the geometry.

☐ Do not show me this message again   Close

Figure 5–50

If the constraint does not display vertically,

click 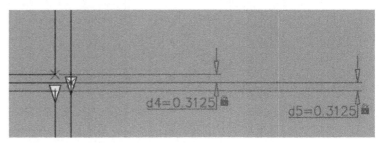 (Vertical) in the

(Linear) drop-down list.

5. Zoom in to a shelf intersection along the right side of the bookcase. Add two linear constraints using the default name and distance, as shown in Figure 5–51. This constrains the shelf geometry to the center line of the shelf.

Figure 5–51

6. Repeat with the other two shelves.

7. In the Parameters Manager, change the name of the three shelf center line location parameters (d1,d2,d3) to Shelf1, Shelf2, and Shelf3. For each of them, set the *Expression* to **Shelf_Height**, as shown in Figure 5–52.

   • As you do this, the shelves value changes and they move into place. The shelf thicknesses also move, because they are constrained to the shelf center line.

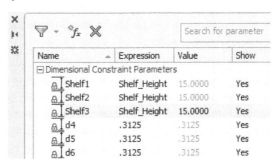

Figure 5–52

8. In the Open/Save panel, click (Test Block).

9. Use grips to modify the height and width of the bookcase. The shelves move correctly, but some constraints are missing, as shown in Figure 5–53.

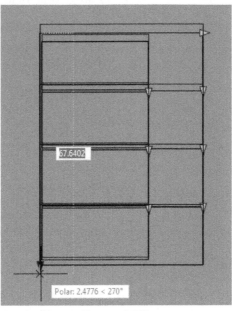

Figure 5–53

10. Undo any changes and close the Test Block Window.

*In the Constraints Settings dialog box> Dimensional tab, use the **Name** format to display only the name of the constraint.*

11. Linear constraints are missing for the thickness of the wood around the outer edge of the bookshelf. Add three constraints near the bottom (left side wall thickness, right side wall thickness, and one bottom wall thickness), as shown in Figure 5–54. Add one more constraint to the top horizontal wall thickness of the bookshelf.

Figure 5–54

12. Test the block again. This time, everything should move correctly.

13. Undo any changes and close the test window to return to the *Block Editor* contextual tab.

Task 5 - Clean up parameters.

You do not need to change the names of these parameters, because no one outside the Block Editor needs to use them.

1. In the Parameters Manager, change all of the *main* bookshelf wall *Expressions* to **Thickness** and all of the shelf *Expressions* to **Half_Thick**, as shown in Figure 5–55. Also, for the top and bottom wall edge thickness, change the *Expressions* to **Thickness**. This enables you to change the thickness of the wood that is used in the bookcase and have all of the related items update.

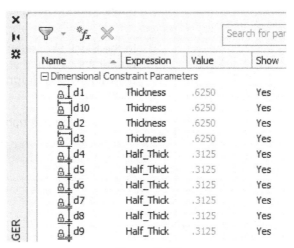

Figure 5–55

2. Test the parameters in the User Parameters list by changing the *Expression* of the **Thickness** parameter to **1/2**. Verify that everything moves correctly.

3. Change it back to **5/8** and check it again.

4. Test the **Height** and **Width** parameters using several different sizes. End with a *Height* of **60** and a *Width* of **30**.

Construction geometry does not plot or display outside the Block Editor contextual tab.

5. In the *Block Editor* contextual tab>Manage panel, click

    (Construction Geometry). Select each of the three shelf center lines. Press <Enter> to end the selection set and <Enter> again to convert them to construction geometry.

Task 6 - Create a block table.

In most cases, an object (such as a bookcase) is available in specific sizes. Creating a Block Table creates a list of sizes that can be used when inserting and manipulating the block.

1. In the Dimensional panel, click ⊞ (Block Table).

2. Select a parameter location near the lower left corner of the bookcase and set it to display **1** grip.

3. In the Block Properties Table dialog box, click ⁺ƒₓ (Add properties...) to add an existing parameter to the table. Select both **Width** and **Height**. (Hold <Ctrl> to select both.) Click **OK**.

    •   The dialog box updates as shown in Figure 5–56.

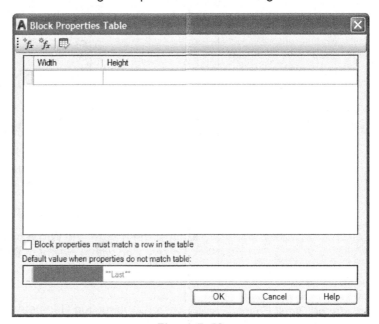

Figure 5–56

4. To add a new parameter, click ⁎ƒₓ (Add parameters). In the New Parameter dialog box, set the following, as shown in Figure 5–57:
    •   *Name*: **Size**
    •   *Value*: **30 x 60**
    •   *Type*: **String**

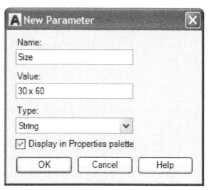

Figure 5–57

5. Click **OK**.

6. In the Block Properties Table dialog box, drag the *Size* column to the beginning before *Width* and *Height* as shown in Figure 5–58.

7. Fill out the table as shown in Figure 5–58.

*Select **Block properties must match a row in the table** to restrict the block to only being resized using the sizes available in the table.*

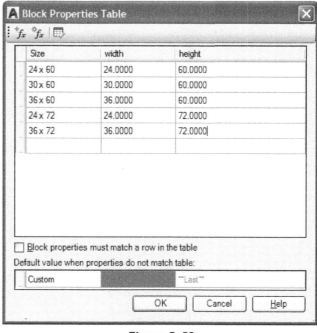

Figure 5–58

8. Click (Audit) to audit the Block Properties Table.

9. If the table contains any errors, the audit can fix them. If the table does not contain any errors, click **Close** and **OK**.

10. Save the block and close the Block Editor.

11. Test the block in the drawing.

12. Insert several copies of the block and set them at different sizes.

13. Save the drawing.

5.4 Additional Visibility Options

When you create a new visibility state you can select from the following options:

Hide all existing objects in new state	Use when you are creating several alternate views of objects, such as the top, front, and side of a mechanical part. This provides a clean slate to on which to work.
Show all existing objects in new state	Use when you are planning to toggle off some objects. You use a different tool to make objects invisible.
Leave visibility of existing objects unchanged in new state	Use if you want to start with the same settings as the current state.

- If objects are visible in a state and you want to make them invisible, click ⬚ (Make Invisible) in the *Block Editor* contextual tab>Visibility panel, and then select the objects. This sets the objects to only be invisible in this state.

- If objects are invisible and you want to make them visible, you need to click ⬚ (Visibility Mode) in the *Block Editor* contextual tab>Visibility panel. This controls the **bvmode** system variable.

  - If *bvmode* is set to **0**, invisible items do not display.
  - If *bvmode* is set to **1**, invisible objects display in gray.

- If Visibility Mode is set so that objects that are invisible display, you can click ⬚ (Make Visible) in the *Block Editor* contextual tab>Visibility panel, and then select the objects to be visible in the current state or in all visibility states.

Chapter Review Questions

1. Which types of grips are available for dynamic blocks? (Select all that apply.)

   a. Lengthen/Shorten

   b. Copy

   c. Flip

   d. List

2. How do you convert a conventional block into a dynamic block?

   a. Explode the block and add attributes.

   b. Create a layer named **Dynamic** and move the block to that layer.

   c. Use the **Wblock** command to export the block to a new drawing.

   d. Open the block in the Block Editor and add parameters and actions.

3. How many blocks can be opened in the Block Editor at a time?

   a. One

   b. Two

   c. Four

   d. Multiple number

4. Which of the following holds true for Constraints in a dynamic block? (Select all that apply.)

   a. Constraints help to retain the correct shape and geometry of the objects in the block.

   b. Constraints are used to create new dynamic block definitions from scratch.

   c. Constraints can be used to add dynamic blocks to the Tool Palettes.

   d. Constraints can be geometric or dimensional.

5. What are parameter sets?

    a. A group of all of the available parameters.

    b. A set of tools that are used to convert a dynamic block into a regular block.

    c. A group of related parameters and associated actions.

    d. A set of tools that are used to add dynamic blocks to a Tool Palette.

6. To test a dynamic block that has constraints, you are required to save the block first.

    a. True

    b. False

7. When creating a dynamic block that stretches in one direction, the required block authoring tools are...

    a. **Linear Parameter** and **Polar Parameter**.

    b. **Stretch Action** and **Linear Parameter**.

    c. **Stretch Action** and **Alignment Parameter**.

    d. **Stretch Action**, **Alignment Parameter**, and **Polar Parameter**.

Command Summary

Button	Command	Location
Dimensional Constraints		
	Aligned	**Ribbon:** *Parametric* tab and *Block Editor* contextual tab>Dimensional panel
	Angle	**Ribbon:** *Parametric* tab and *Block Editor* contextual tab>Dimensional panel
	Convert	**Ribbon:** *Parametric* tab>Dimensional panel
	Diameter	**Ribbon:** *Parametric* tab and *Block Editor* contextual tab>Dimensional panel
	Horizontal	**Ribbon:** *Parametric* tab and *Block Editor* contextual tab>Dimensional panel
	Linear	**Ribbon:** *Parametric* tab and *Block Editor* contextual tab>Dimensional panel
	Radius	**Ribbon:** *Parametric* tab and *Block Editor* contextual tab>Dimensional panel
	Vertical	**Ribbon:** *Parametric* tab and *Block Editor* contextual tab>Dimensional panel
Dynamic Block Specific Tools		
	Block Editor	**Ribbon:** *Insert* tab>Block panel
	Block Table	**Ribbon:** *Block Editor* contextual tab>Dimensional panel
	Construction Geometry	**Ribbon:** *Block Editor* contextual tab>Manage panel
	Constraint Display Status	**Ribbon:** *Block Editor* contextual tab>Manage panel
	Create Block	**Ribbon:** *Insert* tab>Block panel
	Test Block	**Ribbon:** *Block Editor* contextual tab>Dimensional panel
General Constraint Tools		
	Delete Constraints	**Ribbon:** *Parametric* tab and *Block Editor* contextual tab>Manage panel
	Parameters Manager	**Ribbon:** *Parametric* tab and *Block Editor* contextual tab>Manage panel

Geometric Constraints

	Auto Constrain	**Ribbon:** *Parametric* tab and *Block Editor* contextual tab>Geometric panel
	Coincident	**Ribbon:** *Parametric* tab and *Block Editor* contextual tab>Geometric panel
	Colinear	**Ribbon:** *Parametric* tab and *Block Editor* contextual tab>Geometric panel
	Concentric	**Ribbon:** *Parametric* tab and *Block Editor* contextual tab>Geometric panel
	Equal	**Ribbon:** *Parametric* tab and *Block Editor* contextual tab>Geometric panel
	Fix	**Ribbon:** *Parametric* tab and *Block Editor* contextual tab>Geometric panel
	Hide All	**Ribbon:** *Parametric* tab and *Block Editor* contextual tab>Geometric panel
	Horizontal	**Ribbon:** *Parametric* tab and *Block Editor* contextual tab>Geometric panel
	Parallel	**Ribbon:** *Parametric* tab and *Block Editor* contextual tab>Geometric panel
	Perpendicular	**Ribbon:** *Parametric* tab and *Block Editor* contextual tab>Geometric panel
	Show All	**Ribbon:** *Parametric* tab and *Block Editor* contextual tab>Geometric panel
	Show/Hide	**Ribbon:** *Parametric* tab and *Block Editor* contextual tab>Geometric panel
	Smooth	**Ribbon:** *Parametric* tab and *Block Editor* contextual tab>Geometric panel
	Symmetric	**Ribbon:** *Parametric* tab and *Block Editor* contextual tab>Geometric panel
	Tangent	**Ribbon:** *Parametric* tab and *Block Editor* contextual tab>Geometric panel
	Vertical	**Ribbon:** *Parametric* tab and *Block Editor* contextual tab>Geometric panel

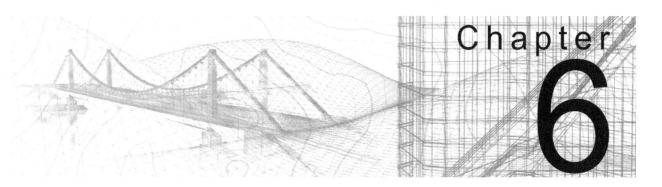

Attributes

Learning how to insert attributes, edit attribute values, and define new attributes enables you to easily associate them with blocks, to redefine blocks containing attributes, and to extract attribute information from a drawing.

Learning Objectives in This Chapter

- Insert blocks with attributes.
- Adjust attribute visibility and other properties.
- Create attribute definitions in new and existing blocks.
- Modify attribute values and definition visibility and display.
- Add a new attribute to an existing block.
- Synchronize attributes after redefining existing blocks.
- Extract attribute information into a database or table.

6.1 Inserting Blocks with Attributes

What Are Attributes?

Attributes are data elements that are associated with blocks. Each time a block with attributes is inserted into a drawing, a new data record is inserted into the master database of the drawing.

From these records in the drawing database, the AutoCAD® software can extract information for creating parts lists and bills of materials, estimating takeoffs, doing inventory counts, and creating schedules. Attributes also enable you to create graphic standards for tasks, such as reference and location numbering. Attributes are also used to assign tag labels on blocks and store information, such as part numbers in a drawing.

How Attribute Values Are Entered

A block that contains attributes inserts them into the drawing database each time the block is inserted. The AutoCAD software prompts you to provide values for each of the attributes that are associated with the block. Figure 6–1 shows an example of attribute tags in a block definition and populated attribute values in a block reference.

Attribute Tags   Inserted Attribute

Figure 6–1

The **attdia** system variable controls how attribute values are entered.

- **attdia** = **0** causes attributes to be entered at the Command Prompt, as shown in Figure 6–2.

- **attdia** = **1** (the default value) causes attributes to be entered in a dialog box, as shown in Figure 6–3.

- Entering the values using a dialog box enables all of the categories of information to be displayed at the same time and enables you to edit a value before closing the dialog box.

- Some blocks with attributes are set to enter the information automatically. You can modify them when they are in the drawing.

Attdia set to 0

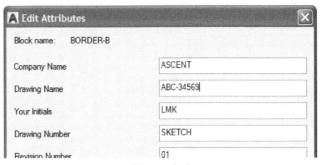

```
Command: _insert
Specify insertion point or [Basepoint/Scale/Rotate]:
Enter attribute values
Voltage <120>: 120/240
KVA <75>:
# of Taps: 4
Coil: Auto
```

Figure 6–2

Attdia set to 1

Figure 6–3

Retain Attribute Display

When inserted as part of a block, some attributes can be visible and some not. The visibility of an attribute is determined when the attribute is created, before it is associated with a block. If you want to display the invisible attributes, you can make them visible temporarily, as shown in Figure 6–4.

Attribute Display set to Normal *Attribute Display set to On*

Figure 6–4

- The **Retain Attribute Display** command enables you to toggle the visibility of attributes on or off.

- In the ribbon, in the *Home* tab>expanded Block panel, or in the *Insert* tab>expanded Block panel, expand the Attribute Display drop-down list.

Command Options

 Retain Attribute Display: Displays attributes according to their defined modes. Invisible attributes do not display, while visible attributes display.

 Display All Attributes: Displays all of the attributes, regardless of their defined visibility modes, making them all temporarily visible.

 Hide All Attributes: Hides all of the attributes, regardless of their defined visibility modes, making them all temporarily invisible.

6.2 Editing Attribute Values

When attributes have been inserted into a drawing, you might need to change their values. For example, the cost of a part might change, or one with a different model number might replace the part number that you originally specified. Attribute values in multiple blocks can be replaced using **Find and Replace**.

Editing Attributes One at a Time

The Enhanced Attribute Editor dialog box (shown in Figure 6–5) enables you to change the attribute values in individual blocks. It also enables you to change the text appearance and properties (layer, color, etc.) for each attribute in a block. The quickest way to start this command is to double-click on the block containing the attributes you want to edit.

Figure 6–5

How To: Edit an Individual Attribute

1. In the *Home* tab>Block panel or *Insert* tab>Block panel, click

   (Edit Attribute) and select the block.

2. In the Enhanced Attribute Editor dialog box, in the *Attribute* tab, select the tag you want to modify from the list, if it is not already selected.

You can also double-click on the attribute that you want to modify.

3. In the *Value* field, change the information as required, as shown in Figure 6–6.

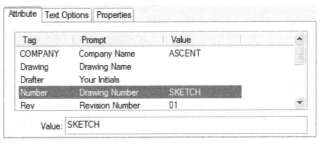

Figure 6–6

4. In the *Text Options* tab (shown in Figure 6–7), you can modify the *Text Style*, *Justification*, *Height*, and other text options that are typically set in the text style.

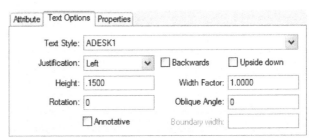

Figure 6–7

5. In the *Properties* tab (shown in Figure 6–8), you can modify the *Layer*, *Linetype*, *Color, Lineweight*, and *Plot style* of the attribute.

Figure 6–8

*Note that it is recommended that you leave these as **ByLayer** in most cases.*

- You can only edit the attributes one block at a time, but you can switch to another block in the Enhanced Attribute Editor using ![icon] (Select block). It displays the drawing window and enables you to select another block with attributes to edit. If you changed the previous attribute, a warning box opens prompting you to save the changes.

- When you edit a multiline attribute, the *Value* field is grayed out. Click 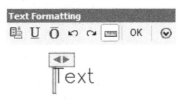 (Browse) to open a simplified version of the Text Formatting toolbar in which you can modify the attribute content, as shown in Figure 6–9.

Figure 6–9

- Tag names and prompts cannot be changed in the Enhanced Attribute Editor dialog box, you must edit the block that contains the attributes to update this information.

- The *Text Options* and *Properties* tabs apply to the attribute that is selected in the list in the *Attribute* tab.

Editing Multiple Attribute Values

To change multiple attribute values, the easiest tool to use is **Find and Replace**, as shown in Figure 6–10. It works on attributes and regular text.

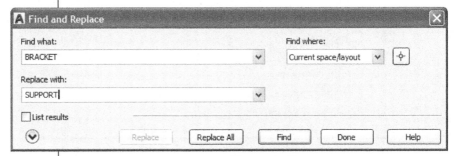

Figure 6–10

For example, you might want to change a department name in all of the related attributes in a drawing or you might want to change a part number. If you know the original information, it is easy for the AutoCAD software to find and replace it for you.

How To: Edit Multiple Attribute Values

*You can also right-click in the drawing window and select **Find** in the shortcut menu.*

1. In the *Annotate* tab>Text panel, type the string you want to find in the *Find text* field and click (Find). The Find and Replace dialog box opens.
2. In the *Replace with:* field, type the string you want to use to replace the existing text.

3. Specify how you want to select the objects to be modified in the Find where: drop-down list. This can be **Entire drawing**, **Current space/layout**, or **Selected objects**.

4. Click 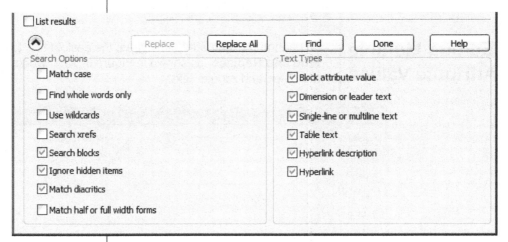 (Select objects) to specify a selection set.

5. Click **Find** to find the first instance of the text in the drawing and display it in the context box on the left. The button changes to **Find Next**.

6. Click **Replace** to replace the instance of the word highlighted in the drawing window or click **Replace All** to replace all of the instances of the word in the drawing.

7. When you are finished, click **Done**.

- Click ⊙ to expand the Find and Replace dialog box and modify the type of objects to be included in the search, as shown in Figure 6–11. You can also set the command to match the case of the letters or to only find whole words.

☐ List results

| Replace | Replace All | Find | Done | Help |

Search Options
- ☐ Match case
- ☐ Find whole words only
- ☐ Use wildcards
- ☐ Search xrefs
- ☑ Search blocks
- ☑ Ignore hidden items
- ☑ Match diacritics
- ☐ Match half or full width forms

Text Types
- ☑ Block attribute value
- ☑ Dimension or leader text
- ☑ Single-line or multiline text
- ☑ Table text
- ☑ Hyperlink description
- ☑ Hyperlink

Figure 6–11

Practice 6a

Inserting and Editing Attribute Values

Practice Objectives

- Insert blocks with attributes.
- Modify both the value and properties of attributes in a title block.

In this practice, you will insert several blocks with attributes. You will also use **Find and Replace** and the Enhanced Attribute Editor to change the value and properties of attributes in a title block.

Task 1 - Insert attributes.

In this task, you will insert several blocks with attributes. The completed drawing is shown in Figure 6–12.

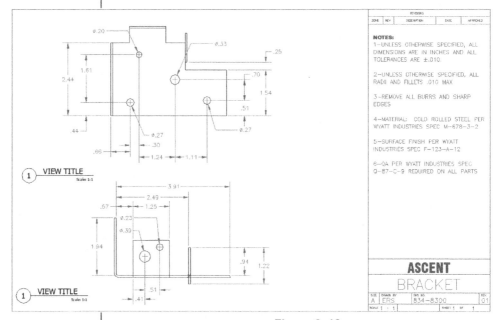

Figure 6–12

1. Open **Bracket-Ad-I.dwg** from the practice files folder. The drawing opens in **Layout1**.

2. Insert the block **BORDER-B** at **0,0**. The Edit Attributes dialog box opens automatically.

*If the Edit Attribute
dialog box does not
open, set attdia to 1.*

3. In the Edit Attributes dialog box, fill out the fields as shown in Figure 6–13, and click **OK**. Note that the information is added to the title block.

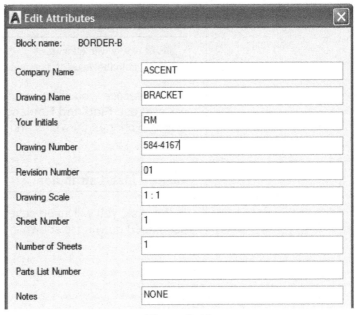

Figure 6–13

4. Open the Tools Palette and select the *Annotation* tab, if required.

5. Insert a copy of **Drawing Title-Imperial** under top and bottom model views. It is inserted without prompting for the values. All of the attribute values in this block have been preset, as shown in Figure 6–14.

Figure 6–14

6. Insert an additional copy of the **Drawing Title-Imperial** block anywhere to one side.

7. Explode it. The information is lost and the attribute tag information displays instead, as shown in Figure 6–15.

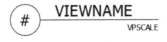

Figure 6–15

8. Erase all the components of the exploded block.

9. Zoom in to the lower right corner of the title block.

10. In the *Insert* tab>expanded Block panel, expand the Attribute Display drop-down list and click (Hide All Attributes). All of the attributes become invisible.

11. In the *Insert* tab>Block panel, expand the Attribute Display drop-down list and click (Retain Attribute Display). All of the attributes return to their normal visibility status.

12. Save the drawing.

Task 2 - Edit attributes.

In this task, you will use **Find and Replace** and the Enhanced Attribute Editor to change the value and properties of attributes in a title block, as shown in Figure 6–16.

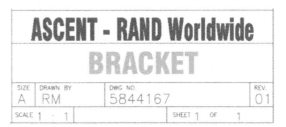

Figure 6–16

1. In the *Annotate* tab>Text panel, type **ASCENT** in the *Find text* field and click (Find).

2. In the Find and Replace dialog box, click to expand it and verify that **Block attribute value** is selected to be included in the search. Ensure the *Find what* string is set to **ASCENT** and in the *Replace with* string, enter **ASCENT - RAND Worldwide**. Click **Replace All** to replace all of the strings.

3. A smaller Find and Replace dialog box opens indicating the number of matches that were found and changed. Click **OK**, and then click **Done** to close the Find and Replace dialog box.

4. In the title block, note that the new company name is bigger than the space provided and extends beyond it. Double-click anywhere on the title block to start the **Edit Attribute** command that opens the Enhanced Attribute Editor dialog box.

5. In the *Attribute* tab, in the list of attributes, select **Company**. In the *Text Options* tab, change the *Width Factor* to **0.7**, as shown in Figure 6–17.

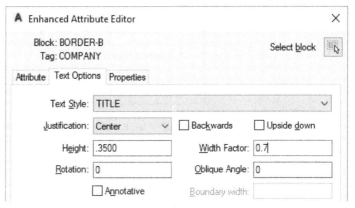

Figure 6–17

6. In the *Attribute* tab, select the **Drawing** attribute. In the *Text Options* tab, change the *Text Style* to **TITLE**. In the *Properties* tab, change the *Color* to **Green**.

If the drawing attribute Bracket is not at the correct location, use grips to move it.

7. Click **OK** to close the Enhanced Attribute Editor dialog box. Note the affected changes in the title block, as shown previously in Figure 6–16.

8. Save and close the drawing.

6.3 Defining Attributes

Attribute definitions are special objects that you include with a block when the block is defined. The **Define Attribute** command creates an attribute definition using a dialog box.

How To: Create a Block with Attributes

1. Draw the objects that you want to include in the block.
2. In the *Home* tab>expanded Block panel or *Insert* tab>Block

   Definition panel, click ⬨ (Define Attributes) to create the attributes.
3. Using the **Block** command, select the attributes and other objects that make up the block.
4. Insert the block and fill in the attribute information.

- Attributes can be annotative.

- A block can contain other objects in addition to the attributes, or just attributes without other objects.

- You can also add attributes using ⬨ (Attribute Definition) in the *Block Editor* contextual tab>Action Parameters panel.

- Block attribute information can contain multiple lines of text while remaining a single attribute. This is very useful for title block information, such as addresses or information that varies in length, but needs to remain in one area in a block.

Attribute Definition

The Attribute Definition dialog box (shown in Figure 6–18) is used to configure attributes before they are associated with a block.

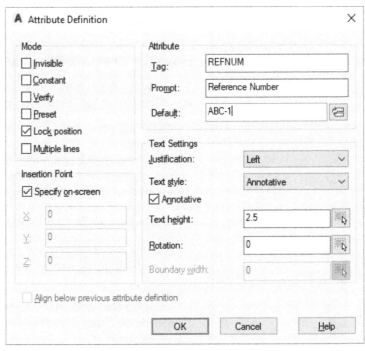

Figure 6–18

Attribute Components

Tag	A label for the category of information that is stored in a particular attribute. Attribute tags in the software are similar to the *field names* or *column labels* in other data systems. Some common tags are *type*, *cost*, *rating*, *manufacturer*, *reference_number*, and *material*. This label cannot be blank or have spaces.
Prompt	The prompt that displays in the Command Line or dialog box when a block with this attribute is inserted. If empty, the Tags name is used for the prompt. Phrase your prompt to help users to enter the correct information. For example, you could write a question for the prompt.
Default	The initial contents or actual data value of a specific block instance. This value is used as a default value and can be blank in the dialog box. You can click ⬔ (Insert field) to insert a field as the value.

Attribute Modes

The Attribute Mode controls how an attribute value displays in a drawing and how much control you have over the value.

Invisible	Controls whether an attribute value normally displays in the drawing, or is just stored in the database. For example, reference numbers and part locations WOULD NOT typically be invisible, while costs, remarks, and manufacturers would be invisible.
Constant	Controls whether the attribute is defined ahead of time or is entered by the operator when the block is inserted. The part number of a specific part can be constant, while a reference number or detail sheet number would not be constant. Constant attributes CANNOT be edited.
Verify	Use for some non-constant attributes, such as serial numbers and costs, which are so important that they need to be confirmed by the operator. The Verify mode causes the software to prompt for the value twice when the block is inserted. If dialog boxes are used, verify does not have an effect.
Preset	Similar to **Constant**, except that values can be edited after insertion. Preset values are not requested at the Command Line when the block is inserted. However, the value displays in the dialog box for editing.
Lock position	Select if you do not want the attributes to move separately from the rest of the block.
Multiple lines	Select if you want to create a multiline attribute. When selected, the *Default* field is grayed out. Click ⬚ (Browse) to specify the location and default text.

Insertion Point and Text Settings

Use these options to determine the attribute text placement and properties. You can specify the *Justification*, *Text style*, *Text height*, and *Rotation* of the text, or make the text *Annotative*. The **Specify On-screen** option is the most common method that is used to place the attribute definition text.

- Once you have placed one attribute, you might want to speed up the process by using the same text options. To do so, select **Align below previous attribute definition**.

- The *Boundary width* setting is only available for multiline attributes.

Associating Attributes with Blocks

Once the attributes have been defined, they must be associated with a block. This is done by including attributes as part of the block while in the **Block** or **Wblock** command or in the Block Editor authoring mode.

Select the attributes individually, rather than with a window or crossing box. The order in which the attribute information displays during block insertion depends on the order in which the attributes were selected for inclusion in the block.

- To edit an attribute before it is associated with a block, double-click on the attribute. This opens the Edit Attribute Definition dialog box (shown in Figure 6–19), which enables you to change the *Tag*, *Prompt*, or *Default* value.

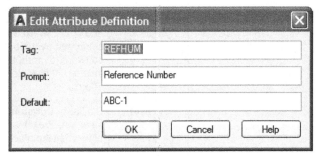

Figure 6–19

Practice 6b

Defining Attributes

Practice Objective

- Define multiple attributes using given values and use them to create a block for use in a drawing.

In this practice, you will create attributes in a block that you will then use in another drawing. The block with attribute definitions is shown in Figure 6–20.

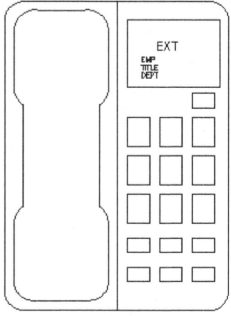

Figure 6–20

1. Open **Attributes-A.dwg** from the practice files folder.

*You need to create each of the attributes separately. Enter the settings for each attribute and click **OK** to place it in the drawing.*

Start [icon] (Define Attributes) again to create other remaining attributes.

2. In the *Insert* tab>Block Definition panel, click [icon] (Define Attributes) to create four attributes using the values given in the table below. In the Attribute Definition dialog box, select the specified *Mode* option and enter the values in the appropriate fields, as shown for the EXT tag in Figure 6–21.

Tag:	EXT	EMP	TITLE	DEPT
Prompt:	Extension	Employee Name	Title	Department
Default:	(blank)	(blank)	(blank)	Design
Mode:	none (all checkboxes cleared)	Invisible and Multiple lines	Invisible	Invisible and Preset
Justification:	Center	Middle left	Click **Align below previous attribute definition** near the bottom of the dialog box.	Click **Align below previous attribute definition** near the bottom of the dialog box.
Text style:	BLOCK	Standard	---	---
Annotative	Yes (select checkbox)	No (cleared)	---	---
Text height:	1/4"	1/8"	---	---
Insertion Point: X, Y, Z	6,7,0	5.25,6.75,0	---	---

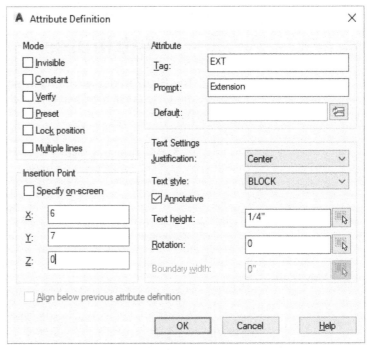

Figure 6–21

3. Use **Wblock** to create a new drawing called **Phone.dwg** containing the drawing of the phone and the attributes. Set the *Source* to **Objects**. Set the *Base point* to the middle of the top of the phone (using the *Pick point*). Set the file path to the practice files folder and *Insert units* to **Inches**.

4. Save and close the drawing.

5. Open **Office-A.dwg** from the practice files folder.

6. Use the *Libraries* tab of the Blocks palette and locate the **Phone.dwg** file (in your practice files folder). Insert the block **Phone** and place it on one of the desks.

7. Double-click on the block **Phone** to open the Enhanced Attribute Editor. Select **Extension** and enter any *Value* for extension. Click **OK**. Note that the extension number is displayed at the place where you had placed the **EXT** attribute in the block Phone.

8. Insert the block **Phone** on each of the remaining three desks and test the attributes by entering the value.

9. Save and close the drawing.

6.4 Redefining Blocks with Attributes

The Block Attribute Manager (shown in Figure 6–22) simplifies the process of modifying attributes in blocks and updating the blocks.

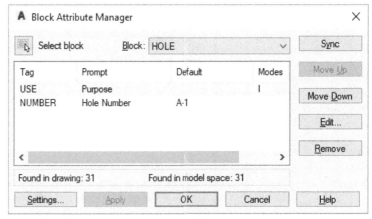

Figure 6–22

*   The Block Attribute Manager does not affect (or enable you to modify) the attribute values in blocks. To modify those values, use the **Edit Attribute** command.

*   You cannot add attributes to a block using the Block Attribute Manager. You need to explode the block, add the new attribute, and redefine the block. Then use the **Synchronize Attributes** command to update the blocks and their attributes.

How To: Use the Block Attribute Manager

1. In the *Home* tab>expanded Block panel, or in the *Insert* tab>Block Definition panel, click (Manage Attributes) to open the Block Attribute Manager dialog box.
2. Expand the Block drop-down list and select a block.

    *   You can also use (Select block) to select a block in the drawing window.
3. The block's attributes display. To modify an attribute, select it in the list and click **Edit**.
4. In the Edit Attribute dialog box, make the required changes.

Only blocks with attributes are listed

5. In the Block Attribute Manager, click **Apply** to apply the changes and stay in the dialog box, or click **OK** to apply the changes and close the dialog box.

• Use **Move Up** and **Move Down** to change the position of an attribute in the list. The location in the list determines the order in which the prompts display when you insert the block and fill in the attribute values. It does not change the physical order of the attributes.

• **Sync** updates existing blocks that were not updated automatically when you made a change using the Block Attribute Manager.

• You can remove an attribute from a block definition by selecting it in the list and clicking **Remove**.

Editing Options

When an attribute is edited, the Edit Attribute dialog box is used as it was when the attribute was defined, as shown in Figure 6–23.

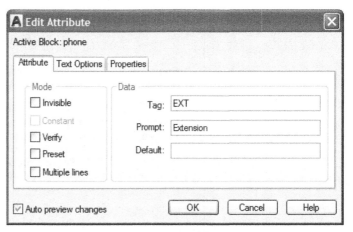

Figure 6–23

• The *Text Options* and *Properties* tabs apply to the attribute selected in the list in the *Attribute* tab.

• **Auto preview changes** makes the changes visible in the drawing immediately. Toggling this off provides a slightly faster performance.

Settings

The Settings control the properties that display in the Block Attribute Manager. By default, only the **Tag**, **Prompt**, **Default**, **Modes**, and **Annotative** properties display, as shown in Figure 6–24.

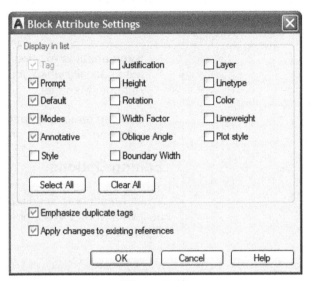

Figure 6–24

Emphasize duplicate tags	If selected, duplicate tag names display in red in the Block Attribute Manager.
Apply changes to existing references	If selected, all of the existing and new instances of the block reference are updated with the changes specified in the Block Attribute Manager. If not selected, only new instances of the block display the changes. You can use the **Synchronize Attributes** command if this option has been toggled off.

Updating Blocks with New Attributes

To add an attribute to a block, open the block definition in the Block Editor authoring environment and add the attribute. Alternatively, you can explode a copy of the block, add the attribute, and redefine the block. New instances of the redefined block include the new attribute, but existing instances of the block do not. You can use **Synchronize Attributes** to update all of the blocks and their attributes.

How To: Synchronize Attributes

1. Open the block in the Block Editor authoring environment, add the required attribute(s), and save the block.
2. In the *Home* tab>expanded Block panel, or in the *Insert* tab>expanded Block Definition panel, click (Synchronize Attributes).
3. Press <Enter> to select a block (type **?** to display a list or **N** to type a name).
4. Select the block.
5. At the *Resync Process* prompt, enter **yes** or **no**.

- This command also works on existing blocks that were not automatically updated when you made a change using the Block Attribute Manager.

- At least one attribute must already be in the block that you are trying to update with other attributes.

Practice 6c

Redefining Blocks with Attributes

Practice Objectives

- Modify block attribute values and block attribute settings using the Block Attribute Manager.
- Redefine a block and then synchronize all of the existing instances of that block in the drawing to be updated.

In this practice, you will use **Edit Attribute**, make changes to existing attributes in the Block Attribute Manager, and use **Synchronize Attributes**. The completed drawing is shown in Figure 6–25.

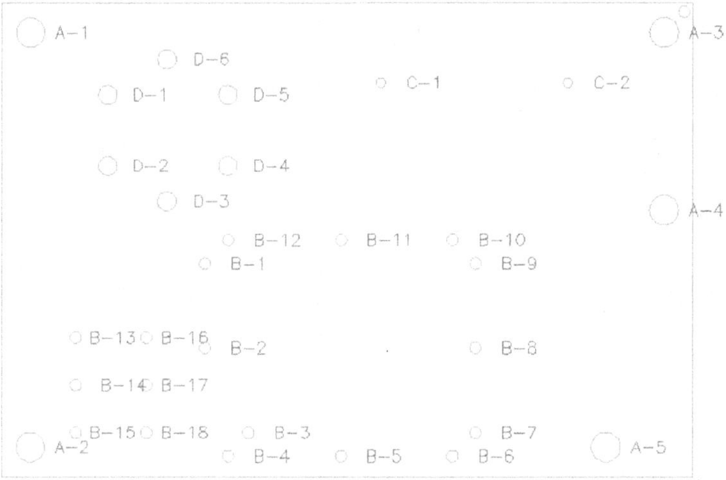

Figure 6–25

1. Open **PCB-I.dwg** from the practice files folder.

2. Double-click on the **A-3** attribute in the bottom right corner of the part to open the Enhanced Attribute Editor.

3. In the *Value* edit box, change the *NUMBER* value to **A-5**, and note that *USE* is listed above *NUMBER*, as shown in Figure 6–26. Click **OK** to close the Enhanced Attribute Editor dialog box. In the drawing, note that the attribute changes to **A-5**.

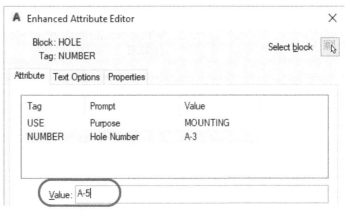

Figure 6–26

4. In the *Insert* tab>Block Definition panel, click (Manage Attributes) to open the Block Attribute Manager. **HOLE** is the selected block, and its attributes are listed. Note that the *USE* attribute has the **I** (Invisible) mode set.

5. Select the *NUMBER* attribute in the list and click **Move Up** to move it above *USE*.

6. With *NUMBER* selected, click **Edit**. In the *Properties* tab, change the *Color* to **Cyan**. Click **OK** to close the Edit Attribute dialog box.

You might need to select a different Block first and then reselect the original Block before you click Sync.

7. If any of the blocks have not updated automatically, click **Sync** to update all of the instances of the block. Click **OK** to close the Block Attribute Manager. The *NUMBER* attribute now displays in cyan.

8. Double-click on any attribute to edit it. Note that *NUMBER* is now at the top of the list, above *USE*. Click **Cancel** to close the Enhanced Attribute Editor.

9. Insert the block **Hole Plus** to one side of the part, using the default values for the attributes, and explode it. It contains three attributes: *NUMBER*, *LOCATION*, and *USE*.

10. In the *Insert* tab>Block Definition Panel, click **Create Block** to start the **Create Block** command. Set the following:
   • In the Block Definition dialog box, name the block **HOLE**.
   • In the *Objects* area, use **Select objects** to select the three attributes (from the Hole Plus block that was exploded) to be used for the block object.
   • In the *Base Point* area, select **Specify On-screen**.
   • In the *Objects* area, select **Delete**, and then clear the **Open in block editor** option.

11. Click **OK** to close the Block Definition dialog box.

12. When prompted, select **Redefine block** to redefine the block **HOLE**.

13. Select a point just to the left of *NUMBER* to specify the insertion base point.

14. Insert a copy of the redefined block **HOLE** to one side, using the default values for the attributes. It includes the *LOCATION* attribute with the default value of **Unknown**. The attributes for the existing blocks named **HOLE** in the part have not changed.

15. In the *Insert* tab>expanded Block Definition panel, click

    (Synchronize Attributes). Press <Enter> and select the new block **HOLE**.

16. At the *ATTSYNC block HOLE?* prompt, select **Yes**. Note that the existing blocks update to include the new attribute with the default value **Unknown**.

17. In the *Insert* tab>Block Definition panel, click (Manage Attributes) to open the Block Attribute Manager dialog box.

18. For the block **HOLE**, select the *Tag* named **LOCATION** in the list, and click **Edit**. The Edit Attribute dialog box opens.

*If the **Auto preview changes** option is toggled on, the drawing changes immediately. If this option is off, the change displays after you exit the Block Attribute Manager.*

19. In the *Attribute* tab, in the *Mode* area, toggle on **Invisible** and then click **OK** to return to the Block Attribute Manager dialog box.

20. Click **OK** to apply the changes and exit the Block Attribute Manager dialog box. The *LOCATION* attribute with the default value **Unknown**, to which all of the other blocks were updated, is now invisible.

21. Save the drawing.

6.5 Extracting Attributes

Attributes can be used in a drawing for labels, tags, etc. They can also be used to extract information into a database or in an AutoCAD table format, as shown in Figure 6–27. The extracted information can then be used for parts lists, inventories, etc.

1084X
Steelcase
Fabric
Red

Furniture Schedule					
QUANITY	TYPE	STYLE	MANUFACTURER	MATERIAL	COLOR
2	CHAIR	1084X	Steelcase	Fabric	Blue
6	CHAIR	1084X	Steelcase	Fabric	Red
2	CHAIR	1084X	Steelcase	Fabric	Green
4	CHAIR	1084X	Steelcase	Fabric	Cherry

Figure 6–27

- In the *Annotate* tab>Tables panel, or in the *Insert* tab>Linking & Extraction panel, click (Extract Data) to start data extraction.

- The **Extract Data** command uses a wizard that automates the process. The major steps in the process are to select the drawing(s) from which to extract the attributes that you want in a table, and select the format to use for the extracted data.

- You can also extract attributes and other data using the **Table** command.

- You can extract information from multiple drawings at the same time.

- Once you have set up the extraction information, you can save it to a *template* so that you do not have to go through the entire wizard again. The template is a text file (Block Template File, .BLK) that specifies the parameters for extraction.

- Data can be exported to a file or made into an AutoCAD table object.

You can create a table by extracting data from objects in the current drawing or from other drawings. In the **Table** command, in the Insert Table dialog box, select **From object data in the drawing (Data Extraction)**, as shown in Figure 6–28. The Data Extraction Wizard opens. It guides you through the selection of objects, whether you want to extract data from the current drawing or another one, and how the data displays in the table.

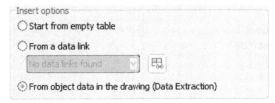

Figure 6–28

How To: Extract Attributes to a Table or File

1. In the *Annotate* tab>Tables panel, or in the *Insert* tab>Linking & Extraction panel, click (Extract Data). Alternatively, you can use the **Table** command.
   - If you are using the **Table** command, select **From object data in the drawing (Data Extraction)** and click **OK**. The Data Extraction Wizard opens.
2. On the *Begin* page, select **Create a new data extraction**, as shown in Figure 6–29.
   - If you have an existing template that was made from another data extraction file (.DXE) or a block template file (.BLK), select the box and then select the template file.

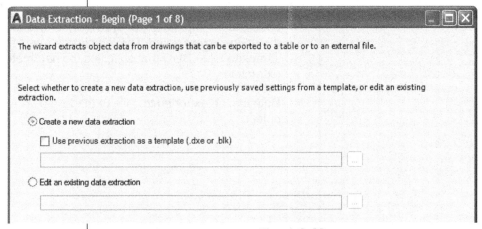

Figure 6–29

3. Click **Next >**.

4. Select a location. In the Save Data Extraction As dialog box, shown in Figure 6–30, type a name for the new data extraction files (.DXE) and click **Save**.

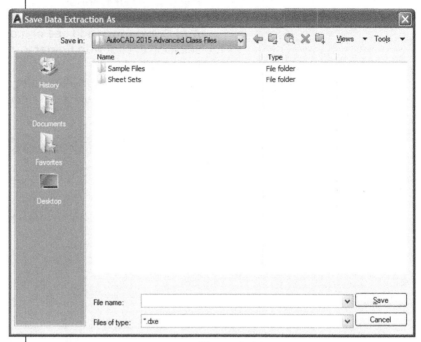

Figure 6–30

5. On the *Define Data Source* page, you can select the file(s) or objects in a drawing from which you want to extract information, as shown in Figure 6–31.

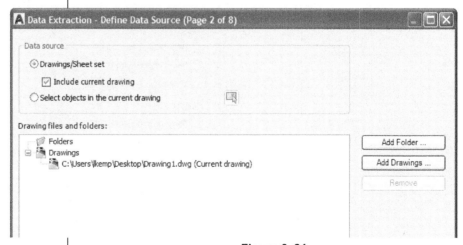

Figure 6–31

- If you select **Select object in the current drawing**, click
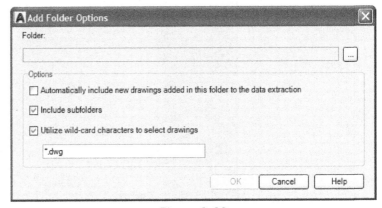 (Select Objects) and select the required objects.
- If you select **Drawings/Sheet set**, you can select **Include current drawing** and add other folders or drawings. Click **Add Drawings** to add one or more drawings to the selection or click **Add Folder** to include all of the drawings in a specified folder.
- In the Add Folder Options dialog box, you can specify the folder and how drawings are added to the list, as shown in Figure 6–32.

Figure 6–32

6. In the Define Data Source dialog box, you should also click **Settings** to verify that you are extracting the correct information, as shown in Figure 6–33.

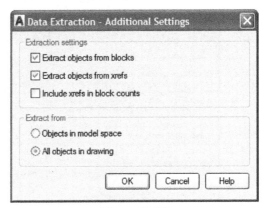

Figure 6–33

7. Click **Next >** when you have finished adding drawings or objects.

8. On the *Select Objects* page, select the objects that you want to include in the data extraction, as shown in Figure 6–34.

   - These include attributes and other objects, such as blocks, lines, and polylines.
   - Use the **Display** options as selection aids.
   - You can also right-click in the *Objects* area and select **Check All**, **Uncheck All**, **Invert Selection**, and **Edit Display Name**.

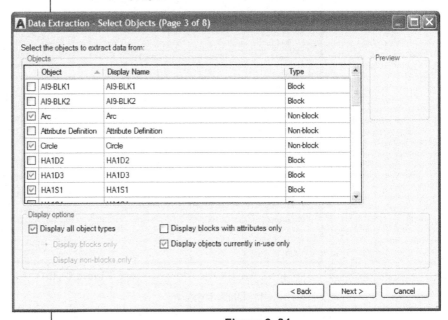

Figure 6–34

9. Click **Next >**.

10. On the *Select Properties* page, all of the properties are selected by default. Select or clear them as required (as shown in Figure 6–35), to select the options you want to use.

- Right-click to clear everything to more easily select only the objects you want to use.
- You can also modify the *Display Name*, which controls the name that displays in the table.

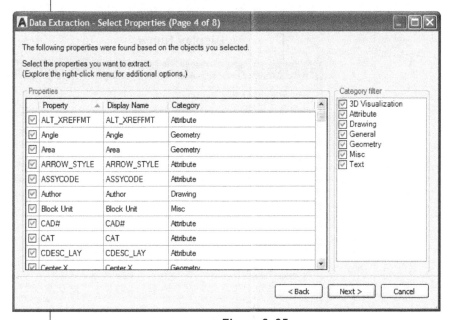

Figure 6–35

11. Click **Next >**.
12. The data is extracted from the drawings and the results display on the *Refine Data* page, as shown in Figure 6–36.

- You can modify the appearance of the columns. Select the options that you want to display. Reorder the column locations by dragging the headers to new locations.
- To reorder the column information alphabetically, click once on the column name.
- To rename a column, right-click on the header.
- If you have additional information stored in a spreadsheet, click **Link External Data** to select the data link.
- Click **Sort Columns Options** to open the Sort Columns dialog box, in which you can also modify the column information.

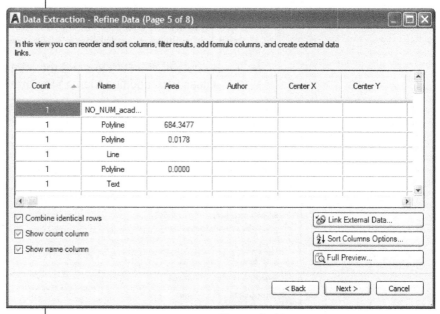

Figure 6–36

13. Click **Full Preview** to display the results.
14. Click **Next >**.
15. On the *Choose Output* page, in the *Output options* area (shown in Figure 6–37), select **Insert data extraction table into drawing** and/or **Output data to external file**.
   - The external files that you can create include XLS, CSV, MDB, and TXT.

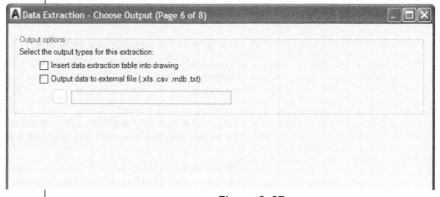

Figure 6–37

16. Click **Next >**.

17. If you select the AutoCAD table option, the *Table Style* page opens, in which you can set up the Table Style information and add a title for the table, as shown in Figure 6–38.

- By default, the Headers are the attribute tag names, unless you modified them in the previous step.

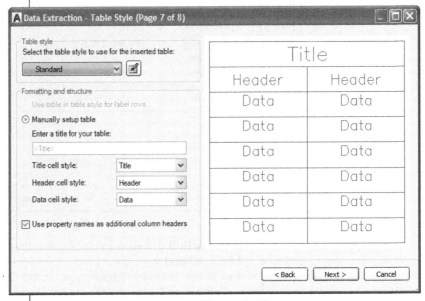

Figure 6–38

18. Click **Next >**.
19. Click **Finish** to close the Data Extraction Wizard. Pick a point in the drawing to insert the table.
20. Use grips to adjust the table to fit in the available space.

- The text in the resulting table is linked to the attribute data. Any manual changes that you make in the table are lost if you refresh the table data. A warning box opens when you place the table.

- You can add data columns from external sources next to those containing the data extracted from the objects.

- To update the table to include any modifications you have made to the data in the drawing, either:

  - right-click on the table and select **Update Table Data Links**, or

  - in the Status Bar, right-click on (Data Link) and select **Update All Data Links**.

Practice 6d

Extracting Object Data to a Table

Practice Objective

- Extract attribute information from blocks and insert that information into a table.

In this practice, you will extract attribute information from blocks in a drawing and insert the information into a table, as shown in Figure 6–39.

Bill of Materials			
Count	Name	Catalog	Manufacturer
1	HTS12	9025–GXW2	SQD
1	HPS12		
1	HLS12	CR115B201	GE
1	HA1S1		
1	HA1D3		
1	PLCIO_9EE	1771–OA	AB
1	PLCIO_7E9	1771–IA	AB
1	AI9–BLK2		
1	AI9–BLK1		
2	HA1S4		
2	HCR1	700–R220A1	AB
2	HPB12	800H–BR6D2	AB
3	HMS1	AN16DN0AB	EATON
3	HLT1G	800T–P16H	AB
3	HCR1	700–P400A1	AB
3	HPB11	800H–BR6D1	AB
4	HA1D2		
5	HCR21		
6	HCR22		

Figure 6–39

1. Open **Control-I.dwg** from the practice files folder.

2. In the *Annotate* tab>Tables panel, click ⬚ (Extract Data). The Data Extraction Wizard opens.

3. Select **Create a new data extraction** (if required) and click **Next >**.

4. In the Save Data Extraction As dialog box, navigate to the practice files folder, enter **BOM** as the *File name*, and click **Save**.

5. In the Data Extraction Wizard, in the *Data source* area, ensure that **Drawings/Sheet Set** and **Include current drawing** are selected, and then click **Next >**.

You can also start the ***Table*** *command, select* ***From object data in the drawing (Data Extraction),*** *and then click* ***OK****. Note that the Files of type is* ****.dxe.***

6. In the *Select Objects* page, clear the **Display all object types** option and select **Display blocks only**, as shown in Figure 6–40.

7. Scroll through the list of blocks and clear **LOGO**, **NO_NUM_acade_title**, and the five blocks starting with **WD**, as shown in Figure 6–40.

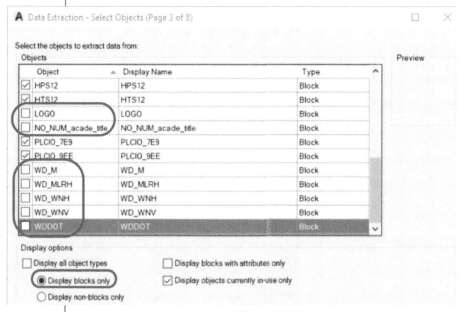

Figure 6–40

8. Click **Next >**.

9. In the *Select Properties* page>*Category filter* area, clear all of the options except **Attribute**, as shown in Figure 6–41.

10. In the *Properties* area, all of the properties are selected by default. Right-click and select **Uncheck all**. Then select **CAT** and **MFG**.

11. Change the display name of CAT to **Catalog** (as shown in Figure 6–41) and display name of MFG to **Manufacturer**.

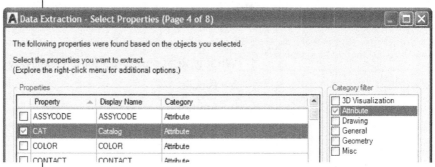

Figure 6–41

12. Click **Next >**.

13. The data is extracted from the drawings and the results display on the *Refine Data* page. Click **Next >**.

14. In the *Choose Output* page, in the *Output options* area, select **Insert data extraction table into drawing**.

15. Click **Next >**.

16. In the *Table Style* page, in the *Formatting and structure* area, type **Bill of Materials** for the title of the table, as shown in Figure 6–42.

Figure 6–42

17. Click **Next >**.

18. Click **Finish** to close the Data Extraction Wizard.

19. Pick a point in the drawing to insert the table. Note that the table contains only the Catalog and Manufacturer information, as shown previously in Figure 6–39.

20. Save and close the drawing.

Chapter Review Questions

1. What type of object are attributes always associated with?

   a. Blocks

   b. Layers

   c. Text objects

   d. Any geometric objects

2. What are possible uses for attributes? (Select all that apply.)

   a. Assign tag labels on blocks.

   b. Store information, such as part numbers in a drawing.

   c. Explode all of the blocks.

   d. Extract information from drawings for parts lists, inventory, etc.

3. What is the quickest way of opening the Enhanced Attribute Editor for changing the attribute values in individual blocks?

   a. Explode the block.

   b. Use **Edit Text**.

   c. From the Block Attribute Manager.

   d. Double-click on the block.

4. Which Attribute Mode controls whether an attribute value normally displays in a drawing?

   a. Invisible

   b. Preset

   c. Constant

   d. Lock Position

5. When extracting attribute information from blocks, what can you write the data to?

   a. An AutoCAD table

   b. A .DWF file

   c. A web page

   d. Another block

6. If you add an attribute to a block after it has been created, which command do you use to update the existing blocks in a drawing?

   a. **Update Block**

   b. **Synchronize Attributes**

   c. **Edit Attributes**

   d. **Data Extraction**

7. To create an attribute that cannot be edited when it is inserted with a block, set the Attribute Mode to...

   a. **Invisible**

   b. **Preset**

   c. **Verify**

   d. **Constant**

Command Summary

Button	Command	Location
	Define Attributes	• **Ribbon:** *Home* tab>expanded Block panel or *Insert* tab>Block Definition panel
	Display All Attributes	• **Ribbon:** *Home* tab>expanded Block panel or *Insert* tab>expanded Block panel
	Edit Attribute	• **Ribbon:** *Home* tab>Block panel or *Insert* tab>Block panel
	Extract Data	• **Ribbon:** *Insert* tab>Linking & Extraction panel or *Annotate* tab>Tables panel
	Find and Replace	• **Ribbon:** *Annotate* tab>Text panel • **Shortcut:** (*right-click in drawing window*) Find...
	Hide All Attributes	• **Ribbon:** *Home* tab>expanded Block panel or *Insert* tab>expanded Block panel
	Manage Attributes	• **Ribbon:** *Home* tab>expanded Block panel or *Insert* tab>Block Definition panel
	Retain Attribute Display	• **Ribbon:** *Home* tab>expanded Block panel or *Insert* tab>expanded Block panel
	Synchronize Attributes	• **Ribbon:** *Home* tab>expanded Block panel or *Insert* tab>expanded Block Definition panel

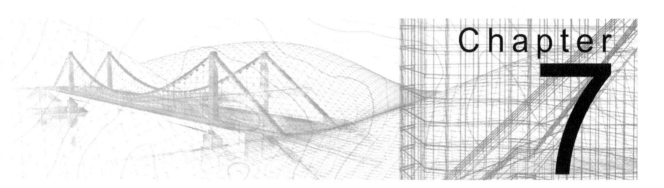

Projects - Advanced Blocks and Attributes

This chapter contains practice projects that can be used to gain additional hands-on experience with the topics and commands covered so far in this training guide. These practices are intended to be self-guided and do not include step-by-step information.

Project Objectives in This Chapter

- Add parameters and actions to a dynamic block.
- Create blocks with attributes to store information in the block.
- Extract attribute information from blocks into a table.

Practice 7a

Dynamic Block Practice - Desk Unit

In this practice, you will create a dynamic block for a desk and chair set. You will add parameters and actions (as shown in Figure 7–1) so that the block aligns automatically and can be flipped, and the chair can rotate separately from the desk.

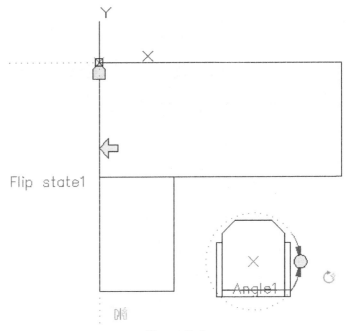

Figure 7–1

Task 1 - Start the block.

1. Open **Dynamic Desk-A.dwg** from the practice files folder.

2. Start the **Create Block** command.

3. Name the block **Desk Unit**.

4. Select the upper left corner of the desk as the base point and select the desk (two rectangles) and the chair as the block objects.

5. Select **Open in block editor** and click **OK**. The desk unit opens in the Block Editor environment with the *Block Editor* contextual tab and the Blocks Authoring Palettes displayed.

Task 2 - Add an alignment parameter.

The **Alignment** parameter is fully functional by itself. Unlike most other parameters, an action does not need to be specified with it. When you apply an alignment to a block it rotates according to the angle of the closest object.

1. In the Block Authoring Palettes, in the *Parameters* tab, select **Alignment**.

2. Place the base point for the alignment at the upper left corner of the desk. The alignment grip will be placed here.

3. Pick the second point for the alignment direction at the upper right corner of the desk.

4. Save the changes to the block and close the Block Editor authoring environment.

5. Insert the new block **Desk Unit** in the center of the room. Select the block and select the alignment grip. Move it close to the angled wall. The **Desk Unit** should align with the wall, as shown in Figure 7–2. Insert another **Desk Unit** along the angled wall and note that the alignment also works while inserting the block.

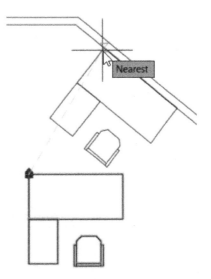

Figure 7–2

Task 3 - Rotate the chair independently of the desk.

1. Double-click on a **Desk Unit** block and then click **OK** in the Edit Block Definition dialog box to open it in the Block Editor authoring environment.

You might need to scroll down in the palette to display this set.

2. In the Block Authoring Palettes, in the *Parameter Sets* tab, select **Rotation Set**.

3. Specify the base point at the center of the chair.

4. Specify the radius of the parameter to be slightly outside the right edge of the chair. The rotation grip is placed here.

5. Press <Enter> to accept the default rotation angle of **0**.

6. Right-click on 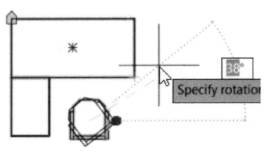 (Rotate), expand Action Selection Set, and select **New Selection Set**. You are prompted to select the objects to be included in the rotation. Select the chair objects and press <Enter>.

7. Save the changes to the block and close the Block Editor.

8. Test the new Rotation action in the block, as shown in Figure 7–3. You should be able to rotate the chair without rotating the rest of the block.

Figure 7–3

Task 4 - Add a flip set.

1. Open the block **Desk Unit** in the Block Editor authoring environment again.

2. In the Block Authoring Palettes, in the *Parameter Sets* tab, select **Flip Set**.

3. For the base point of the reflection line, select the lower left corner of the desk.

4. For the endpoint of the reflection line, select the upper left corner of the desk.

5. Pick near the line to place the label location.

6. Move the flip arrow near the middle of the left side of the desk.

7. Right-click on 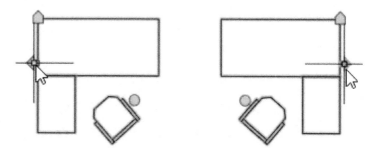 (Flip), expand **Action Selection Set**, and then select **New Selection Set**.

8. Select all of the objects, including the parameters and actions. They are included in the Flip action.

9. Save the changes to the block and close the Block Editor.

10. Test the new Flip action in the block, as shown in Figure 7–4.

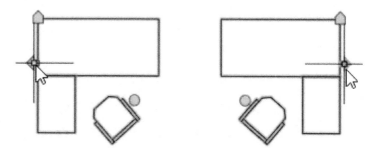

Figure 7–4

11. Save and close the drawing.

Practice 7b | Mechanical Attribute Project - Amplifier

In this practice, you will create and insert blocks with attributes (as shown in Figure 7–5), to store information about components in a drawing and then extract the attributes to a table. The commands to be used include: **Insert (Blocks palette)**, **Attribute Define**, **Attribute Edit**, **Synchronize Attributes**, and **Extract Attributes**.

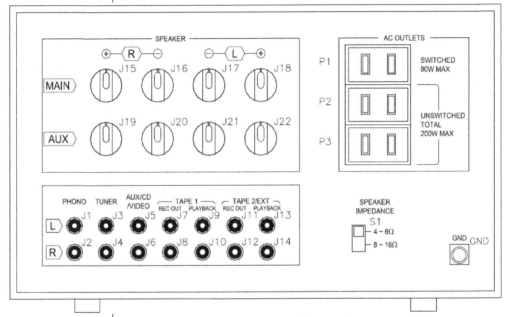

Figure 7–5

1. Open **Amplifier-I.dwg** from the practice files folder.

2. Insert the blocks **Speaker-Pos**, **Speaker-Neg**, **Phono-L**, and **Phono-R**, as shown in Figure 7–5. Each of these blocks has an attribute that you designate using the numbers J1 through J22.

*In the Blocks palette> Current Drawing tab, use the **Repeat Placement** option.*

3. Create the blocks with the attributes shown in Figure 7–6 for **Ground**, **Switch**, and **AC-Outlet**. Use the following parameters:

- Draw the objects on layer **0**
- Draw the attributes on layer **Text**
- Set the *Text height* to **0.125**
- Place the *DESIG* attribute over and above the upper right corner of the object and make it visible (leave all of the other Modes cleared).
- The other attributes should be aligned below the first one and be invisible. They are the same for all four items but with different defaults. Therefore, you can make one set and copy it to the other two objects before creating the blocks.

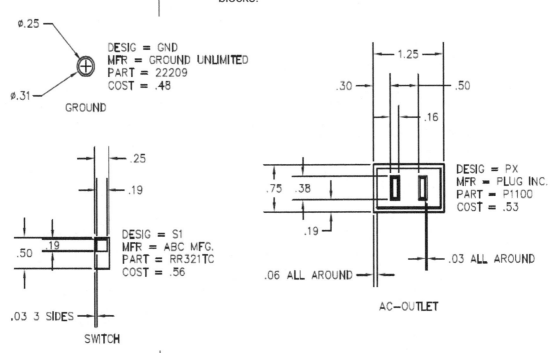

Figure 7–6

4. Insert the blocks on layer **Components** and fill in the attribute information, as shown in Figure 7–7.

5. Use grips to move the visible plug attributes (P1, P2, and P3) to the left side of the plugs, as shown in Figure 7–7.

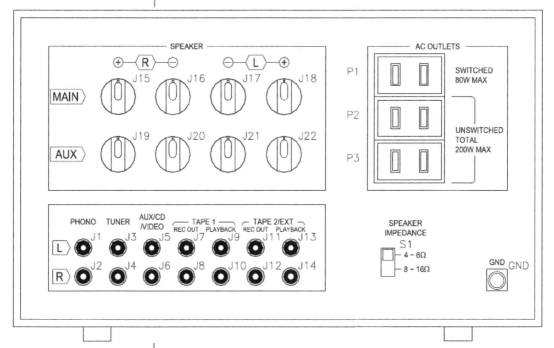

Figure 7–7

6. If time permits, create the **Speaker-Pos**, **Speaker-Neg**, **Phono-L**, and **Phono-R** blocks again that you inserted earlier with the added attributes shown in Figure 7–8. The *DESIG* attribute already exists.

```
DESIG = JX
MFR = SMITH CONNECTORS
PART = 601228-WHT
COST = .28
```
PHONO-L

```
DESIG = JX
MFR = SMITH CONNECTORS
PART = 601228-RED
COST = .28
```
PHONO-R

```
DESIG = JX
MFR = H.R. JONES CO.
PART = 2819ORG
COST = .32
```
SPEAKER-POS

```
DESIG = JX
MFR = H.R. JONES CO.
PART = 2819BLK
COST = .32
```
SPEAKER-NEG

Figure 7–8

7. Use **Synchronize Attributes** to update the existing blocks with the new block definitions so that they include the new attributes.

8. Use **Edit Attributes** to fill in the attribute values for the blocks where they have already been inserted.

9. Use the **Data Extraction** command to create an AutoCAD® table for a parts list of the components, as shown in Figure 7–9. When selecting the attributes, include all of the blocks, except the *DESIG* attribute. Use the Standard table style and place the table in the layout.

PART LIST				
Quantity	PART	Name	COST	MFR
1	22209	GROUND	.48	GROUND UNLIMITED
1	RR321TC	SWITCH	.56	ABC MFG.
3	P1100	AC−OUTLET	.53	PLUG INC.
4	28190RG	SPEAKER−POS	.32	H.R. JONES CO.
4	2819BLK	SPEAKER−NEG	.32	H.R. JONES CO.
7	601228−WHT	PHONO−L	.28	SMITH CONNECTORS
7	601228−RED	PHONO−R	.28	SMITH CONNECTORS

Figure 7–9

10. Save the drawing.

Practice 7c | Architectural Attribute Project - Door Schedule

In this practice, you will create an annotative door symbol block with attributes for door specifications. You will then insert the block into a floorplan (as shown in Figure 7–10), extract the attribute information, and put the information into the drawing as a door schedule table.

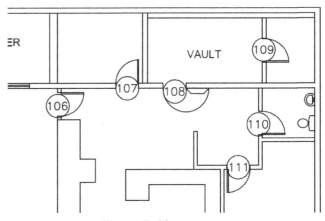

Figure 7–10

1. Open **Door Schedule-A.dwg** from the practice files folder.

2. Create a layer called **Symbols** and make it current.

3. Zoom in on a very small area and draw a **3/16"** radius circle in the middle of the Drawing Window. Note that it is a tiny circle compared to the rest of the drawing.

4. Use (Define Attributes) to create the following attributes, as shown on the left of Figure 7–10:

Do not make the individual attributes annotative. That is done when you create the block.

Tag:	Prompt:	Default:	Mode:	Text Settings:
DOORNUM	Door Number	<none>	<none>	*Justification*: **Middle Center** *Text Style*: **Standard** *Text Height*: **1/8"** *Insertion Point*: Specify on Screen (select the center of the circle)
SIZE	Door Size	3' x 6'8	Invisible	Align below previous attribute definition

MATL	Door Material	Steel	Invisible	Align below previous attribute definition
FRAME	Frame Type	12	Invisible	Align below previous attribute definition
HARDWARE	Hardware Set	1	Invisible	Align below previous attribute definition
FIRE	Fire Rating	A	Invisible	Align below previous attribute definition
REMARKS	Remarks	<none>	Invisible	Align below previous attribute definition

Remember to select the attributes in the order in which you want them to display; do not use a window or crossing.

5. Start the **Create Block** command, then do the following:
   - Name the block **Door Symbol**.
   - Select the center of the circle as the base point of the block.
   - Select the circle and the attributes as the objects in the block.
   - Select **Annotative** and **Match Block orientation to layout**.
   - Do not open the block in the Block Editor authoring environment.
   - Click **OK**.

6. Switch to the **Plans and Sections** layout.

7. Make the floor plan viewport active and zoom in until it displays more clearly.
   - The viewport should be set to **1/8"=1'-0"** and locked.

8. Insert the block **Door Symbol** in the doorways. Number them as **101**, **102**, **103**, etc.
   - In the Blocks palette, use the **Repeat Placement** option to insert multiple doors.

9. Return to Paper Space and zoom out to display the full sheet.

10. Use the **Data Extraction** command to create a table with the door attributes.

- Use only the attributes for the block **Door Symbol**.
- Hide the *Name* and *Count* columns, and reorganize the other columns as shown in Figure 7–11.
- Use the title **DOOR SCHEDULE** and the *Standard* table style.
- Place the table in the layout. It displays as shown in Figure 7–11.

DOOR SCHEDULE						
DOORNUM	SIZE	MATL	FRAME	HARDWARE	FIRE	REMARKS
101	3' x 6'8	Steel	12	1	A	
102	3' x 6'8	Steel	12	1	A	
103	3' x 6'8	Steel	12	1	A	
104	3' x 6'8	Steel	12	1	A	
105	3' x 6'8	Steel	12	1	A	
106	3' x 6'8	Steel	12	1	A	
107	3' x 6'8	Steel	12	1	A	
108	3' x 6'8	Steel	12	3	A	
109	3' x 6'8	Steel	10	4	A	Vault Door
110	3' x 6'8	Steel	12	1	A	
111	3' x 6'8	Steel	12	1	A	
113	3' x 6'8	Steel	12	1	A	

Figure 7–11

11. Change the attribute information for several doors (for example, the Vault door). In the Status Bar, right-click on

⌒ (Data Link) and select **Update All Data Links**. Verify that the table updates with the new information.

12. Save and close the drawing.

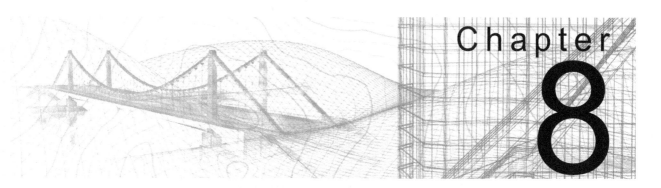

Output and Publishing

Knowledge on how to plot and export DWF, DWFx, and PDF files enables you to easily view DWF and DWFx files in the Autodesk® Design Review software, create a markup in the Autodesk Design Review software, and view it in a drawing. Additionally, you also learn how to publish drawing sets from multiple drawings.

Learning Objectives in This Chapter

- Share information in an AutoCAD® drawing electronically with users that do not have the AutoCAD software.
- View and create markups in DWF and DWFx files in the Autodesk Design Review software.
- View markups made to DWF files in the Autodesk Design Review software in the associated DWG file in the AutoCAD software.
- Batch Plot/Publish multi-sheet and multi-drawing electronic or paper drawing sets.
- Share views in the cloud.

8.1 Output for Electronic Review

You often need to share information in an AutoCAD drawing electronically with users who do not have the AutoCAD software or who only need to view (and not edit) the information. There are two main options for this: creating a DWF or DWFx file that can be viewed and marked up in the Autodesk Design Review software or creating a PDF file that can be viewed in Adobe Reader.

- Autodesk Design Review is a free program from Autodesk. You can download the software from: *http://www.autodesk.com/products/design-review/*.

- Adobe Reader is a free third-party program and can be downloaded from *http://get.adobe.com/reader/*.

- You can create DWF, DWFx, and PDF files using the **Plot** command, **Batch Plot/Publish** command, or **Export DWF/DWFx/PDF** commands, as shown in Figure 8–1.

Figure 8–1

> **Hint: DWF vs DWFx**
>
> **DWF** (**Design Web Format**) is a compressed vector format that loads and displays faster than normal DWG files.
>
> **DWFx** can create multiple page DWF files with the **Batch Plot/Publish** command. It enables you to open DWFx files in Internet Explorer without having any Autodesk products installed.

Plotting Electronic Files

Layouts can be set up to create DWF, DWFx, or PDF files, or you can specify the plotter type in the **Plot** command. Multiple PDF plotters are available. Each one sets the level of print quality.

How To: Plot to a DWF, DWFx, or PDF File

*You can also access the **Plot** command in Application Menu>Print.*

1. In the Quick Access Bar or in the *Output* tab>Plot panel, click

   ![printer icon] (Plot).

   - If the software detects multiple drawings or layouts open, a Batch Plot dialog box displays. You can either use **Batch Plot** or plot a single sheet.

2. Select the appropriate plotter from the list, as shown in Figure 8–2:

   - **DWF6 ePlot.pc3** for DWF files
   - **DWFx ePlot (XPS Compatible).pc3** for DWFx files
   - Any of the **AutoCAD PDF** printers for PDF files

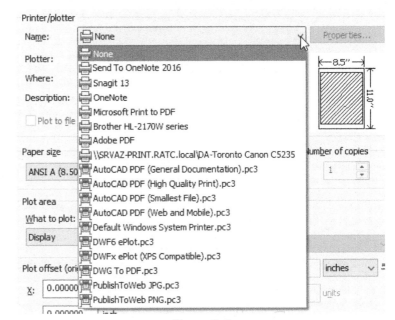

Figure 8–2

3. Click **OK** to plot the file.

- DWF, DWFx, and PDF files cannot be opened directly in the AutoCAD software, but can be accessed using DWF or PDF Overlays or the Markup Set Manager (for DWF).

- Normal DWF plots are in 2D. A separate command, **3DDWF**, enables you to create DWFs of 3D models, so that you can change the viewing angle in the DWF viewer.

Exporting DWF or PDF Files

Exporting to DWF, DWFx, or PDF is another way of creating electronic files to share with other companies or within your company.

How To: Export Layouts to DWF, DWFx, or PDF

- If you want to create a multi-sheet DWFx or PDF, use <Ctrl> or <Shift> to select multiple layout tabs before you start the **Export** command.

*You can also access the required **Export** command in Application Menu>Export.*

1. In the ribbon, in the *Output* tab>Export to DWF/PDF panel, click the required **Export** command,  (DWFx)/ ⬤ (DWF)/ 📄PDF (PDF).

2. Review the information in the Save As dialog box, as shown in Figure 8–3.

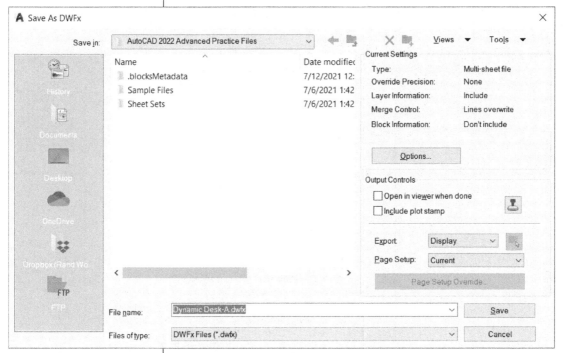

Figure 8–3

3. Click **Options** to modify any of the settings that need to be changed.
4. Select the required Output Controls.
    - If you selected the **Open in viewer when done** option, the associated viewer program opens, enabling you to view the exported file.
5. Specify whether you want to export the current layout or all of the layouts and the associated Page Setup.
6. Assign the correct filename and location and click **Save**.

In the ribbon, in the *Output* tab>Export to DWF/PDF panel. you can set the following options:

- For the *Model* tab, you can set up what to export (**Display**, **Extents**, and **Window**

- For the layout tabs, you can set up what to export, (**Current layout** or **All layouts**), and the Page Setup.

- Click ⌕ (Preview) to display the proposed export.

- Click ⊞ (Export to DWF Options) or ⊞ (Export to PDF Options) to modify any of the options.

Export to PDF Options

When exporting drawing files to PDF files, you can control the quality of vectors, rasters, and merge control (enables lines to merge or overwrite each other), as shown in Figure 8–4.

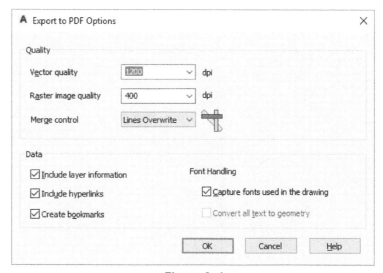

Figure 8–4

You can also include information about data, such as:

Layer information	Layer information can be included in PDF files.
Hyperlinks	Hyperlinks in the drawing file works inside the PDF file. This works for sheets that are linked and weblinks.
Bookmarks	Bookmarks are enabled. Each sheet and each sheet view becomes a bookmark in the PDF.
Fonts	TrueType fonts are embedded in the PDF file and do not have to be available in the PDF viewer. If this option is not selected, the PDF viewer uses substitute fonts. If you have a PDF file with shx fonts, they are converted to geometry and display as a comment in the PDF file. You can also convert all text to geometry during the export process.

The AutoCAD PDF printers provide various print qualities. The table below lists the output settings for each PDF printer.

Printer/Plotter	Vector Quality	Raster Image Quality	Merge Control	Include Layer Info.	Include Hyperlinks	Create Bookmarks	Capture fonts used in the drawing
General Documentation	1200	400	Lines Overwrite	X	X	X	X
High Quality	2400	600	Lines Overwrite	X	X	X	X
Small Files	200	400	Lines Overwrite				
Web and Mobile	200	400	Lines Overwrite	X	X	X	X

Hint: SHX Text Recognition

When a PDF file that contains SHX text is imported into the AutoCAD software, the text is converted into separate geometric objects, such as polylines, as shown in Figure 8–5. This makes editing the text extremely difficult. Various tools are available to help you to work with imported AutoCAD SHX objects and convert them to MText objects.

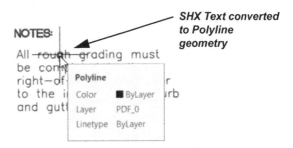

Figure 8–5

In the *Insert* tab>Import panel, three tools are available:

- (Recognize SHX Text) enables you to convert SHX geometry to Mtext string objects (as shown in Figure 8–6) based on the font and other settings provided in the PDF Text Recognition Settings dialog box.

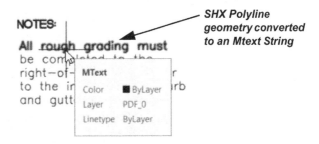

Figure 8–6

- (Recognition Settings) opens the PDF Text Recognition Settings dialog box, which enables you to control the various settings for conversion of SHX geometry to text

- (Combine Text) enables you to combine multiple individual text objects to create a single multiline text object as a paragraph.

8.2 Autodesk Design Review

Once you have created a DWF or DWFx file, you can view it using the Autodesk Design Review software, as shown in Figure 8–7. The viewer is a separate utility that is a free download from the Autodesk website. You can create markups in the Autodesk Design Review software and then view them in the associated drawing file using **Markup Set Manager**.

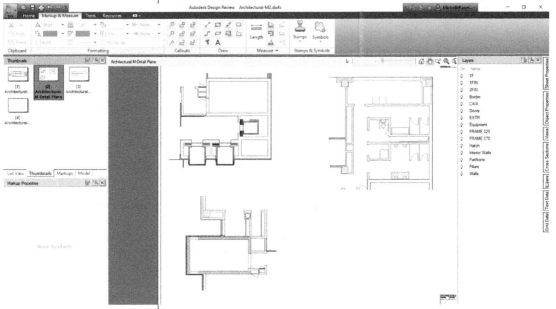

Figure 8–7

- Drawing (DWG) files automatically have DWFx files created when opened in the Autodesk Design Review software.

The Design Review software must already be installed. You can download it from autodesk.com/products/ design-review/overview.

- To open the Autodesk Design Review software from the AutoCAD software, right-click on the plot icon in the Status Bar and select **View Plotted File**, as shown in Figure 8–8.

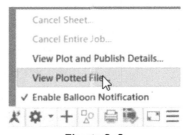

Figure 8–8

- You can also open the viewer from Windows by selecting **Start>Autodesk>Autodesk Design Review**. Alternatively, in Windows Explorer, double-click on the DWF or DWFx file to open it.

Viewing Sheets in Autodesk Design Review

The active sheet displays in the Viewer. A Thumbnails palette (shown in Figure 8–9) provides access to other sheets if they exist.

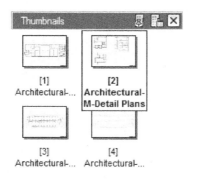

Figure 8–9

- At the top of each view are **Zoom** and **Pan** commands similar to their corresponding tools in the AutoCAD software, as shown in Figure 8–10. You can also use the arrow keys on the right to scroll through multiple sheets.

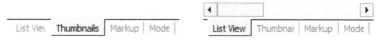

Figure 8–10

Layers in Autodesk Design Review

The Layers palette (shown in Figure 8–11), provides control over the visibility of layers. Select the light bulb to toggle the layers on and off in the current view.

Palettes can be pinned to remain displayed or unpinned so that they auto-hide, much like AutoCAD palettes.

Figure 8–11

- To have access to layers in the DWF file, the layer information must be included when the DWF file is created. If you use the **Export** command, this option is preset. If you use the **Plot** command, you need to set the option in the Properties of the DWF plotter (in the Plotter Configuration Editor, click **Custom Properties**). Select **Include layer information**, as shown in Figure 8–12.

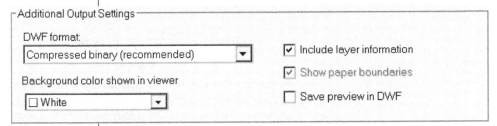

Figure 8–12

Creating Markups

The *Markup & Measure* tab contains tools for redlining and marking up DWF files including text, symbols, stamps, etc., as shown in Figure 8–13.

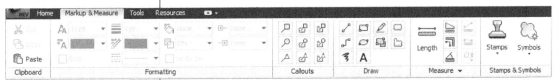

Figure 8–13

When you have added markups, they display in the Markups palette, as shown in Figure 8–14.

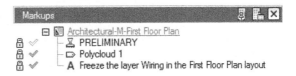

Figure 8–14

Viewing Markups in AutoCAD

The markups can be viewed in the AutoCAD software using the **Markup Set Manager** located in the *View* tab>Palettes panel.

In the **Markup Set Manager**, you can view the markup and automatically open the associated DWG file to make revisions as required. You can then republish the DWF with the corrections.

How To: View a Markup in AutoCAD

1. In the *View* tab>Palettes panel, click (Markup Set Manager).
2. In the Markup Set Manager, select **Open...**, as shown in Figure 8–15.

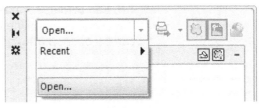

Figure 8–15

3. Select the DWF markup file from the appropriate folder.
4. In the Markup Set Manager, expand the list of markups, as shown in Figure 8–16.

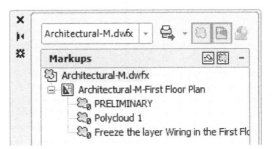

Figure 8–16

---

5. Double-click on one of the markups to display it in the drawing.
6. Make changes to the drawing as required.
7. To indicate to the reviewer that something has been done with the drawing, change the Markup status as shown in Figure 8–17.

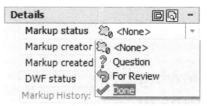

Figure 8–17

8. Repeat the process for any additional markups.

9. In the Markup Set Manager, expand (Republish Markup DWF) and select **Republish All Sheets or Republish Markup Sheets**.

10. The Specify DWF file dialog box automatically displays the associated DWF file. Click **Select** and replace the existing file or create a new file.

Hint: Autodesk Viewer

You can also use Autodesk Viewer to view the DWF files. The Viewer is a free online file viewer provided by Autodesk and can be opened from *https://viewer.autodesk.com/.*

8.3 Publishing Drawing Sets

The **Batch Plot/Publish** command provides an easy way to create either electronic or paper drawing sets using the interface shown in Figure 8–18. With **Batch Plot/Publish** you can create multi-sheet and multi-drawing DWFx or PDF files that can be viewed using the Autodesk Design Review software or Adobe Reader. The same list of drawing sheets can also be plotted directly to paper.

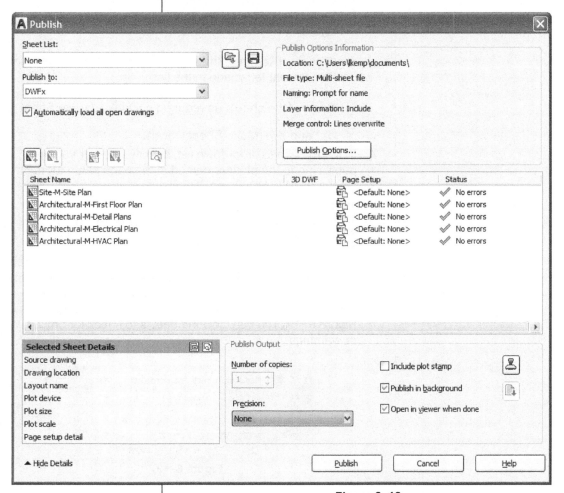

Figure 8–18

You can add layouts to the list for publishing from any drawing while controlling the order in which they are printed or presented. Once the list of sheets has been created, you can save it and easily reload it later to publish the same set of sheets again.

How To: Publish a Set of Drawings

1. Open a drawing containing multiple layouts that you want to publish.
2. In the ribbon, in the *Output* tab>Plot panel, click 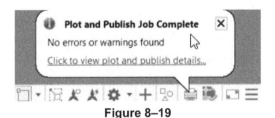 (Batch Plot).
3. In the Publish dialog box, a list of drawing sheets that were automatically created from the existing layouts in the drawing displays.

   - Click (Add Sheets) to include other drawings. Selecting a drawing file automatically imports all of its layouts.

   - Click (Remove Sheets) to remove any sheets that you do not want to include in the list.

   - Reorder the sheets as required using (Move Sheet Up) and (Move Sheet Down).

4. In the Publish to drop-down list, specify whether you are publishing to the plotters named in the page setup for each layout: a DWF, DWFx, or PDF file.
5. Click **Publish**.
6. You might be prompted to save the current list of sheets. Do so if you are planning to print the same group of layouts again. A DSD file is created.

- The publishing process takes place in the background, enabling you to continue with other projects. When it is finished, an alert balloon opens in the Status Bar, as shown in Figure 8–19. You can view the details to check for any errors or warnings.

Figure 8–19

- Click (Preview) to display the plot preview of the sheet that has been selected in the list.

- In the Publish Options dialog box you can specify the output, type of file (single or multi-sheet), prompt or default name for the multi-sheet file, security, and layer information, as shown in Figure 8–20.

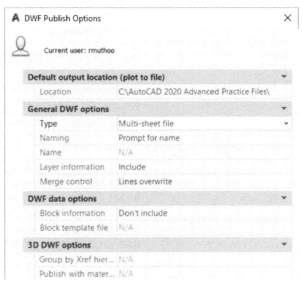

Figure 8–20

- **Show Details** displays additional information about the selected sheet details, number of copies, plot stamp, publish in background, and viewer options. Click **Hide Details** to close the additional options.

How To: Work with Sheet Lists Files

1. In the ribbon, in the *Output* tab>Plot panel, click ▭ (Batch Plot).

2. In the Publish dialog box, click ▭ (Load Sheet List).
3. Select the DSD file that you want to load.
4. In the Load Sheet List dialog box (shown in Figure 8–21), select to either replace or append sheets to the current list.

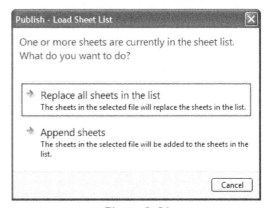

Figure 8–21

5. In the Publish dialog box, make any required changes and click **Publish**.

- You can change the default page setup in the list of page setups in the drawing. You can also import page setups from another drawing or template that contains named page setups. To change the page setup for a sheet, select its default setup in the list and then select from the drop-down list.

- The **Batch Plot** command automatically adds all of the open drawings to the Sheet list, including their Model tabs. This might create a problem when several drawings are open. An alert box opens and prompts you to change the names of the model sheets. To keep this from happening, clear the **Automatically load all open drawings** option.

Practice 8a

Reviewing and Publishing Drawing Sets

Practice Objectives

- Plot and export a single layout and multi-sheets to DWF and DWFx files, and view and mark them up in the Autodesk Design Review software.
- View DWF markups to revise its associated DWG file in the AutoCAD software using the Markup Set Manager.
- Set up a list of multiple layouts from multiple drawings to batch plot them.

To complete this practice, you must have the Autodesk Design Review software. The software must be installed before you start the practice.

In this practice, you will plot a layout to a DWF file and open the file in the Autodesk Design Review software. You will also export a multi-sheet DWFx file, view it in the Autodesk Design Review software, and make several markups. Finally, you will import the DWFx file into the original drawing file using the Markup Set Manager and make a change based on the markup. You will then republish the DWFx and review the changes in the Autodesk Design Review software, as shown in Figure 8–22. Finally, you will Batch Plot multiple drawings.

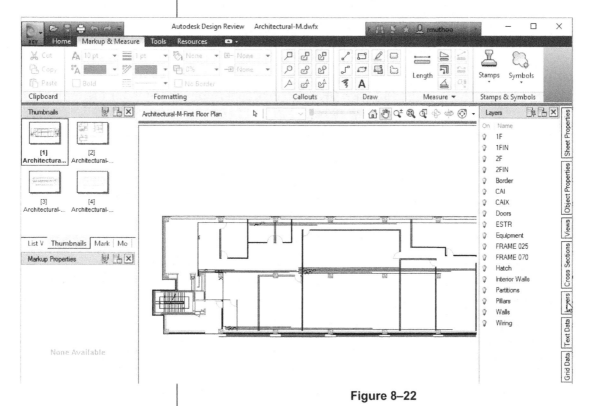

Figure 8–22

Task 1 - Plot a DWF file.

1. Open **Architectural-M.dwg** from the practice files folder.

2. Switch to the **First Floor Plan** layout.

3. Start the **Plot** command. In the Batch Plot warning dialog box, click **Continue to plot a single sheet**.

4. In the Plot dialog box, verify that the *Printer/plotter* is set to **DWF6 ePlot.pc3**. (It was set in the page setup for the layout.)

5. Click **Properties** to open the Plotter Configuration Editor.

6. Select **Custom Properties** in the list. In the *Access Custom Dialog* area, click **Custom Properties**.

7. In the DWF6 ePlot Properties dialog box, in the *Additional Output Settings* area, select **Include layer information**, as shown in Figure 8–23. Click **OK** twice.

Figure 8–23

8. Click **OK** again to accept **Apply changes for the current plot only**.

9. The **Plot to file** option is on by default for this plotter. Set the *Plot Area* to **Layout**.

10. Click **OK** to create the plot. Save the DWF file in the practice files folder and name it **First Floor Plan.dwf**.

11. Close the *Plot and Publish Job Complete* balloon in the Status Bar.

*The Autodesk Design Review software must already be installed. If Windows prompts you to select which application to use to open the file, select **Autodesk DWF Application.***

12. In the Status Bar, right-click on 🖨 (Plot/Publish Details) and select **View Plotted File...** to open the **First Floor Plan.dwf** in the Autodesk Design Review software.

13. Pan and zoom to view the image.

14. Along the right side of the drawing window, expand the Layers palette. A list of layers are displayed.

15. Close the Autodesk Design Review software.

Task 2 - Export a multi-sheet DWFx file.

Note that the selected layouts are highlighted.

1. Select all four layout tabs by pressing <Ctrl> or <Shift> as you select each one.

2. Start the 🔍 (Export DWFx) command (*Output* tab>Export to DWF/PDF panel).

3. In the Save as DWFx dialog box, browse to the practice files and click **Options**, as shown in Figure 8–24.

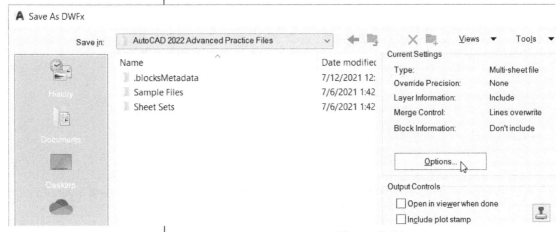

Figure 8–24

4. Verify that *Layer information* is set to **Include**, as shown in Figure 8–25. Click **OK**.

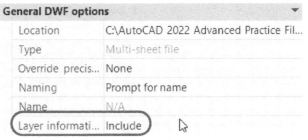

Figure 8–25

*Export is automatically set to **All layouts** because you selected more than one layout before starting the command.*

5. In the Save as DWFx dialog box, in the *Output Controls* area, select **Open in viewer when done**.

6. Verify that you are still in the practice files folder and use the drawing name as the filename. Click **Save**.

If the exported DWFx file opens in Internet Explorer, close it and open the file in the Autodesk Design Review software manually.

7. The Autodesk Design Review software opens after the file is exported. Click on the *Thumbnails* tab to display the four thumbnails, one for each layout. Select the *Layers* tab to display the list of layers, as shown in Figure 8–26.

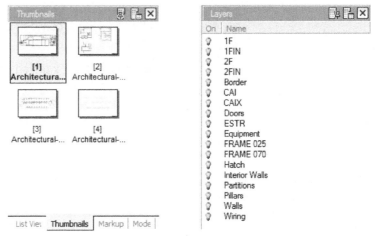

Figure 8–26

8. Open each of the thumbnails.

9. In the First Floor Plan layout, toggle off several layers to display the change. Toggle them back on.

Task 3 - Create a markup.

1. In the Autodesk Design Review software, ensure that you are in the First Floor Plan layout. In the ribbon, open the *Markup & Measure* tab.

2. In the Stamps & Symbols panel, expand ⚱ (Stamps) and select **PRELIMINARY**. Place it near the top of the title block, as shown in Figure 8–27.

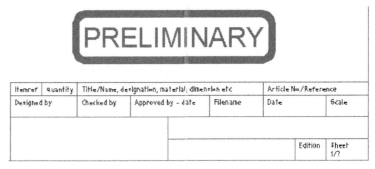

Figure 8–27

3. Zoom in to the middle of the First Floor Plan layout, where you see some long horizontal lines and small tick marks, as shown in Figure 8–28.

4. In the *Markup & Measure* tab>Draw panel, click

   (Polycloud) and add a revision cloud (click four points of the polygon) around some of the objects, as shown in Figure 8–28.

5. In the Draw panel, click **A** (Text Box), place a text box near the cloud, and type the words shown in Figure 8–28. Set the size of the text in the Formatting panel as required.

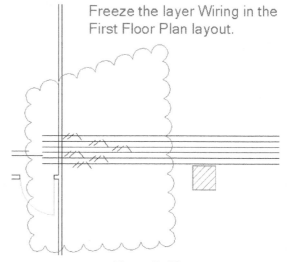

Freeze the layer Wiring in the First Floor Plan layout.

Figure 8–28

6. Save the DWFx file.

7. Close the Autodesk Design Review software.

Task 4 - Use the Markup Set Manager.

---

1. In the AutoCAD software, select the First Floor Plan layout if you are not already in it.

2. In the *View* tab>Palettes panel, click (Markup Set Manager), if it is not already open.

3. In the Markup Set Manager, click **Open...**, as shown in Figure 8–29.

Figure 8–29

4. In the Open Markup DWF dialog box, select **Architectural-M.dwfx** from the practice files folder and click **Open**.

5. In the Markup Set Manager, expand the list of markups, as shown in Figure 8–30.

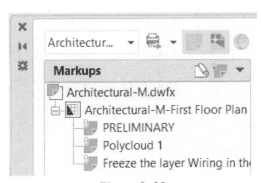

Figure 8–30

6. Double-click on one of the markups to display it in the drawing.

7. Double-click on **Polycloud 1** and zoom in on the revision cloud that is now displayed in the drawing.

8. Double-click inside the viewport to activate it.

9. In the *Home* tab>Layers panel, click ⛄ (Freeze).

10. Select the horizontal lines or small tick marks to freeze the layer. Press <Enter> to end the command.

11. Zoom out to display the entire layout.

12. In the Markup Set Manager, select **Polycloud 1**.

13. In the *Details* area, change the *Markup status* to **Done**, as shown in Figure 8–31.

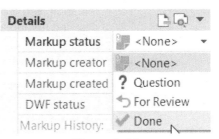

Figure 8–31

14. Repeat the process for the text **Freeze the layer Wiring...**.

15. Save the drawing.

16. In the Markup Set Manager, expand 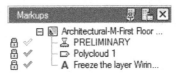 (Republish Markup DWF) and select **Republish All Sheets**.

17. The Specify DWFx file dialog box should automatically list the associated DWFx file. Click **Select** and then click **Yes** to replace the existing file.

18. When the file has finished printing, open the Autodesk Design Review software. The changes are displayed and the markups are checked, as shown in Figure 8–32.

Figure 8–32

19. Close the Autodesk Design Review software.

20. Save the drawing.

Task 5 - Publish drawing sets.

In this task, you will use the **Batch Plot** command to set up a list of drawing layouts using two different drawings, as shown in Figure 8–33, and to create a multi-sheet DWF file. You will also view the file in the Autodesk Design Review software.

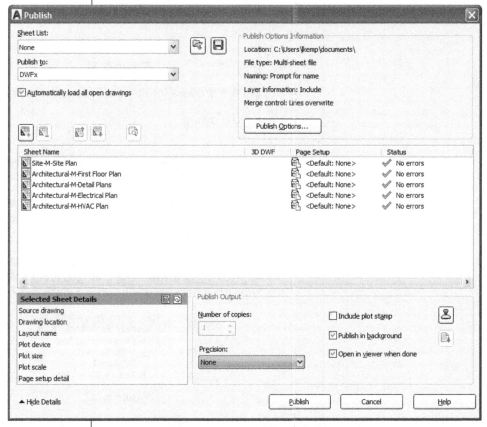

Figure 8–33

1. Verify that **Architectural-M.dwg** is open.

2. Save the drawing. Note that all of the sheets must be saved before saving the sheet list in the **Batch Plot** command.

3. In the ribbon, in the *Output* tab>Plot panel, click (Batch Plot). In the Publish dialog box, the drawing file *Model* tab and the layouts are listed as sheets.

4. Select the **Architectural-M-Model** sheet and click (Remove Sheets) to remove it from the list.

5. To add a sheet, click ⊞ (Add Sheets) and select the file **Site-M.dwg** in the Practice Files folder. Two sheets from this drawing (the *Model* tab and one layout tab) are added to the list.

6. Remove the **Site-M-Model** sheet.

7. Select **Site-M-Site Plan**. Click ⊞ (Move Sheet Up) and move it to the top of the list, as shown in Figure 8–34.

Figure 8–34

8. In the Publish to drop-down list, select **DWFx**.

   • Publishing to DWFx creates individual files for each layout, even if you have set multi-sheet files using the **Publish Options**.

9. Click ⊟ (Save Sheet List) and save the list in the practice files folder (**Architectural-M.dsd**). This makes it easy to publish the same set of sheets again.

10. Click **Publish**, type a new filename, and specify the practice files folder as the location of the file. Click **Select**.

11. If the Plot - Processing Background Job alert box opens, click **Close**. The job is then processed in the background and wait till the *Plot and Publish Job Complete* balloon displays indicating that the job is finished.

12. In the Status Bar, right-click on ⊟ (Publish Details) and select **View Plotted File...**.

13. In the Autodesk Design Review software, zoom and pan as required.

14. Close the Autodesk Design Review software.

15. Close the drawing file.

8.4 Shared Views

Creating shared views are a great alternative to printing .PDF and .DWF files for sharing your designs with stakeholders. Shared views are stored in the cloud and can be viewed and commented on by any web enabled desktop, tablet, or mobile device. The links created for sharing views expire after thirty days, but can be extended or terminated at any time.

When sharing views, you can determine if you only share 2D views and whether you share the model view along with all the layout views. You can also include object properties with the view to better communicate object information.

Shared Views Palette

A history of the published shared views displays in the Shared Views palette, as shown in Figure 8–35. Click on the ellipsis next to the Shared View to see a list of available commands. You can also create new sheets from here. In the *Collaborate* tab>Share

panel, click ![icon] (Shared Views) to display the Shared Views palette.

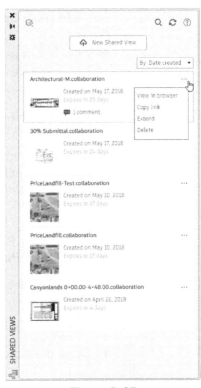

Figure 8–35

How To: Create a Shared View

1. Sign in to your Autodesk account, if you are not already signed in.

2. Expand **A** (Application Menu)>Publish and click (Share View).

3. In the Share View dialog box, type a name, select which views to share, and whether or not to share object properties, as shown in Figure 8–36. Click **Share**.

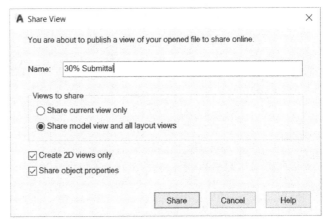

Figure 8–36

4. In the Share View - Processing Ready to Start dialog box, click **Proceed**.

5. When the *Share View Upload Complete* balloon displays in the Status Bar (as shown in Figure 8–37), click **View in Browser**.

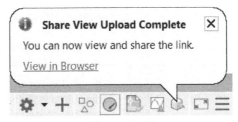

Figure 8–37

You can continue working in the background until the upload is complete.

Autodesk Viewer

The Autodesk Viewer opens the temporary view link in a browser on your desktop, tablet, or other mobile device. This enables you to share the view with stakeholders who do not have AutoCAD software, without having to email files back and forth or install other viewing software. Using an Internet browser, they can review and markup the design for better communication. Figure 8–38 shows the Autodesk Viewer interface.

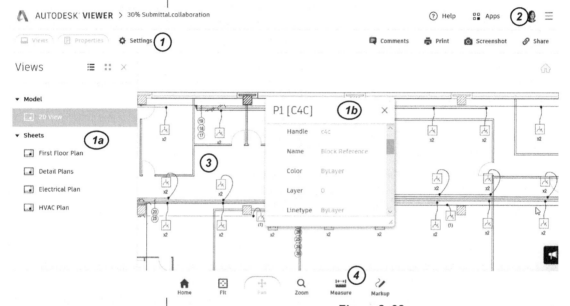

Figure 8–38

1. Palettes Bar

Multiple palettes are available to help navigate, share, and analyze the model. Palettes include: Views, Properties, Settings, Comments, Print, Screenshot, and Share.

1a - Views: Lists all the model and sheet views shared when the view link was created.

1b - Properties: Lists the properties of the currently selected object in the active view. Properties can include: color, layer, linetype, material, length, and more.

2. Autodesk Sign in

Typically, you must already be signed in. If you are not, you are required to sign in to your Autodesk account to be able to open views and save markups.

3. Active View

The active view displays the model or sheet shared from AutoCAD.

4. Tool Bar

The Tool Bar contains navigation and communication tools, as shown in Figure 8–39. The Fit, Pan, and Zoom tools help you quickly navigate the active view. The Measure and Markup tools help you communicate with other team members about the design.

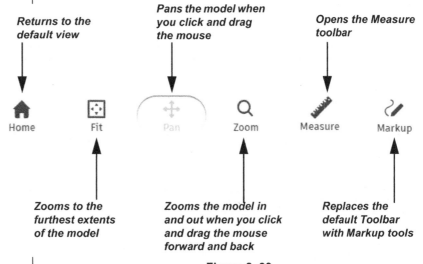

Figure 8–39

Measure and Markup

Measure

The Measure tool contains additional tools for measuring shared view objects including: distance, angle, and area. You can also calibrate distances by placing a distance measurement and defining the distance you measured, as shown in Figure 8–40.

The following object snap options are available for more accurate measurements:

Tooltip	Osnap	Tooltip	Osnap
	Endpoint		Nearest
	Midpoint		Perpendicular

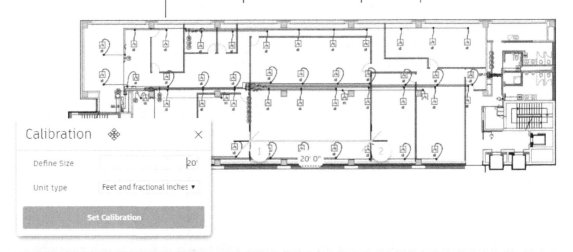

Figure 8–40

How To: Set Which Units Display

1. In the Toolbar, click Measure (Measure).

2. In the Measure toolbar, click ⚙ (Settings).

3. In the Settings dialog box, select the unit type and precision, as shown in Figure 8–41.

| Unit type | Feet and fractional inch ▼ |
| Precision | 1/8 ▼ |

Figure 8–41

How To: Measure Objects

1. In the Toolbar, click Measure (Measure).
2. In the Measure tools, select the type of measurement you want to make: (|←→| Distance, ◣ Angle, or ▦ Area)

3. Click on the points you want to measure. Note that Object snaps are enabled automatically, as shown in Figure 8–42.

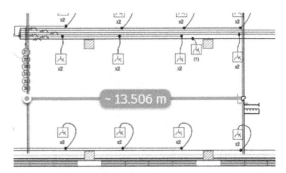

~ 13.506 m

Figure 8–42

How To: Calibrate Measurements

1. In the Toolbar, click Measure (Measure).

2. In the Measure toolbar, click  (Calibrate).

3. Click on the points you want to measure. In the Calibration dialog box, define the size and set the unit type, as shown in Figure 8–43. Click **Set Calibration**.

Calibration ✕

Define Size		40
Unit type	Feet and fractional inches	▼

Set Calibration

Figure 8–43

Markup

The Markup tool contains tools for redlining and marking up shared views including text, arrows, clouds, etc., as shown in

Figure 8–44. When you click Markup (Markup), the Markup toolbar replaces the original toolbar. Markups must be saved or canceled before the original toolbar can reappear. In order to save a markup, you must be signed into you Autodesk account.

Free draw lines and shapes

Add rectangular shaped revision clouds

Set the markup color

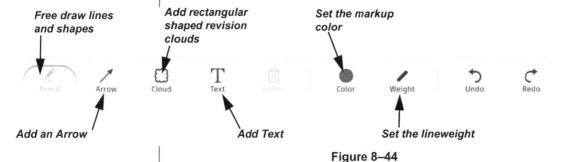

Pencil   Arrow   Cloud   Text   Delete   Color   Weight   Undo   Redo

Add an Arrow

Add Text

Set the lineweight

Figure 8–44

Practice 8b

Create Shared Views

Practice Objectives

- Create shared views and inspect them in the Autodesk Viewer browser,
- Mark up shared views in the Autodesk Viewer browser.
- Review a shared view in AutoCAD software and add a comment.

In this practice, you will create shared views and inspect the file in the Autodesk Viewer browser. You will also make multiple markups, as shown in Figure 8–45. Finally, you will display the shared view in the AutoCAD software and add comments to the shared view.

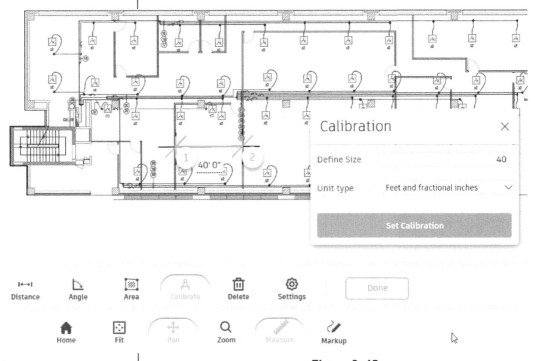

Figure 8–45

Task 1 - Create a shared view.

1. Typically, you must be signed in to your Autodesk account. You can confirm if you are signed in by looking at the InfoCenter, which displays your Autodesk user name when you are signed in. If you are not already, sign in to your Autodesk account.

2. Open **Architectural-MShare.dwg** from the practice files folder.

3. Expand  (Application Menu)>Publish and click

    (Share View).

4. In the Share View dialog box, do the following, as shown in Figure 8–46:

    - *Name*: Type **30% Submittal**
    - *Views to share* area: Select **Share model view and all layout views**.
    - Select **Create 2D views only** and **Share object properties**.
    - Click **Share**.

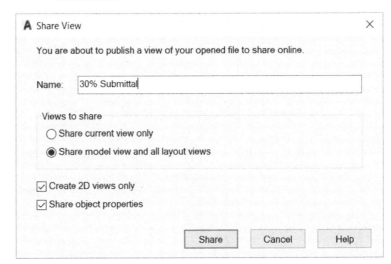

Figure 8–46

5. In the Share View - Processing Ready to Start dialog box, click **Proceed**.

6. When the *Share View Upload Complete* balloon displays in the Status Bar (as shown in Figure 8–47), click **View in Browser**.

    •   The Autodesk Viewer opens the temporary view link in a browser with the view displayed.

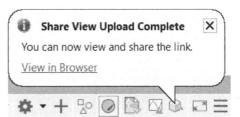

Figure 8–47

Task 2 - Set the units to display.

1. In the Autodesk Viewer toolbar, click Measure (Measure) to display the Measure tools.

2. In the Measure tools, click (Settings).

3. In the Settings dialog box, select **Feet and fractional inch** for the unit type and **1/8** for precision, as shown in Figure 8–48.

Figure 8–48

4. Press <Esc> to exit the command.

Task 3 - Measure objects.

1. In the Autodesk Viewer toolbar, click Measure (Measure) to display the Measure tools.

2. In the Measure tools, click |↔| (Distance).

Note that the cursor snaps to the relevant object snaps.

3. Click a few different points to measure various rooms and objects to get an idea of how they relate to one another.

4. Click the points similar to that shown in Figure 8–49. Press <Esc> to exit the command.

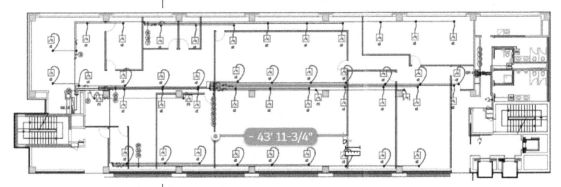

Figure 8–49

Task 4 - Calibrate measurements.

---

1. In the Autodesk Viewer toolbar, click Measure (Measure).

2. In the Measure toolbar, click Ａ (Calibrate).

3. Click on the points that you checked in Step 4 of Task 3. In the Calibration dialog box, verify that the unit type is set to **Feet and fractional inches** and define the size as **40**, as shown in Figure 8–50. Click **Set Calibration**.

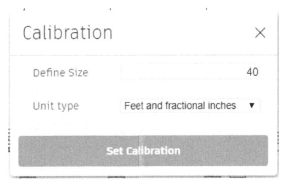

Figure 8–50

4. Measure the distance again and note the difference.

Task 5 - Analyze the model using palettes.

1. In the Palettes bar, click (Properties).

2. In the Active View, click on a column, as shown in Figure 8–51. Review its properties, then close the Properties palette.

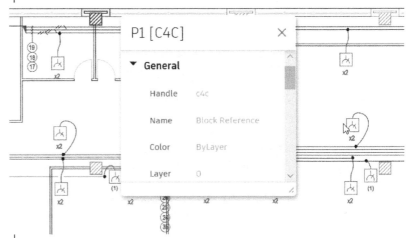

Figure 8–51

Task 6 - Create a markup.

1. In the Autodesk Viewer toolbar, click ^{Markup} (Markup).

2. In the Markup toolbar, click T (Text).

3. In the Active View, click a point near a column, as shown in Figure 8–52. Type **Create a column layer and place all columns on that layer**.

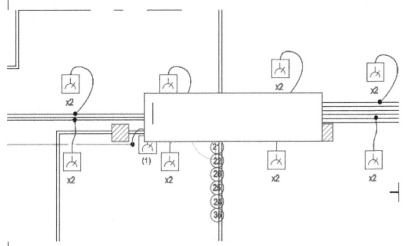

Figure 8–52

4. In the Markup toolbar, click ✐ (Arrow) and add a arrows pointing from the text box to a few of the columns, as shown in Figure 8–53. Adjust the arrows as required.

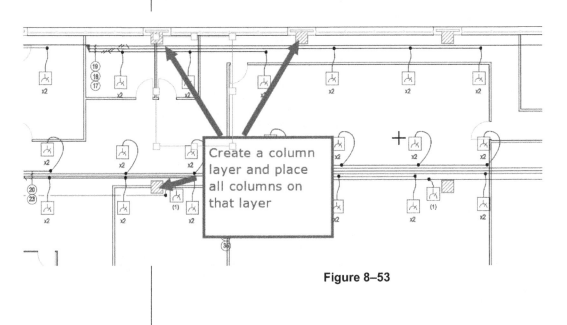

Figure 8–53

5. In the Markup toolbar, click 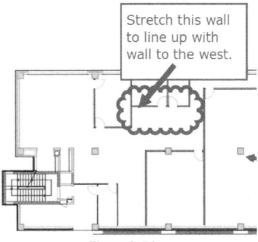 (Cloud) and add a cloud, as shown in Figure 8–54. Then, add the text and arrow shown.

Figure 8–54

6. Click **Save** to make markups available to others with the view link.

7. Close the Autodesk Viewer.

Task 7 - Open shared views.

1. In the AutoCAD software, in the *Collaborate* tab>Share panel, click (Shared Views) to display the Shared View palette.

2. In the Shared View palette, if the view is not already displayed, click **New Shared View**. A new **30% Submittal** shared view displays, as shown in Figure 8–55.

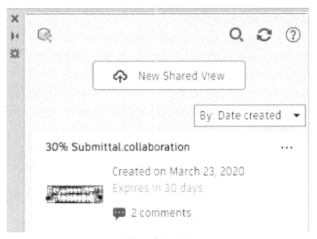

Figure 8–55

3. Click on  to open the drop-down list shown in Figure 8–56.

Figure 8–56

4. Click **View in browser**. The shared view opens in the Autodesk Viewer browser.

5. In the top right of the view, click **Comments**.

   • Note: To add comments, you must be signed in to an Autodesk account. You are required to have a subscription.

6. In the comment field, type **Reviewed on April 6** (as shown in Figure 8–57), and then click **Post**.

Figure 8–57

7. Close the Autodesk Viewer.

8. In the Shared Views palette, click ⟳ (Refresh). The comment and drawing displays as shown in Figure 8–58.

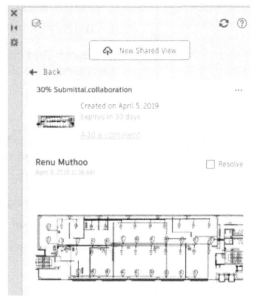

Figure 8–58

9. Save and close the files.

Chapter Review Questions

1. What is a DWF file?

    a. A plot style table file.

    b. An AutoCAD system file that controls plot settings.

    c. A backup copy of a drawing file.

    d. A compressed file format for viewing drawings.

2. What information about data can be included when exporting drawing files to PDF files? (Select all that apply.)

    a. **Layer information**

    b. **Linetype information**

    c. **Fonts**

    d. **Hyperlinks**

3. Which tool can you use to plot several drawings at once to a DWF file, to a PDF file, or to paper?

    a. **Plotter Manager**

    b. **Plot**

    c. **Plotter Wizard**

    d. **Batch Plot/Publish**

4. The **Batch Plot** command can add all the open drawings to the Sheet list, excluding their *Model* tabs.

    a. True

    b. False

5. If you do not have the AutoCAD software installed, which application would you use to view a DWF file?

    a. Microsoft Word

    b. Autodesk Design Review

    c. Adobe Acrobat

    d. Microsoft Excel

6. How do you share your design with someone who does not have AutoCAD or any viewing software and enable them to measure it, mark it up, and send back valuable electronic feedback?

   a. This is not possible without installing a viewing software.

   b. Print a .DWF and have them use Autodesk Design Review.

   c. Share views and have them provide feedback in the Autodesk Viewer browser.

   d. Take screen shots of the design and email them.

Command Summary

Button	Command	Location
	Batch Plot	• **Ribbon:** *Output* tab>Plot panel • **Application Menu:** Print • **Command Prompt:** publish
	Export DWF	• **Ribbon:** *Output* tab>Export to DWF/PDF panel • **Application Menu:** Export>DWF • **Command Prompt:** exportdwf
	Export DWFx	• **Ribbon:** *Output* tab>Export to DWF/PDF panel • **Application Menu:** Export>DWFx • **Command Prompt:** exportdwfx
	Export PDF	• **Ribbon:** *Output* tab>Export to DWF/PDF panel • **Application Menu:** Export>PDF • **Command Prompt:** exportpdf
	Export to DWF/PDF Options	• **Ribbon:** *Output* tab>Export to DWF/PDF panel
	Markup Set Manager	• **Ribbon:** *View* tab>Palettes panel • **Command Prompt:** markup
	Plot	• **Quick Access Toolbar** • **Ribbon:** *Output* tab>Plot panel • **Application Menu:** Print • **Command Prompt:** plot or <Ctrl>+<P>
	Preview	• **Ribbon:** *Output* tab>Plot panel • **Application Menu:** Print
	Republish Markup DWF	• **Markup Set Manager**
	Share View	• **Application Menu:** Publish • **Ribbon:** *Collaborate* tab>Share panel • **Command Prompt:** ShareView

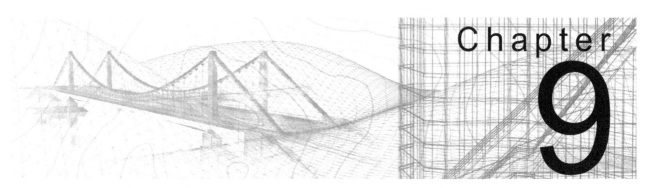

Other Tools for Collaboration

Sharing drawings with other team members has become a necessity. Learn how to package a drawing and related files with eTransmit to ensure that team members have everything they need to work with the drawings you send. In addition, learn how to add hyperlinks to a drawing to quickly reference images, documents, or other material.

Learning Objectives in This Chapter

- Create a single compressed file that includes all of the associated files for easy transmittal.
- Create and save transmittal setups with specific properties for easy reuse later.
- Work with hyperlinks for specific objects in a drawing for easy access to any information.
- Compare drawings to highlight differences between versions.

9.1 eTransmit

The **eTransmit** utility (shown in Figure 9–1) packs an open drawing with all of its associated files (such as drawing reference files, images, fonts, etc.) into a single compressed file or transmittal set. This makes it easy to email all of the files associated with a project to clients, partners, members of a design team, etc.

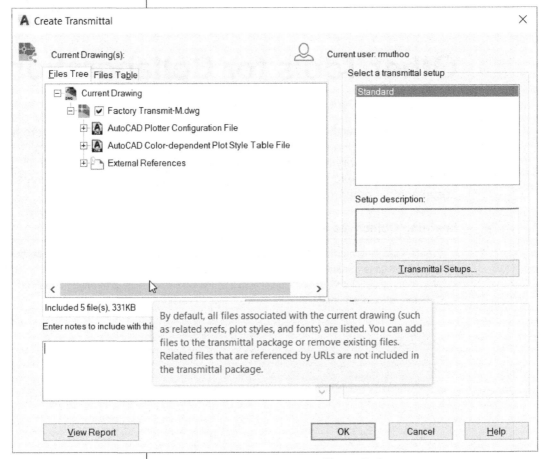

Figure 9–1

- It is recommended that you save all open files before using the **eTransmit** utility to pack them.

- The *Files Tree* tab lists the actual drawing files and other files that are going to be packaged. The files are listed hierarchically under the current drawing with font maps, image files, plotter configuration files, and drawing reference files listed in separate categories.

- The *Files Table* tab lists all of the files that are going to be packaged alphabetically, as shown in Figure 9–2. You can use **Add File** to include other files in the transmittal set.

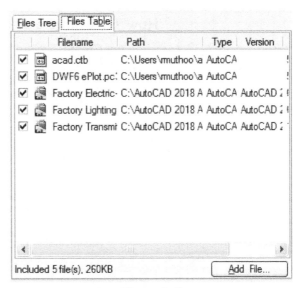

Figure 9–2

- **eTransmit** works well with Sheet Set Manager.

How To: Create a Transmittal Set

1. Open a drawing that you want to transmit. Save the file if any changes are made.
2. In **Application Menu>Publish**, click 💾 (**eTransmit**).
3. The Create Transmittal dialog box opens displaying a list of all of the associated files.
4. Add additional files as required.
5. Select a Transmittal Setup (you can create a new one as required).
6. Add notes in the *Notes* area as required.
7. Click **View Report** to see details of the transmittal. The text of the report is included in the transmittal set.
8. Click **OK** to create the transmittal set. The next steps depend on the options selected in the Transmittal Setup file. You might be prompted for a filename or to override another transmittal file.

Transmittal Setups

You can create *Transmittal Setups* with specific properties and save them to easily generate future transmittals using the same properties. If you often use eTransmit, this is a big time-saver.

How To: Create a Transmittal Setup

1. In the Create Transmittal dialog box, click **Transmittal Setups**.
2. In the Transmittal Setups dialog box (shown in Figure 9–3), click **New** to create a new setup.
   - Or select a setup you want to change and click **Modify**.

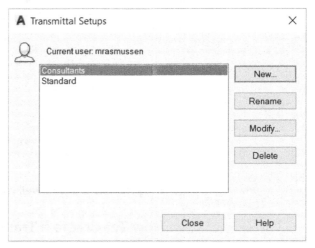

Figure 9–3

3. If creating a new setup, you are prompted for a new name, as shown in Figure 9–4. A Transmittal Setup uses an existing setup style as a starting point.

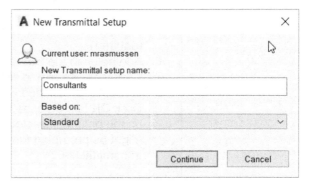

Figure 9–4

4. In the Modify Transmittal Setup dialog box, define the settings and options for the setup, as shown in Figure 9–5.

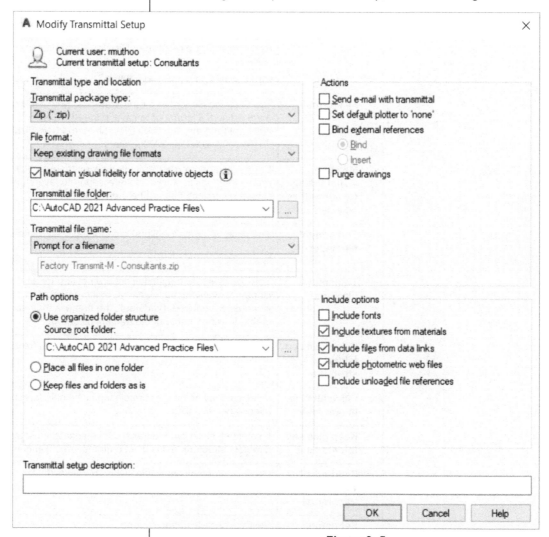

Figure 9–5

5. Click **OK** and then **Close** to create the setup. The new setup becomes the default setup for the current transmittal set.

Transmittal Setup Options

Transmittal package type	Select the type of file for the transmittal set: **Folder:** Creates a set of uncompressed files in a folder. **Self-extracting executable:** Creates a compressed .EXE file. **Zip:** Creates a compressed Zip file.
File format	Specifies the file format for the drawings. Select to keep the existing file format or to save in the AutoCAD® software (and the AutoCAD LT® software) 2018, 2013, 2010, 2007, 2004, or 2000 formats.
Maintain visual fidelity for annotative objects	Separates annotative objects and saves them as scaled representations in blocks into new separate layers (for software versions that are before 2010).
Transmittal file folder	The folder in which the file(s) are created. You can click ⬚ (Browse) and specify a folder.
Transmittal file name	You can have the transmittal set prompt you for a filename, overwrite the filename, or increment the filename as required. By default, the name is the <name of the drawing - name of the transmittal setup>.
Use organized folder structure	If selected, you can also specify the *Source* root folder.
Place all files in one folder	If selected, all of the files are placed in a single target folder when installed.
Keep files and folders as is	If selected, files from the transmittal are installed in the directory structure that is used on the source computer.
Send email with transmittal	Opens your email application when a transmittal is created.
Set default plotter to 'none'	Sets the default plotter to **none**.
Bind external references	Inserts all of the external references to the base drawing file and detaches the drawing reference files.
Prompt for password	Enables you to specify a password to be required to open the transmittal set.
Purge Drawings	Runs the **Purge** command on drawings before including them in the transmittal set.

Include fonts	Includes all of the font files. If you know that the company you are sending the file to uses the same fonts, you can save space in the set by not sending them.
Include textures from materials	Includes textures with materials that are attached to faces.
Include files from data links	Includes external files that are referenced by data links.
Include photometric web files	Includes photometric web files that are associated with web lights in the drawing.
Include unloaded file references	Includes all of the unloaded referenced files in the set and keeps them unloaded in the package.
Transmittal setup description	Type a description for this setup.

Practice 9a | eTransmit

Practice Objective

- Create a compressed transmittal set of all of the files related to a drawing, using the **eTransmit** command.

In this practice, you will use **eTransmit** to create a compressed transmittal set of all of the files related to a drawing, as shown in Figure 9–6.

Figure 9–6

1. Open **Factory Transmit-M.dwg** from the practice files folder.

2. Open the External References palette. Verify that **Factory Electric-Adv-M.dwg** and **Factory Lighting-Adv-M.dwg** are attached, as shown in Figure 9–7.

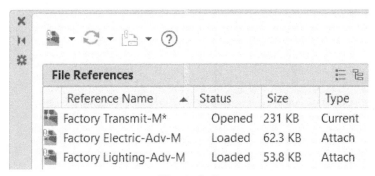

Figure 9–7

If prompted, save the drawing.

3. In the Application Menu, expand **Publish** and click

   (eTransmit) to start the **eTransmit** command.

4. In the Create Transmittal dialog box, click **Transmittal Setups**.

5. Click **New** to create a new transmittal setup (based on **Standard**) named **Consultants**. Click **Continue**.

6. In the Modify Transmittal Setup dialog box, for the *Transmittal package type*, verify that **Zip (*.zip)** is selected.

7. For the *Transmittal file folder*, select the practice files folder. Leave the default settings for the other options.

8. Click **OK** and then click **Close** to create the setup. Ensure that **Consultants** is current.

9. In the Create Transmittal dialog box, click **View Report** to preview the report that is going to be generated. Click **Close** to close the View Transmittal Report dialog box.

10. Click **OK** and save the transmittal set in the practice files folder.

11. Open Windows Explorer and, in the practice files folder, locate **Factory Transmit-M - Consultants.zip**. Double-click on this file to open the zip file. Extract the files to *C:\Factory Files* (or another path that your instructor specifies).

12. Navigate to the folder in which you extracted the files and note the files that were included. Double-click on **Factory Transmit-M.txt** to open the report.

9.2 Hyperlinks

A hyperlink is a pointer to a file that opens when the link is activated. The file can be on the Internet or a local drive.

You can add hyperlinks to specific objects in a drawing, as shown in Figure 9–8. They can be used for easy access to any information you want to associate with the drawing, such as technical information in a document file, an inventory in a spreadsheet, a project proposal, or other AutoCAD drawings. You can also have a hyperlink point to a named view or layout in a drawing, or send a message to an email address.

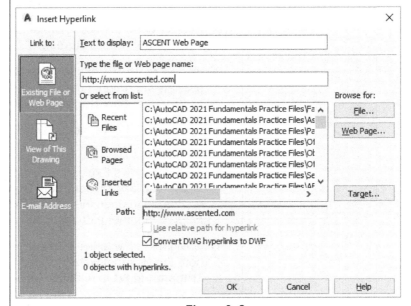

Figure 9–8

How To: Insert a Hyperlink

1. In the *Insert* tab>Data panel, click (Hyperlink).
2. Select the object(s) to which you want to attach the link and press <Enter>. The Insert Hyperlink dialog box opens.
3. In the *Link to:* area on the left side of the dialog box, select the type of link you want to use:
   - To a file or web address,
   - To a named view in the drawing, or
   - To an email address (send a message to that address).

4. In the *Text to display:* area, type the text you want to display in the drawing as the hyperlink's tag or description.
5. Depending on the type of link that you selected in Step 3, specify one of the following:
   - A URL for a web address or a filename with a path,
   - A named view or layout in the drawing, or
   - An email address.
6. Click **OK** to end the command.

- When linking to an existing file or Web page, **Target** enables you to specify a location in the file, as shown in Figure 9–9. For example, this could be a named view or layout in an AutoCAD drawing.

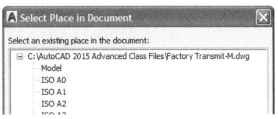

Figure 9–9

- When linking to a file, the path can be relative or absolute. If **Use Relative Path for Hyperlink** is selected, only the filename is stored with the hyperlink. The AutoCAD software uses the current drawing path or the path stored in the **hyperlinkbase** system variable.

- When linking to a file, hyperlinks can be converted. With **Convert DWG hyperlinks to DWF** selected, and when publishing to a DWF, the DWG hyperlink is converted to a DWF hyperlink.

- If you link to an email address, activating the link opens a new email message in your default email software to that address.

- Hyperlinks can be added to blocks using the **Create Block** command or using **Hyperlink** in the *Insert* tab>Data panel.

- You can add a hyperlink to text by inserting a hyperlink **Field**.

Using a Hyperlink

When you move the cursor near an object with an attached hyperlink, a small hyperlink icon displays, and the tooltip containing the hyperlink description or path, as shown in Figure 9–10.

Figure 9–10

- To activate the hyperlink, hold <Ctrl> and select the object. Alternatively, you can select the object with the hyperlink, right-click, expand Hyperlink and select **Open "<name of hyperlink>"**. The associated file opens.

- To edit the hyperlink information, select the object, right-click in the drawing window, expand Hyperlink and select **Edit Hyperlink**.

- To remove a hyperlink, open the Edit Hyperlink dialog box, and click **Remove Link**.

Hint: Sharing Drawings on a Network Using the WhoHas Command

Only one person at a time can access a drawing for editing. If you share drawings with others on a network and discover that a drawing you need is currently open by another user, you can use the **WhoHas** command to determine who has the file.

- Type **WhoHas** at the Command Line and select the drawing that you want to query.

- The software reports the user name and computer name in which the drawing is open, and the time it was opened.

Practice 9b

Hyperlinks

Practice Objective

- Attach hyperlinks to objects in a drawing, which are used to open another drawing and access a site on the internet.

In this practice, you will attach hyperlinks to objects in a drawing and use them to open a drawing and access a site on the Internet. One of the hyperlinks is shown in Figure 9–11.

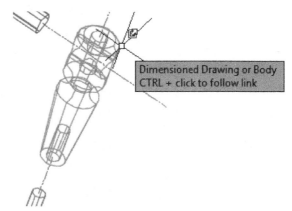

Figure 9–11

1. Open **Trammel-M.dwg** from the practice files folder.

2. In the *Insert* tab>Data panel, click (Hyperlink). In the title block, select the text **ASCENT – Center for Technical Knowledge** and press <Enter>.

3. In the Insert Hyperlink dialog box, set the following:
   - *Link to:* Ensure that **Existing File or Web Page** is selected.
   - *Text to display*: **ASCENT Web Page**
   - *Type the file or Web page*: **http://www.ascented.com**

4. Click **OK** to set the hyperlink.

5. Hover the cursor near the text **ASCENT – Center for Technical Knowledge**. The hyperlink icon and its description display as shown in Figure 9–12.

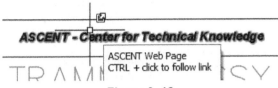

Figure 9–12

6. Double-click on the assembly to enter Model Space.

7. Start the Hyperlink command and do the following:
   - Select the magenta part of the assembly and press <Enter> to open the Insert Hyperlink dialog box.
   - *Text to display*: **Dimensioned Drawing of Body**.
   - In the *Browse for:* area, click **File**.
   - Navigate to the practice files folder and open **Body-M.dwg**.
   - Click **OK** in the Insert Hyperlink dialog box.

8. Hover the cursor over the magenta part to display the hyperlink icon and its description.

9. Select the magenta part. With the object highlighted, right-click, expand Hyperlink, and select **Open "Dimensioned Drawing of Body"**, as shown in Figure 9–13. **Body-M.dwg** opens in a separate window. Close the file and return to **Trammel-M.dwg**.

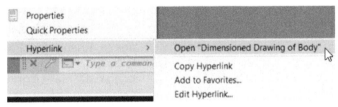

Figure 9–13

10. Return to Paper Space.

11. Hold <Ctrl> and select the ASCENT text to which you applied the hyperlink. The web page opens in your web browser if you have Internet access on your computer.

12. Close the browser.

13. Save and close the drawing.

9.3 Revision Clouds

Revision clouds are cloud-shaped objects that can be used to designate areas that you need to draw attention to in the drawing. The revision cloud creation options are located in the *Annotate* tab>Markup panel, as shown in Figure 9–14.

The revision cloud creation options are Rectangular, Polygonal, Freehand, and then you can also convert an object into a revision cloud.

Figure 9–14

How To: Create a Revision Cloud from an Object

1. In the *Annotate* tab>Markup panel, click (Revision Cloud).
2. Select **Object** from the <Down arrow> menu (as shown in Figure 9–15) or in the Command line.

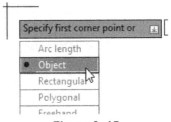

Figure 9–15

3. In the drawing, select the closed object. A preview of the revision cloud is displayed.

4. Select **Yes** or **No** to the set direction of the revision cloud arcs and end the command. The revision cloud is created, as shown in Figure 9–16.

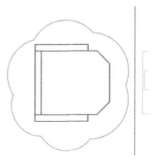

From Object (Circle)

Figure 9–16

Revcloud Properties

• When you hover your cursor over a revision cloud object, the Quick Properties now displays a **Revcloud** object type (as shown in Figure 9–17) instead of *Polyline* object type as in the previous versions of AutoCAD.

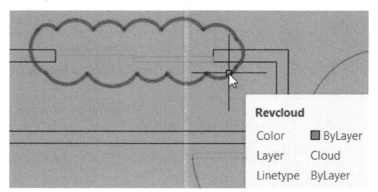

Figure 9–17

• Revision clouds are created using an approximate single value for the length of the arc chord. It is also called as the **Arc Length** and is the distance between the two endpoints of a single arc segment, as shown in Figure 9–18.

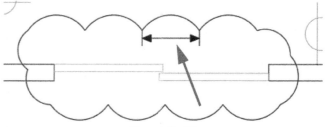

Figure 9–18

- You can now change the arc length of the arcs in the revision cloud. The arc length can be changed either from the Properties palette (as shown in Figure 9–19) or by using the new **REVCLOUDPROPERTIES** command.

- When you select a revision cloud, **Revcloud** object type is displayed in the Properties palette (as shown in Figure 9–19) instead of being picked as a *Polyline* in the previous AutoCAD releases.

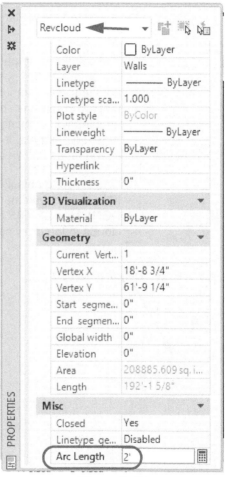

Figure 9–19

- **REVCLOUDARCVARIANCE** (system variable): It controls whether the revcloud arcs are created with varying or uniform chord lengths. This system variable can be set to On/Off. **Off** restores the previous way that revision clouds were created with less vertexes. **On** results in a more hand-drawn appearance with more vertexes.

9.4 Compare Drawings

Shared files have a higher chance of edits made by one user being overwritten by another user who might be making edits at the same time. The **Drawing Compare** command provides a way to quickly highlight the differences between two versions of the same drawing file or two different drawing files.

You can also modify the drawing while in the compare state. While in compare state, the changes that you make are compared in real-time and the differences are dynamically highlighted.

The software compares documents by displaying the objects that are unique to the open drawing in one color, and the objects unique to the comparison drawing in another color. The objects that are common in both the drawings are displayed in gray. This enables you to easily visualize the differences and import the required changes. It also places a revision cloud around the changes, as shown in Figure 9–20.

Only drawing objects are supported during the compare process. If there are coordination models, underlays (PDF, DWF, and DGN), Map 3D GIS objects, images, OLE objects, or point clouds in the drawing, they are ignored during the comparison process.

Only in drawing 1   *Only in drawing 2*   *Only in drawing 2*

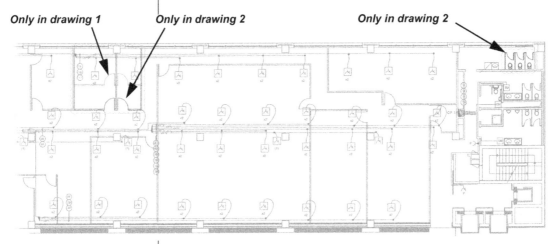

Figure 9–20

How To: Compare Two Drawings

1. Open one of the drawings that you want to compare.

2. In the *Collaborate* tab>Compare panel, click  (DWG Compare).

3. In the Select a drawing to compare dialog box, select the other drawing that you want to compare to the current drawing.

4. Review and edit the comparisons in the open drawing.

Compare Toolbar

The comparison is displayed in the Compare window, which is enclosed in a thick blue border. The Compare toolbar (shown in Figure 9–21) displays in the Compare window with the drawings displayed in the compare state.

Figure 9–21

- The ⚪ (On/Off) icon controls the visibility of the objects that are different and highlighted in either one of the comparison colors.

- To jump and zoom to the previous or next comparative difference, click on the ⇐/ ⇒ (Previous/Next) arrows.

- Click 📄 (Import Objects) to import the changes from the compared drawing into the current drawing. Once the objects are imported, they are no longer highlighted in the compared drawing color, and are displayed in gray.

- 📄 (Export Snapshot) creates a new drawing that contains all of the similarities and differences in both of the drawings, maintaining the colors of the differences.

- Select ⚙ (Settings) to display the detailed tools that can be used on the comparison objects, as shown in Figure 9–22.

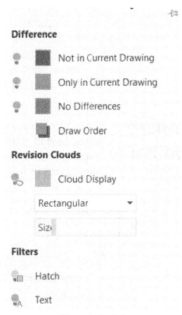

Figure 9–22

- Using the color blocks, you can customize the color of the compared objects.

- You can toggle the display of a revision cloud around the different objects using 🔲 (Revision Cloud). You can set these revision clouds to be either **Rectangular** or **Polygonal** using the Revision Cloud drop-down list, as shown in Figure 9–23.

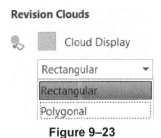

Figure 9–23

Practice 9c | Compare Drawings

Practice Objectives

- Compare two versions of the same drawing file for differences.
- Use the various Compare options provided.

In this practice, you will compare two drawings to find the differences shown in Figure 9–24.

Only in drawing 1 *Only in drawing 2* *Only in drawing 2*

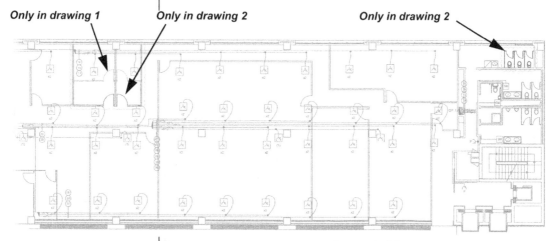

Figure 9–24

Task 1 - Compare two versions of the same drawing file.

1. In the practice files folder, open **Compare-1.dwg**. This is the DWG1 file. In the top right area, note that only the sink is displayed.

2. In the *Collaborate* tab>Compare panel, click [icon] (DWG Compare).

3. In the Select a drawing to compare dialog box, navigate to the practice files folder and open **Compare 2.dwg**.

The comparison colors can vary based on the selected colors in the Settings toolbar.

4. Note that the comparison is displayed in the Compare window in the current drawing (**Compare-1.dwg**). Review the comparison and note the differences shown in Figure 9–24.

   - Green objects are specific to **Compare-1.dwg**, red objects are specific to **Compare-2.dwg**, and common objects are displayed in gray.
   - A revision cloud displays around the differences.

5. Draw a circle anywhere in the drawing and note that it is drawn in green (as shown in Figure 9–25) because it is being dynamically compared and is drawn in the current drawing (**Compare-1.dwg**).

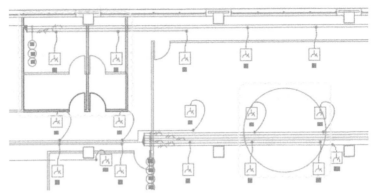

Figure 9–25

Task 2 - Use the Compare options.

---

1. In the DWG Compare toolbar, click ⚙ (Settings) to display the detailed tools and pin it for further use.

2. Click on the color block beside **Not in Current Drawing**. In the Select Color dialog box, select the color blue and click **OK**. Note that the red objects have changed to blue in the drawing.

3. In the Settings display of the DWG Compare toolbar, click 💡 beside **Only in Current Drawing** and **No Differences** to toggle off their display. Note that only the objects that are specific to **Compare-2.dwg** are displayed in the drawing, as shown in Figure 9–26.

Figure 9–26

4. Click 💡 beside **Only in Current Drawing** and **No Differences**, to toggle on their display.

5. In the Settings display of the DWG Compare toolbar, ensure that 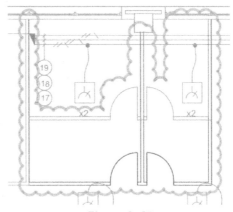 (Revision Cloud) is set to **On**. In the drawing, note that the colored areas have a yellow rectangular revision cloud around them.

6. Zoom into the left revision cloud and note that the shape is a rectangle.

7. In the Revision Clouds drop-down list, select **Polygonal**. Note that a revision cloud changes its shape and displays around the colored objects. Select the revision cloud to highlight it, as shown in Figure 9–27.

Figure 9–27

8. Press <Esc> to exit the selection of the revision cloud.

9. In the DWG Compare toolbar, click (Import Objects).

10. Using a selection window, select the 3 toilet stalls (along the right side of the drawing). Press <Enter> to complete the selection. Note that the objects change from blue to gray indicating that they are now a part of both the drawings.

11. In the DWG Compare toolbar, click (Exit Compare). The drawing ends compare mode. Note that only the objects that were imported from the other drawing are added to the current drawing. All other comparison changes are discarded.

12. Save and close **Compare-1.dwg**.

Chapter Review Questions

1. What types of files are automatically included in a transmittal set using **eTransmit**? (Select all that apply.)

   a. Loaded External Reference files

   b. Associated Plotter Configuration files

   c. Hyperlinked spreadsheets

   d. Associated Font files

2. What is the purpose of **eTransmit**?

   a. Packages a drawing and associated files in a single .ZIP file.

   b. Sends information about a drawing across the Internet.

   c. Sends attribute information in an email message.

   d. Makes a drawing file viewable on the Internet.

3. It is recommended that all open files be saved before you use them in the **eTransmit** utility.

   a. True

   b. False

4. How do you activate a hyperlink in an AutoCAD drawing?

   a. Double-click on the object.

   b. Hold <Shift> and click on the object.

   c. Hold <Ctrl> and click on the object.

   d. Hold <Ctrl> and right-click on the object.

5. Which of the following objects does the **Drawing Compare** command work on?

   a. Coordination models

   b. Drawing objects

   c. AutoCAD Map 3D GIS objects

   d. Images

Command Summary

Button	Command	Location
	Compare	• **Ribbon:** *Collaboration* tab>Compare panel
	eTransmit	• **Ribbon:** Application Menu>Publish
	Hyperlink	• **Ribbon:** *Insert* tab>Data panel

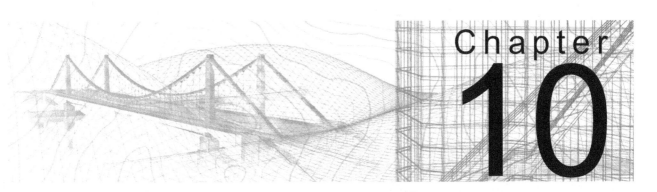

Introduction to Sheet Sets

Most projects require more than one drawing sheet to communicate the project design. Sheet sets provide a way to gather all the required sheets for a project in one location for ease of printing and publishing. In this chapter, you learn about sheet set concepts, creating sheet sets and sheets, using Sheet Views and Model Views for sheets, and using existing layouts as sheets.

Learning Objectives in This Chapter

- Open and close existing sheet sets.
- Navigate the Sheet Set Manager palette.
- Create new sheet sets based on a template or by importing existing layouts.
- Set default templates in Sheet Set Properties to automate block and file creation.
- Generate new sheets using the Sheet Set Manager.
- Organize sheets by adding subsets in the Sheet List.
- Add views with callout blocks to sheets in a sheet set.
- Optimize projects to work with sets by importing layouts from existing drawings into the Sheet Set Manager.

10.1 Overview of Sheet Sets

Sheet sets integrate document management with viewing and plotting features. They automate such functions as creating layouts (sheets) with views, coordinating XREFs, and linking information across a set of files. Sheet sets can contain multiple views, sheets, and model views. Sheet sets also enable you to quickly publish, transmit, and archive multiple drawing files.

- If you work on a project that requires the output of multiple coordinated drawings, sheet sets can solve many of the day-to-day headaches of managing the drawings and keeping them up-to-date.

- Sheet sets ensures that all of the sheets in a set have a consistent format. You can also print all of the sheets in the set at the same time.

- The central feature of sheet sets is the **Sheet Set Manager** (as shown in Figure 10–1), which enables you to coordinate the information as files and views. In this palette you open a sheet set and then work with all of the drawings and sheets in that set.

- You can open the Sheet Set Manager in the *View* tab> Palettes panel by clicking 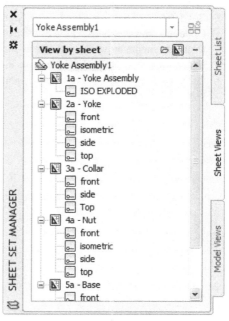 (Sheet Set Manager).

Figure 10–1

How To: Open an Existing Sheet Set

If the Sheet Set Manager is not open:

*You can also open a sheet set from the **Start** tab window by selecting **Open a sheet set** in the Open drop-down list.*

1. In the Application Menu, expand **Open** and select **Sheet Set**.
2. The Open Sheet Set dialog box opens. By default, it searches for sheet sets in the *User\Documents\AutoCAD Sheet Sets* folder. However, when you have previously opened a sheet set, it remembers the location of the last used folder.
3. Select the sheet set that you want to open and click **Open**.

If the Sheet Set Manager is open:

- Select a sheet set from the Open drop-down list in the Sheet Set Manager, as shown in Figure 10–2.

  - Sheet sets that are currently open are listed at the top of the drop-down list.
  - You can also create new sheet sets or select from a list of recently opened ones.

Figure 10–2

The Sheet Set Manager can still be open if no drawings are open.

- As with other palettes in the software, the Sheet Set Manager can be resized and set to auto-hide.

- Sheet sets are stored in DST files. These files contain project information and pointers to other files that actually make up the sheet set. Typically, sheet sets are stored on a server so that multiple designers can access them.

An example of a locked sheet set:

- You can work in a sheet set if someone else has it open. The only exception is if they are changing the sheet set in some way, such as creating a new sheet. In this case, the sheet set is locked. However, you can still display the sheet set, publish or create transmittal sets, and edit drawings that are referenced by the sheet set.

Understanding the Sheet Set Manager

The Sheet Set Manager contains three tabs: *Sheet List*, *Sheet Views*, and *Model Views*.

Sheet List

The *Sheet List* tab (shown in Figure 10–3) tracks the sheets and enables you to create new ones. Each sheet is actually a separate layout in a drawing file. Sheets hold views of XREFs and anything else you normally add to a layout.

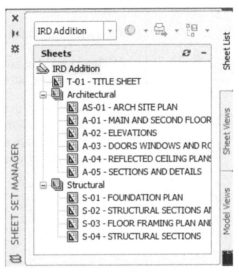

Figure 10–3

- To open a sheet, double-click on its name in the Sheet Set Manager. The drawing file that contains the layout opens.

- Sheets in the list can be organized in subsets and nested subsets.

Sheet Views

The *Sheet Views* tab displays the views that have been placed on the sheets, as shown in Figure 10–4. Views are listed here as you add them to sheets. If you have not placed any views, this area is empty.

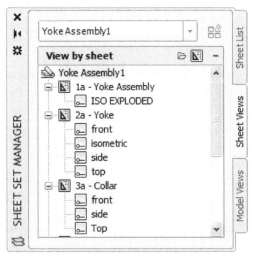

Figure 10–4

- You can list the views, such as Elevation, Floor Plan, etc. Use (View by category) or (View by sheet) at the top of the view panel to organize the list.

- You can modify the name and number of a view in this tab. However, you cannot place views on sheets from here. That is done in the *Model Views* tab.

- To open a view, double-click on it in the list. The sheet that displays the view opens.

Model Views

The *Model Views* tab (shown in Figure 10–5) has a dual purpose. It is where you can specify the locations of the drawing files that are used in the sheet set. Once the files are listed in this tab, you can select the named views that are defined in the drawings to place the views on sheets.

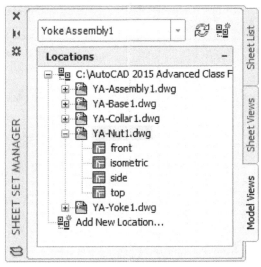

Figure 10–5

- To open a drawing in the *Model Views* tab, double-click on it.

- You can define multiple drawing folder locations for a single sheet set.

Details and Preview Information

When you hover over a sheet in the Sheet Set Manager, a tooltip displays, as shown in Figure 10–6. You can also hover over sheet views, model views, and other objects in the various tabs to display tooltips for those objects.

A-01 - MAIN AND SECOND FLOOR PLAN

Status: Accessible
Sheet: A-01 - MAIN AND SECOND FLOOR PLAN
Description: MAIN FLOOR PLAN, SECOND FLOOR PLAN, WALL TYPE NOTES

Views:
Floor Plans - Main Floor Plan
Floor Plans - Second Floor Plan

File Name: A-01.dwg
Location: C:\AutoCAD 2020 Advanced Practice Files\Sample Files \Sheet Sets\Architectural
File Size: 129KB (132,128 bytes)

Figure 10–6

- The tooltip for a sheet includes a preview of the sheet, its status, the sheet name and its description, views used on the sheet, filename, location, size, last time saved, last edited by, and sheet size.

- The status of a sheet, view, or drawing is either **Accessible** or **Locked for Edit** (because someone else is working in it). If the file is locked it displays the details of the person who has it open.

Closing Sheet Sets

To close a sheet set, save and close any files in the set. In the Sheet Set Manager, in the *Sheet List* tab, right-click on the name of the sheet set and select **Close Sheet Set**, as shown in Figure 10–7.

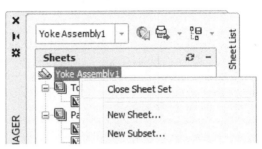

Figure 10–7

Sheets that are opened using the Sheet Set Manager retain additional information about the sheet set. If you change the sheet set information (i.e., change the client name for the project), you can update it in all of the sheets using **Resave All Sheets**.

Practice 10a | Overview of Sheet Sets

Practice Objectives

- Create new sheet sets using the Sheet Set Wizard, based on a template or by importing existing layouts.
- Understand the use of Sheet Set Properties as default templates.

In this practice, you will use the Sheet Set Manager to open an existing sheet set, as shown in Figure 10–8. You will note the information stored in the sheet set and open several sheets.

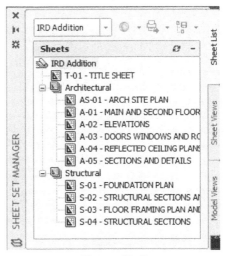

Figure 10–8

1. Open the Sheet Set Manager.

   - If no drawing is open, click 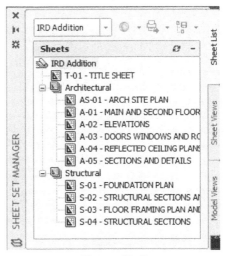 (Sheet Set Manager) in the Quick Access Toolbar.

   - If a drawing is open, you can also click (Sheet Set Manager) in the *View* tab>Palettes panel.

2. Close any open drawings.

3. Ensure that the sheet set list is empty. If a sheet set name displays in the list, right-click on the sheet set name in the Sheet Set Manager and select **Close Sheet Set**.

4. In the Sheet Set Manager drop-down list, select **Open** to open the Open Sheet Set dialog box.

The practice files folder contains an established folder structure for sheet sets.

5. Select the sheet set **IRD Addition.dst**, in the practice files folder under ...*Sample Files\Sheet Sets\Architectural*.

6. In the *Sheet List* tab of the palette, identify the sheets and subsets.

7. Click once on the sheet **A-01 MAIN AND SECOND FLOOR PLAN** to select it. Hover the cursor over the sheet name to display the tooltip with the preview and details for this sheet, as shown in Figure 10–9. Which drawing file contains this sheet?

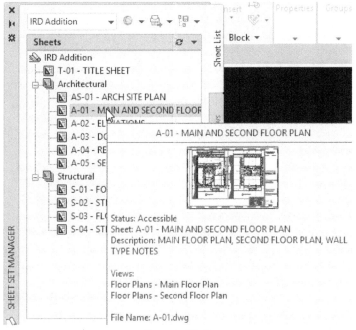

Figure 10–9

8. Double-click on the sheet **A-01 MAIN AND SECOND FLOOR PLAN** to open it. The drawing **A-01.dwg** (from the subfolder *Sheet Sets>Architectural*), opens in the *MAIN AND SECOND FLOOR PLAN* layout tab. The sheet consists of a title block, a table, and views in a layout.

9. Double-click inside one of the viewports to activate Model Space.

10. Select an object in the model. All of the objects are selected because they are part of a reference file (XREF). Press <Esc> to clear the selection.

11. In the Sheet Set Manager, switch to the *Sheet Views* tab.

12. Hover the cursor over the **Main Floor Plan** view to display a tooltip with the preview and details for this sheet, as shown in Figure 10–10. Note that the status is locked for editing because you have it open.

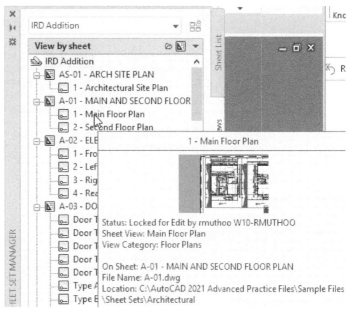

Figure 10–10

13. In the Sheet Set Manager, switch to the *Model Views* tab.

14. Two locations should be listed. Expand the first location, to display the list of drawing files it contains.

15. In the Sheet Set Manager, hover the cursor over several drawings to preview them. Double-click on one of the drawings to open it.

16. Right-click on any drawing tab in the *File tabs* bar and click **Close All**. Do not save any changes.

17. In the Sheet Set Manager, in the *Sheet List* tab, right-click on IRD Addition and select **Close Sheet Set**.

18. If time permits, open one of the other sample sheet sets in the *Sheet Sets* subfolder and look at the way it is laid out.

19. Close all of the sheet sets.

10.2 Creating Sheet Sets

The AutoCAD software provides a wizard (shown in
Figure 10–11) to help you create new sheet sets. There are two
basic methods to creating a sheet set, and each one provides a
very different result. They are described as follows:

An example sheet set	Similar to using a template to create a new drawing. The example sheet set that you select provides the organizational structure and other basic settings for the new sheet set, but no actual sheets are created. You generate them in the sheet set after it has been created.
Existing drawings	you import existing layouts to use as sheets. Sheets created in this way do not have all of the features of sheets generated in the sheet set.

Figure 10–11

How To: Create a Sheet Set by Example

1. In the *Start* tab window, select **Create sheet set** in the New drop-down list.
   - Alternatively, if you have the Sheet Set Manager open, expand the drop-down list and select **New Sheet Set...**.
2. The Create Sheet Set wizard opens. On the *Begin* page, select **An example sheet set** and click **Next >**.
3. In the Sheet Set Example page, select **Select a sheet set to use as an example** to use an existing sheet set as an example as shown in Figure 10–12. Several sheet sets are supplied with the software. If **Browse to another sheet set to use as an example** is selected, you can click ⊡ (Browse) and locate the required sheet set.

Figure 10–12

4. Click **Next >** to continue.

   - You can set the default location where the software looks for example sheet sets. Use **Template Settings>Sheet Set Template File Location** in the *Files* tab in the Options dialog box, as shown in Figure 10–13.

Figure 10–13

5. In the Sheet Set Details dialog box (shown in Figure 10–14), enter a name and description for the sheet set (optional), and specify the location in which you want to store the data (DST) file. Click **Next >** to continue.

Name of new sheet set:

New Sheet Set (4)

Description (optional):

Use the Architectural Imperial Sheet Set to create a new sheet set with a default sheet size of 24 x 36 inches.

Store sheet set data file (.dst) here:

C:\Users\lkemp\Documents\AutoCAD Sheet Sets

Note: The sheet set data file should be stored in a location that can be accessed by all contributors to the sheet set.

☐ Create a folder hierarchy based on subsets

Sheet Set Properties

Figure 10–14

- You can click **Sheet Set Properties** to set the properties for the sheet set, or do it after the sheet set has been created.

6. In the Confirm dialog box shown in Figure 10–15, the *Sheet Set Preview* area displays the predefined subsets for the sheets and other information for the new sheet set. Click **< Back** if you need to make changes. If not, click **Finish** to create the new sheet set. The Sheet Set Manager opens with the new sheet set active.

Figure 10–15

Sheet Set Properties

The Sheet Set Properties (shown in Figure 10–16) can be specified when the sheet set is created or after it has been created. In the Sheet Set Manager, right-click on the sheet set name and select **Properties**.

Figure 10–16

- The properties include the label blocks, callout blocks, and page setups that are used in the sheet set. Assigning customized selections here provides a level of continuity for your projects. The Sheet Set Properties also controls the defaults for creating sheets (which drawing template and layout are used) and additional information about the project. Here, you specify the template file that you want to use for the creation of new sheets in the sheet set. You can also create additional custom properties.

- Sheet sets are often used by multiple designers on a design team. Set the default location for the templates to be a network location where they can be accessed by all of the team members. The **Template Settings>Sheet Set Template File Location** and **Default Template for Sheet Creation and Page Setup Overrides** options are located in the *Files* tab in the Options dialog box

10.3 Creating Sheets in Sheet Sets

Sheets are electronic versions of drawing plots. Each sheet in a sheet set is actually a layout in a drawing file, as shown in Figure 10–17.

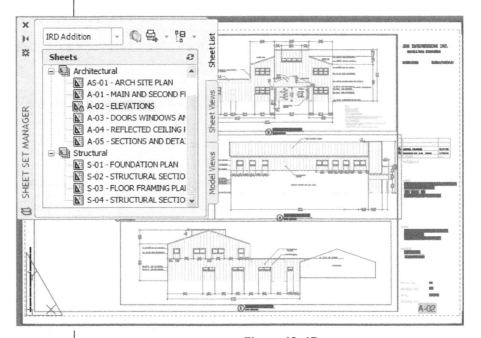

Figure 10–17

Instead of creating a new layout and applying the required information to the base drawing, the Sheet Set Manager can be used to generate new sheets. This applies project-wide information (such as a job name) and adds automatic numbering to each sheet.

- In the Sheet Set Manager, in the *Sheet List* tab, you can display and modify sheets, create new sheets, organize sheets into subsets, and display or preview the sheet details.

- You can drag-and-drop sheets in the Sheet Set Manager to reorder them in the list.

- When you create a sheet, the AutoCAD software creates a new drawing file with a layout that has been set up according to the default template that has been specified for the sheet set.

- Each sheet can have multiple viewports. The views to be displayed on the sheet are referenced from other drawing files using the *Model Views* tab.

How To: Create a Sheet

1. Open the Sheet Set Manager and a sheet set if they are not already open.
2. In the *Sheet List* tab, right-click on the sheet set name (or a subset name) and select **New Sheet...**
3. Fill out the New Sheet dialog box as required, as shown in Figure 10–18.

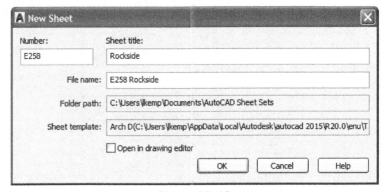

Figure 10–18

4. Click **OK** to create the sheet.

- If you have not set up the default templates an alert box opens prompting you that *To create a new sheet you must first specify a template (DWT) file. Click **OK** to browse to a sheet creation template file.* Default templates should be assigned in the Sheet Set Properties.

- The *Folder path* and *Sheet template* are defined in the Sheet Set Properties. They cannot be changed in the New Sheet dialog box.

Removing Sheets

You can remove a sheet from a sheet set by right-clicking on it in the sheet list and selecting **Remove Sheet**. This removes the sheet from the sheet set, but the actual drawing file and layout are not deleted. The confirmation box (shown in Figure 10–19) opens before the sheet is removed.

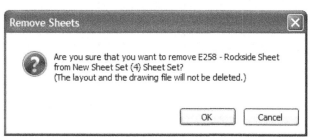

Figure 10–19

Organizing Sheets in Subsets

If your sheet set contains many sheets, it helps to organize them into subsets. These subsets might be based on types of drawings (as shown in Figure 10–20), or they might be different floors of a building or components of an assembly. You can include subsets in your example sheet sets to help establish an office standard.

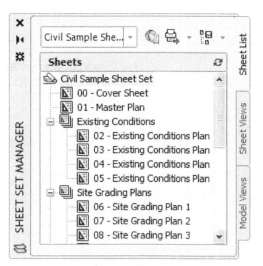

Figure 10–20

How To: Create a Subset in the Sheet List

1. In the Sheet Set Manager, in the *Sheet List* tab, right-click on the sheet set name and select **New Subset**.
2. In the Subset Properties dialog box, type a Subset name, as shown in Figure 10–21. If required, set a storage location and template for new sheets in this subset.

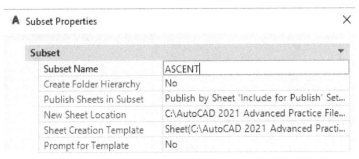

Figure 10–21

3. Click **OK** to create the subset.

- You can set a location in which to store any new sheet files for this subset, which is different from the main folder that has been defined for new sheets in the set. If the *Create Folder Hierarchy* property is set to **Yes**, a subfolder with the same name as the subset is created in the main folder.

- New sheets for the subset can be based on a different template than the general template for new sheets in the set.

- To add new sheets to the subset, right-click on the subset name (rather than on the sheet set name) and select **New Sheet**.

- To move an existing sheet to a subset, drag-and-drop the sheet to the subset or between subsets.

Hint: Creating a Sheet List Table

A special table is associated with sheet sets, as shown in Figure 10–22. It creates a list of sheets that can be placed on a cover sheet. As you add, remove, or renumber/rename sheets, the table can be updated automatically.

Sheet List Table	
Sheet Number	Sheet Title
AS-01	ARCH SITE PLAN
A-01	MAIN AND SECOND FLOOR PLAN
A-02	ELEVATIONS
A-03	DOORS WINDOWS AND ROOMS
A-04	REFLECTED CEILING PLANS
A-05	SECTIONS AND DETAILS

Figure 10–22

1. Open the sheet in which you want to insert the Sheet List Table.
2. In the Sheet Set Manager, right-click on the sheet set name and select **Insert Sheet List Table**.
3. Select the Table Style and change the title as required. You can also select **Show Subheader** if you want to distinguish between sheet categories.
4. Click **OK**. An alert box opens the first time you use this, prompting you that the sheet list table is created by the Sheet Set Manager and that any manual changes are lost when you update it. You can toggle off this alert option.
5. Place the table on the sheet.

If you make a change to the sheet list, such as renaming, reordering, or deleting a sheet(s), you need to select the table, right-click and select **Update Table Data Links**.

10.4 Adding Views to Sheets

The *Model Views* tab is used to add views to sheets, as shown in Figure 10–23. In this tab you can define the folder location(s) for the drawings that you want to reference to the sheet set. You then select a view (named view) in a drawing and place it on the sheet.

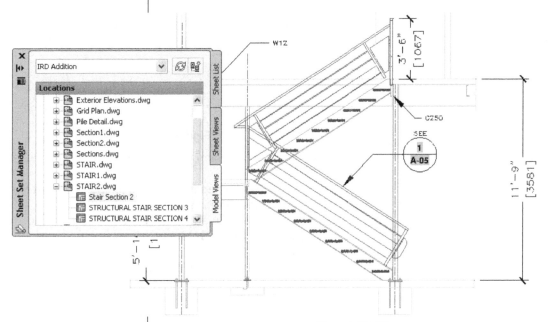

Figure 10–23

To add a view to a sheet, you must have *Named Views* defined in the *Model Views* tab.

- When you add a view, it attaches the referenced drawing as an XREF in the sheet drawing.

- Views placed on sheets include a title and scale callout that is linked to the view using fields.

- You can open drawing files from the *Model Views* tab by double-clicking on the filename.

- If the drawing you want to use does not contain a *named view*, you need to open the drawing, define the view, and save and close the drawing. You can then add the view to a sheet.

How To: Set Up Model Views

Model view locations (shown in Figure 10–24) can be established in the Sheet Set Properties, or you can add locations when you are ready to add a view.

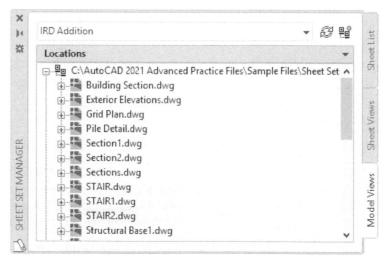

Figure 10–24

1. In the Sheet Set Manager, switch to the *Model Views* tab.
2. Double-click on **Add New Location...**.
3. Select the folder in which the drawings you want to use are stored. You must select a folder and not a file; the files that you need should be located in a specific folder. All of the files in the folder display. You can use multiple folder locations with multiple drawings.

How To: Place a View on a Sheet

1. Open a sheet file.
2. In the *Model Views* tab, find the drawing that contains the named view that you want to use.
3. Click the **+** symbol next to the drawing to expand its list of views, as shown in Figure 10–25.

Figure 10–25

4. Drag-and-drop the view onto the sheet.

   • You can also right-click on the view that you want to use and select **Place on Sheet**.)

You can right-click and change the scale as required.

5. The named view displays attached to the cursor. A tooltip displays the current scale, as shown in Figure 10–26.

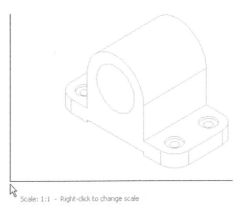

Scale: 1:1 – Right-click to change scale

Figure 10–26

6. Pick in the drawing window to place the view. A label with the view title and scale (which are defined by fields) is automatically placed with the view.

• You can resize or move the viewport as required, once you have placed the view in the drawing.

• The view label is a separate object from the view. It is a block that can be moved or deleted if it is not required.

Fields and Sheet Sets

You can use fields to define much of the standard information that is required on sheets. There is a special category of fields that is designed to integrate with sheet sets. This includes the fields related to the sheet number, title, or views. Using fields for this information helps to automate the information and to coordinate it across sheets.

The labels that are applied to views on a sheet use fields to define the view name, number, and scale of the viewport, as shown in Figure 10–27. If the view name and number are changed in the Sheet Set Manager, the fields in the labels update after regeneration. The scale is linked to the viewport. Therefore, if the viewport scale is changed, the scale field in the label changes as well.

Figure 10–27

- Some fields have links to the sheet or view. If you hover the cursor over one of the links, a hyperlink icon displays, as shown in Figure 10–28. Hover over the object field, hold <Ctrl>, and click to follow the link. In the example shown in Figure 10–28, clicking the link opens the Assembly sheet.

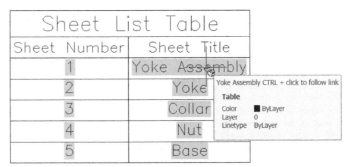

Figure 10–28

Sheet Views Tab

After you have added views from the drawings listed in the *Model Views* tab to a sheet, a list of the views displays in the *Sheet Views* tab, as shown in Figure 10–29. In this tab, you can open a view on a sheet, rename views, or place callout blocks and label blocks. You can also create categories to organize the list of views.

Figure 10–29

- You cannot place views on sheets from this tab. That is done from the *Model Views* tab.

- Views from imported sheets are not included in the view list.

- Views can be listed by either sheet or category. Use the buttons at the top of the View panel to sort the list.

Right-click on a view name in the list to display the shortcut menu shown in Figure 10–30.

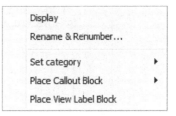

Figure 10–30

Display	Opens the sheet in which the view is located and zooms in on the view.
Rename & Renumber	Opens a dialog box in which you can change the name and number of a view. When a view is inserted from a resource drawing it is automatically assigned the name of the named view and does not include a number. **Regen** to display the change.

Rename & Renumber View	
Number:	View title:
1	Architectural Site Plan
< Previous	Next >	OK

Set Category	Reassigns the selected sheet view to a specified category.
Place Callout Block	A callout block references another view. For example, you can place a callout block of an elevation on a plan but it is linked to an elevation on a different sheet. If the elevation number or sheet number change, the callout also changes. The list of callout blocks is specified in the Sheet Set Properties.
Place View Label Block	Adds a title label referencing the selected view. It can be placed anywhere in the drawing but continues to have a connection to that view.

- Do not try to modify the actual block that holds the title name and number, because doing so results in it losing its connection to the sheet set.

- Changing the scale of the viewport updates the *Scale* field in the Title callout.

View Category

If you have many views, you can create View Categories to help organize them by drawing file or by type, as shown in Figure 10–31. When the categories have been created, you can drag-and-drop views from the list into the appropriate category.

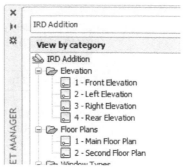

Figure 10–31

How To: Create a View Category

1. Click 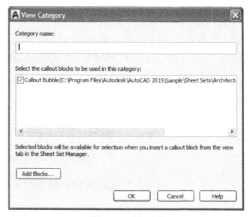 (View by category) to display the views organized according to category.

2. In the *Sheet Views* tab, click 🔲 (New View Category) or right-click on the sheet set name and select **New View Category**.

3. In the View Category dialog box (shown in Figure 10–32), enter a name for the category. You can also add blocks using **Add Blocks…**, which can be used as callout blocks in this category. Select the block(s) that you want to include and click **OK**.

Figure 10–32

Practice 10b | Introduction to Sheet Sets

Practice Objectives

- Create a new sheet set from an example.
- Create new sheets in a sheet set and set specific properties.
- Add views to sheets.

In this practice, you will create a new sheet set by example, create new sheets in a sheet set, and add views to sheets.

Task 1 - Create sheet sets.

In this task, you will create a new sheet set by example, as shown in Figure 10–33.

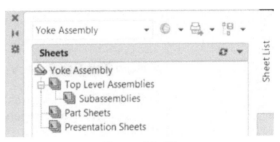

Figure 10–33

1. Open the Sheet Set Manager if it is not already open.

2. Close any sheets sets that might be open.

3. In the Sheet Set Manager, expand the drop-down list and select **New Sheet Set**.

4. In the Sheet Set Wizard, on the *Begin* page, select **An example sheet set**, if required, and click **Next >**.

5. On the *Sheet Set Example* page, select **Manufacturing Imperial Sheet Set** and click **Next >**.

6. In the *Sheet Set Details* page, name the new sheet set **Yoke Assembly**, and add a description, as required. Store the sheet set data file in the *\Sheet Sets\Projects\Yoke Assembly* folder in the practice files folder

   - Use ⟦...⟧ (Browse) to locate the folder.

7. Click **Sheet Set Properties**.

The practice files folder contains an established folder structure for sheet sets.

When you click inside the Model view row, it changes into an edit box and 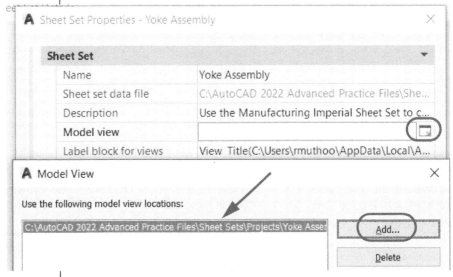 displays along with it.

8. In the *Sheet Set* area, click the *Model view* edit box browser to open the Model View dialog box. In the Model View dialog box, click **Add** and set the *Model view* location to **Sheet Sets\Projects\Yoke Assembly\Resource Drawings** in the practice files folder, as shown in Figure 10–34. Click **OK**.

Figure 10–34

9. In the *Sheet Creation* area, set the *Sheet storage location* to **Sheet Sets\Projects\Yoke Assembly\Sheets** in the practice files folder. New files created for sheets in this set are saved here.

10. In the *Sheet Creation* area, set the *Sheet creation template* to the template **SS-MECH-C-SIZED.dwt** in *Sheet Sets\ Templates* in the practice files folder. New sheets in this set are based on this template.

11. In the *Sheet Set Custom Properties* area, set the *Job Name* to **Yoke Assembly**, type a value for *Job Number* (such as **ABC-14_24**), and type **<your name>** as the *Owner*.

12. Click **OK** to close the Sheet Set Properties dialog box and click **Next >** to continue.

13. Review the information in the *Confirm* page and click **Finish**. The new sheet set displays in the Sheet Set Manager. The *Sheet List* tab currently displays subset categories but does not contain any sheets.

14. Do not close the sheet set.

Task 2 - Create sheets in sheet sets.

In this task, you will create new sheets in a sheet set, as shown in Figure 10–35.

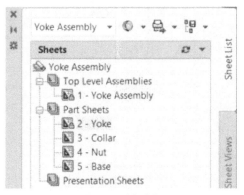

Figure 10–35

A drawing must be open to work with a sheet set.

1. If a drawing is not open, start a new drawing based on the default template.

2. Right-click on the subset **Subassemblies** and select **Remove Subset**. It is not required in this sheet set.

3. Right-click on the subset **Top Level Assemblies** and select **Properties**. In the Subset Properties dialog box, change the *Sheet Creation Template* to **SS-MECH-C-SIZED.dwt** in *Sheet Sets\Templates* in the practice files folder, as shown in Figure 10–36. Once set, in the Subset Properties dialog box, click **OK**. New sheets in the subset are based on this template.

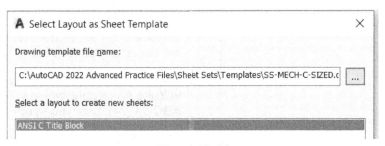

Figure 10–36

4. Repeat Step 3 for the subset **Part Sheets**.

The File name is automatically created using the number and title.

5. Right-click on the subset **Top Level Assemblies**, select **New Sheet**, and set the following, as shown in Figure 10–37:
   - *Number*: **1**
   - *Sheet title*: **Yoke Assembly**

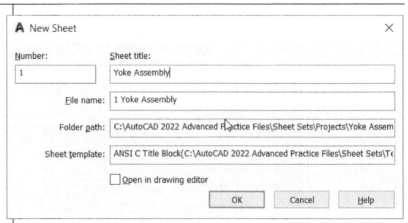

Figure 10–37

6. Click **OK** to create the sheet.

7. Right-click on the subset **Part Sheets**, select **New Sheet**, and set the following:

   - *Number* to: **2**
   - *Sheet title*: **Yoke**

8. Click **OK** to create the sheet.

The AutoCAD software has now created a new DWG file for each sheet that you have created.

9. In **Part Sheets**, create three new sheets numbered and title them as follows:

   - **3–Collar**
   - **4–Nut**
   - **5–Base**

   The Sheet Set Manager displays all of the sheets, as shown in Figure 10–38.

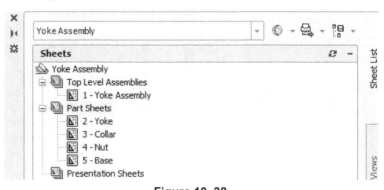

Figure 10–38

10. Double-click on each new sheet to open the file and save each of the sheet files. Note the title block information, as shown in Figure 10–39. Views are not yet displayed on the sheets.

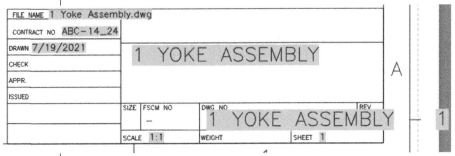

Figure 10–39

Task 3 - Add views to sheets.

In this task, you will add views to sheets. One of the completed drawings is shown in Figure 10–40.

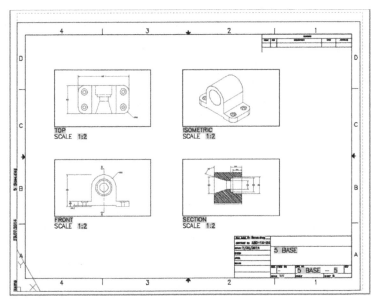

Figure 10–40

1. In the *Sheet List* tab, double-click on the sheet **1-Yoke Assembly** to open it.

2. In the Sheet Set Manager, switch to the *Model Views* tab.

3. You should already have a location for *Sheet Sets\ Projects\Yoke Assembly\Resource Drawings* in the practice files folder. Review the location and if it is not set as above, add it.

4. Expand this location (click the **+** symbol next to it) and find **YA-Assembly.dwg**.

5. Expand **YA-Assembly.dwg**, as shown in Figure 10–41. Note that one view named **ISO Exploded** has already been defined in this drawing.

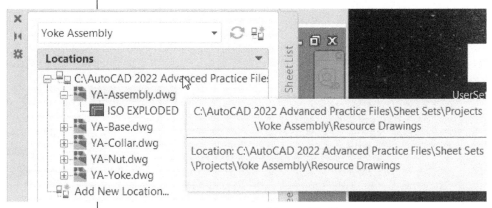

Figure 10–41

6. Drag the **ISO Exploded** view onto the *1 Yoke Assembly* layout sheet (do not click). A preview of the view and a tooltip display at the cursor, as shown in Figure 10–42.

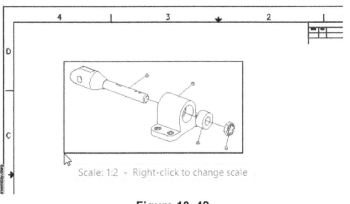

Figure 10–42

After right-clicking, you might need to wait for a short time for the scale list to display clearly.

7. Note that the view scale is set to 1:2, which needs to be changed to 1:1. With the preview attached to the cursor, in the viewport, right-click and set the *scale* to **1:1.** Note the bigger preview with the cursor. Pick a point to place the view in the layout, as shown in Figure 10–43.

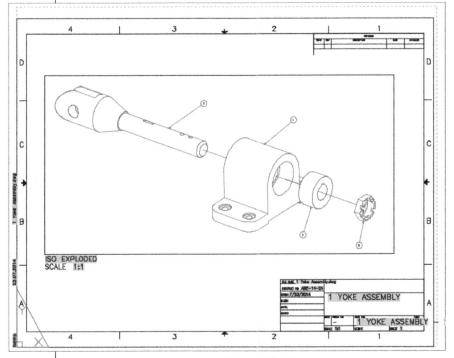

Figure 10–43

8. Save the **1 Yoke Assembly** sheet file.

9. In the Sheet Set Manager, switch back to the *Sheet List* tab. Double-click on the sheet **2-Yoke** to open it.

10. In the Sheet Set Manager, switch to the *Model Views* tab and find and expand **YA-Yoke.dwg** to display its views. Four views should be listed.

11. Drag the **front** view to the *2 Yoke* layout sheet, and pick a point to place it in the lower left portion of the layout, as shown in Figure 10–44.

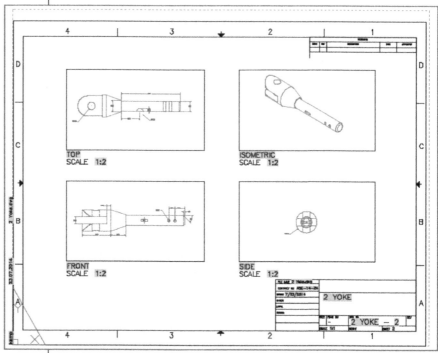

Figure 10–44

Once you have placed the views, you can move the viewports using Object Snap Tracking to align the objects, as required.

12. Repeat this to place the other three views on the sheet, as shown in Figure 10–44. Save the sheet.

13. Switch back to the *Sheet List* tab and open the sheet **3-Collar**.

14. Switch to the *Model Views* tab and add the appropriate views to the sheet from the drawing **YA-Collar.dwg**.

15. Repeat the process to add views to the other two part sheets from the corresponding model views.

16. Save and close all of the drawings.

17. Close the **Yoke Assembly** sheet set.

10.5 Importing Layouts to Sheet Sets

The process of setting up sheets (starting from **An example sheet set** and creating the sheets in it) is the preferred method. However, what if you already have a project well underway? You can optimize your projects to work with sheet sets by importing layouts from **Existing drawings** into the Sheet Set Manager, as shown in Figure 10–45.

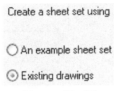

Figure 10–45

This method does not provide every benefit that is available with sheet sets. For example, your existing layouts probably do not have fields set up to work in sheet sets for sheet numbering, etc. However, this method does give you access to streamlined plotting and publishing, transmittal creation, and the archive feature. Opening your layouts as sheets through the Sheet Set Manager should make XREF handling easier.

- Each layout is linked as a sheet in the Sheet Set Manager, but is not made into a separate drawing. It remains part of its existing drawing.

- The views in imported sheets are not linked in the sheet set. They are not listed in the *Sheet Views* tab.

- In a sheet set based on existing layouts, you can create additional sheets and add views from model views to sheets. These new sheets and views have full sheet set functionality.

Create a Sheet Set from Existing Layouts

When you import layouts from existing drawings you can specify the folders in which the drawings are located and then select the layouts in the drawings that you want to include.

How To: Create a Sheet Set from an Existing Layout

1. In the Sheet Set Manager, expand the drop-down list and select **New Sheet Set**. The Create Sheet Set wizard opens.
2. Select **Existing Drawings** (as shown in Figure 10–46), and click **Next >**.

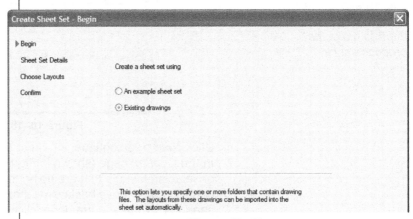

Figure 10–46

3. In the *Sheet Set Details* page, enter the name, description, and file location. This is also where you set up the properties for model views and blocks. If you are going to add other new sheets and use sheet set options and fields, you need to set up these properties.
4. Click **Next >** to continue.
5. In the *Choose Layouts* page, click **Browse** and select the folder in which your drawings are stored. You can then select the drawing files that hold the layouts that you want to import as sheets. Each layout in a drawing is listed, as shown in Figure 10–47. Select the ones you want to use. Set up the **Import Options** before you select the file.

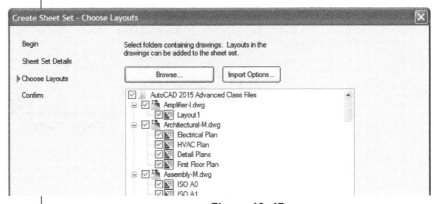

Figure 10–47

You might want to move your files to specific folders before importing them to make the process easier.

- **Import Options** controls how the sheets are named, as shown in Figure 10–48. You can prefix each layout name with the filename. You can also create subsets for sheets based on an existing folder structure.

Figure 10–48

6. Click **Next >** to continue.
7. In the *Confirm* page (shown in Figure 10–49), review the list of selected layouts that are going to be imported. You can use **< Back** to move backwards through the wizard and make changes. When you are done, click **Finish**.

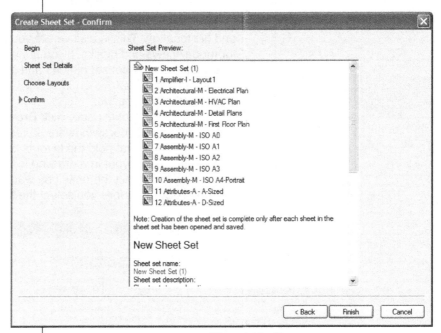

Figure 10–49

8. The Sheet Set Manager opens with the new sheet set active, as shown in Figure 10–50.

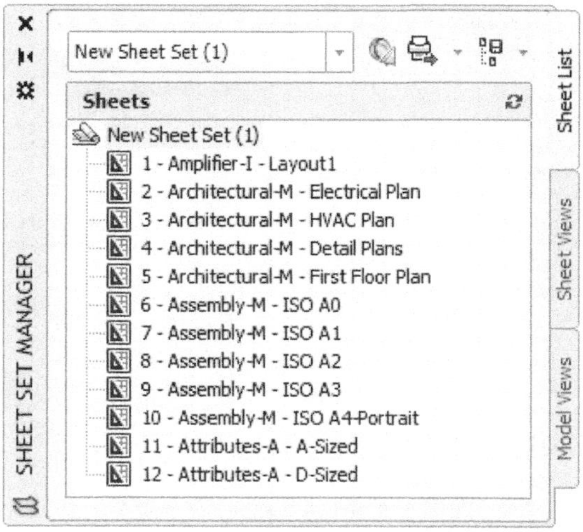

Figure 10–50

- Once your layouts are listed as sheets, you can add subsets to organize them, rename and renumber the sheets, and drag them into the required order.

Importing a Layout to a Sheet Set

Layouts from any drawing can be imported into a new or existing sheet set using the **Import Layout as Sheet** command, or by dragging and dropping the layout from the current drawing onto the *Sheet List* area.

- You must ensure that a printer has been assigned to the layout and that you have viewed the layout and saved the drawing before you attempt to import it into a sheet set.

How To: Import a Layout into Sheet Set Manager

1. Create a layout, assign a printer to it, and save the current drawing.
2. Open the Sheet Set Manager.
3. Open a sheet set or create a new one.
4. In the *Sheet List* tab, right-click on the sheet set name and select **Import Layout as Sheet**.
5. The Import Layouts as Sheets dialog box opens.

6. Click **Browse for Drawings** to browse for drawings and then select the layouts to be added to the sheet set, as shown in Figure 10–51.

Figure 10–51

7. Each layout in the drawing is listed. Clear the check from the layouts that you DO NOT want to import as sheets.
8. If you want the sheet name to include the filename, select **Prefix sheet titles with file name**.
9. Click **Import Checked**. The layouts are added to the sheet set.
10. To add a number to the sheet and rename it as required, right-click on the sheet in the list and select **Rename and Renumber…**. Fill out the Rename & Renumber Sheet dialog box as required.

• The **Import Layout as Sheet** command is also available in the shortcut menu in the layout tab of the active drawing.

• If the file you select has multiple layouts, they are all displayed but only the layout(s) that you select are linked to the sheet set.

Practice 10c | Importing Layouts to Sheet Sets

Practice Objectives

- Create a sheet set from existing drawings.
- Add additional sheets to a sheet set from other drawings.

In this practice, you will create a sheet set from existing drawings and add an additional sheet to the set from another drawing, as shown in Figure 10–52.

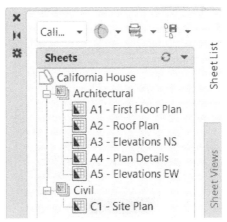

Figure 10–52

Task 1 - Create a sheet set from existing drawings.

1. Start a new drawing based on the **acad.dwt** template (provided with AutoCAD software).

2. Open the Sheet Set Manager and close any sheets sets that are open.

3. In the Sheet Set Manager, select **New Sheet Set**.

4. In the *Begin* page, select **Existing drawings** and click **Next >**.

The practice files folder contains an established folder structure for sheet sets.

5. Name the sheet set **California House** and set *Sheet Sets\Projects\California House* in the practice files folder as the location in which to store the .DST file.

6. Click **Sheet Set Properties**.

7. Add and set the *Model view* location to be *Sheet Sets\Projects\California House\Resource Drawings* in the practice files folder.

---

8. Click **OK** to close the Sheet Set Properties dialog box.

9. Click **Next >** to continue.

10. In the *Choose Layouts* page, click **Import Options**.

11. Clear the **Prefix sheet titles with file name** option and click **OK**.

12. Click **Browse** and open *Sheet Sets\Projects\California House\Resource Drawings* in the practice files folder, as shown in Figure 10–53. Click **OK**.

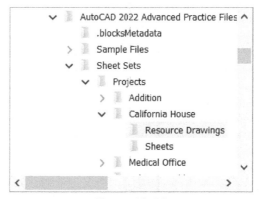

Figure 10–53

13. Select **C-House-A.dwg** and all of its layouts (verify that they have a checkmark). Clear **C-Site-F.dwg**.

14. Click **Next >** to continue.

15. In the *Confirm* page, note that the *Sheet Set Preview* displays five sheets.

16. Click **Finish**.

17. In the Sheet Set Manager, in the *Sheet List* tab, right-click on the sheet set name (California House) and select **New Subset**. Name the new subset **Architectural** and click **OK**.

18. Drag and drop the sheets into the *Architectural* subset. Arrange the sheets in the order shown in Figure 10–54.

   • Arrange them in the order of the names, not by number. You will renumber them later.

Figure 10–54

19. Right-click on the first sheet and select **Rename & Renumber**. In the Rename & Renumber Sheet dialog box, change the *number* to **A1** and click **Next >**. Number the following sheets as **A2**, **A3**, etc.

20. In the Sheet Set Manager, hover the cursor over each sheet to display its tooltip and preview.

Task 2 - Add a sheet from an existing layout.

---

1. In the *Sheet List* tab, right-click on the sheet set name (California House) and select **New Subset**. Name the new subset **Civil**.

2. Right-click on the Civil subset and select **Import Layout as Sheet**.

3. Click **Browse for Drawings**. In the practice files folder, in *Sheet Sets\Projects\California House\Resource Drawings*, select **C-Site-F.dwg**. It contains one layout called **Site Plan**.

4. Click **Import Checked** to import the layout.

5. Right-click on the new sheet and select **Rename & Renumber**. Name it **C1 – Site Plan**.

6. Close the sheet set.

Chapter Review Questions

1. What are the advantages of using sheet sets? (Select all that apply.)

   a. Enables you to get online access.

   b. Helps ensure a consistent format for all of the sheets in the set.

   c. Enables you to easily print all of the sheets in the set at the same time.

   d. Helps coordinate the information on the sheets.

2. Each sheet in a sheet set is a separate layout in a drawing file.

   a. True

   b. False

3. Which part of the Sheet Set Manager would you use to place a view on a sheet?

   a. *Sheet List* tab

   b. *Sheet Views* tab

   c. *Model Views* tab

   d. *Insert* tab

4. Where do you specify the template file that is used for the creation of new sheets in a sheet set?

   a. Drawing Properties

   b. *Resource Drawings* area

   c. Sheet Set Properties

   d. Options dialog box

5. When you are attaching Model Views to a sheet using the Sheet Set Manager, what type of object must be available in the drawing file?

   a. Layouts

   b. Named Views

   c. Viewports

   d. Page Setups

6. If you have many views in the Sheet Set Manager, what can you create to organize them by drawing file or by type?

   a. View Layouts

   b. View Categories

   c. Model views

   d. Renumber views

Command Summary

Button	Command	Location
	Sheet Set Manager	• **Ribbon:** *View* tab>Palettes panel • Quick Access Toolbar (when no drawing is open)

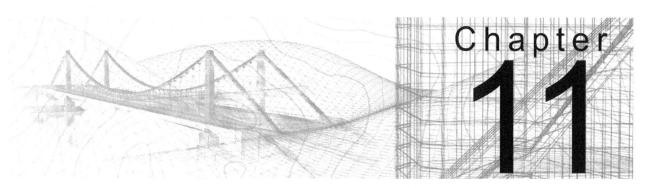

Publishing and Customizing Sheet Sets

Sheet sets provide the ability to quick share and print an entire project. Even if the project contains multiple drawing files, you can quickly package all the project files using one command. In this chapter, you learn how to transmit, archive, and publish sheet sets. You also learn how to set up sheet set templates and create custom blocks for sheet sets.

Learning Objectives in This Chapter

- Package a select group or all of the files related to an entire sheet set.
- Publish and plot groups of files or the entire sheet set in various formats.
- Define custom properties for different types of information to be included in a sheet set.
- Create custom properties to be used as fields to create title blocks, label blocks, and callout blocks that work specifically with sheet sets.

11.1 Transmitting and Archiving Sheet Sets

The **eTransmit** command can be used in a sheet set to package all of the files that are related to the entire drawing set. The **Sheet Sets Archiving** command works in a similar manner to **eTransmit**. While transmittal sets are designed to be sent out of the office, archive sets are saved in the office at specific stages in a project, such as Design Development and Construction Documents.

How To: Create a Transmittal Set from a Sheet Set

1. Save any open drawing files that are related to the sheet set.
2. In the Sheet Set Manager, right-click on the sheet set name and select **eTransmit**. Alternatively, in the **Application Menu>Publish**, click ⬚ (eTransmit).

- The AutoCAD® software gathers information about the files that are used in the sheet set. When the information has been gathered, the Create Transmittal dialog box opens, as shown in Figure 11–1.

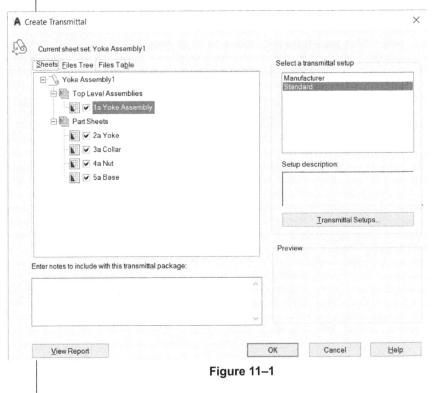

Figure 11–1

- The standard Transmittal dialog box contains tabs for *Files Tree* and *Files Table*. If you start the command from the Sheet Set Manager, there is also a *Sheets* tab. This is where you can select the sheets to be included in the transmittal. By default, all of the sheets are selected.

3. Select a Transmittal Setup.
4. In the *Notes* area, add notes as required.
5. Click **View Report** to display the details of the transmittal. The text of the report is included in the transmittal set.
6. Click **OK** to create the transmittal set.

- The *Files Tree* tab lists the actual drawing files and other files that are going to be packaged, including the Sheet Set Data File (DST and any templates related to the sheets). The files are listed hierarchically. For example, XREFs attached to a sheet are listed under that sheet.

- The *Files Table* tab lists all of the files that are going to be packaged alphabetically.

- You can use **Add File** to include other files in the transmittal set.

- You can **eTransmit** a subset of the sheets and their related files. Right-click on the subset in the sheet list and select **eTransmit**.

- Any open files must be saved before you can use **eTransmit** with them.

Archiving Sheet Sets

Archiving sheet sets is similar to creating transmittal sets. The difference is that archive sets are intended to be saved in your office.

- To start the archive process, right-click on the sheet set name in the Sheet Set Manager and select **Archive**, or in the

  Application Menu>Publish, click 🖾 (Archive).

- The output options for the archive package are the same as for transmittal sets (ZIP, EXE, or folder).

- You can modify the archive setup, but cannot save them as you would save transmittal setups.

- Unlike **eTransmit**, you can only archive the entire sheet set and not the individual subsets.

11.2 Publishing Sheet Sets

In the Sheet Set Manager, you can quickly publish and plot groups of files or the entire sheet set. There are icons at the top of the *Sheet List* tab that facilitate this process.

Publish to DWFx

Select the sheet, sheet subset, or sheet set that you want to publish. When you click ⟳ (Exports the selection to DWFx files), the software checks the Sheet Set Publish Options and publishes the set using the current page setup of each sheet.

🖶 ⯆ (Publish) opens a menu (as shown in Figure 11–2) in which you can select the process that you want to use.

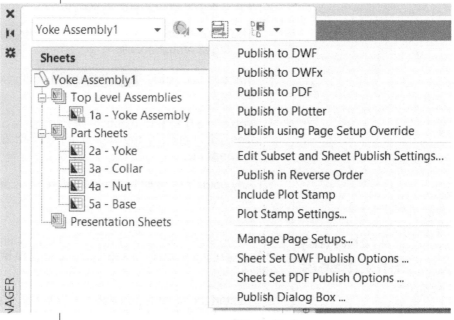

Figure 11–2

Publish to DWF	Publishes the sheets to a DWF file.
Publish to DWFx	Publishes the sheets to a DWFx file.
Publish to PDF	Publishes the sheets to a PDF file.
Publish to Plotter	Publishes the selected sheets directly to the plotter that is set up in the sheet's page setup.

Publish using Page Setup Override	Overrides the individual sheet's page setup. A list of available page setups displays in the extended menu. WARNING: Using this method creates individual plot files even if the page setup is designed to create a multi-page DWF. If you need to apply a different page setup to a group of sheets, use the Publish dialog box.
Edit Subset and Sheet Publish Settings...	Opens the Publish Sheets dialog box for quick check selections of sheets and subsets to include for publishing.
Publish in Reverse Order	Enables you to publish sheet sets to plot in default or reverse order, depending on your requirements.
Include Plot Stamp	Adds a plot stamp to all of the sheets.
Plot Stamp Settings...	Opens the Plot Stamp dialog box.
Manage Page Setups...	Opens the Page Setup Manager in which you can create or modify page setups without having to go to a layout.
Sheet Set DWF Publish Options...	Sets the defaults for Publishing to DWFx or DWF, including the output directory, single or multi-sheet settings, security, and whether to include layer information.
Sheet Set PDF Publish Options...	Sets the defaults for Publishing to PDF, including the output directory, single or multi-sheet settings, security, and whether to include layer information.
Publish Dialog Box...	Opens the Publish dialog box in which you can assign the sheets that you want to publish. This is where you would need to create multi-sheet DWF files when you use Page Setup overrides.

Hint: Sheet Selections

You can group sheets together using ⯊ (Sheet Selections) in the Sheet Set Manager. Select the sheets that you want to group, expand ⯊ (Sheet Selections), and select **Create…** This opens the New Sheet Selection dialog box in which you can enter a name for the group. You can access the group from here. The group names are at the top of the list, as shown in Figure 11–3. The **Manage…** option opens the Sheet Selections dialog box in which you can rename or delete the sheet selections. Sheet Selection groups are very useful when you need to publish groups of sheets without printing the full set.

Figure 11–3

Control Plotting Output

You can use the system variable **publishcollate** to disable homogeneous plotting. This enables drawings or sheet sets to enter the plot spool when another sheet set is being printed. It is controlled by the **Publish Using Page Setup Override** option in the Sheet Set Manager. This can save time by enabling you to put a small print job in the middle of a large one without having to wait for the large one to finish printing. You can also use the **Publish Using Page Setup Override** option to publish a multi-sheet DWF file.

Practice 11a

Transmitting, Archiving, and Publishing Sheet Sets

Practice Objectives

- Create a transmittal set for all of the files that are related to a sheet set.
- Configure the publish options for and publish an entire sheet set to a single DWFx file.
- Publish a single sheet from a sheet set, using preconfigured options.

In this practice, you will create a transmittal set for all of the files that are related to a sheet set, configure the publish options for a sheet set, and publish the sheet set to a single DWFx file. You will then publish a single sheet using preconfigured options.

The practice files folder contains an established folder structure for sheet sets.

Task 1 - Transmit and archive sheet sets.

In this task, you will create a transmittal set for all of the files that are related to a sheet set, as shown in Figure 11–4.

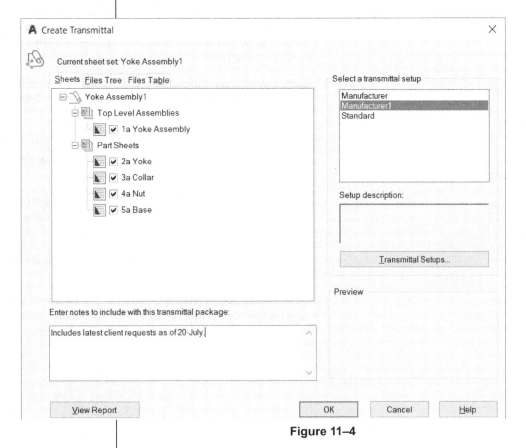

Figure 11–4

Close any other open sheet set.

*At least one drawing must be open to use **eTransmit**.*

1. In the Sheet Set Manager, open the sheet set **Yoke Assembly1** from *Sheet Sets\Projects\Yoke Assembly1* folder in the practice files folder.

2. Double-click on one of the sheets in the list to open it.

3. Save the drawing.

4. Right-click on the sheet set name (**Yoke Assembly1**) and select **eTransmit...**

5. In the Create Transmittal dialog box, select each of the three tabs (*Sheets*, *Files Tree*, and *Files Table*) and note which files are going to be included in the transmittal package.

6. Click **Transmittal Setups**.

7. In the Transmittal Setups dialog box, verify that **Standard** is selected. Click **New** and create a copy of the Standard setup named **Manufacturer1**. Click **Continue**.

8. In the Modify Transmittal Setup dialog box, set the *Transmittal package type* to **Zip (*.zip)** and verify that both *Transmittal file folder* and *Use organizational folder structure* are set to **Sheet Sets\Projects\Yoke Assembly1** in the practice files folder.

9. Click **OK** to create the setup file. In the Transmittal Setups dialog box, click **Close** to return to the Create Transmittal dialog box.

10. In the Create Transmittal dialog box, in the *Enter notes to include...* area, type **Includes latest client requests as of <today's date>**.

11. Click **View Report** and review the details of the transmittal. In the View Transmittal Report dialog box, click **Close**.

12. Click **OK** to create the setup. In the Specify Zip File dialog box, accept the default name and save the zip file in the practice files folder.

13. Using Windows Explorer, locate the zip file in the practice files folder. If you have Winzip available, you can also view the contents of the zip file. Do not extract the files.

Task 2 - Publish sheet sets.

In this task, you will configure the publish options for a sheet set and publish the sheet set to a single DWFx file, as shown in Figure 11–5. You will then publish a single sheet using preconfigured options.

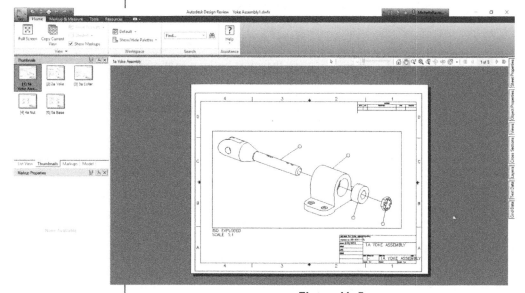

Figure 11–5

1. If a file is not already open, in the Sheet Set Manager, double-click on one of the sheets to open it. Note that a drawing must be open to use the publishing tools.

2. In the Sheet Set Manager, expand ☺ (Publish) and select **Sheet Set DWF Publish Options**.

3. Change the *Default output location* to the practice files folder.

4. In the *General DWF options* area, set the following:
    *   *Type*: **Multi-sheet file**
    *   *Naming:* **Prompt for name** (This enables you to name the DWFx file when it is generated.)

5. Click **OK** to close the Publish Options dialog box.

6. Select the sheet set name (**Yoke Assembly1**) at the top of the sheet list.

7. In the Sheet Set Manager, click (Exports the selection to DWFx files). Save the file in the practice files folder with the name **Yoke Assembly1**.

   - It should publish in the background without requiring further input.
   - The printing icon in the Status Bar is animated while publishing is in progress.

8. Close the alert balloon that opens when the process is finished.

9. View the plot files using the Autodesk® Design Review software.

11.3 Customizing Sheet Sets

Most offices have an idea of the range of drawings that might be required for a project. A major architectural project can have 100 or more drawings divided into various disciplines and subsets in each discipline.

A mechanical project can have an assembly drawing and associated drawings for each part of the assembly. You can establish office standards by creating prototype sheet sets in which many typical details have already been created. These can include: subsets to organize the sheets, preset Properties and Custom Properties, and templates with label blocks, callout blocks, and page setups.

- Start by developing a naming and storage scheme for sheet sets. The storage location is normally a library folder on a server with subfolders for each project and then subfolders under the project folder for resource drawings and subsets of sheets.

- Several existing prototypes are available for Architectural, Civil, and Manufacturing templates in either Metric or Imperial units. You can use one of them as the base for your prototype sheet set or use one you have already set up as your office standard.

- When you start a sheet set using **An example sheet set**, only the subsets and some of the properties are copied over into the new sheet sets. You need to add the sheets themselves.

Sheet Set Properties

In the Sheet Set Properties dialog box (shown in Figure 11–6), some of the options are only set when you create the specific sheet set, such as the *Name* and *Model view* location. Other options should be defined in the prototype sheet set, including *Label block for views*, *Callout blocks*, and *Sheet creation template*.

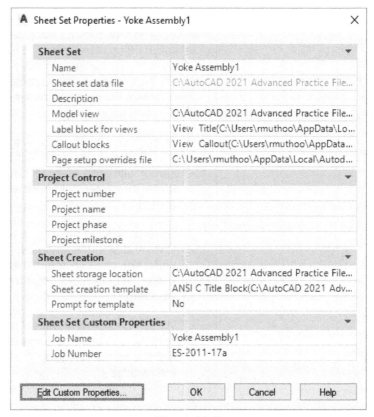

Figure 11–6

Sheet Set

Name	Name of sheet set that is entered when the sheet set is created. You can change it here.
Sheet set data file	Location of DST file (determined when sheet set is created).
Description	Description of sheet set. Can be added when sheet set is created or added here later.
Model view	Specify folder location(s) for drawings that are used in the sheet set. You can also set these locations in the *Model Views* tab. You can have several folder locations.

Label block for views	Block is used as view title when view is inserted on a sheet from a Model view drawing. Uses fields to automatically update information. Block can be stored in drawing file or template file.
Callout blocks	Blocks for callout bubbles. The Mechanical template includes one named **View Callout**. Architectural and Civil templates have several, including **Callout bubble** and several Elevation indicators for interior and exterior views. These blocks can be stored in a drawing file or template file.
Page setup overrides file	File that includes any page setups you might want to use for plotting. It must be a template file.

- The **Label block for views**, **Callout blocks**, and **Page setup overrides file** properties should all be created in the same DWT file.

Sheet Creation

Sheet storage location	Folder in which sheets in a sheet set are stored. Can be same folder used for the *Model view* location, but is often a different one. If working on a network, you need to make these available to everyone working on the project. You can also specify separate folder locations for subsets when you create them.
Sheet creation template	Template that is used when you create a sheet in the Sheet Set Manager. Must contain a layout and the layout should include the standard title block used for the project. Typically the same template in which your label, callout blocks, and page setup overrides are stored.
Prompt for template	In most cases, use the default Sheet creation template, with this option set to **No**. If using several different paper sizes in a sheet set, change the option to **Yes**. Each time you create a new sheet, you are prompted to select a template.

- When you create a subset for sheets you can assign a separate folder in which the sheets are stored, typically a subfolder under the main folder. You can also assign a different sheet creation template to each subset as required for consultants' title blocks or various sheet sizes.

Creating Custom Properties

The *Sheet Set Custom Properties* in Sheet Set Properties enable you to define the types of information to be included, such as a project owner or release date. Once defined in a sheet set, these custom properties are available as fields that can be used in blocks and text throughout the set of drawings.

When creating custom properties, you need to determine whether they are going to be linked to the entire sheet set (such as a project owner) or to specific sheets (such as *drawn by* initials). Properties *Owned by* the **Sheet Set** have the same value across sheets, while properties *Owned by* the **Sheet** can have different values on different sheets.

How To: Create Custom Properties

1. In the Sheet Set Properties dialog box, click **Edit Custom Properties**.
2. In the Custom Properties dialog box, click **Add**.
3. The Add Custom Property dialog box opens, as shown in Figure 11–7. Type a *Name* and a *Default value* and specify the *Owner* of the property – either the **Sheet Set** or **Sheet**.

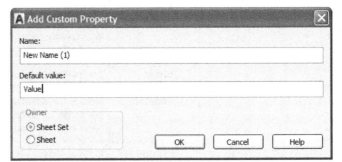

Figure 11–7

4. Click **OK**.
5. Continue adding custom properties as required. Finish by closing the Sheet Set Properties dialog box.

- If the custom properties are not displayed correctly in a sheet set, type **regen** or **regenall**.

11.4 Custom Blocks for Sheet Sets

After you have created custom properties, you can use them as fields, along with the other fields supplied with the software, to create title blocks (as shown in Figure 11–8), label blocks, and callout blocks that work specifically with sheet sets. These blocks should be defined in your sheet set templates so that they are available in new sheets.

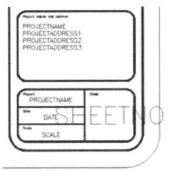

Figure 11–8

- Create any custom properties in Sheet Set Properties that you might need before you start editing or creating the new blocks.

- It helps to work in a sheet set when you are creating these blocks so that you can see how they are working. Create a sheet (using the existing sheet template), make changes to the blocks as required, and save the sheet file as your new template.

- Fields can be inserted as text objects or attributes in blocks.

Attributes and Fields

You can modify existing attribute definitions by double-clicking on the exploded attribute text. Right-click in the *Default* field and either edit or insert a field, as shown in Figure 11–9.

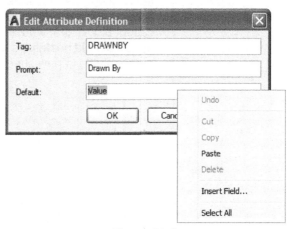

Figure 11–9

To specify a field as the value when you create an attribute (as shown in Figure 11–10), either click  (Insert field) or right-click in the *Default* field and select **Insert Field**.

Figure 11–10

Sheet Set Fields

Several fields are already defined to work with sheet sets, such as *CurrentSheetTitle* and *CurrentSheetNumber*, as shown in Figure 11–11. Fields related to sheet sets are located in the *SheetSet* field category in the Field dialog box.

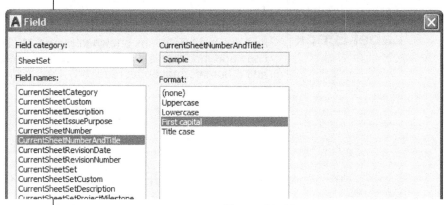

Figure 11–11

- Custom Properties that you have defined are listed in the *CurrentSheetCustom* and *CurrentSheetSetCustom* categories.

- Fields related to views, such as *ViewTitle* and *ViewportScale*, are located under the field name *SheetSetPlaceholder*.

- You can also use normal fields, such as *CreateDate* or *PlotDate*, in title blocks or plot stamps for sheet sets.

How To: Create a Sheet Title Block

1. Draw the title block graphics. You can also use an existing title block that includes attributes.
2. Decide which attributes need to be connected to a sheet set or can use fields as values to be automatically updated.
3. Create a sheet using the existing sheet template and open it.
4. Explode the title block.
5. Add fields in text or attribute values, as required.
6. Redefine the block.
7. Change some of the Sheet Set Properties to verify that the fields are updating in the block correctly.

Ensure that you determine the location of the insertion point before you explode the block

- You might want to include a plot stamp as part of your title block. The fields used by plot stamps are not specifically linked to a sheet set but provide more freedom of placement than the **Plot Stamp** tool in the **Plot** command.

Creating a Title Label Block

The title label supplied with the software's standard sheet set template includes information for the View Number, View Name, and Viewport Scale, as shown in Figure 11–12. You can make a copy and modify this block with your font styles and sizes and add other information as required.

Figure 11–12

- You can modify label and callout blocks using **Refedit** rather than exploding the block. If you added attributes, use **Synchronize Attributes** to synchronize the new information with the existing blocks.

Creating a Callout Block

The callout blocks supplied with the software's standard sheet set template include information for the View Number and Sheet Number, as shown in Figure 11–13. You can make a copy and modify these blocks with your font styles and sizes and add other information as required.

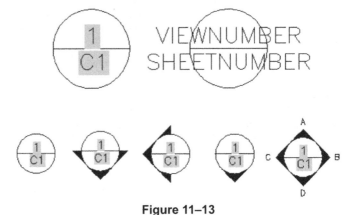

Figure 11–13

- The Architectural and Civil templates contain several callouts that are typically used for interior and exterior elevations.

Practice 11b | Customizing Sheet Sets

Practice Objectives

- Create a template drawing with a standard layout and several page setups, for use in sheet sets.
- Add and remove subsets, set up properties, and create custom properties, to create a prototype sheet set and use it to create a new sheet set (starting from an existing sheet set).
- Add fields to a title block for a template file.

In this practice, you will create a template drawing to use in sheet sets with a standard layout and several page setups. You will start a prototype sheet set from an existing sheet set, add and remove subsets, set up properties, and create custom properties. You will also set up a template file by adding fields to the title block. You will then create a new sheet set based on a prototype sheet set, as shown in Figure 11–14.

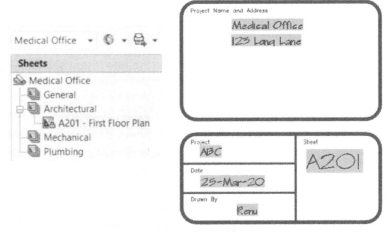

Figure 11–14

The practice files folder contains an established folder structure for sheet sets.

Task 1 - Create a template for sheet creation.

1. Start a new drawing based on **AEC-Imperial.dwt**, found in the practice files folder.

2. Delete the *A-sized* layout.

3. Switch to the *D-sized* layout. Right-click on the *D-sized* layout tab and select **Page Setup Manager**.

Note the available page setups.

4. Modify the page setup called **Arch D-Mono** by selecting it and clicking **Modify**. The Page Setup dialog box opens.

5. Set the *Plot style table* to **monochrome.ctb**, if required. Verify that the *Printer/plotter* name is set to **DWF6 ePlot.pc3** and that the *Paper size* is **ARCH D (24.00 x 36.00 Inches)**. Click **OK**. If you are prompted to update all of the layouts that reference this page setup, click **Yes**.

6. Set the current setup to **Arch D-Mono** by selecting it and clicking **Set Current**. Click **Close**.

7. Save the drawing as a drawing template file (DWT) named **SS-AEC-Imperial.dwt** in *Sheet Sets\Templates* in the practice files folder. Add a description, as required.

8. Close the newly created template file.

Task 2 - Create a prototype sheet set.

---

1. Create a new sheet set based on **An example sheet set**.

2. Use the **Architectural Imperial Sheet Set**.

3. Name the new sheet set **SS-AEC-Imperial** and store its DST file in *Sheet Sets\Templates* in the practice files folder.

4. Click **Sheet Set Properties**.

5. In the Sheet Set Properties dialog box, do the following:
    *   Leave the *Model view* location field blank.
    *   Set the *Page setup overrides file* to the template **SS-AEC-Imperial.dwt** that you have saved in *Sheet Sets\Templates* in the practice files folder.
    *   Set the *Sheet creation template* to the template **SS-AEC-Imperial.dwt**.

6. In the Sheet Set Properties dialog box, click **Edit Custom Properties**.

7. Click **Add** to add two custom properties named **Drawn By** and **Checked By**. Set the *Owner* to **Sheet Set**. Keep the *Default value* set to **Value**.

8. Click **OK** to finish the custom properties and click **OK** again to close the Sheet Set Properties dialog box.

9. Click **Next** and **Finish** to complete the sheet set creation.

Task 3 - Set up subsets for sheets.

1. In the Sheet Set Manager>*Sheet List* tab, note the existing subset categories that were defined in the example sheet set.

2. Delete subsets **Structural**, **Electrical**, **Fire Protection**, **Civil**, and **Landscape** by right-clicking on each subset name and selecting **Remove Subset**.

3. For each of the four remaining subsets, right-click on the subset name and select **Properties**. Change the *Sheet Creation Template* to **SS-AEC-Imperial.dwt** in *Sheet Sets\Templates* in the practice files folder.

Task 4 - Customize title block for sheet set.

In this task, you will set up the template file by adding fields to the title block. You will then create a new sheet set based on a prototype sheet set. The completed title block with properties is shown in Figure 11–15.

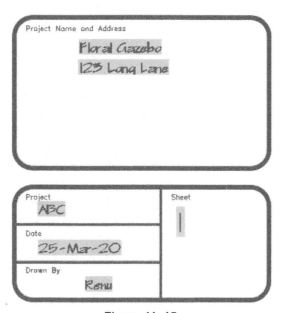

Figure 11–15

1. In the Sheet Set Manager, right-click on the sheet set name (**SS-AEC-Imperial**) and select **New Sheet**. Enter **1** as the *Number*, **Sample** as the *Sheet Title*.

2. Open **1-Sample** by double-clicking on it.

3. Explode the title block.

4. Zoom in on the lower right corner of the title block. You are going to add fields to this section.

5. Change the current layer to **Border**.

6. Double-click on the text **Scale**. Change it to **Drawn By**.

7. Start the **Define Attributes** command in the *Insert* tab>Block Definition panel.

8. Set the *Tag* and *Prompt* to **Drawn By** (no space in the tag text).

9. Next to *Default*, click ⊟ (Insert Field) and set the following:

   - *Field category*: **SheetSet**
   - *Field names:* **CurrentSheetSetCustom**
   - *Custom property name:* **Drawn By**
   - Click **OK**.

10. Continue by setting the following:

    - *Justification*: **Left**
    - *Text style*: **Hand**
    - *Text height*: **0.125**
    - *Insertion Point*: select **Specify on-screen**

11. Click **OK** and place the attribute in the *Drawn By* space.

12. Repeat the process to add the following fields in their respective attributes:

    - *Project Name*, *Project Address 1*, and *Project Number* (all found under *CurrentSheetSetCustom*)
    - *Sheet Number* (*CurrentSheetNumber*): Use a *Text height* of **0.25**.
    - *Date* (in the *Date & Time* category): Use the *Save Date* field.

13. Start the **Create Block** command.

14. Expand the Name drop-down list and select **TBLK-ARCH D (24.00 x 36.00)**.

15. Set the *Base point* at **0,0,0**.

16. Using **Select objects**, select all of the objects in the layout, except the viewport. Select the **Convert to block** option. Click **OK** and redefine the block.

17. Accept the default values for the attributes. These fields are controlled by the sheet set **Properties**. The Date displays a specific value at this point, as shown in Figure 11–16.

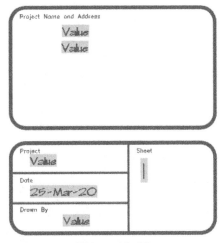

Figure 11–16

18. In the Sheet Set Manager, right-click on the sheet set name, select **Properties…**, and then select **Edit Custom Properties**.

19. Change the values of several custom properties used in the title block.

- You can use generic terms such as **Client** and **Address 1**, since this is going to be the template and not a specific project.

20. **Regen** to display the new values in the title block.

21. **Zoom All** to display the entire layout.

22. Use **Save As>Drawing Template** to save the drawing as a template with the name **SS-AEC-Imperial.dwt** (in *Sheet Sets\Templates* in the practice files folder), overwriting the existing template. Close the file.

23. Remove the 1 - Sample sheet file from the sheet set. This only removes the connection to the sheet set; it does not delete the drawing file.

24. Close the sheet set.

Task 5 - Create a new sheet set from a prototype.

1. Open the Options dialog box. In the *Files* tab, select **Template Settings>Sheet Set Template File location**.

2. Select the default path and click **Browse**. Set the *Sheet Set Template File Location* to be *Sheet Sets\Templates* in the practice files folder, as shown in Figure 11–17.

Template Settings

    Drawing Template File Location

    Sheet Set Template File Location

        C:\AutoCAD 2022 Advanced Practice Files\Sheet Sets\Templates

    Default Template File Name for QNEW

Figure 11–17

3. Similarly, change the *Default Template for Sheet Creation and Page Setup Overrides* to the template **SS-AEC-Imperial.dwt**, located in the *Sheet Sets\Templates* folder in the practice files folder.

4. Click **OK** to close the Options dialog box.

5. Create a new sheet set with **An example sheet set**, using **SS-AEC-Imperial**.

6. Name the new sheet set **Medical Office** and store the DST file in *Sheet Sets\Projects\Medical Office* in the practice files folder.

7. Open **Sheet Set Properties**. Set the following locations in the practice files folder:

   - *Model view:* **Sheet Sets\Projects\Medical Office\ Resource Drawings**
   - *Sheet storage location:* **Sheet Sets\Projects\ Medical Office\Sheets**

8. Click **Edit Custom Properties** and type some information for the *Project Name*, *Project Number*, and other custom properties.

9. Click **OK** to close Sheet Set Properties and apply the changes. Complete the Create Sheet Set wizard.

10. In the Architectural subset, create a new sheet named **A201-First Floor Plan**. Verify that it is based on **SS-AEC-Imperial.dwt**.

11. Open the new sheet.

12. The title block has been populated with the information stored in the properties, as shown in Figure 11–18.

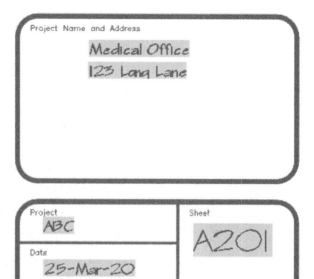

Figure 11–18

13. Save and close the sheet.

14. Close the sheet set.

15. Change the default sheet set template location back to its original default location. In the Options dialog box>*Files* tab, expand Template Settings and set the *Sheet Set Template File Location* to *C:\Users\<user name>\AppData\Local\ Autodesk\AutoCAD <version>\<release>\<language>\ Template* for Windows 10.

Chapter Review Questions

1. How would you **eTransmit** a subset of the sheets and their related files to a consultant?

   a. Right-click on a subset of the sheet list and select **eTransmit**.

   b. Start **eTransmit**, select the sheet set, and select the subset.

   c. You cannot **eTransmit** only part of a sheet set.

   d. In the Sheet Set Manager, right-click on the sheet set name and use the option for selecting a subset in the sheet set.

2. What is the quickest way of plotting a full sheet set to a DWF file?

   a. There is no quick way.

   b. Select **Plot** in the Quick Access Toolbar.

   c. Select **Publish to DWF** in the Sheet Set Manager.

   d. Select **Batch Plot** in the Application Menu.

3. Where do you create a custom field for use in sheet sets, such as *Drawn By*?

   a. In the Attribute Definition dialog box.

   b. In the Custom Properties of Sheet Set Properties.

   c. In the Fields dialog box.

   d. In the Drawing Properties.

4. The custom properties are available as fields but cannot be used in blocks and text.

   a. True

   b. False

5. The title label supplied with the software's standard sheet set template includes information for:

   a. **Viewport Color**

   b. **Font Style**

   c. **Font Size**

   d. **Viewport Scale**

6. When you create Custom Properties in a Sheet Set, they can be used in individual sheets or across the entire project. What types of objects are these?

   a. Hyperlinks

   b. Text

   c. Blocks

   d. Fields

Command Summary

Button	Command	Location
	Archive	• **Application Menu:** Publish • **Shortcut:** (*right-click on a sheet set name*)
	eTransmit	• **Application Menu:** Publish • **Shortcut:** (*right-click on a sheet set name*)
	Exports the selection to DWFx files	• **Sheet Set Manager**
	Publish	• **Sheet Set Manager**

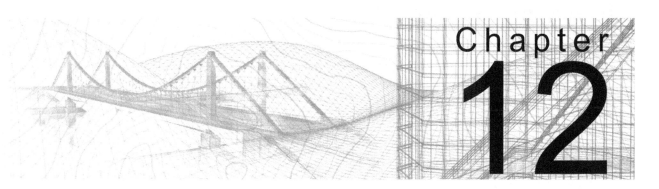

Projects - Sheet Sets

This chapter contains a practice project that can be used to gain additional hands-on experience with the topics and commands covered so far in this training guide. This practice is intended to be self-guided and does not include step-by-step information.

Project Objectives in This Chapter

- Set up Sheet Set Properties to automate multiple tasks.
- Publish a sheet set to a DWF file.

Practice 12a | Sheet Sets

In this project, you will create a sheet set and set up the Sheet Set Properties. You will create sheets and add information, such as views, door and window tags, and a schedule. You will also publish the sheet set to a DWF file. One of the completed sheets is shown in Figure 12–1.

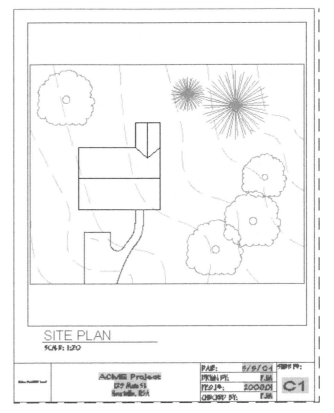

SITE PLAN
SCALE: 1:20

ACME Project
125 Main St
Anywhere, USA

DATE:	9/9/01
DRAWN BY:	PJM
PROJ#:	2008.01
CHECKED BY:	PJM

SHEET NO:
C1

Figure 12–1

Task 1 - Create a sheet set.

In the Options dialog box>*Files* tab, expand Template Settings and verify that the default *Sheet Set Template File Location* is set to *C:\Users\<user name>\AppData\Local\Autodesk\AutoCAD <version>\<release>\<language>\Template* for Windows 7 and Windows 10.

1. Create a new sheet set based on the **Architectural Imperial** example sheet set.

2. Name the new sheet set **Addition**. Store the sheet set data file in *Sheet Sets/Projects/Addition* in the practice files folder.

3. Click **Sheet Set Properties**.

4. Set the *Model View* location to **Sheet Sets\Projects\ Addition\Resource Drawings** in the practice files folder.

5. Change the *Label block for views* to the block **TITLE** in the template **SS-Small-Imperial-1.dwt** found in *Sheet Sets/Templates* in the practice files folder.

6. Change the *Callout blocks* to the block **CALLOUT** in the template **SS-Small-Imperial-1.dwt**.

7. Change the *Sheet creation template* to **SS-SMALL-Imperial-1.dwt** (**A-Sized Vertical** layout).

8. Fill out the custom properties as required. Add custom properties (owned by Sheet) for *Drawn By* and *Checked By*. Set the default values for these to your initials.

9. Finish the sheet set.

10. This is a very small project so you do not need all of the subcategories. Remove them from the *Sheet List* tab.

Task 2 - Create sheets.

---

1. Create the sheets shown in Figure 12–2 in the sheet set **Addition**.

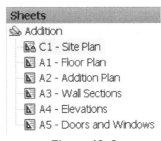

Figure 12–2

2. Open the sheet **C1 – Site Plan**.

3. In the Sheet Set Manager, in the *Model Views* tab, locate **Addition Site-A.dwg**.

4. Drag the view **Site Plan** from the drawing onto the sheet. Adjust the scale as required and accept the defaults for the title.

5. Save and close the sheet.

6. Open the sheet **A1 – Floor Plan**.

7. In the *Model Views* tab, locate **Addition-Plan-A.dwg**.

8. Select the view **Overall** and drag it onto the sheet. Set the *scale* to **1/8"=1'-0"**. Accept the defaults for the title.

9. Modify the viewport so that it fits inside the border if required. Lock the viewport.

10. In the viewport, toggle off any extra layers other than walls, windows, doors, and tags for the active file and the XREF file.

11. In Paper Space, using the **Insert Block** command, add door and window tags, as shown in Figure 12–3.

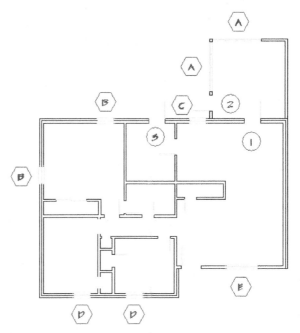

Figure 12–3

12. Save and close the sheet.

13. Open the sheet **A2-Addition Plan**.

14. In the *Model Views* tab, locate **Addition-Plan-A.dwg**.

15. Select the view **Addition** and drag it onto the sheet. Set the *scale* to **1/4"=1'-0"**. Accept the defaults for the title.

16. Add dimensions. They can be placed in Paper Space.

17. Save and close the sheet.

18. Open the sheet **A5 – Doors And Windows**.

19. Create the schedules shown in Figure 12–4 on this sheet. Use the *Schedules* table style.

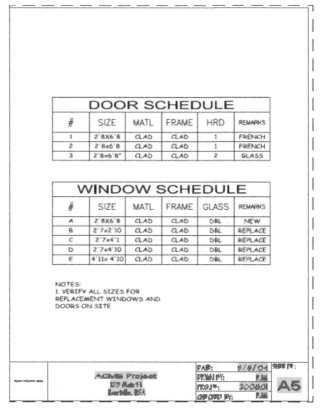

Figure 12–4

20. Save and close the sheet.

21. Publish the entire sheet set to DWF and view the sheet set in the Autodesk® Design Review software.

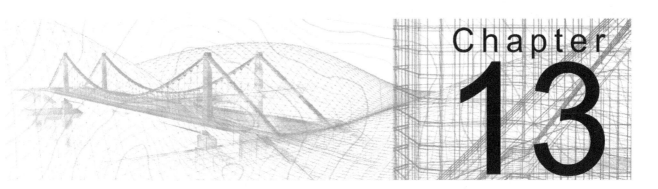

13

Managing Layers

The Layer Properties Manager controls which linework is displayed and how it is displayed in the drawing. Using this powerful tool, you can filter layers and control their status in each view independently. In this chapter, you learn how to work with the Layer Properties Manager and its settings, create layer filters, and set up layer states.

Learning Objectives in This Chapter

- Control the properties columns and the layer settings using the Layer Properties Manager.
- Create settings that override Layer Properties in viewports.
- Define groups of layers based on specified properties.
- Manipulate layers as a group using the Group Filter.
- Manage specific configurations of layers to be restored later using the Layer States Manager.
- Import and export layer states for use in other drawings.

13.1 Working in the Layer Properties Manager

The Layer Properties Manager (shown in Figure 13–1) can be used to create new layers and to work with layer property overrides in viewports.

- The Layer Properties Manager contains other tools that can be use to manage layers, including controlling the properties columns and the layer settings.

You can resize the Layer Properties Manager by dragging its edges.

- The Layer Properties Manager can be opened by clicking 📇 (Layer Properties Manager) in the *Home* tab>Layers panel or *View* tab>Palettes panel.

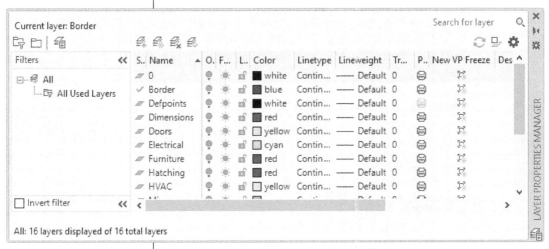

Figure 13–1

Displaying Columns in the Layer Properties Manager

The Layer Properties Manager column display order can be rearranged to suit your needs. Select a column header and drag it to a new location, as shown in Figure 13–2. The AutoCAD® software retains the new location of the column.

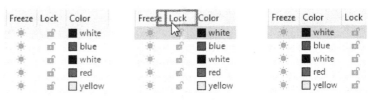

Figure 13–2

Note that if the name is grayed out, it cannot be removed.

Columns that you do not want to display can also be removed. Right-click on a column header and select a column name to clear the check and remove it from the display, as shown in Figure 13–3.

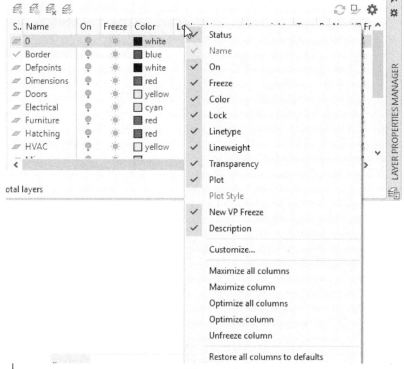

Figure 13–3

- Additional column names display if you are in a layout. These provide access to the viewport layer property overrides.

- Other selections in the shortcut menu include:
  - **Maximize column** and **Maximize all columns:** The maximize options change the column width so that the full header name displays.
  - **Optimize all column** and **Optimize column:** The optimize options change the column width based on the length of the column content
  - **Freeze/Unfreeze column:** The *Freeze* column acts like freeze panes do in Excel. It causes the selected column and columns to the left of it to constantly display. When scrolling to the right to show other columns, the frozen column remains visible.
  - **Restore all columns to defaults:** Sets the column display back to the default options.

- **Customize...:** Enables you to modify more than one column at a time.
- Selecting **Customize...** opens the Customize Layer Columns dialog box (shown in Figure 13–4), in which you can clear the checkmark from any columns that you do not want to display. Use **Move Up** and Mo**ve Down** to change a selected column's position in the display.

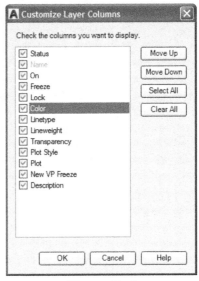

Figure 13–4

- Freezing keeps the column visible even if you scroll to the end of the options. For example, you might want to freeze the *Name* column (shown in Figure 13–5), so that it displays when you make changes to the plot columns.

Figure 13–5

- The tooltips for the column headers display the column name and a description of the information displayed in the column, as shown in Figure 13–6.

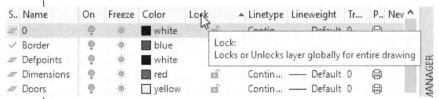

Figure 13–6

Layer Settings

Click ⚙ (Settings) to open the Layer Settings dialog box, as shown in Figure 13–7. These options are helpful when you use reference files that have different layer property overrides or might impact the created Layer States.

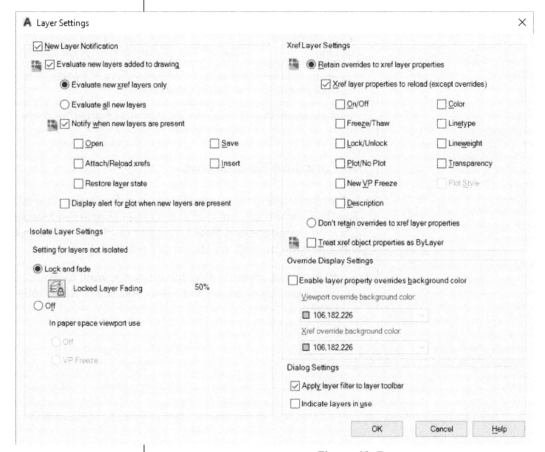

Figure 13–7

Layer Settings Options

Evaluate new layers added to drawing	If selected, evaluates and detects whether new XREF layers or new layers have been added to the drawing based on the setting.
Notify when new layers are present	Notifies you that new layers (or XREF layers) have been added to the drawing and enables you to customize the actions that trigger the display of the notification. Options include **Open**, **Attach/Reload xrefs**, **Restore layer state**, **Save**, and **Insert**.
Display alert for plot when new layers are present	Layer Notification Warning box opens when you use **Plot** in a drawing containing new layers.
Settings for layers not isolated	Controls the behavior of layers that are not selected when using **Layer Isolate**.
Xref Layer Settings	Control the layer properties that you want to reload. These properties are stored in the **VISRETAINMODE** system variable.
Override Display Settings	Sets color of background highlight indicating that viewport settings override overall layer settings.
Apply layer filter to layer toolbar	Layer filter set in Layer Properties Manager is also applied to Layer Control.
Indicate layers in use	Displays icon in list view to indicate layers that contain objects.

Reconciling New Layers

When there are unreconciled layers in a drawing, a new layer filter is automatically created in the Layer Properties Manager. Click on **Unreconciled New Layers t**o display only the layers that are unreconciled, as shown in Figure 13–8.

- To reconcile layers, select the ones you want to accept into your main list of layers, right-click and select **Reconcile Layer**.

Figure 13–8

Freezing Layers in New Viewports

The *New VP Freeze* column displays whether or not the layer is frozen in new viewports, as shown in Figure 13–9. For example, you might want to create a layer that is only displayed in one viewport. Select **New VP Freeze** so that layer is not displayed in any additional viewports that you create.

Figure 13–9

Freezing Layers in All Viewports Except Current

You can freeze selected layers in all viewports except the current viewport. Activate the viewport in which you want to keep the layer(s) visible. In the Layer Properties Manager, select the layer(s), right-click and select **VP Freeze Layer>In All Viewports Except Current**, as shown in Figure 13–10. Select **VP Thaw Layer in All Viewports** to return the layer back to normal.

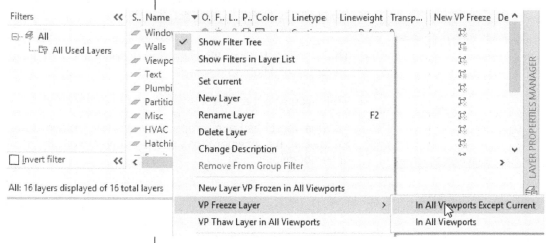

Figure 13–10

Overriding Layer Properties in Viewports

You can change layer properties (such as color, linetype, lineweight, and plot style) in a viewport without that change being made in other viewports. The changes only affect the current viewport and not the model or other viewports.

- The viewport-specific options include:
  - New VP Freeze
  - VP Freeze
  - VP Color
  - VP Linetype
  - VP Lineweight
  - VP Transparency
  - VP Plot Style
- To create these changes, you must be in a layout tab (Status Bar) and working through a viewport.

How To: Modify Layer Properties in a Viewport

1. In a layout tab, double-click in a viewport to activate Model Space.
2. Open the Layer Properties Manager and modify the viewport properties as required. They are highlighted as they are modified.

- The 🔲 (Toggle Override Highlight) option must be toggled on for the highlight to display

- When you select a viewport with Layer property overrides, 🔲 (Viewport has Layer property overrides) displays in the Status Bar. If a viewport does not have layer overrides, it does not display.

- The **Viewport Overrides** layer filter is automatically created when you have viewport overrides and you maximize a specific viewport, as shown in Figure 13–11.

Figure 13–11

- The layer name and any viewport-specific modifications are highlighted in the Layer Properties Manager.

Practice 13a | Working in the Layer Properties Manager

Practice Objective

- Modify the layer settings and the way in which columns display in the Layer Properties Manager.

In this practice, you will change the way the columns display in the Layer Properties Manager, modify the Layer Settings, and reconcile new layers in a drawing. The Layer Properties Manager is shown in Figure 13–12.

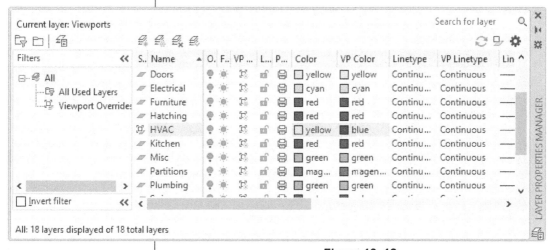

Figure 13–12

1. Open **Small House-A.dwg** from the practice files folder.

2. In the *Home* tab>Layers panel, click 🖹 (Layer Properties). In the Layer Properties Manager, the layers and their properties are listed in the columns.

This option maximizes to either the column's heading or its contents, whichever is larger.

3. Right-click on any of the column titles and select **Maximize all columns**. The columns shift so that the information listed in each column is completely displayed.

4. For the layers **Electrical** and **Furniture**, click 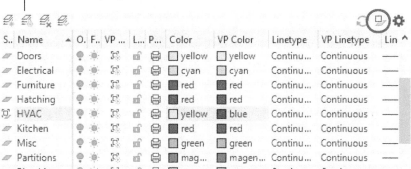 (New VP Freeze) to freeze them.

5. Auto-hide the Layer Properties Manager.

6. Switch to the **Proposal** layout. The existing viewport displays all of the layers as thawed.

7. In the Layer Properties Manager, right-click on the **Viewports** layer and select **Set current**.

*The **Electrical** and **Furniture** layers are frozen in this viewport, but not in the already existing viewport.*

8. Create a new viewport in the right half of layout. Note that the objects on the **Furniture** (red colored) and **Electrical** (cyan colored) layers are not displayed.

9. Make the new viewport active and display the Layer Properties Manager.

10. More properties are now available for Layer Property Overrides. Override the layer **HVAC** by making the *VP Color* **blue**.

- Verify that the (Toggle Override Highlight) is toggled on for the highlight to display.
- Note that the change is highlighted in blue, as shown in Figure 13–13.
- Note that (Viewport has Layer property overrides) displays in the Status Bar.

S..	Name	▲	O.	F..	VP ...	L...	P...	Color	VP Color	Linetype	VP Linetype	Lin ^
	Doors							☐ yellow	☐ yellow	Continu...	Continuous	—
	Electrical							☐ cyan	☐ cyan	Continu...	Continuous	—
	Furniture							■ red	■ red	Continu...	Continuous	—
	Hatching							■ red	■ red	Continu...	Continuous	—
	HVAC							☐ yellow	■ blue	Continu...	Continuous	—
	Kitchen							■ red	■ red	Continu...	Continuous	—
	Misc							☐ green	☐ green	Continu...	Continuous	—
	Partitions							■ mag...	■ magen...	Continu...	Continuous	—

Figure 13–13

11. Click (Settings) to open the Layer Settings dialog box.

12. Select **Evaluate all new layers**, **Notify when new layers are present**, and **Save**, as shown in Figure 13–14.

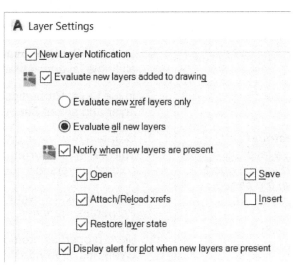

Figure 13–14

13. In the *Override Display Settings* area, select **Enable layer property overrides background color** and change the *Viewport override background color* to **green**, as shown in Figure 13–15.

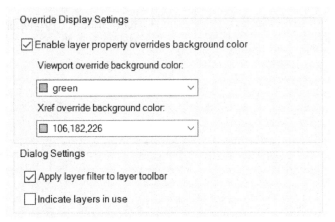

Figure 13–15

14. Click **OK** to return to the Layer Properties Manager and note that the override changes are highlighted in green.

15. Create three new layers using the default layer settings.

16. Save the drawing.

17. The Layer Properties Manager displays with the *Unreconciled New Layers* filter active. Select the **Unreconciled New Layers** filter to display only the layers that are unreconciled, as shown in Figure 13–16.

Figure 13–16

18. Select the layers, right-click and select **Reconcile Layer**. The layers are reconciled. Note that the **Unreconciled New Layers** filter is removed.

19. Save and close the drawing.

13.2 Creating Layer Filters

As you set up your layer standards, several additional tools in the Layer Properties Manager can help coordinate multi-layer systems.

- *Property filters* provide a way to define lists of layers based on specified properties.

- *Group filters* enable you to group any layers you specify so that you can manipulate them as a group.

Using the Filter Tree

In drawings with large numbers of layers, finding the ones that you want to manipulate in the list can be time-consuming. Layer Filters enable you to control which layers display in the layer list in the Layer Properties Manager, as shown in Figure 13–17. The Filter tree (the pane to the left of the layer list) displays the Property and Group Filters.

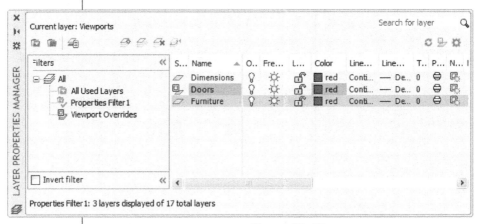

Figure 13–17

- Select a filter name to only display the layers in that filter.

- There are predefined filters for *All* and *All Used Layers* as well as a filter for each XREF in a drawing and if applicable, *Unreconciled New Layers*.

- Right-click on a filter to change its **Visibility**, **Lock**, **Viewport** (**Freeze/Thaw**), or **Isolate Group** (freeze all layers not in the filter) options, as shown in Figure 13–18. This enables you to use filters to control the display of layers in the drawing.

Figure 13–18

- You can create a temporary filter using Search for layer 🔍 in the top right corner of the Layer Properties Manager. When you click in the field, the cursor is placed in front of an asterisk (*) wildcard character. You can type a letter or group of letters and have the software look for layers that have those letter(s) at the beginning of their names.

- The Filters pane can be collapsed if you do not want to use it by clicking **《** (Collapses Layer filter tree), as shown in Figure 13–19.

Click 》 (Expands Layer filter tree) to restore it.

Figure 13–19

- When the Filters pane is collapsed, you can still specify a filter by expanding 📁 ▾ (Expands or collapses the Layer filter tree) in the lower left corner of the Layer Properties Manager, as shown in Figure 13–20.

Figure 13–20

- The **Invert Filter** option below the filter list enables you to reverse the currently applied filter. For example, selecting **Invert Filter** with the filter *All Used Layers*, lists all of the unused layers.

Property Filters

Property filters include any layers that match a specified property. For example, you can define property filters for all of the layers that are frozen (as shown in Figure 13–21), all of the layers of a specific color, or all of the layers whose names begin with a specific prefix.

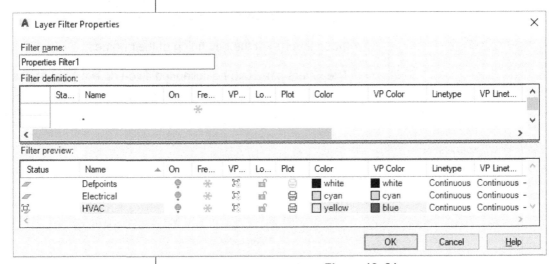

Figure 13–21

How To: Create a Property Filter

1. In the Layer Properties Manager, click (New Property Filter). The Layer Filter Properties dialog box opens.
2. Type a name for the filter.
3. Add the Filter definition information. You can expand the drop-down lists and select an option. For example, if you click the field under the *Freeze* column, you can select an empty space (no property), a ❄ (Freeze), or a ☀ (Thaw), as shown in Figure 13–22.

Filter definition:

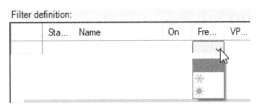

Figure 13–22

- If you are typing a name, you can use standard wildcards, such as * (asterisk), for everything. For example, **D*** would list all of the layer names that start with D, as shown in Figure 13–23. The bottom pane displays a preview of the Filter.

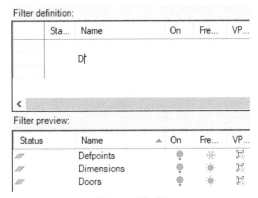

Figure 13–23

4. Click **OK** to continue.

- Double-click on a property filter to modify it or right-click on its name and select **Properties...**.

- If you add several filter properties in one row (such as **A*** and **Freeze**), the filter works as an **AND** operation (the layer must start with A and be frozen).

- If you add filter properties on separate rows (such as **A*** on one row and **Freeze** on another) the filter works as an **OR** operation (the layers must either start with A or be frozen).

Group Filters

A group filter can include a number of specified layers, as shown in Figure 13–24. The layers do not have to have a name or state in common, as is required for Property filters. You can add layers to a group filter by dragging-and-dropping the layer name from the list or by selecting objects in a layer in the drawing.

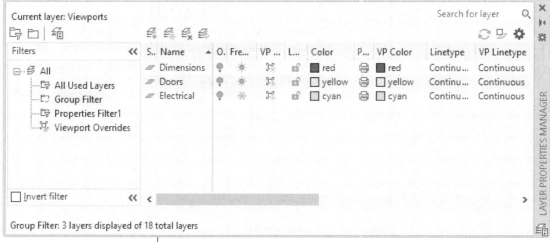

Figure 13–24

How To: Create a Group Filter

1. Open the Layer Properties Manager.
2. Click ☐ (New Group Filter) and give the filter a name.
3. Apply the *All* filter to display the complete layer list.
4. Drag and drop layers from the layer list into the group. You can also right-click on the filter name and select **Select Layers>Add** (or **Replace**).

   • The AutoCAD software switches to the drawing window in which you can select objects on the required layers. Press <Enter> when you complete the selection set. You return to the Layer Properties Manager in which the layers in the group display in the layer list.

5. You can then use the group to quickly modify the state or properties of all of the layers it contains.

   • You can remove a layer from a group filter by right-clicking on it in the group filter list in the Layer Properties Manager and selecting **Remove from Group Filter**.

   • Layers that are added to an existing group filter do not automatically use the visibility settings or other settings that you have already applied to the filter. You need to reapply these settings using the shortcut menu in the filter.

- Group filters can be nested under other group filters. You can also nest property filters under group filters.

- You can convert a property filter to a group filter by right-clicking on the filter and selecting **Convert to Group Filter.**

13.3 Setting Layer States

Layer States enable you to save a specific configuration of layers (their status of on/off, thawed/frozen, etc.) and later restore it. Layer States can be created, edited, saved, and renamed in the Layer States Manager, as shown in Figure 13–25. You can also import and export layer states to use in other drawings.

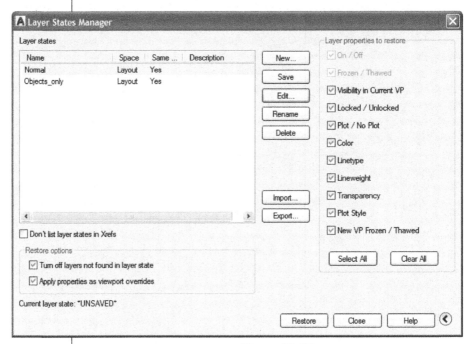

Figure 13–25

For example, in a floor plan drawing you could set up a layer state to display the appropriate layers for the Reflected Ceiling Plan, another state with the appropriate layers displayed for dimensions, etc. Restoring the saved state is easier than adjusting the individual layers each time you need to view or print the drawing in different ways.

How To: Create a New Layer State

The layer state also saves which layer is active.

1. Set the status of the layers in the drawing (on or off, thawed or frozen, etc.) as required.
2. In the *Home* tab>expanded Layers panel>Layer State drop-down list, select **Manage Layer States**.
3. In the Layer States Manager, click **New**.

You can also open the Layer States Manager

by clicking ⊞ (Layer States Manager) in the Layer Properties Manager.

4. Type a name and description for the Layer State and click **OK**.
5. You can create additional states and click **Edit** to modify them.
6. When you are finished, select the layer state that you want to use and click **Restore**. If you do not want to restore a layer state at this time, click **Close**.

- Layer States can be saved and restored in the model or in a layout view.

- By default, all of the layer settings, such as on/off, color, and lineweight, are included in the layer state.

Click ⊘ (Less Restore Options) to hide it again.

- You can modify the *Layer properties to restore* area in the Layer States Manager by expanding ⊘ (More Restore Options).

- The **Don't list layer states in Xrefs** option, filters the list of layer states to only display those in the current drawing.

- If you expect other layers to be added after you create a layer state and you do not want the new layers to be included in the layer state, select **Turn off layers not found in layer state**. When you restore the state, the new layers are toggled off.

- By default, the **Apply properties as viewport overrides** option is selected. After selecting a viewport, you can select this option and save a layer state that overrides the viewport's layer properties.

- To rename a Layer State, select it and click **Rename**. The layer state's name highlights in blue and you can type a new name.

- The *Same as Dwg* column displays **Yes** or **No** depending on whether the Layer State settings match those in the drawing.

Restoring a Layer State

Layer States can be restored from the Layer States Manager. Double-click on the Layer State name or select the name and click **Restore**.

You can also restore a layer state using the Layer State drop-down list in the *Home* tab>Layers panel, as shown in Figure 13–26.

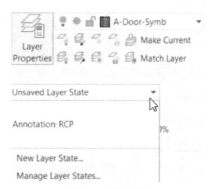

Figure 13–26

How To: Edit a Layer State

You can modify the information saved by a layer state including the current layer, layer status, layer properties, etc. For example, you might want the layer **Walls** in an electrical plan to be gray so that the walls fade into the background while the electrical layers have a heavier lineweight.

1. Open the Layer States Manager.
2. Select the Layer State that you want to modify and click **Edit**. The Edit Layer State dialog box opens, as shown in Figure 13–27.

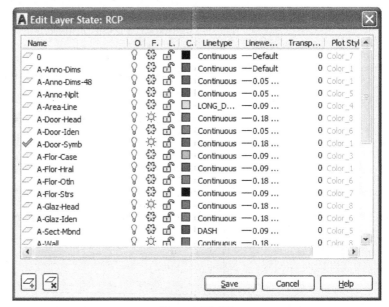

Figure 13–27

3. Modify the layers, as required.
4. If you want to add a layer that is not included in the state, click 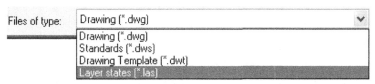 (Add layer to layer state). The Select Layers to Add to Layer State dialog box opens, in which you can select the layers that you want to add.
5. To delete a layer from the layer state, select the layer(s) and click 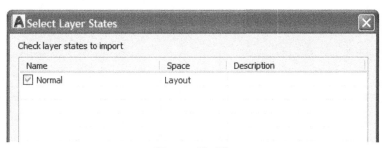 (Remove layer from layer state).
6. When you are finished, click **Save** to save the changes and close the Edit Layer State dialog box. You can also click **Cancel** to exit without saving changes.

How To: Import a Layer State

Layer states can be imported from other drawing files, drawing template files, and drawing standards files, as well as from layer states files, as shown in Figure 13–28.

Files of type: | Drawing (*.dwg)
Drawing (*.dwg)
Standards (*.dws)
Drawing Template (*.dwt)
Layer states (*.las)

Figure 13–28

1. Open the Layers States Manager and click **Import**.
2. The Import Layer State dialog box opens. In the Files of Type drop-down list, select **Drawing (.dwg)**, **Standards (.dws)**, **Drawing Template (.dwt)**, or **Layer states (.las)**.
3. Browse to the location of the file that you want to import, select it, and click **Open**. The Select Layer States dialog box opens.
4. Select the Layer States that you want to import, as shown in Figure 13–29.

Figure 13–29

5. Click **OK**.

6. If a Layer State of the same name exists in the drawing, a warning box opens. Click **Replace** to replace the existing Layer State and **Cancel** to cancel importing the new Layer State.

*   You can click **Export** to export a Layer State to an .LAS file. It can then be imported into other drawings. If the layers are not defined in a drawing, they are automatically created when the Layer State is imported.

Hint: Layer Previous

If you make a quick, temporary change to the status of your layers and want to return to the previous status, use **Layer Previous**, as shown in Figure 13–30. Similar to **Zoom Previous**, this tool can step back repeatedly through a series of layer changes. The only layer changes that it does not affect are the renaming of layers and creating new ones.

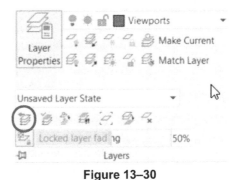

Figure 13–30

Practice 13b | Layer Filters and Layer States

Practice Objectives

- Create layer property and layer group filters.
- Create and restore layer states.

In this practice, you will create layer property and layer group filters and create and restore several layer states.

Task 1 - Create layer filters.

In this task, you will create layer property and layer group filters, as shown in Figure 13–31.

Figure 13–31

1. Open **Layer Plan-A.dwg** from the practice files folder.

2. Open the Layer Properties Manager (if it is not already open). All of the layers are on and thawed except for **A-Door-Head** and **A-Glaz-Head**.

3. Click (New Property Filter). Name the filter **Architectural Layers**. In the *Filter definition* area, in the *Name* field, type **A-***. The layers that match the filter should be displayed in the *Filter preview* area. Click **OK** to set the filter.

4. Click (New Group Filter) and name the new filter **Annotations**.

5. Click on **All** in the *Filters* list to display all of the layers. Drag and drop the layers **A-Anno-Dims** and **A-Door-Iden** from the layer list into the **Annotations** group.

6. Click on **Annotations** in the *Filters* list and verify that only those two layers are displayed.

7. In the drawing window, select any of the red grid bubbles along the right side of the drawing, the blue vertical center line, and the blue section callout at the bottom left of the drawing.

8. In the Layer Properties Manager, select the *Annotations* filter.

9. Right-click on the **Annotations** filter, expand **Select Layers** and select **Add**. Five layers are listed in the **Annotations** filter.

*The layers that are part of the **Annotations** filter are frozen.*

10. In the Layer Properties Manager, right-click on the **Annotations** filter again, expand **Visibility** and select **Frozen**. Note that the objects on these layers are not displayed in the drawing anymore.

11. Save the drawing.

Task 2 - Set up layer states (Architectural).

In this task, you will create and restore several layer states. The final layer state is shown in Figure 13–32.

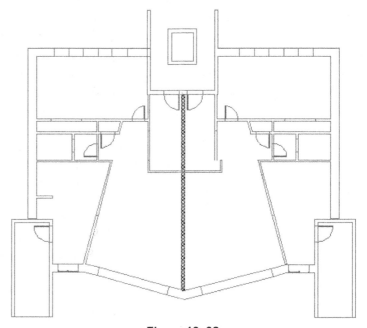

Figure 13–32

1. Use the **Annotations** layer filter to verify that all of the annotations are frozen.

2. Click ⬚ (Layer States Manager) and create a new layer state called **Annotations Off**.

3. Create another new layer state and name it **RCP** with the description **Reflected Ceiling Plan**.

4. Select the new layer state **RCP** and click **Edit**.

5. In the Edit Layer State dialog box, freeze all of the layers except the current layer (**A-Door-Symb**), **A-Wall**, **A-Door-Head**, **A-Glaz-Head**, **Defpoints**, and **E-lite-Eqpm**. Change the *color* of these layers to **gray** and click **Save**.

You might need to ***Regen*** *to refresh the screen after switching layer states.*

6. Close the Layer States Manager.

7. In the *Home* tab>Layers panel, use the Layer State drop-down list to try the two new layer states in your drawing.

8. Save and close the drawing.

Practice 13c | Setting Up Layer States (Mechanical)

Practice Objective

- Set up layer states.

In this practice, you will restore and edit layer states and then create a new layer state. Two of the layer states are shown in Figure 13–33.

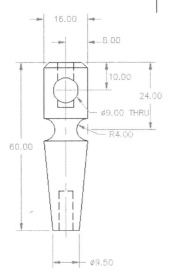

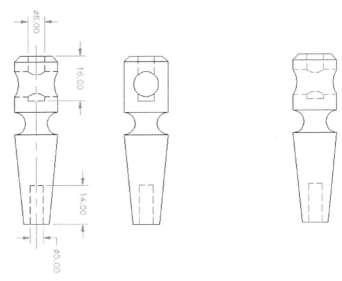

Figure 13–33

Task 1 - Work with layer states.

1. Open **Spindle Detail-M.dwg** from the practice files folder.

2. In the *Home* tab>expanded Layers panel, use the Layer State drop-down list to set the layer state to **Normal**, as shown in Figure 13–34.

    - In the drawing, note that the current layer is **0**, the hidden lines are black/white, and objects and dimensions are displayed.

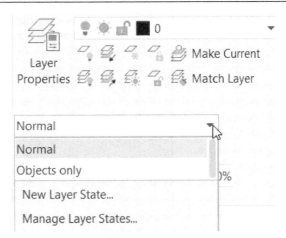

Figure 13–34

3. Switch the Layer State to **Objects only**, as shown in Figure 13–35.

   - The layer **Object** is current and layers with hidden linetypes are blue with no dimensions.

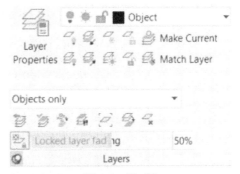

Figure 13–35

4. Open the Layer States Manager by expanding the Layer State drop-down list and selecting **Manage Layer States**.

5. Select **Objects only** and then click **New** to create a new layer state.

6. In the *New layer state name* field, type **Visible Objects only** and click **OK**.

7. In the Layer States Manager, select the layer state **Visible Objects only** and click **Edit**.

8. In the Edit Layer State dialog box, freeze the layers **Hidden-Front** and **Hidden-Side**, as shown in Figure 13–36.

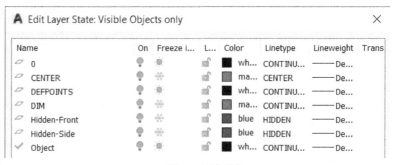

Figure 13–36

9. Click **Save** to close the Edit Layer State dialog box.

10. Click **Close** to close the Layer States Manager.

You might need to use REGEN to refresh the screen after switching layer states

11. Check each layer state using the Layer State drop-down list to see the changes.

Task 2 - Import layer states.

1. Open the Layer States Manager and click **Import**.

2. Browse to **Mech Part-M.dwg** in the practice files folder and click **Open**.

3. Verify that the layer state **heavy objects** is checked, as shown in Figure 13–37. Click **OK**.

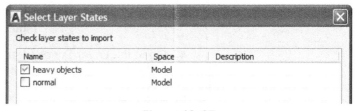

Figure 13–37

You might need to toggle on the

(Show/Hide LineWeight) option in the Status Bar.

4. In the Layer States Manager, select the layer state **heavy objects** and click **Restore**. Note the thick lineweight of the objects.

5. Switch the layer state to **Normal**.

6. Save and close the file.

Chapter Review Questions

1. How do you remove columns that you do not want to display in the Layer Properties Manager?

   a. Select the column and press <Delete>.

   b. Right-click on the column and select **Delete**.

   c. Drag-and-drop the column out of the Layer Properties Manager.

   d. Right-click on the header and clear the checkmark next to the column name.

2. How do you add layers to a layer group filter?

   a. In the Layer Properties Manager, drag-and-drop layers into the filter.

   b. Edit the properties that are associated with the filter.

   c. Change the properties of the layers to match the properties of the filter.

   d. Double-click on the layers in the Layer Properties Manager.

3. What are the two types of Layer Filters?

   a. Property filters and color filters.

   b. Property filters and group filters.

   c. Color filters and group filters.

   d. Model filters and layout filters.

4. What is the purpose of Layer States?

   a. To save a configuration of layers and layer properties.

   b. To control the objects on a layer.

   c. To control which layers are contained in a drawing.

   d. To change the names of layers in a drawing.

5. You cannot import layer states from drawing templates.

   a. True

   b. False

Command Summary

Button	Command	Location
	Layer Properties Manager	• **Ribbon:** *Home* tab>Layers panel or *View* tab>Palettes panel
	Layer States Manager	• **Ribbon:** *Home* tab>Layers panel>Layer State drop-down list

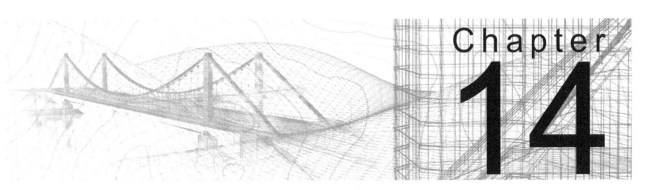

Chapter

14

CAD Standards

It is extremely important that all drawings produced by a firm are consistent throughout and follow the same method of production. That is why many firms have standards that they expect employees to follow. In this chapter, you learn how to configure standards, check drawings for standards compliance, and translate layers.

Learning Objectives in This Chapter

- Create an AutoCAD® Drawing Standards file.
- Associate the standards file to the current drawing.
- Check a drawing for compliance after it has been associated with a standards file.
- Translate layers automatically to match the CAD standards file.

14.1 CAD Standards Concepts

The CAD Standards tools are designed to help establish consistency from drawing to drawing. Standards can be established for layers, linetypes, text styles, and dimension styles. With the CAD Standards tools, you can quickly check an existing drawing to ensure that it matches an established scheme for any of the standard components.

Using the CAD Standards tools involves several steps:

1. Create a standards file that is an AutoCAD drawing containing the appropriate layers, linetypes, text, and dimension styles, saved in the .DWS format.
2. Use the **Configure Standards** command to associate the standards file with a drawing to apply the standards.
3. Use **Check Standards** to compare the current drawing to the standards and to fix any discrepancies.

Creating a Standards File

The process of creating a standards file is similar to the process of creating a drawing template file.

How To: Create a Standards File

1. Start a new drawing or open an existing drawing.
2. Set up the layers, linetypes, text styles, and dimension styles as required to meet your standards.
3. Save the drawing as an AutoCAD Drawing Standards (.DWS) file.
4. Select the location in which you want to save the file, and click **Save**.

- You can open a standards file to change it the same way that you would to change a drawing file. In the Select File dialog box, in the Files of type drop down list, select **Standards** (*.DWS). You can define several standards files for different sets of standards or different projects.

- In many cases, the standards file is required to have the same settings as your template drawing. Create a new drawing based on the template and save it as a standards file.

14.2 Configuring Standards

Once you have created the standards file, you need to associate it to the drawing(s) to which you want to apply the standards. The **Configure Standards** command controls the standards files that are associated with a drawing, as shown in Figure 14–1.

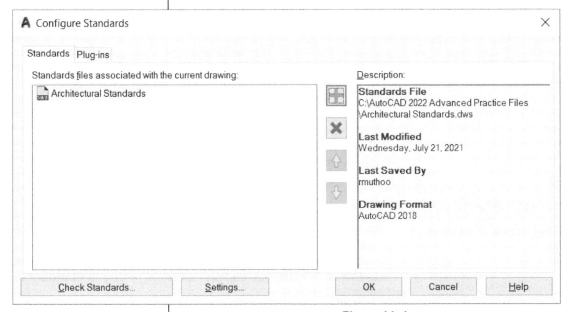

Figure 14–1

1. Open the drawing to which you want to apply the standards.
2. In the *Manage* tab>CAD Standards panel, click ⬚ (Configure Standards).
3. Click ➕ (Add Standards File) and select the standards file that you want to use.
4. To use the standards immediately, click **Check Standards**. You can also click **OK** to close the Configure Standards dialog box and check the standards later.

Plug-ins

Plug-ins are applications that specify how properties are checked for a named object. The AutoCAD software currently includes plug-ins for layers, linetypes, dimension styles, text styles, and multileader styles, as shown in Figure 14–2.

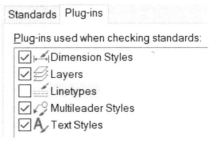

Figure 14–2

The *Plug-ins* tab enables you to select which standard components to check. For example, if you are not concerned about linetype standards, clear the check from this option.

CAD Standards Status Bar Icon

(Associated standards file(s)), located near the right end of the Status Bar, displays by default when a standards file is associated with the drawing, as shown in Figure 14–3. An alert balloon might also display to notify you of standards violations. It contains a link that you can click to start the **Check Standards** command.

Figure 14–3

* One standards file can be associated with multiple drawing files.

* A drawing can be associated with more than one standards file. If any of the standards conflict, the standards file listed first in the Configure Standards dialog box takes precedence. Use ⬆ (Move Up) or ⬇ (Move Down) to change the order of the standards files in the list.

* To remove a standards file from the drawing, select it in the list, and click ⊠ (Remove Standards File).

14.3 Checking Standards

After a standards file has been associated with a drawing, you can check the drawing for compliance. In the ribbon, in the

Manage tab>CAD Standards panel, when you click 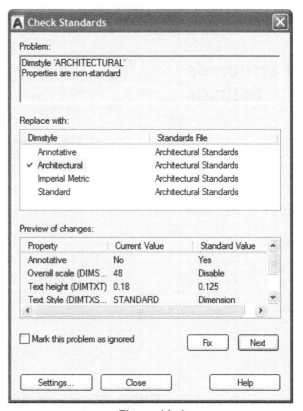 (Check Standards), the software compares the standard components in the current drawing with the settings in the standards file. For each discrepancy it finds, it prompts you to select how to fix the problem, as shown in Figure 14–4.

Figure 14–4

- If the software finds a non-standard object in the drawing, it displays a *Replace with* area containing the available standard objects. For example, this could be a layer that is not one of your standard layers, or one that uses a different color than your standard layer. Select a standard layer or style to substitute for the non-standard one, and click **Fix**.

- The *Preview of changes* area displays the properties that are going to change when you replace the non-standard object.

- When you replace a non-standard object with a standard one, drawing objects are converted and non-standard objects are purged. For example, **Partition** is a non-standard layer name that can be fixed by replacing it with the standard layer **Wall**. All objects on the layer **Partition** are moved to the layer **Wall** and the layer **Partition** is purged from the drawing.

- To leave a non-standard object unchanged, click **Next** to ignore it.

- If you select the **Mark this problem as ignored** option, the problem prompts you with *Ignored by: (your username)* the next time the drawing is checked.

CAD Standards Settings

In the Check Standards dialog box, click **Settings** to open the CAD Standards Settings dialog box. This is where you can adjust how the checking process works and control the notifications about standards violations, as shown in Figure 14–5.

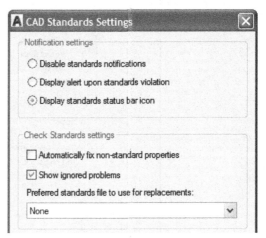

Figure 14–5

Check Standards Settings

Automatically fix non-standard properties	When a non-standard object has the same name as a standard object, the standard object's properties are automatically substituted.
Show ignored problems	Problems that were marked as ignored display when the standards are checked.
Preferred standards file to use for replacements	If more than one standards file is attached, specify which one is to be used for replacements.

Notification Settings

You can have the AutoCAD software provide *real-time* notification when you create or edit named objects that do not conform to the associated standards. For example, an alert box opens if you create a new, non-standard layer in the drawing.

- **Disable standards notifications:** Toggles off the notifications feature and toggles off the display of

  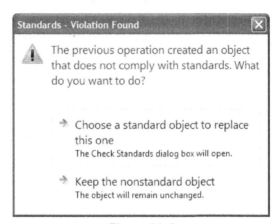 (Associated standards file(s)) in the Status Bar.

- **Display alert upon standards violations:** Opens an alert

  box, as shown in Figure 14–6. (Associated standards file(s)) does not display in the Status Bar.

Figure 14–6

- **Display standards status bar icon:** The (Associated standards file(s)) icon is displayed in the Status Bar. If there is a standards violation, a balloon is also displayed, as shown in Figure 14–7.

Figure 14–7

Practice 14a

Creating, Configuring, and Checking Standards

Practice Objective

- Create a Standards file, associate it with a drawing, and check the drawing for compliance against it.

In this practice, you will create a standards file that is based on a template and associate a standards file with a drawing. You will also check a drawing for compliance to standards and fix any discrepancies.

Task 1 - Create a standards file.

In this task, you will create a standards file based on a template. The layers for the standards file are shown in Figure 14–8.

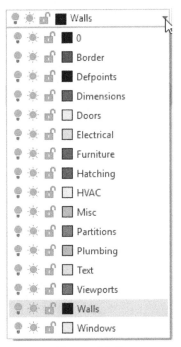

Figure 14–8

1. Start a new drawing based on **AEC-Imperial.dwt** located in the practice files folder.

2. Expand the Layer Control and note the layers in the drawing.

3. Open the Dimension Style Manager. Note the appearance of the **Architectural** style in the preview window. Close the Dimension Style Manager.

4. Open the Text Style dialog box and note the text styles that have been defined in the drawing. Close the dialog box.

5. Expand the Application Menu, expand 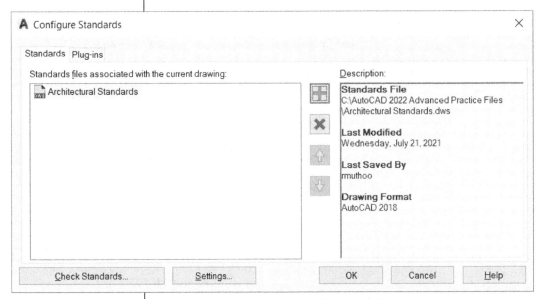 (Save As), and select **Drawing Standards**.

6. in the *Files of type* box, ensure that the **AutoCAD Drawing Standards (*.dws)** file is displayed. Name the file **Architectural Standards** and save it in the practice files folder.

7. The new .dws file containing the same standard components as the template opens. Close the file.

Task 2 - Configure standards.

In this task, you will associate a standards file with a drawing, as shown in Figure 14–9.

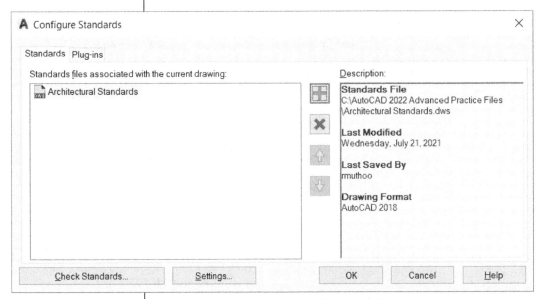

Figure 14–9

1. Open **Model Home 1-A.dwg** from the practice files folder.

2. In the *Manage* tab>CAD Standards panel, click

   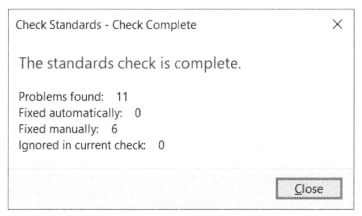 (Configure). In the Configure Standards dialog box, note that no standards files are currently associated with this drawing.

3. In the Configure Standards dialog box, click (Add Standards File) to add a standards file.

4. In the practice files folder, select **Architectural Standards.dws** and click **Open**.

5. In the *Plug-ins* tab, clear the **Linetypes** option and verify that the other options are selected.

6. Click **OK** to close the Configure Standards dialog box.

   (Associated standards file(s)) displays in the Status Bar indicating that a standards file is attached to the drawing.

7. Save the drawing.

*In the CAD Standards Settings dialog box, the Notification settings should be set to **Display standards status bar icon**.*

Task 3 - Check standards.

In this task, you will check a drawing for compliance to standards and fix any discrepancies, as shown in Figure 14–10.

Check Standards - Check Complete   ✕

The standards check is complete.

Problems found: 11
Fixed automatically: 0
Fixed manually: 6
Ignored in current check: 0

Close

Figure 14–10

1. In the Layer Control, note that there are several non-standard layers, including **Balcony**, **Chairs**, and **Outlets**.

2. Start the **Configure Standards** command.

3. Click **Settings** to open the CAD Standards Settings dialog box. In the *Check Standards settings* area, verify that the **Automatically fix non-standard properties** option is not selected. Click **OK** to close the CAD Standards Settings dialog box.

4. Click **OK** to close the Configure Standards dialog box.

5. In the *Manage* tab>CAD Standards panel, click  (Check).

6. The first problem encountered is with the dimension style **Architectural**, which has non-standard properties, as shown in Figure 14–11. In the *Replace with* area, ensure that **Architectural** is selected, and then click **Fix**.

Figure 14–11

Objects in the layer
Swing *are moved to the layer* ***Doors****, and the layer* ***Swing*** *is purged.*

7. The next problem is that the layer **Swing** is non-standard. In the *Replace with* area, select the layer **Doors**, and click **Fix**.

8. The properties of the layer **Electrical** are non-standard. Click **Fix** to make them match the standard properties.

9. The layer **Balcony** is non-standard. Click **Next** to leave it unchanged in the drawing.

10. Fix the layer **Plumbing** to give it the standard properties.

11. Click **Next** to leave the layer **Kitchen** unchanged.

12. Replace the layer **Chairs** with the layer **Furniture**, and click **Fix**.

13. Replace the layer **Outlets** with the layer **Electrical**, and click **Fix**.

14. Click **Next** to leave the **Multileader Style** unchanged.

15. Click **Next** to leave the text style **LOGO** unchanged.

16. Click **Next** to leave the text style **Hand** unchanged.

17. Close both the Check Complete dialog box and the Check Standards dialog box. Many objects have changed color to reflect their new layer assignments. Also expand the Layers control and note that many layers, such as **Swing** and **Chairs**, have been purged.

18. Open the Layer Properties Manager. Create a new layer called **Switches** with the default properties. Close the Layer Properties Manager.

19. In the Status Bar, the ▯ (Associated standards file(s)) icon and an alert balloon displays, indicating there is a standards violation, as shown in Figure 14–12. Select the **Run Check Standards** link to check the standards.

Figure 14–12

20. Click **Next** for the issues that were previously ignored.

21. Replace the layer **Switches** with **Electrical**.

22. After check complete, close all dialog boxes and verify that the newly created layer **Switches** no longer exists in the Layer Properties Manager.

23. Save and close the drawing.

14.4 Layer Translator

When you receive drawings from contractors or other sources, they might not match your standard layering scheme. The Layer Translator (shown in Figure 14–13) automates the process of converting layers to match the layer standards that you want to use.

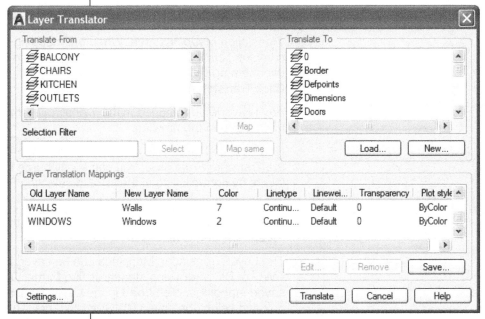

Figure 14–13

Both the **Check Standards** and **Layer Translator** commands can help in the process of converting layers to meet a standard. The advantage of the Layer Translator is greater automation. Once you have set up the layer mappings for the translation, you can easily translate layers from one standard to another in many drawings.

How To: Translate Layers in a Drawing

1. Open the drawing containing the layers that you want to translate.
2. In the *Manage* tab>CAD Standards panel, click 🗄 (Layer Translator).
3. The drawing's existing layers are listed in the *Translate From* area in the Layer Translator dialog box.

4. In the *Translate To* area, click either **Load** (to load existing layers from a DWG, DWT, or DWS file) or **New** (to define a new layer). Continue until you have loaded and/or created all of the required layers.

5. To map the translation, select one or more layers in the *Translate From* list and one layer in the *Translate To* list, and click **Map**.

   - You can also click **Map Same** to automatically map all of the pairs of layers that have the same name.

6. The Layer Translation Mappings are listed in the *Layer Translation Mappings* area. When the mappings are complete, click **Save** (if you want to save these mappings to use them again).

7. Click **Translate** to convert the layers.

- Any layers left unmapped in the *Translate From* area remain unchanged in the drawing.

- Unreferenced (empty) layers are indicated by 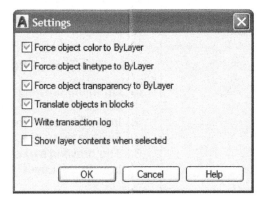 (Unfilled) in the *Translate From* area. You can easily purge the unused layers by right-clicking in the list and selecting **Purge layers**.

- You can edit the properties of the translated layers in the *Layer Translation Mappings* area by selecting the layer in the list and clicking **Edit**.

- The Layer Translation Mappings can be saved in either the DWG or DWS (drawing standards file) format. To use the saved mappings, click **Load** in the Layer Translator dialog box and select the saved DWG or DWS file. The saved mappings are automatically listed in the dialog box.

Settings

Use the Settings dialog box (shown in Figure 14–14) to control the optional features of the layer translation process.

Settings

☑ Force object color to ByLayer
☑ Force object linetype to ByLayer
☑ Force object transparency to ByLayer
☑ Translate objects in blocks
☑ Write transaction log
☐ Show layer contents when selected

[OK] [Cancel] [Help]

Figure 14–14

Force object color to ByLayer	Color definition for all objects is changed to **ByLayer** (the object's color is determined by the layer's color).
Force object linetype to ByLayer	Linetype definition for all objects is changed to **ByLayer** (the object's linetype is determined by the layer's linetype).
Force object transparency to ByLayer	Transparency definition for all objects is changed to **ByLayer** (the object's transparency is determined by the layer's transparency setting).
Translate objects in blocks	Objects nested in block definitions are translated to the new layer definitions.
Write transaction log	A transaction log of the translation is generated. The log is a text file (.LOG) that lists the layers that were translated and the new layer assignments.
Show layer contents when selected	Only objects in the layer selected in the *Translate From* area display in the drawing window. Enables you to quickly note the objects that are on a specific layer.

- Even if you are not translating layers, the **Show layer contents when selected** option is useful for understanding the layer scheme of a drawing.

Hint: Selection Filter

In the *Selection Filter* field, you can select areas based on a naming pattern using wildcard characters. Valid wildcard characters include * (matches any string), ? (matches any single character), and ~ (matches anything except the pattern). For example, to select all of the layers that begin with the letters **A-Wall**, type **A-Wall*** in the field and click **Select**.

Practice 14b | Layer Translator

Practice Objective

- Translate layers in a drawing and then save the translation mappings for use in another drawing.

In this practice, you will use **Layer Translator** to translate layers in a drawing (as shown in Figure 14–15), save the translation mappings, and then use them in another drawing.

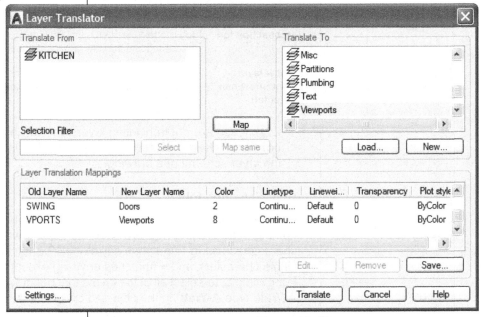

Figure 14–15

1. Open **Model Home 2-A.dwg** from the practice files folder.

2. Expand the Layer Control and note the layers in the drawing.

3. In the *Manage* tab>CAD Standards panel, click (Layer Translator). In the Layer Translator dialog box, the current layers are listed in the *Translate From* area.

4. Click **Load**. In the Select Drawing File dialog box, change *Files of type* to **Drawing Template (*.dwt)** and select **AEC-Imperial.dwt** from the practice files folder. Click **Open**.

5. In the Layer Translator dialog box, click **Map same**. All layers with the same names are listed in the *Layer Translation Mappings* area.

6. In the *Translate From* area, select **BALCONY**. In *Translate To* area, select **Misc**. Click **Map**. The layers are added to the *Layer Translation Mappings* area.

7. Continue to map the following pairs:

   - *CHAIRS* to **Furniture**
   - *OUTLETS* to **Electrical**
   - *SWING* to **Doors**
   - *VPORTS* to **Viewports**

8. The only layer left in the *Translate From* area should be **KITCHEN**. Leave this layer so that it remains unchanged in the drawing.

9. Click **Save** to save the mappings. Save them as a drawing file (DWG) with the name **Model Mappings** in the practice files folder.

10. Click **Translate** to complete the command. Expand the Layer Control. Note that the layers that were mapped to other layers (such as **CHAIRS** and **OUTLETS**) are gone.

11. Save and close the drawing.

12. Open **Model Home 3-A.dwg** from the practice files folder and note the layers. Layers such as **CHAIRS** and **OUTLETS** are present.

13. Start **Layer Translator** and click **Load**. Load **Model Mappings.dwg**. The mappings saved in that drawing are automatically restored.

14. Click **Translate** to translate the layers in this drawing using the same mappings. Click **Translate only** as you do not need to save the mapping information again.

15. Check the layers in the Layer Control. The layers such as **CHAIRS** and **OUTLETS** have been mapped and do not display any longer.

16. Save and close the drawing.

Chapter Review Questions

1. With the CAD Standards tools, you can establish standards for which type of drawing components?

   a. Table styles

   b. Blocks

   c. Text spelling

   d. Layers

2. You cannot associate one standards file with multiple drawing files.

   a. True

   b. False

3. When checking standards, if the AutoCAD software finds a non-standard layer called **Switches** and you replace it with the layer **Electrical**, what happens to the layer **Switches** and the objects on it?

   a. Objects stay on the layer **Switches**, but change color to match the color of the layer **Electrical**.

   b. Objects are moved to the layer **Electrical** and the layer **Switches** is purged.

   c. The layer **Switches** is attached as a single XREF.

   d. Both layers are merged into one named **Electrical Switches**.

4. In the Layer Translator, what types of files can you load layers from in the *Translate To* area?

   a. BMP, TIFF, and JPG

   b. DWT and DWG

   c. DWT, DWG, and DWS

   d. DWS and DWG

5. When checking a file using the **Check Standards** command, and replacing a non-standard layer with a standard one, the objects on the non-standard layer are...

   a. Frozen on the non-standard layer.

   b. Moved to a selected standard layer.

   c. Deleted from the drawing.

   d. Copied to a selected standard layer.

Command Summary

Button	Command	Location
	Check Standards	• **Ribbon:** *Manage* tab>CAD Standards panel
	Configure Standards	• **Ribbon:** *Manage* tab>CAD Standards panel
	Layer Translator	• **Ribbon:** *Manage* tab>CAD Standards panel

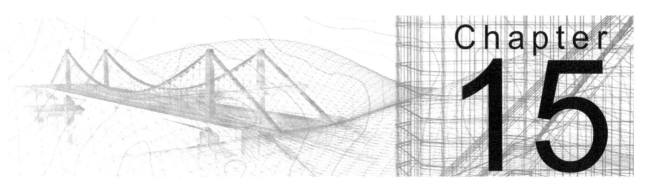

System Setup

Setting up the AutoCAD® system, before starting any drawings, helps reduce the amount of time spent on repetitive tasks. In this chapter, you learn how to set up plotters and plot styles to ensure that all drawings print correctly every time. You use drawing utilities to gain information about the drawing or to fix a corrupt file. You also learn how to customize the environment through system variables and dynamic input settings to create a more efficient work environment.

Learning Objectives in This Chapter

- Change system variables to control the way many features behave.
- Adjust Dynamic Input settings for interacting with the cursor and its display.
- Analyze data in a drawing file and correct any possible problems.
- Report a variety of drawing file information, including number of objects, drawing limits, latest version, etc.
- Add and configure a plotter.
- Define visual effects, lineweights, and colors for plot styles.
- Assign a plot style to a layouts page setup.

15.1 Options Dialog Box

Many aspects of the AutoCAD environment (i.e., screen appearance, default file locations, or system variables that affect performance) can be set in the Options dialog box, as shown in Figure 15–1.

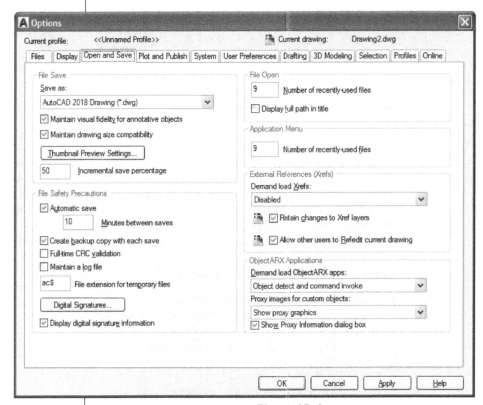

Figure 15–1

- You can open the Options dialog box by clicking **Application Menu>Options**, or by right-clicking in blank space in the drawing window and selecting **Options**.

- If (AutoCAD drawing symbol) displays next to an option, it indicates that those settings are saved *in the drawing*. Other settings are saved *in the registry* and applied to all of the drawings used during a session of the AutoCAD software.

- Options stored in the registry can be saved in a profile so that you can easily switch between different configurations of options.

- Many of the settings in the Options dialog box can also be set using system variables.

Options

The following table describes the Options dialog box tabs:

Files tab	View and change the software's search paths, filenames, and file locations (e.g., you can specify where the software looks for template files). You can either type a path or browse to select the location. ⊟····📄 Template Settings 　⊟····📑 Drawing Template File Location 　　⌐····⇨ C:\AutoCAD Template 　⊞····📑 Sheet Set Template File Location 　⊞····📄 Default Template File Name for QNEW
Display tab	Controls the screen display, including the visibility of items (such as scroll bars, tooltips, and layout elements), screen colors and fonts, and variables for display performance.
Open and Save tab	Controls the default format for saving a file, automatic saving and backup, file security, and how XREFs and ObjectARX applications are loaded. Safety options enable you to password-protect a drawing and apply a digital signature (requires a 3rd-party product).
Plot and Publish tab	Determines several plotter settings and the default plot device for new drawings. Also enables you to edit the Plot Style Table and Plot Stamp Settings.
System tab	Regulates the graphics display and pointing device, database options, and other miscellaneous options, such as the default Startup dialog box and trusted sources for security.
User Preferences tab	Governs various preferences, such as the use of accelerator keys, how typed coordinates are handled, the default units for block insertion, field settings, etc.
Drafting tab	Specifies the visual settings for AutoSnap and AutoTrack, and sets the aperture size and object snap options. Related settings are in the Drafting Settings dialog box.
3D Modeling tab	Specifies the options used for 3D objects, navigation, crosshairs, and for the ViewCube or **UCS** icon.
Selection tab	Controls settings related to object selection and grips. The Visual Effect Settings for object selection include the selection preview effect and display of Window/Crossing selection modes.
Profiles tab	Saves the registry settings in Options under a name so that they can be restored easily. The profile does not include settings that are saved in the drawing file. Click **Add to List** to create a new profile. Set it to be current and set up the Options required. Changes in Options are saved in the current profile.

Selection Highlighting

A system variable that controls the glowing selection highlighting effect color found in the *Selection* tab of the Options dialog box.

How To: Change the Selection Effect Color

1. Open the **Options** dialog box.
2. Click the *Selection* tab to make it active.
3. Expand the Selection effect color drop-down list (as shown in Figure 15–2) and select a new color.

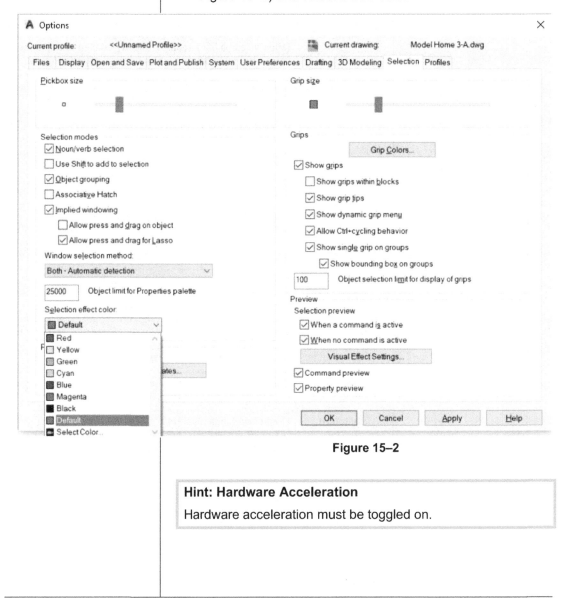

Figure 15–2

Hint: Hardware Acceleration

Hardware acceleration must be toggled on.

Improve Graphics Performance

You can take advantage of the improved graphics with a control accessed from the *Systems* tab, in the Graphics Performance dialog box.

How To: Improve Graphics Performance

1. Open the **Options** dialog box.
2. Click the *System* tab to make it active.
3. Click **Graphics Performance**.
4. In the Graphics Performance dialog box, click **Details** and select the mode depending on which **Video Memory Caching Level**. You can select **Basic Mode**, **Intermediate Mode**, or **Advanced Mode**, as shown in Figure 15–3.

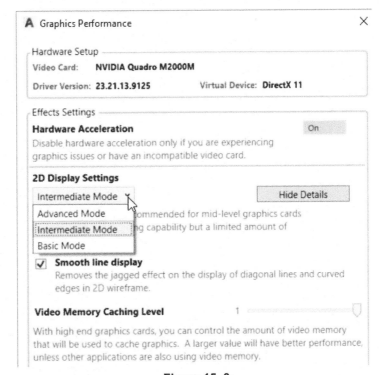

Figure 15–3

Security Options

A Security Options dialog box (accessed from the *System* tab in the Options dialog box) enables you to make adjustments to the security level using a control slider, as shown in Figure 15–4. In the Security Options dialog box, you can add and remove trusted folders for executable files. When searching for executable files, you can select from the following two options:

- **Exclude the Start In or drawing folders (recommended)**

- **Include the Start In and drawing folders**

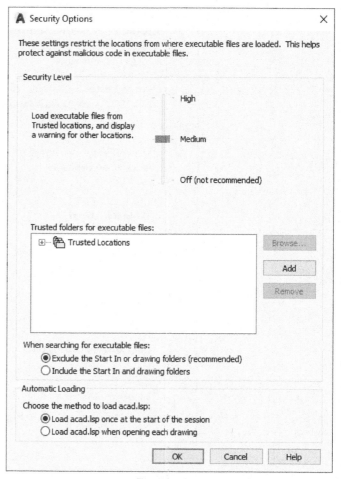

Figure 15–4

These controls or similar controls can also be found in the CAD Manager Control Utility and Deployment Wizard or by using the system variable **LegacyCodeSearch**.

Practice 15a | Options Dialog Box

Practice Objective

- Modify option settings and save the result as a profile to easily be restored later.

In this practice, you will set options for several different aspects of the AutoCAD software and save the settings in a profile, as shown in Figure 15–5.

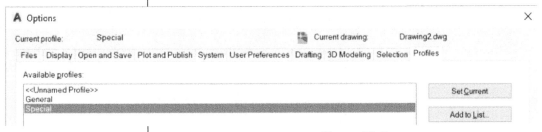

Figure 15–5

Task 1 - Save a new profile.

1. In any open drawing, open the Options dialog box (Application Menu>**Options**) and select the *Profiles* tab.

2. Note the current profile and select it in the list.

3. Click **Add to List**. Name this profile **General** with the description **General default settings**. Click **Apply & Close**.

4. Click **Add to List**. Name this profile **Special** with the description **My preferences**. Click **Apply & Close**.

5. Select the **Special** profile in the list and click **Set Current**. Any changes that you now make in the Options dialog box are saved in this profile.

6. In the *Display* tab, change the *Crosshair size* to **20**.

7. In the *Window Elements* area, click **Colors**. Set the following:

   - In the *Context* area, select **Command line**.
   - In the *Interface element* area, select **Active prompt background.**
   - Expand the Color drop-down list and select **Blue**.
   - In the *Interface element* area, select **Active prompt text.**
   - Expand the Color drop-down list and select **White**.

8. Click **Apply & Close**.

9. In the *Open and Save* tab, in the *File Safety Precautions* area, set *Automatic save* to **15**, and clear the **Create backup copy with each save** option.

10. In the *Files* tab, expand *Template Settings.* Expand *Default Template File Name for QNEW,* select **None,** and then click **Browse**. Set it to **AEC-Imperial.dwt** in the practice files folder.

11. Click **OK** to close the Options dialog box. Note the changes on the screen. The cross hair has become big and the Command Line is a blue band with white text.

12. Open the Options dialog box again. In the *Profiles* tab, select the **General** profile and click **Set Current**. Look in the other tabs and verify that the General settings have been restored. Click **OK** to close the Options dialog box.

13. Note the changes on the screen.

Task 2 - Change the selection effect color.

1. Open **Office-M1.dwg** from the practice files folder.

2. Start the **Move** command.

3. Select all the objects in the model. Note how they are all highlighted in blue. Press <Esc>.

4. Open the Options dialog box.

5. Click the *Selection* tab.

6. Note that the *Selection effect color* displays **Default** (blue color). Expand the Selection effect color drop-down list and select **Red**, as shown in Figure 15–6. Click **OK**.

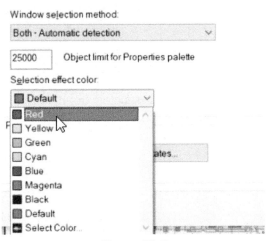

Figure 15–6

7. Start the **Move** command.

8. Select all the objects in the model. Note how they all turn red.

9. Click the basepoint near the bottom left corner of the model, and move it to the right, as shown in Figure 15–7.

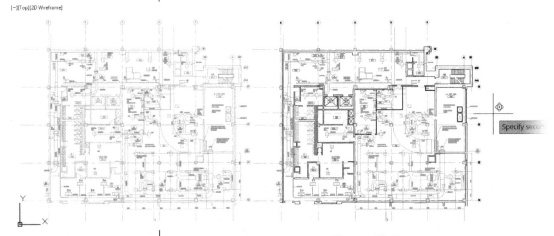

Figure 15–7

10. Press <Esc> to cancel the command.

11. Close the drawing without saving.

15.2 System Variables

System variables are values that are stored by the software that control the way the software behaves. Almost every setting that can be changed in the software is stored as a system variable, such as: from

- the default fillet radius (**filletrad**),

- the size of dimension text (**dimtxt**),

- the way File dialog boxes display (**filedia**).

The AutoCAD software has hundreds of system variables. For a complete list, see *Command Reference* in Help or use the System Variables Editor (**sysvdlg**), as shown in Figure 15–8.

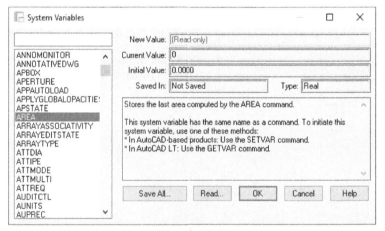

Figure 15–8

- You can also display a list of all of the system variables and their current values by typing **setvar**.

- Many system variables can be set in the Options dialog box or other dialog boxes. Most system variables can be changed, but some are read-only, such as **dwgname**.

- System variables are saved to either the individual drawing or to the Registry. Some are not saved.

- Most system variables are stored as strings (text), reals (real numbers, such as 2.25), integers (round numbers, such as 2), 2D or 3D points (0,0,0), or switches (on/off).

- System variables can be used in macros, scripts, and AutoLISP routines.

Some Common System Variables

Some common system variables are as follows.

clayer	Sets the current layer in the drawing.
expert	Controls whether or not the software issues prompts and warnings in various situations, such as when you toggle off the current layer, redefine a block, etc. Values range from 0 to 5. See Help for details.
lastpoint	Saves the coordinates of the last point picked or entered.
mirrtext	Controls whether text is reversed in the **Mirror** command. When set to **0**, text is not reversed. When set to **1**, text is reversed. The default setting is **1**.

ltscale	Controls the linetype scale for the entire drawing. Increasing **ltscale** increases the scale of all of the parts (dashes and spaces) of any linetype that is not continuous. Decreasing the scale decreases all of the parts. The default **ltscale** is 1. However, it can be modified as required. For example, changing it to 5 makes the dashes and gaps 5 times as long. It can also be set in the Linetype Manager (*Home* tab> Properties panel, expand Linetype Control and select **Other...** In the *Details* area, set the *Global scale factor*).

celtscale	Sets the linetype scale for newly created objects as a scale factor of the **ltscale**. By default, it is set to **1**. For example, if the **ltscale** is 10 and the **celtscale** is 2, the actual linetype scale for new objects is 20 (the dashes and gaps look twice as long as in other lines). You can change the scale for existing objects using the **Properties** command rather than by setting the **celtscale**.
msltscale	Sets the linetype scale in the *Model Space* tab according to the annotation scale. If set to **0** (in drawings created in versions of the AutoCAD software from 2007 and earlier), the linetype scale is not affected by the annotation scale. If it is set to **1** (in drawings created by default in versions of the AutoCAD software from 2008 and later), the linetype scale is scaled according to the annotation scale.

| **CURSOR BADGE** | Controls the display of cursor badges.
• Visible: To toggle cursor badges on, set the variable to **2**.
• Hidden: To toggle cursor badges off, set the variable to **1**. |

CURSORBADGE=2   CURSORBADGE=1

System Variable Monitor

The System Variable Monitor enables IT and CAD managers to quickly identify and edit variables that do not conform to a company's standards. When the **SYSVARMONITOR** command is active, a table displays indicating which system variables are selected to be monitored, as shown in Figure 15–9.

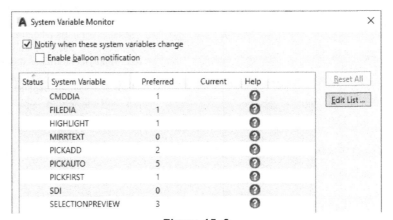

Figure 15–9

If a change is made to a system variable that is under the monitored category, the ☐ (System Variable Monitor) icon displays in the Status Bar.

- Selecting the option to **Notify when these system variables change** evokes a notification at the command line when a monitored system variable violates a preferred setting, as shown in Figure 15–10.

```
**** System Variable Changed ****
1 of the monitored system variables has changed from the preferred value. Use SYSVARMONITOR
command to view changes.
    ▸ Type a command
```

Figure 15–10

- Selecting the option to **Enable balloon notification** displays a notification bubble at the Status Bar when a monitored system variable violates a preferred setting, as shown in Figure 15–11.

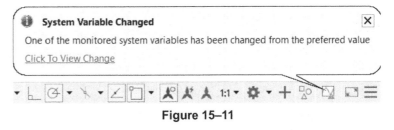

Figure 15–11

Status **column**	Displays ⚠ (Warning) next to monitored system variables which deviate from the preferred value.
System Variable **column**	Provides the names of those variables that are currently being monitored.
Preferred **column**	Indicates the preferred setting for the system variable.
Current **column**	Lists the current value for any system variables that are not equal to the preferred value.

Right-clicking on ⬚ (System Variable Monitor) displays the options shown in Figure 15–12.

Figure 15–12

- **Configure System Variable Monitor:** Opens the System Variable Monitor dialog box.

- **Reset System Variables:** Enables you to reset all of the system variables to their preferred settings, without needing to open the System Variable Monitor dialog box.

- **Display Notification:** When selected (displayed with a checkmark), if the preferred setting is violated, a notification displays in the command line, and a bubble notification with the System Variable Monitor icon displays in the Status Bar.

How To: Monitor System Variables

1. Type **SYSVARMONITOR** to open the System Variable Monitor dialog box.
2. In the System Variable Monitor dialog box, click **Edit List**.
3. In the Edit System Variable List dialog box, select the variable you want to monitor from the available system variables list on the left, as shown in Figure 15–13. The list can be narrowed by typing in the *Search list* field at the top.

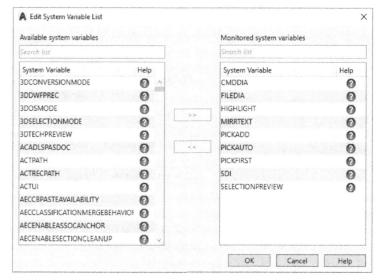

Figure 15–13

4. Click **>>** (Add Selected) to add the variable to the Monitored system variable list on the right.
5. Continue adding system variable to the list on the right and click **OK** when done.

Practice 15b | System Variables

Practice Objective

- Modify various system variable values and note their effects.

In this practice, you will set several different types of system variables. The different polylines are shown in Figure 15–14.

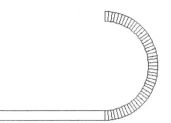

Figure 15–14

1. Start a new drawing based on the template **acad.dwt** provided with the software.

2. At the Command prompt, type **setvar** and press <Enter>. Type **?** and press <Enter>. Then, press <Enter> again to display a list of the system variables.

3. Press <Enter> a few times to scroll down the list and note which system variable names you recognize. Press <Esc> to cancel the command. If the Text window was opened, close it.

*FILEDIA is a monitored system variable. The preferred setting is **1**.*

4. At the Command prompt, enter the system variable **FILEDIA**.

5. At the *Enter new value for FILEDIA* prompt, enter **0** and press <Enter>. In the Status Bar, note that ⬚ (System Variable Monitor) displays.

6. Right-click on ⬚ (System Variable Monitor) and select **Display Notification**. A checkmark displays next to the selected option, as shown in Figure 15–15.

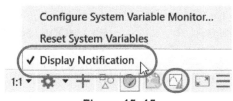

Figure 15–15

---

7. Right-click on 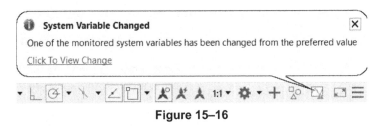 (System Variable Monitor) and select

   Reset System Variables. Note that (System Variable Monitor) does not display in the Status Bar, as all of the monitored system variables have been reset to their preferred settings.

8. At the Command prompt, enter the system variable **FILEDIA** again.

9. At the *Enter new value for FILEDIA* prompt, enter **0** and press

   <Enter>. In the Status Bar, note that (System Variable Monitor) displays along with a notification bubble, as shown in Figure 15–16.

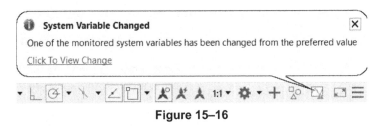

Figure 15–16

10. In the command line (you might have to expand it), note that the System Variable Changed notification displays, as shown in Figure 15–17.

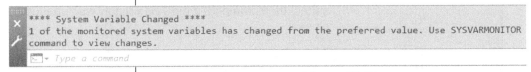

Figure 15–17

11. In the bubble, click on **Click to View Change** to open the System Variable Monitor dialog box. Note that the *Status* of FILEDIA displays ⚠, indicating that it has been changed.

12. In the System Variable Monitor dialog box, click **Reset All**. Click **Edit List**.

The list can be narrowed by typing in the Search list field at the top.

13. In the Edit System Variable List dialog box, in the *Available system variables* list, select the variables **CURSORSIZE**, **FILLMODE**, and **PLINEWID**. Click **>>** (Add Selected) to add the variables to the *Monitored system variables* list on the right, as shown in Figure 15–18. Click **OK** twice when done.

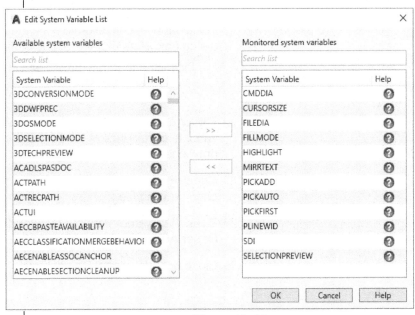

Figure 15–18

14. Draw a polyline with an arc. Note the current line width.

Note the notification above the command line.

15. At the Command prompt, type **plinewid** (**Polyline width**). This system variable can be set to any real number. Change the *value* to **0.5** and draw another polyline. A notification at the command line indicates that a monitored system variable violates a preferred setting.

16. Type the system variable **fillmode**, which controls the fill display of polylines and other objects. The system variable is a switch, where 1 = on and 0 = off. Change the *value* to **0**.

17. Regen the drawing to display the change. Toggling the fill off can speed up system performance in large drawings.

18. Type the system variable **dwgname**. This system variable, which stores the drawing name, is read-only.

19. Type the system variable **cursorsize**. Change the *value* to **10** to increase the size of the cursor crosshairs.

20. Type **SYSVARMONITOR** or click on **Click to View Change** in the bubble notification to open the System Variable Monitor dialog box. Note that the Status of these variables displays ⚠, indicating that they have been changed.

21. Start another new drawing based on the template **acad.dwt**.

22. The crosshairs are large in this drawing as well. The system variable **cursorsize** is saved in the system and applies to all drawings.

23. Check the value of **plinewid** in this drawing. It is specific to each drawing file.

24. Open the System Variable Monitor dialog box, and then click **Reset All**.

25. Close both drawings. Do not save changes.

15.3 Dynamic Input Settings

You should already be familiar with the settings that are used to control the software's drafting aids, such as Osnap, Polar, and Otrack. The Drafting Settings dialog box in which you can adjust these features also defines the settings for Dynamic Input. You can set up the dynamic command prompting, dimension input, pointer input for typed coordinates, and tooltip appearance. To open the Drafting Settings dialog box (shown in Figure 15–19), right-click on 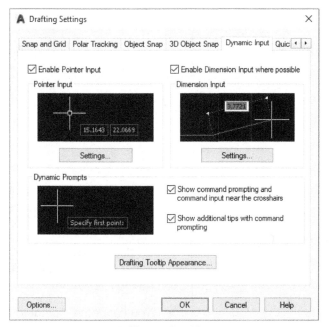 (Dynamic Input) in the Status Bar and select **Dynamic Input Settings...**. The settings are system variables that apply to all of the drawings.

Figure 15–19

Enable Pointer Input	Typed input (such as command names) displays at the pointer, rather than in the Command Line.
Enable Dimension Input where possible	Dynamic dimensions display in commands when available.
Show command prompting and command input near the crosshairs	Command prompts display at the crosshairs. Should be on if you want to use Dynamic Input as the primary interface for command input.

Use **Settings** and **Drafting Tooltip Appearance** to open dialog boxes in which you can make further adjustments.

Pointer Input Settings

Click **Settings** in the *Pointer Input* area to open the Pointer Input Settings dialog box (shown in Figure 15–20).

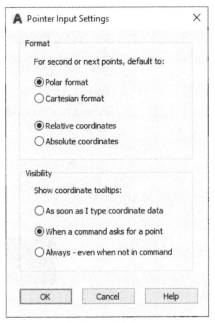

Figure 15–20

- You can type coordinates in any format (x, y, or dist<angle) and override the default Polar/Cartesian setting.

- By default, **Relative coordinates** are used. Typing **2,2** for a second point is equivalent to typing **@2,2**. You do not need to use the @ symbol.

- You can force a point to be absolute rather than relative by prefixing it with **#**, such as **#2,2**.

- Changing the default format to Cartesian does not affect the distance and angle format that displays for the next point when drawing lines. However, it does change the default for the second point in commands, such as **Move** and **Stretch**.

Dimension Input Settings

Click **Settings** in the *Dimension Input* area to open the Dimension Input Settings dialog box (shown in Figure 15–21). These settings control the dimensions that display when drawing and when editing with grips.

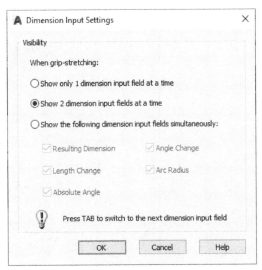

Figure 15–21

- For stretching with grips, you can specify whether to display the **Resulting Dimension** (i.e., the new length), the **Length Change**, or both, as shown in Figure 15–22.

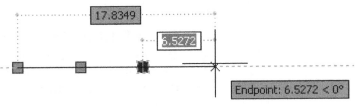

Figure 15–22

Tooltip Appearance Settings

Click **Drafting Tooltip Appearance** to open the Tooltip
Appearance dialog box (shown in Figure 15–23). You can apply
these settings to all of the drafting tooltips (such as Polar and
Osnap tooltips) or just the Dynamic Input tooltips.

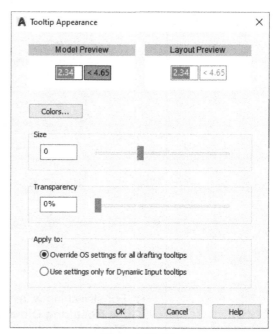

Figure 15–23

Hint: Hiding the Command Line

With the new dynamic input tools, you might not use the
Command Line as often. You can toggle it off to increase
screen space if you prefer not to use it. Type
commandlinehide or press <Ctrl>+<9> to toggle it off. Toggle
it back on again by pressing <Ctrl>+<9> or typing
commandline. You can also toggle the Command Line on and
off by clicking ⌨ (Command Line) in the *View* tab>Palettes
panel.

Practice 15c | Dynamic Input Settings

Practice Objective

- Modify settings for Dynamic Input and note their effects.

In this practice, you will note the effect of various changes to the Dynamic Input settings, as shown in Figure 15–24.

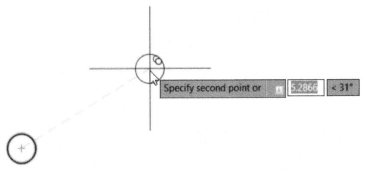

Figure 15–24

1. Open **Dynamic-I.dwg** from the practice files folder.

2. Verify that 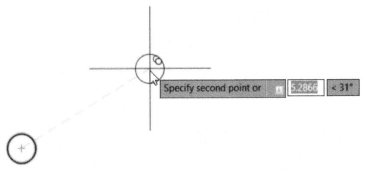 (Dynamic Input) is toggled on in the Status Bar.

3. Draw a line anywhere. The command prompts near the pointer and dynamic dimensions display on the line as you draw.

4. Right-click on (Dynamic Input) and select **Dynamic Input Settings**. In the Drafting Settings dialog box>*Dynamic Input* tab, clear the **Show command prompting and command input near the crosshairs** option to toggle it off and click **OK**.

5. Draw another line. The dynamic dimensions display, but the prompts do not display near the pointer.

6. In the Drafting Settings dialog box, change the settings again to toggle command prompting back on.

7. Erase the lines that you just drew.

8. Start the **Copy** command, select the circle, and pick its center as the base point. For the second point, the coordinates at the pointer display the polar format (**Distance<Angle**). Enter **5** for the distance, press <Tab>, and then enter **45** for the angle. A copy is placed 5 units away at an angle of 45 degrees.

9. In the Dynamic Input settings, change the *Pointer Input* settings to use the **Cartesian format** for the second points.

10. Copy the original circle again. The coordinates for the second point default to the Cartesian (X,Y) format. Type **10**, press <Tab>, and type **1** to place the copy 10 units to the right and 1 unit up. You can also type **10,1** directly. (With dynamic input, the default for the second point is relative coordinates. Therefore, the @ symbol is not required).

11. Save the file.

15.4 Drawing Utilities

The AutoCAD software includes several utilities to help you manage and maintain your drawing data.

Renaming Named Objects

Occasionally, you need to rename a named object that you or someone else has defined, such as a layer or block. The **Rename** command enables you to change the name of any named objects in the drawing, including blocks, layers, dimension styles, etc., as shown in Figure 15–25.

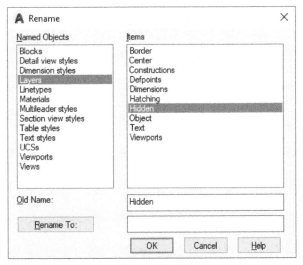

Figure 15–25

How To: Rename an Object

1. At the Command prompt, type **Rename** to open the Rename dialog box.
2. In the *Named Objects* pane, select the category.
3. In the *Items* pane, select the name to change.
4. In the *Rename To:* field, type the new name and click **Rename To:** to rename the object and remain in the Rename dialog box. Click **OK** to rename the object and close the dialog box.

- Names can be up to 255 characters long, including spaces.

- You cannot rename certain standard AutoCAD objects, such as the layer **0** or the linetype **Continuous**.

- Layers can also be renamed directly in the Layer Properties Manager.

Drawing Recovery and Repair

If your computer crashes you might need to determine which file is the latest version of a drawing. Is it the DWG file that you have been working on or the most recent BAK (backup file) or the SV$ file created when the automatic save feature is on? The Drawing Recovery Manager helps you make this decision.

To open the Drawing Recovery Manager (shown in Figure 15–26), expand the Application Menu, expand **Drawing Utilities**, and click  (Open the Drawing Recovery Manager). The Drawing Recovery Manager opens automatically when you restart the software after a crash.

Figure 15–26

In the *Backup Files* area in the Drawing Recovery Manager, a list of the drawing files affected by the crash displays. The available versions of the file display under each drawing name. Select the name of the file to display its details, such as when the drawing was last saved and to display a preview of the file.

You can use the Drawing Recovery Manager to open the files. Double-click on a filename in the list to open it. You can open DWG, BAK, DWS, and SV$ files using this method. You can then decide which file holds the most current information and use **Save As** to rename it as the primary drawing filename and set the location.

If the data in a drawing file has been corrupted because of a system crash, two additional commands can help to restore the data.

- **Audit:** Scans and fixes problems in an open drawing.

- **Recover:** Audits and opens (if possible) any drawing file.

In the Application Menu, expand **Drawing Utilities**, and click

(Audit) to start the **Audit** command. The *Fix any errors detected?* prompt displays at the cursor. Select **Yes** to automatically fix any errors. The results of the audit display at the Command Line, as shown in Figure 15–27.

```
Command: audit
Fix any errors detected? [Yes/No] <N>: Y
Auditing Header
Auditing Tables
Auditing Entities Pass 1
Pass 1 700      objects audited
Auditing Entities Pass 2
Pass 2 700      objects audited
Auditing Blocks
  12       Blocks audited
Total errors found 0 fixed 0
Erased 0 objects
```

Figure 15–27

In the Application Menu, select **Drawing Utilities**, and then click

(Recover) to start the **Recover** command, which prompts you to select a drawing file. It then analyzes the data in the file, recovers as much of it as possible and audits it for errors, and (if possible) opens the recovered file.

- Click (Recover with Xrefs) to include all of the attached XREFs.

Checking a Drawing's Status

The **Status** command reports a variety of useful information about the current drawing and your system as shown in Figure 15–28. Drawing information includes the number of objects, drawing limits, and current settings for **Snap**, **Grid**, layer, color, etc. System information includes free disk space and memory. In the Application Menu, expand **Drawing Utilities** and click (Status) to start the **Status** command

```
Command: _STATUS 707 objects in C:\AutoCAD Advanced 2011 Exercise Files\
Model Home 1-A-11.dwg
Model space limits are X: 16'-5 1/2"   Y: 19'-10 5/8"   (Off)
                        X: 65'-2 3/4"   Y: 55'-4 1/8"
Model space uses        X: 19'-3 9/16"  Y: 23'-3 1/8"
                        X: 65'-3 5/8"   Y: 56'-5 1/8" **Over
Display shows           X: 20'-11 5/16" Y: 24'-11 1/16"
                        X: 63'-7 15/16" Y: 54'-9 1/8"
Insertion base is       X:     0'-0"  Y:     0'-0"  Z:      0'-0"
Snap resolution is      X:     0'-1"  Y:     0'-1"
Grid spacing is         X:     0'-0"  Y:     0'-0"

Current space:       Model space
Current layout:      Model
Current layer:       "Walls"
Current color:       BYLAYER -- 7 (white)
Current linetype:    BYLAYER -- "CONTINUOUS"
Current material:    BYLAYER -- "Global"
Current lineweight:  BYLAYER
Current elevation:     0'-0"  thickness:     0'-0"
Fill on  Grid off  Ortho off  Qtext off  Snap off  Tablet off
Object snap modes:    Center, Endpoint, Midpoint
Free dwg disk (C:) space: 7034.6 MBytes
Free temp disk (C:) space: 7034.6 MBytes
Free physical memory: 2475.8 Mbytes (out of 3679.4M).
Free swap file space: 5346.8 Mbytes (out of 6591.6M).
```

Figure 15–28

Practice 15d | Drawing Utilities

Practice Objective

- Use various drawing utilities to rename a dimension style, check for errors, and review drawing information.

In this practice, you will use several of the drawing utilities. The results of the **Audit** command are shown in Figure 15–29.

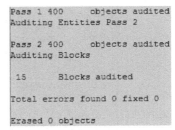

```
Pass 1 400      objects audited
Auditing Entities Pass 2

Pass 2 400      objects audited
Auditing Blocks

 15        Blocks audited

Total errors found 0 fixed 0

Erased 0 objects
```

Figure 15–29

1. Open **Body2-M.dwg** from the practice files folder.

2. In the *Annotate* tab>Dimensions panel, note the current dimension style name, **20TO1**.

3. At the Command prompt, type **Rename**.

4. In the Rename dialog box, in the *Named Objects* pane, select **Dimension styles**. Then in the *Items* pane, select **20TO1**.

5. In the *Rename To:* field, type **Mechanical 20**, as shown in Figure 15–30.

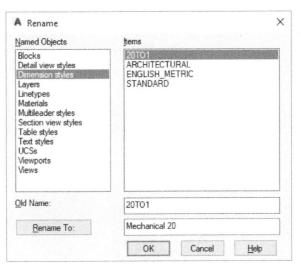

Figure 15–30

6. Click **Rename To:** to rename the dimension style *20TO1* as **Mechanical 20**. In the *Items* pane, note that **Mechanical 20** replaces **20TO1**. Click **OK** to close the Rename dialog box and note that the dimension style name in the ribbon has changed.

   • You might need to expand the Dimension Style control to refresh the list.

7. In the Application Menu, expand **Drawing Utilities**, and click (Audit). Select **Yes** to fix any errors. Press <F2> to open the Text Window to display the Audit information. Did the software find any errors in this file? Close the Text window.

8. In the Application Menu, expand **Drawing Utilities**, click (Recover) and select **Recover**. Open the drawing **2403-HVAC-M.dwg** from the practice files folder. The software scans the drawing and opens it. Were any invalid objects found?

9. In the Application Menu, expand **Drawing Utilities**, and then click (Status) and review the information. How many objects are in this drawing? How much free physical memory is available on your system?

10. Close both drawings. Do not save changes.

15.5 Managing Plotters

When you add a plotter to your system, it must be *configured* before you can use it with the AutoCAD software. Plotters are configured using the Add Plotter Wizard and the plotter configurations are stored in the Plotter Manager.

- The AutoCAD software also supports Windows plotters, so this step might not be a required in your office.

Add Plotter Wizard

The Add Plotter wizard (shown in Figure 15–31) guides you through the process of configuring a plotter for the software.

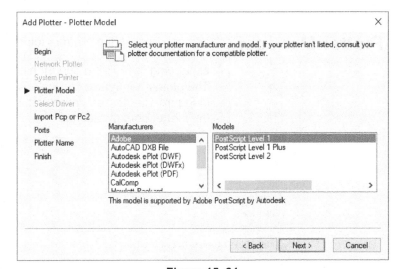

Figure 15–31

- To open the Add Plotter wizard, expand the Application Menu, expand (Print) and click (Manage Plotters). It opens the Autodesk Plotters window (Windows Explorer window with *Autodesk Plotters* folder opened). Double-click on the **Add-A-Plotter Wizard** shortcut. You can also open the wizard by clicking **Add or Configure Plotters** in the *Plot and Publish* tab in the Options dialog box.

- The configuration information is stored in a plotter configuration file with the extension PC3. These files are automatically placed in the *Plotters* folder. You can change the location by expanding the Application Menu and clicking **Options**. Then, select the *Files* tab, expand *Printer Support File Path*, and enter the new path in the *Printer Configuration Search Path*.

- The default *Plotters* folder location varies depending on the operating system.

  - **Windows 7 and Windows 10:** *C:\Users\<User name>\appdata\roaming\Autodesk\AutoCAD <version>\ <release>\<language>\Plotters*

- The wizard can import plotter settings from a PCP or PC2 configuration file that was used with earlier releases.

- You can create a PC3 configuration file for a non-system plotter or for a Windows system printer. For a Windows system printer, you can also control its default properties in the Windows Control Panel, without configuring it in the AutoCAD software.

Plotter Manager

You can access the *Plotters* folder from the Application Menu, expanding (Print) and then clicking (Manage Plotters). The plotter configuration files (.PC3) are stored here, as shown in Figure 15–32. You can delete unnecessary plotters and edit the plotter configurations.

)ws (C:) > Users > hwaraich > AppData > Roaming > Autodesk > AutoCAD 2022 > R24.1 > enu > Plotters >

Name	Date modified	Type	Size
Plot Styles	4/5/2021 8:28 AM	File folder	
PMP Files	4/5/2021 8:28 AM	File folder	
Add-A-Plotter Wizard	4/5/2021 8:28 AM	Shortcut	2 KB
AutoCAD PDF (General Documentation)....	10/10/2014 10:39 PM	AutoCAD Plotter ...	2 KB
AutoCAD PDF (High Quality Print).pc3	10/10/2014 10:39 PM	AutoCAD Plotter ...	2 KB
AutoCAD PDF (Smallest File).pc3	10/10/2014 10:39 PM	AutoCAD Plotter ...	2 KB
AutoCAD PDF (Web and Mobile).pc3	10/10/2014 10:39 PM	AutoCAD Plotter ...	2 KB
Default Windows System Printer.pc3	3/3/2003 7:36 PM	AutoCAD Plotter ...	2 KB
DWF6 ePlot.pc3	7/29/2004 3:14 AM	AutoCAD Plotter ...	5 KB
DWFx ePlot (XPS Compatible).pc3	6/21/2007 10:17 AM	AutoCAD Plotter ...	5 KB
DWG To PDF.pc3	10/10/2014 10:39 PM	AutoCAD Plotter ...	2 KB
PublishToWeb JPG.pc3	12/7/1999 8:53 PM	AutoCAD Plotter ...	1 KB
PublishToWeb PNG.pc3	11/21/2000 11:18 PM	AutoCAD Plotter ...	1 KB

Figure 15–32

- To edit a plotter configuration, double-click on its icon in the folder.

- To delete a plotter configuration, delete the PC3 file from the folder.

- The *PMP Files* folder contains files that are related to the **Publish to Web** command.

Plotter Configuration Editor

The Plotter Configuration Editor enables you to set up or change the plotter description, port used, and many plotter-specific settings.

- To open the Plotter Configuration Editor (shown in Figure 15–33), double-click on the plotter's icon in the *Plotter Manager* folder, or click **Properties** next to the plotter name in the Plot dialog box.

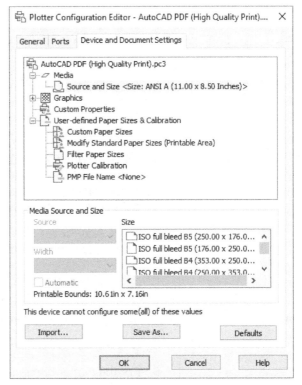

Figure 15–33

General tab	Displays information about the plotter and enables you to add or edit a description.
Ports tab	Enables you to change the way you plot the drawing: to a specific port, plot to a file, or AutoSpool.
Device and Document Settings tab	Enables you to set up specifics for the plotter including: Media (paper types), Physical Pen Configuration, Graphics and Calibration, and User Defined sizes.

- In the *Device and Document Settings* tab, you can set up Custom Paper Sizes to use with the plotter. You can also *filter* the paper sizes, so that only the sizes you use are listed in the Plot or Page Setup dialog box.

Practice 15e | Managing Plotters

Practice Objective

- Add a plotter configuration and then modify its settings.

In this practice, you will add a plotter configuration and then edit it to change the available paper sizes, as shown in Figure 15–34.

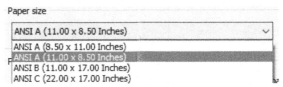

Figure 15–34

1. In any drawing, start the **Add Plotter** wizard, by clicking

   (Manage Plotters) in **Application Menu>Print**. In the Autodesk Plotters window (Windows Explorer window with *Autodesk Plotter* folder opened), double-click on the **Add-A-Plotter Wizard** shortcut.

2. In the Add Plotter dialog box, Introduction page, click **Next >**. Select **My Computer** and click **Next >** again.

3. Select **Hewlett-Packard** in the *Manufacturers* list and select **DraftMaster RX Plus 7596C** in the *Models* list. Click **Next >**.

Do not import a PCP or PC2 file.

4. In the Import Pcp or Pc2 page of the wizard, Click **Next >**.

5. Use the default setting for the Ports. Click **Next >**.

6. For the plotter name, use **DraftMaster** followed by your initials. Click **Next >** and **Finish** to complete the wizard.

7. Start the **Plot** command. Change the *Plotter* to the **DraftMaster** device that you just configured, as shown in Figure 15–35.

8. Note the paper sizes that are listed. Click **Properties** next to the plotter name (as shown in Figure 15–35) to open the Plotter Configuration Editor.

Figure 15–35

9. In the *Device and Document Settings* tab, under *User-defined Paper Sizes & Calibration*, select **Filter Paper Sizes**.

10. Click **Uncheck All** to clear all of the selected sizes and select only the sizes that start with **ANSI A**, **ANSI B**, and **ANSI C**. Click **OK**.

11. In the Changes to a Printer Configuration File dialog box, select **Save changes to the following file** and accept the default to save the changes in the PC3 file for the plotter you created.

12. Open the list of paper sizes again and note how many are available.

13. Cancel the **Plot** command.

15.6 Plot Styles

Concepts

Plot styles enable you to plot objects with a different appearance (color, linetype, lineweight, etc.) from their appearance in the drawing. Plot styles also enable you to control the plotted properties of objects. For example, in one layout, you might want to plot the room walls in grayscale and the ductwork in a heavier lineweight to have it stand out. In another layout, you might want to have the reverse. One way this can be accomplished is to use plot styles, so you can plot the same drawing with different display settings to highlight specific features.

You can use plot styles to control the appearance of the plot including:

- Color, linetype, and lineweight

- End, join, and fill styles for wide lineweights

- Gray-scaling and dithering (combining color dots to give the impression of displaying more colors than are actually available)

- Pen assignments

Notes

- A drawing can use a *color-dependent plot style table*, a *named plot style table*, or *neither*. When a plot style table is used, the objects are plotted as defined by the plot style table.

- New drawings use either color-dependent or named plot styles depending on the template that is used to create them. There are two versions of each predefined template with the AutoCAD software: one that uses color plot styles and one that uses named plot styles.

- A plot style table can be used for any output device. Some output devices might not be able to plot exactly as the plot style table dictates. For example, even if you use a plot style table to plot all of the black lines in the drawing in green, a black-and-white laser printer is still only able to plot the lines in black.

- Plot style tables are stored in files with the extensions CTB (for color-dependent) or STB (for named). These files are stored in the *Plot Styles* folder.

- A drawing can only use one type of table (color-dependent or named) at a time. Only one plot style table can be used per layout.

- You can edit the tables to add new styles (for named plot style tables) and assign properties (for both types of plot styles).

Types of Plot Style Tables

Color-Dependent Plot Style Tables

A color-dependent plot style table contains 255 styles, one for each ACI color. You can specify the plotted effects that you want to use for each color. You cannot rename, add, or delete the color-dependent styles.

- Think of the styles in a color plot style table as a set of pens. A pen has specific characteristics, such as thickness and color. You can assign a pen to each color in the drawing file. For example, you could assign a wide black pen to the color green. Everything green in the drawing is then plotted in wide black lines.

- The plot style table for a drawing can be assigned in the Page Setup or Plot dialog box. The *Plot style table* area is located in the *Plot Device* tab.

Named Plot Style Tables

With named plot styles, you can define any combination of color, linetype, lineweight, dithering, etc. that you need and give it a name (for example, **New Construction** or **Demolition**). You can define as many named styles as required and apply them in the drawing.

- Using named plot styles can be more involved than using color plot styles, since named styles can be assigned by layer or by object.

- To assign a named plot style for a layer, open the Layer Properties Manager, and select the plot style icon of the layer that you want to set. This is the same way that you assign a layer's color or linetype.

- To assign a named plot style for an object, select the object and access Properties. You can also select the object (it displays grips) and select the plot style in the *Home* tab> Properties panel.

How To: Use a Plot Style Table in a Drawing

Color-Dependent Plot Style Table

1. Create a plot style table that specifies the effect of plot styles.
2. Assign the plot style table in the Page Setup of a layout.

Named Plot Style Table

1. Create a plot style table that specifies the effect of plot styles.
2. Assign the plot style table in the Page Setup in a layout.
3. Assign plot styles to layers or specific objects in the drawing.

Creating Plot Style Tables

You can define the visual effects for your plot styles in plot style tables using the Add Plot Style Table wizard, as shown in Figure 15–36.

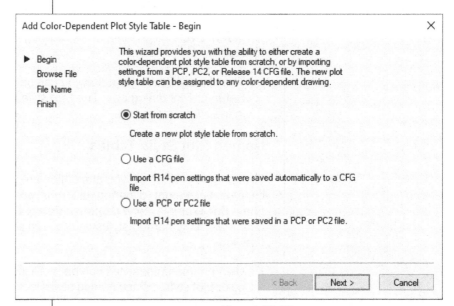

Figure 15–36

How To: Create a Plot Style Table

1. Open the Page Setup Manager in **Application Menu>Print** by clicking 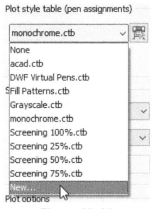 (Page Setup), or by right-clicking on a layout and selecting **Page Setup Manager**.
2. In the *Page setups* area, select a page setup and click **Modify**.
3. In the Page Setup dialog box, in the Plot style table (pen assignments) drop-down list, select **New**, as shown in Figure 15–37.

Figure 15–37

4. Select whether to start a new table from scratch or based on an existing table. You can import pen table properties from an R14 CFG file or PCP/PC2 files as the basis of your new table.
5. Select whether to create a **Color-Dependent Plot Style Table** or **Named Plot Style Table**.
6. In the *File name* field, type a name for the plot style table file.
7. Click **Plot Style Table Editor** to edit the table to suit your needs. For named plot style tables, you can add styles and for color plot style tables, you can edit the existing styles.
8. Click **Finish**.

Attaching Plot Style Tables to Layouts

Plot styles are assigned to a layout in the layout's Page Setup. You can also assign a plot style table in the Plot dialog box when you plot.

How To: Attach a Plot Style Table to a Layout

1. Open the Page Setup Manager (right-click on a layout and select **Page Setup Manager**).
2. In the *Page setups* area, select a page setup and click **Modify**.

3. In the Page Setup dialog box, in the Plot style table (pen assignments) drop-down list, select the plot style table that you want to use, as shown in Figure 15–38.

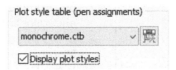

Figure 15–38

4. To display the plot style effects in the drawing window, select **Display plot styles**. The effects display when you use **Regenall**.
5. Click **OK** and close the Plot Style Manager.
6. For named plot styles, after the table has been attached you must also assign plot styles to the layers or objects to which you want the effects to be applied.

Notes

- You can use a different plot style table for each layout, but a table attached to a layout applies to all of the viewports in that layout.

- Several predefined plot style tables are supplied with the software, such as **Grayscale** and **Monochrome**.

- You can edit the selected plot style table in Page Setup by

  clicking (Edit) to the right of the drop-down list.

- If a plot style does not display in the drawing window, you might need to **Preview** the plot first. After you see the changes in the plot, try the **Regenall** command again.

- For plot styles to take effect in the plotted output, verify that the **Plot with plot styles** option is selected in the Plot dialog box.

Practice 15f | Color Plot Styles

Practice Objective

- Create a color plot style table and apply it to a layout.

In this practice, you will create a color plot style table and apply it to a layout, as shown in Figure 15–39.

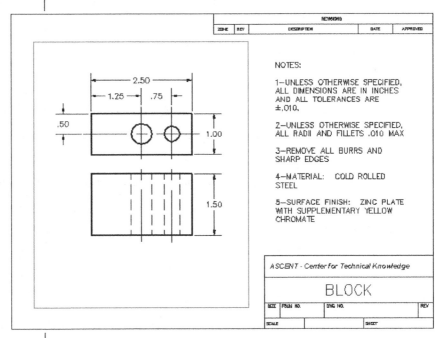

Figure 15–39

- If the effects of the plot styles do not display, use **Plot Preview** to view the effects. The layout view might not always display the effects correctly, especially if you have different plot style tables applied in different layouts.

1. Open **Block-I.dwg** from the practice files folder. It contains two identical layouts **A-Sized** and **A-Sized (2)**.

2. Select **Application Menu>Print>Page Setup** to open the Page Setup Manager.

3. In the *Page setups* area, select **A-Sized** and click **Modify**.

4. Set the *Plot style table (pen assignments)* to **Grayscale.ctb** (one of the tables supplied with the software). Select the **Display plot styles** option and click **OK**. Click **Close** in the Page Setup Manager. The layout should display in grayscale.

5. In the Status Bar, toggle on ▤ (Show/Hide Lineweight). Zoom in to examine the objects. They have the same lineweights.

6. Switch to the second layout (**A-Sized (2)**). A plot style table has not yet been assigned to this layout.

7. Open the Page Setup Manager by right-clicking on the **A-Sized (2)** layout and selecting **Page Setup Manager**.

8. In the *Page setups* area, select **A-Sized (2)** and click **Modify**.

9. In the Page Setup dialog box, in the Plot style table (pen assignments) drop-down list, select **New**.

10. On the Add Color - Dependant Plot Style Table - Begin page, select **Start from scratch** and click **Next >** to continue.

11. On the *File name* page, name the new table **Mechanical** and click **Next >**.

12. Click **Plot Style Table Editor** to edit the new table. Select the Color in the *Plot styles* area and then change the settings in the *Properties* area, as follows:

*If the lineweight is not in the list, click **Edit Lineweights**.*

Plot styles	Color 1	Color 2	Color 4	Color 5	Color 7
Color	Black	Black	Black	Black	Black
Lineweight	0.5000mm	0.3000mm	0.3000mm	0.5000mm	0.7000mm

13. Click **Save & Close** to close the Plot Style Table Editor.

14. Clear the **Use this plot style table for new and pre-AutoCAD <version-language> drawings** option. Click **Finish** to complete the process.

15. Modify the Page Setup for the **A-Sized (2)** layout. Select **Mechanical.ctb** as the *Plot style table (pen assignments)* and select **Display plot styles**. Click **OK** and **Close**.

16. Verify that ▤ (Show/Hide Lineweight) is toggled on.

17. Zoom in to examine the objects, which should all be black with different lineweights for the centerlines, dimension lines, and object lines.

18. Save and close the drawing.

Practice 15g | Named Plot Styles

Practice Objective

- Create a named plot style table and apply the styles to a drawing.

In this practice, you will create a named plot style table and apply the styles in a drawing, as shown in Figure 15–40.

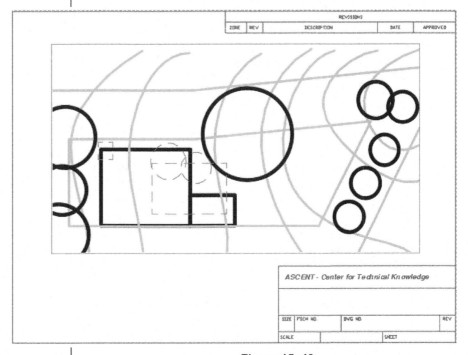

Figure 15–40

1. Open **Lot-F.dwg** from the practice files folder.

2. Open the Page Setup Manager by right-clicking on the *Layout1* tab and selecting **Page Setup Manager**.

3. In the *Page setups* area, select a page setup and click **Modify**.

4. In the Page Setup dialog box, in the Plot style table (pen assignments) drop-down list, select **New**.

5. Start the table from scratch. Click **Next>**.

6. Set the name to **Lot**. Click **Next>**.

7. Click **Plot Style Table Editor** and add the following styles, as shown in Figure 15–41:

*Click **Add Style** to create additional columns for each style and then edit the new style column.*

Name	Guide lines	Finished	Remove
Description	Contour and boundary lines	Final lines	Objects to be removed
Color	Green	Black	Magenta
Linetype	Solid	Solid	Dashed
Lineweight	1.0000mm	1.5800mm	0.0000mm

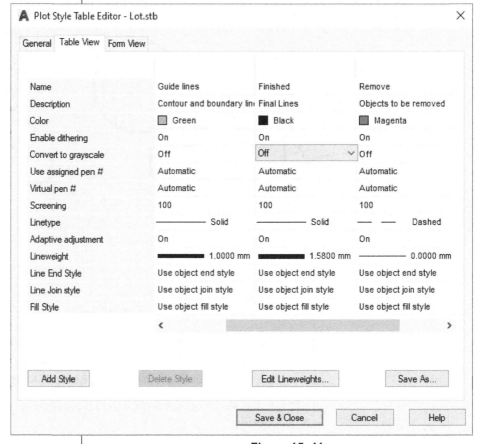

Figure 15–41

8. Click **Save & Close** and **Finish**.

9. In the Page Setup Manager, set the Plot style table to **Lot.stb**. Select **Display plot styles**. Click **OK** and **Close** the Page Setup Manager.

10. Switch to Model space, if required.

11. Open the Layer Properties Manager and apply plot styles to the layers as follows, as shown in Figure 15–42:

Plot Style	Layers
Guide lines	Boundary, Buildable Area, Contours
Finished	New, Road, Trees
Remove	Existing

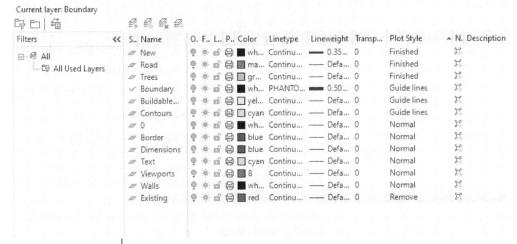

Figure 15–42

12. Switch to **Layout1**. Note the colors and lineweights of the different objects in the viewport. Double-click in the viewport to switch to Model Space.

13. Type **regenall**. The plot styles are applied to the objects in the viewport.

14. In the Status Bar, toggle on ▤ (Show/Hide Lineweight) and note that the lineweights were applied by the plot styles.

15. Select the two trees (circles) that overlap the building and use Properties to change the plot style of the selected objects to **Remove**. Click on **PLOT>PREVIEW** and note that they become magenta and dashed, as defined by this plot style.

16. Switch back to Paper Space.

17. Save and close the drawing.

Chapter Review Questions

1. Where can you set the background color of the AutoCAD drawing window?

   a. **Options>Display>Colors**

   b. **Options>Files>Template Settings**

   c. **Options>User Preferences>Background**

   d. **Options>System>Performance**

2. How do you tell the AutoCAD software where to look for template (DWT) files?

   a. **Options>Open and Save>Template Settings**

   b. **Options>Files>Template Settings**

   c. **Options>User Preferences>Template Settings**

   d. **Options>System>Quick New**

3. How do you improve the graphics performance for capable devices?

   a. Type **Graphics Performance** in the command line to change the variable.

   b. Right-click in the drawing and select **Graphics Performance**.

   c. On the *View* tab>Interface panel, click **Graphics Performance**.

   d. In the Options dialog box, *System* tab, click **Graphics Performance**.

4. Which command enables you to display the values of all of the system variables?

   a. **List**

   b. **Filter**

   c. **Setvar**

   d. **Style**

5. Which command displays a list of drawing information, such as the number of objects, drawing limits, and current layer?

    a. **Drawing Recover Manager**

    b. **Recover**

    c. **Audit**

    d. **Status**

6. Which of the following are true when Dynamic Input is active?

    a. You cannot pick points using the mouse.

    b. The Command Line is toggled off.

    c. Relative coordinate entry is the default.

    d. The length of the objects is not shown.

7. What is the extension of the plotter configuration file where the configuration information is stored?

    a. PCP

    b. PC3

    c. PCR

    d. PC1

8. Different plot style tables can be used for each layout, but a table attached to a layout applies to all of the viewports in that layout.

    a. True

    b. False

Command Summary

Button	Command	Location
	Audit	• **Application Menu:** Drawing Utilities • **Command Prompt:** Audit
	Command Line	• **Ribbon:** *View* tab>Palettes panel • **Command Prompt:** commandline
	Dynamic Input Settings	• **Status Bar:** (*right-click on Dynamic Input*) Settings...
	Manage Plotter	• **Application Menu:** Print
	Open the Drawing Recovery Manager	• **Application Menu:** Drawing Utilities
Options	Options	• **Application Menu** • **Shortcut Menu:** (*right-click in drawing window*)
	Recover	• **Application Menu:** Drawing Utilities> Recover • **Command Prompt:** Recover
	Recover with Xrefs	• **Application Menu:** Drawing Utilities> Recover
NA	Rename	• **Command Prompt:** rename *or* ren
	Show/Hide Lineweights	• **Status Bar**
	Status	• **Application Menu:** Drawing Utilities • **Command Prompt:** Recover

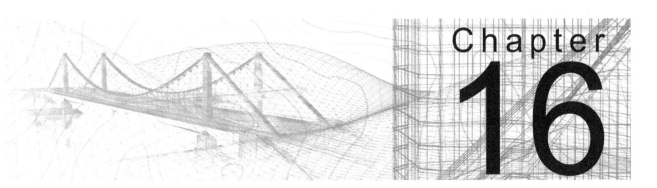

Chapter

16

Introduction to Customization

Since the AutoCAD® software is used in a variety of industries, each of which use different workflows, many people like to customize their workspaces. In this chapter, you learn how and why to customize the AutoCAD software and how to determine which aspects of the software can be customized. You also learn how to create a custom workspace.

Learning Objectives in This Chapter

- List some of the goals of customizing the software.
- Set up the user interface to streamline workflows and save it as a personal workspace.
- Organize frequently used palettes to maximize space in the drawing window.

16.1 Why Customize?

People use the AutoCAD software for many different disciplines. Since it is not designed for a specific industry, it is not optimized for your application. Customizing the software to suit your specific needs can greatly increase the speed and quality of your work. With customization you can:

- Streamline repetitive tasks.

- Maintain drawing standards.

- Increase productivity by limiting options for those who are less experienced.

Customization Guidelines

- The main goal of customizing the software is to make it easier and faster to use for everyone involved.

- Use a systematic and thoughtful approach. Do not just sit down one day and start customizing.

- Think of all those who might benefit from your efforts. You might be able to add one or two lines to a macro that can be used by other departments to speed up everyone's work.

- Ensure that the customized version of the software can easily be used by even the most inexperienced person in your organization.

- Save the original of any support files you customize before you make any changes.

- Do not keep your customized information in the ACAD directory structure. Keep the custom files in a separate directory and ensure that the ACAD search path is set to find them.

- Always test your customizations on more than one computer.

What Can Be Customized?

Drawing Features

- Use Template drawings with predefined Layers, Text Styles, Table Styles, Dimension Styles, Units, etc.

- Create or use custom Blocks, Linetypes, Hatch Patterns, and Fonts.

AutoCAD Environment

- Set up multiple configurations for Plotters and Layouts.

- Save AutoCAD Options in User Profiles.

AutoCAD User Interface

- Create custom Workspaces that provide the tools required for a specific task.

- Get quick access to commands, blocks, and hatches with customized Tool Palettes, Ribbon panels, and Toolbars, and by adding commands to the Quick Access Toolbar.

- Customize the AutoCAD menus to focus on the options you need.

- Display the ribbon with the panels arranged to suit your workflow.

- Create keyboard shortcuts for often-used commands (Command Aliases and shortcut keys).

Programming Features

- Automate repetitive tasks using Scripts, Macros at the Command Line, or from drop-down menus and toolbars, and the Action Recorder.

- Write AutoLISP or Visual Basic routines that define new commands for the software.

16.2 Creating a Custom Workspace

As you learn the various ways of working with the software you need to set up your personal workspace. You can specify how you want your palettes to be organized, the order in which you want to arrange the panels (in tabs), what you want the ribbon to contain, and which, if any, toolbars you might want open. When you are finished, create a new workspace to save the arrangement.

For example, you might want to create a workspace that maximizes the drawing area. Start with the **Drafting & Annotation** workspace active. Toggle on Properties and Tool Palettes and other palettes that you use frequently. Dock and hide them on the same side of the screen. If you are using Dynamic Input you can also dock and auto-hide the Command Line below the other palettes. Limit the number of options you have in the Status Bar to the ones that you commonly use.

- Arrange the panels in the ribbon tabs in any order and set the ribbon to be docked to the side, or set to a specific auto-hide setting.

- Another powerful way to maximize the drawing area is to use

  (Clean Screen) (as shown in Figure 16–1), which toggles the ribbon and the *File tabs* bar on and off. The Quick Access Toolbar, Application Menu, Status Bar, and Command Line are still displayed. It also maximizes the AutoCAD application on the whole display screen. At the Command prompt, use the **cleanscreenon** or **cleanscreenoff** commands, or you can press <Ctrl>+<0>.

Figure 16–1

Organizing Palettes

As you continue working in the software, numerous palettes are available to help you work with greater precision and effectiveness. However, they tend to use a lot of space in the drawing window. If you do not have two monitors to work on you might find it frustrating to keep moving palettes around or toggling them on and off when you need them. Instead, you can organize all of the palettes that you typically need to one side of the screen, dock them, and set each of them to **Auto-hide**. This process is also referred to as *anchoring* a palette, as shown in Figure 16–2.

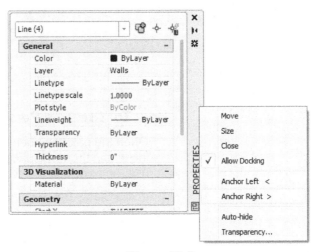

Figure 16–2

When you auto-hide a palette, it minimizes to display a bar to one side of the drawing window. Palettes stack if more than one is docked. Moving the cursor over the title bar displays the full-size palette.

To save space on the screen, you can auto-hide all of the palettes to any side of the window and set the view to **Icons only**, as shown in Figure 16–3. Hover the cursor over the icon to display the entire palette. The settings for **Icons only** and **Text Only** can be set independently on the left or right side of the screen.

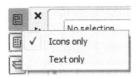

Figure 16–3

Lock User Interface

The **Lock UI** command locks the position and size of toolbars and dockable windows such as the DesignCenter or Properties palette. The **Lock UI** command enables you to check/uncheck multiple UI elements at a time rather than reopening the flyout each time. By checking an item, it locks that specific type of user interface element. Figure 16–4 shows all elements checked (locked).

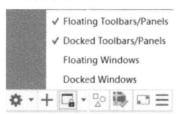

Figure 16–4

How To: Create a Personal Workspace

1. Open the palettes, menus, and toolbars that you want to include in the workspace, close the ones you do not want to use, and arrange the screen and ribbon, as required.
2. In the Status Bar, expand ✿ ˅ (Workspace) and select **Save Current As...**.
3. In the Save Workspace dialog box, type a name for the new workspace and click **Save**. The new workspace becomes the current workspace.

• You can also create, modify, and remove workspaces using the Customize User Interface dialog box.

Hint: Workspace Settings

In the Status Bar, ⚙ ˅ (Workspace) and select **Workspace Settings**. The Workspace Settings dialog box opens, as shown in Figure 16–5. You can specify the workspace that is linked to My Workspace in the Workspace Settings dialog box and control the display and order of workspaces in the *Menu Display and Order* area.

Figure 16–5

- If you want the workspace to save the changes when you modify the screen, select **Automatically save workspace changes**.

- If you want the workspace to return to its default arrangement when you change workspaces, select **Do not save changes to workspace**. You should select this option when you have finished customizing your workspace.

- All of the ribbon panels, palette windows, and toolbars are available in any workspace, even if they are defined as not displayed in the workspace.

Practice 16a | Setting Up Workspaces

Practice Objective

- Create a custom workspace and note the effects of switching between different workspaces.

In this practice, you will create a custom workspace and note the effects of switching workspaces, as shown in Figure 16–6.

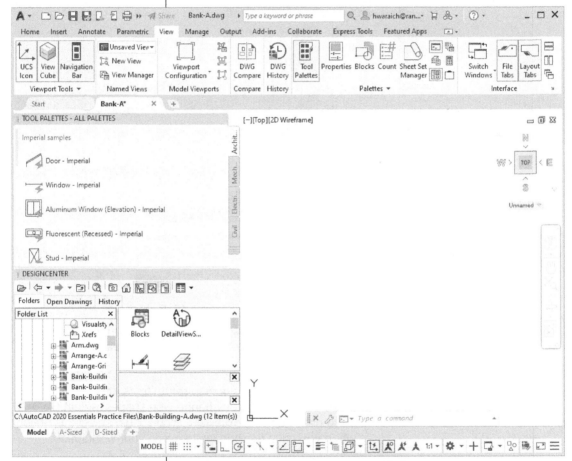

Figure 16–6

1. Start a new drawing based on the default AutoCAD template.

2. In the Status Bar, expand ⚙ ˅ (Workspace) and select **3D Modeling**. Switch back to the **Drafting & Annotation** workspace. Note the differences between the two workspaces.

3. Switch back to the **3D Modeling** workspace. Open any palettes that you want to use. For instance, you could open Properties, Tool Palettes, and DesignCenter.

4. Toggle the ribbon display to **Minimize to Panel Buttons**.

5. Arrange the palettes in the drawing area by docking and auto-hiding them.

6. Open the Layer Properties Manager and anchor it on the right. Right-click in the title bar of the Layer Properties Manager and select **Icons only**.

7. In the Status Bar, expand ✿ ˅ (Workspace) and select **Save Current As**. Type **My 2D Workspace** and click **Save**. The new workspace becomes current.

8. Switch to the **3D Modeling** workspace. What are the differences? Finish by selecting the default **Drafting & Annotation** workspace.

9. Close the file. Do not save it. Your workspace is still available to use in other drawing files.

Chapter Review Questions

1. Which of the following is NOT a valid method of toggling off all ribbon tabs, panels, and tool palettes at the same time?

   a. Toggle **Clean screen On** in the Status Bar.

   b. Type **Cleanscreenon** in the Command Line.

   c. Right-click in the drawing window and select **Maximize Drawing Area**.

   d. Use the short-cut keys, <Ctrl>+<0> (zero).

2. Which of the following options enables you to only display a palette when you hover the cursor over the titlebar?

   a. **Icons Only**

   b. **Auto-hide**

   c. **Minimize**

   d. **Show Palette**

3. Which of the following can be controlled using the Workspace Settings dialog box? (Select all that apply.)

   a. Specify the workspace that is linked to My Workspace.

   b. Control which workspaces are listed when working in the AutoCAD software.

   c. Control the order in which workspaces are listed when working in the AutoCAD software.

   d. Right-click on customization.

4. One of the customization guidelines is to not keep your customized information in the ACAD directory structure but to keep the custom files in a separate directory and set the ACAD search path to find them.

   a. True

   b. False

5. A Workspace controls the _____.

   a. Default file locations for your drawings.

   b. Display of ribbon tabs and panels.

   c. Settings, such as layers, units, and annotation styles.

   d. Default color scheme for the interface.

Command Summary

Button	Command	Location
	Cleanscreen	• **Status Bar** • **Command line:** **cleanscreenon/cleanscreenoff**
	Workspace Settings	• **Quick Access Toolbar** • **Status Bar**

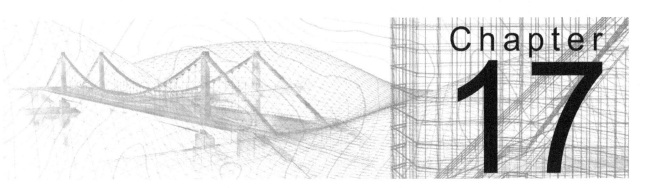

Customizing the User Interface

In this chapter, you learn how to use the tools in the Customize User Interface dialog box, customize the ribbon, customize a menu, create a toolbar, and create custom shortcut keys.

Learning Objectives in This Chapter

- Access the central location for all interface customization.
- Navigate through the various panes of the Customize User Interface (CUI) dialog box.
- Modify the ribbon by changing the location of the panels, customize tabs and panels, and add them to a workspace.
- Customize the available commands in the Quick Access Toolbar.
- Associate different Quick Access Toolbars to specific workspaces.
- Manage drop-down menus, shortcut or context menus, and custom menus from previous releases of the software.
- Modify the action of specific mouse buttons and keyboard keys using the CUI.

17.1 Using the Customize User Interface (CUI) Dialog Box

The Customize User Interface dialog box (shown in Figure 17–1) is the central place for all of the interface customization. You can customize the ribbon to display standard and custom commands, control how panels display in tabs, and create and modify ribbon tabs and panels. You can also create custom toolbars, keyboard shortcuts, drop-down menus, shortcut menus, and workspaces.

Figure 17–1

- Interface customizations are saved in a Customize User Interface (CUIx) file. The default is **acad.cuix**. Changes made in the Customize User Interface dialog box are stored in either the main CUI file or partial CUI files.

- By default, any changes made to the CUI are made to the main customization file supplied with the AutoCAD® software. However, you can also create and distribute an enterprise wide CUI to maintain company standards. The Enterprise Customization File location is stored in the Options dialog box, in the *Files* tab, under **Customization Files**.

- You can open the Customize User Interface dialog box by clicking  (User Interface) in the *Manage* tab> Customization panel.

- The CUI dialog box can be displayed in two states. The **Quickcui** command only opens the *Command List* pane in the CUI dialog box, while the standard **CUI** command opens the full dialog box. Both methods enable you to toggle to the other state.

- The full CUI is opened when you type **cui** at the Command Line or select it in the *Manage* tab>Customization panel.

- The partial CUI (shown in Figure 17–2), opens when you type **quickcui** or select **Customize Commands** in the Tool Palette's shortcut menu.

Figure 17–2

- To expand or collapse any pane in the CUI dialog box, click the pane's title bar. To expand the partial CUI interface, click ⊙ to expand the entire CUI dialog box. You can click ⊙ to hide the right side of the dialog box.

Overview of the CUI Interface

The CUI interface consists of several panes. Depending on what you have selected, one or more of these sets of options is displayed.

Customizations in All Files Pane

The *Customizations in All Files* pane (shown in Figure 17–3), displays the various types of objects that can be customized. These include workspaces, ribbon tabs, ribbon panels, toolbars, and menus. Click the **+** and **–** symbols to expand and hide the various components in the tree.

Figure 17–3

For example, if you want to modify the *Annotate* tab in the ribbon, click the + symbols next to *Ribbon*, *Tabs*, and *Annotate*, as shown in Figure 17–4. The various panels are displayed in the list.

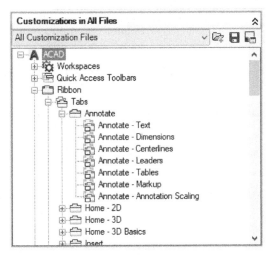

Figure 17–4

- You can duplicate toolbars, menus, panels, and commands within the CUI dialog box using copy and paste.

Command List Pane

The *Command List* area (shown in Figure 17–5), includes all commands in the software displayed in alphabetical order. To refine the display, search for a command or select an option in the All Commands Only drop-down list.

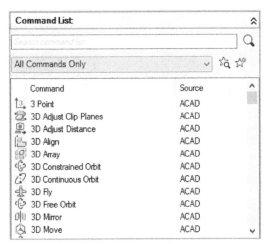

Figure 17–5

The *Search* field at the top of the *Command List* area helps you to filter command names as you type. The more you type, the more specific the displayed list becomes, as shown in Figure 17–6. Click 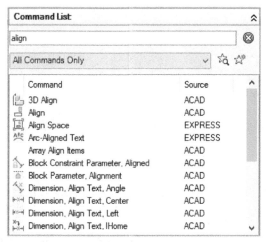 to display the full list again.

Figure 17–6

- In the *Command List* area, you can view a command's related macro by hovering over the command name, as shown in Figure 17–7.

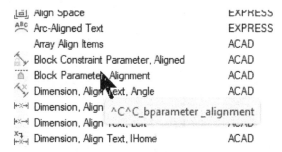

Figure 17–7

- To create a new command, click ☆ (Create a new command) and fill out the information in the *Properties* pane in the expanded CUI dialog box.

Preview Area

The *Preview* area (shown in Figure 17–8) includes representations of the panel or toolbar that you are working on. You can drag and drop commands to it and rearrange the location of the buttons in the panel or toolbar.

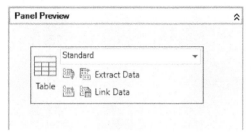

Figure 17–8

- When using the *Toolbar Preview* pane, dragging a button off the toolbar causes (Cloud) to display, indicating that the button is being removed. This does not work in the *Panel Preview* pane.

Button Image Pane

If the selected tool is associated with a button, the *Button Image* pane opens, as shown in Figure 17–9.

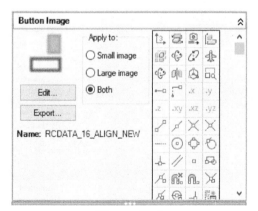

Figure 17–9

You can select a different button from the list or click **Edit** to open the Button Editor, as shown in Figure 17–10. This is a basic graphic editor with a limited number of pixels. To create more complex button designs you need to use a different program.

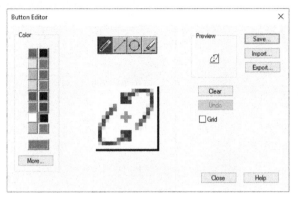

Figure 17–10

Properties Pane

The *Properties* pane displays the *Name*, *Description*, *Macro*, and other information that is associated with the selected tool, as shown in Figure 17–11. These items can be modified.

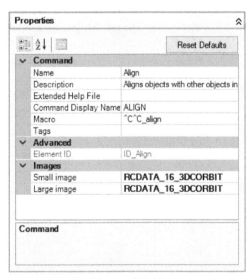

Figure 17–11

Hint: Customizing Palettes

You can create custom command tools in Tool Palettes by dragging a button from a toolbar or the CUI window to a Tool Palette while the Customize User Interface is open, as shown in Figure 17–12.

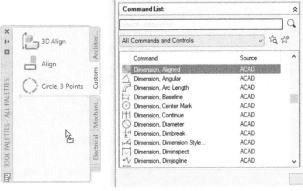

Figure 17–12

Right-click on a palette to access two customize options:

- **Customize Palettes** opens the Customize dialog box in which you can specify palette groups.

- **Customize Commands** opens the Customize User Interface dialog box.

17.2 Customizing the Ribbon

The default tabs and panels in the ribbon can be modified to include different commands, change the order in which the panels or tabs are displayed, or change which panels are contained in a tab. You can add new tabs and panels and then add rows, flyouts, sub-panels, and separators to them.

The simplest way to modify the ribbon is to drag and drop the panels within a tab to change the order in which they are listed. You can also drag the panel to the application window to display it as a floating panel.

How To: Move a Panel

1. Press and hold the mouse button on a panel's title bar.
2. Drag the panel to the new location.
3. Release the mouse button.

- You cannot drag and drop a panel from one tab to another in the drawing window.

- If the panel is dragged off the ribbon, it displays as a floating panel in the drawing window, as shown in Figure 17–13. The panel is visible in the drawing window, whether or not the tab to which it belongs is active. You can expand the panel as if it is still in the ribbon.

Figure 17–13

- Hover the cursor over the floating panel to display the options for moving the panel, as shown in Figure 17–14.

Figure 17–14

Floating Panel Options

⊤	Return the floating panel to its original position in the ribbon.
⊫	Toggle the orientation of the panel's **Expand** button.

- Right-click on a floating panel to display the options that toggle the visibility of panels and tabs.

Customize User Interface Dialog Box

You can use the Customize User Interface (CUI) dialog box to further modify the ribbon. Create or modify panels and tabs and add them to workspaces, and drag and drop or copy and paste objects to add them to existing panels or tabs.

How To: Create a Panel

1. In the *Manage* tab>Customization panel, click (User Interface) to open the Customize User Interface dialog box.
2. In the *Customizations in All Files* pane, expand the **Ribbon** node, right-click on the **Panels** node, and select **New Panel**.
3. Type a name for the panel and press <Enter>.

As the panel is being created, it displays in the Panel Preview pane.

4. Drag and drop commands from the *Command List* pane to the new panel. Arrange them in the order in which you want them to be displayed.
5. Right-click on the **Panel** node and select **New Row** to add a new row.
6. Right-click on a Row and select an option to add a new item: **New Panel**, **New Row**, **New Sub-Panel**, **New Fold Panel**, **New Drop-down**, and **Add Separator**.
7. Drag and drop to arrange the items as needed.

8. In the *Panel Preview* pane, verify that the items are displayed correctly, as shown in Figure 17–15.

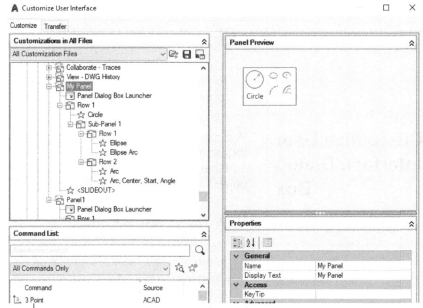

Figure 17–15

9. Click **OK** to close the Customize User Interface dialog box.

- To add another row to the *Customizations In All Files* pane, right-click on the panel name, or on the name of an existing row under which you want to place the new row, and select **New Row**.

- Each panel has one <SLIDEOUT>. You can move rows under it so that they do not display by default, but only when you click on the title of the panel. You can move the row, or the <SLIDEOUT>, as shown in Figure 17–16.

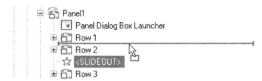

Figure 17–16

How To: Create a Tab

1. Open the Customize User Interface dialog box.
2. In the *Customizations in All Files* pane, expand the **Ribbon** node, right-click on the **Tabs** node, and select **New Tab**.

3. Type a name for the tab and press <Enter>.
4. Drag and drop panels from the **Panels** node to the new tab.
5. Click **OK** to close the Customize User Interface dialog box.

• A panel must be associated with a tab to be displayed in a workspace. **Copy** the panel to the clipboard and then **Paste** it into the associated tab.

How To: Add a Tab to a Workspace

1. Open the Customize User Interface dialog box.
2. Create the necessary panels and tabs.
3. In the *Customizations in All Files* pane, select the required workspace. The *Workspace Contents* pane displays on the right side of the CUI dialog box.
4. Drag and drop tabs onto the **Ribbon Tabs** node in the *Workspace Contents* pane.
5. Right-click on a tab name and select **Remove from Workspace** to remove a tab from the workspace.
6. Drag and drop the tabs to change their display order.
7. Click **OK** to close the Customize User Interface dialog box.

• In the *Workspace Contents* pane, if you click **Customize Workspace**, you can then, in the *Customization in All Files* pane, toggle on or off the tabs you want to have included in the workspace. Click **Done** when complete.

• The tab and panel display is controlled in the shortcut menus. Right-click anywhere on the ribbon, expand Tabs, and select a tab name to toggle its display on or off. Right-click, expand Panels, and select a panel name to toggle its display on or off.

Ribbon Contextual Tabs

You can add contextual tabs that display when you select specific objects in an AutoCAD drawing. For example, the *Block Editor* contextual tab (shown in Figure 17–17) opens when you open the Block Editor.

Figure 17–17

• Contextual tabs display a different color scheme than standard tabs.

- Contextual tab states can be set up in the CUI dialog box in the *Customizations in All Files* pane. In the example shown in Figure 17–18, under the **Ribbon** node, the **Block editor mode** node is expanded.

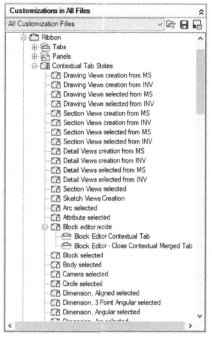

Figure 17–18

How To: Create Contextual Ribbon Tabs

1. Open the CUI dialog box.
2. Create the tab and panels needed for the contextual tab.
3. With the tab name selected, set the *Display Type* to **Full** or **Merged**, as shown in Figure 17–19.

*The **Full** display type only displays the panels for the contextual menu, while the **Merged** display type adds the panels to the current tab.*

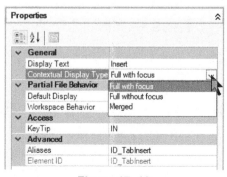

Figure 17–19

4. Drag and drop the new contextual tab to the related **Contextual Tab States** node, as shown in Figure 17–20. The newly created tab is named **Circle_Line_Selected Context Tab** and is copied to the **Circle selected** node. You can also copy this contextual tab to the **Line selected** node.

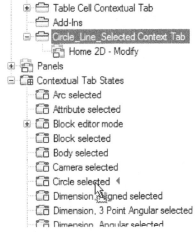

Figure 17–20

Ribbon Fold Panels

In the CUI dialog box, ribbons can be customized to include Fold panels. Fold panels automatically resize horizontally to fit into the available space when the AutoCAD window is resized, or other panels are added or removed from the tab. The sizes can range from small to medium to large, as shown in Figure 17–21.

Figure 17–21

How To: Create Fold Panels

1. Open the CUI dialog box.
2. Create the panel to be used as the Fold panel.
3. Right-click on the Row and select **New Fold Panel**, as shown in Figure 17–22.

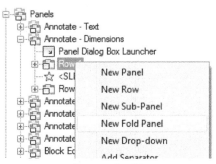

Figure 17–22

4. Add the required commands to the Fold panel by dragging and dropping them from the *Command List* pane.
5. In the *Customizations in All Files* pane, select the Fold panel.
6. In the *Properties* pane, set the *Default*, *Maximum*, and *Minimum Size[s]* to be **Small**, **Medium**, or **Large**, as shown in Figure 17–23.

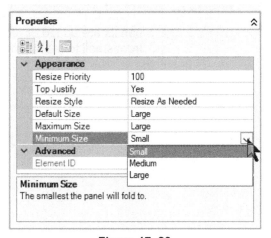

Figure 17–23

7. Close the CUI dialog box.

Ribbon Galleries

Various drop-down lists in the ribbon can be replaced with galleries in which images of the available options are displayed. The variable **GALLERYVIEW** can toggle ribbon galleries on or off.

- The **GALLERYVIEW** variable set to **0** (zero) toggles off the preview as, shown in Figure 17–24.

- The **GALLERYVIEW** variable set to **1** toggles the preview on, as shown on the right in Figure 17–25.

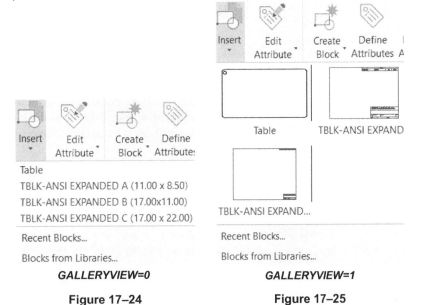

GALLERYVIEW=0

Figure 17–24

GALLERYVIEW=1

Figure 17–25

17.3 Customizing the Quick Access Toolbar

You can customize the Quick Access Toolbar in the Customize User Interface dialog box by dragging and dropping commands from the *Command List* pane to the **Quick Access Toolbar** node. You can also create multiple Quick Access Toolbars containing different collections of commands.

How To: Add a Command to the Quick Access Toolbar

1. Open the CUI dialog box.
2. In the *Customizations in All Files* pane, expand the **Quick Access Toolbar** node.
3. Drag and drop commands from the *Command List* pane to the **Quick Access Toolbar** node.
4. Drag and drop to arrange the commands in the required order.
5. Click **OK** to close the CUI dialog box.

Multiple Quick Access Toolbars

Instead of modifying one Quick Access Toolbar, you can create multiple Quick Access Toolbars, each containing different collections of commands. Add a new toolbar to the **Quick Access Toolbars** node, as shown in Figure 17–26. You can add and remove commands and then select the one you want to associate with a specific workspace. You can also delete Quick Access Toolbars from the node.

Figure 17–26

How To: Create a Quick Access Toolbar and Associate It with a Workspace

1. Open the CUI dialog box.
2. Right-click on the **Quick Access Toolbars** node and select **New Quick Access Toolbar**.
3. The new toolbar name highlights. Type a new name.
4. Expand the new toolbar. A list of default commands displays.
5. In the *Command List* pane, select a command and drag it to the **Quick Access Toolbar** node. You can drag and drop commands within the node.
6. Add as many commands as needed and click **Apply**.
7. In the *Customizations in All Files* pane, expand the **Workspaces** node and select the workspace in which you want to place the new Quick Access Toolbar.
8. Drag and drop the new Quick Access Toolbar to the *Workspace Contents* pane next to the existing Quick Access Toolbar, as shown in Figure 17–27.

Only one Quick Access Toolbar is current in a workspace. Therefore, copying a new one replaces the original one.

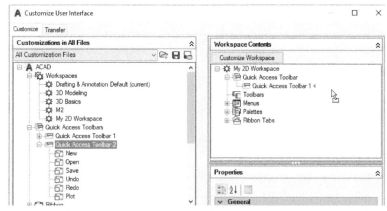

Figure 17–27

9. Click **OK** to close the CUI dialog box.
10. Set the modified workspace to be active. The new Quick Access Toolbar opens. The example shown in Figure 17–28 includes Workspaces and the Layer Control drop-down list.

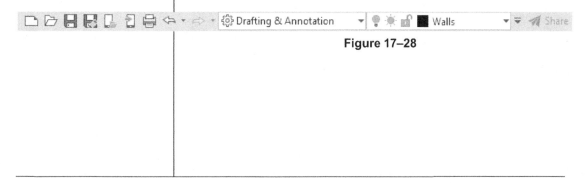

Figure 17–28

- The Quick Access Toolbar can be located above or below the ribbon when it is docked horizontally. To change the location, select the top **Quick Access Toolbar** node in the *Workspace Contents* pane. In the *Properties* pane, set the **Orientation** parameter, as shown in Figure 17–29.

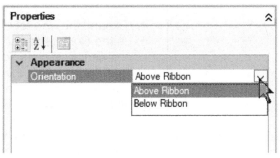

Figure 17–29

17.4 Customizing Menus

You can create custom pull-down menus with the commands or settings that you want to use, as shown in Figure 17–30. You can also specify which menus should display in specific workspaces.

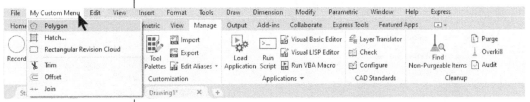

Figure 17–30

- To display the menus, expand Customize Quick Access Toolbar and select **Show Menu Bar**.

How To: Create a Custom Menu

1. Open the CUI dialog box.
2. In the *Customizations in All Files* pane of the dialog box, right-click on Menus and select **New Menu**.
3. A new menu name is added at the bottom of the existing list. Type a new name for the menu.
4. In the *Command List* pane, select a category for the type of command you want to use, or search for one in the *Search command list* field.
5. Select a command and drag it to the new menu name in the *Customizations in All Files* pane. Repeat this procedure until you have added all of the required commands.
6. Drag and drop the tools to arrange them in the required order.
7. Click **OK** to close the CUI dialog box.

- If icons and keyboard shortcuts for a command have been defined, they are displayed in the menu to which the command has been added.

- You can modify the command's properties.

Controlling Menus in Workspaces

When you create a new menu, it is added to all of the existing workspaces. In the CUI dialog box, you can control which menus or other interface items to include in a workspace. Select the workspace in the *Customizations in All Files* pane. In the *Workspace Contents* pane, the toolbars, menus, palettes, and ribbon tabs in the workspace are displayed, as shown in Figure 17–31.

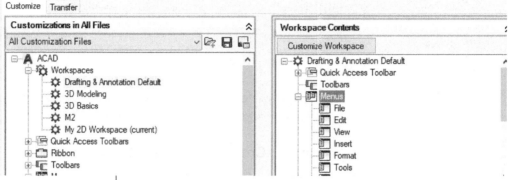

Figure 17–31

- In the *Workspace Contents* pane, drag and drop menus in the list to reorder them.

- To remove a menu from the workspace, right-click on it in the *Workspace Contents* pane and select **Remove from Workspace**.

- To add a menu to a workspace, click **Customize Workspace**. You can then select items from the list of all of the available menus in the *Customizations in All Files* pane, as shown in Figure 17–32. Select the items that you want to include and click **Done** in the *Workspace Contents* pane.

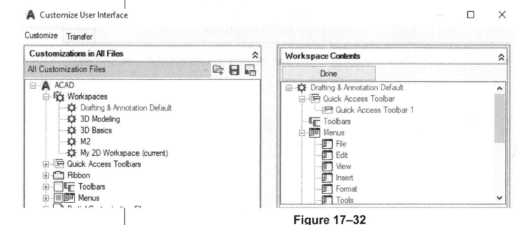

Figure 17–32

Modifying Shortcut Menus

Shortcut menus (also called *context* menus) display next to the cursor when you right-click. The menu that displays is dependent on where you right-click, what object is selected, etc. A variety of shortcut menus are defined in the software. You can modify them to suit your needs and add new shortcut menus, as shown in Figure 17–33.

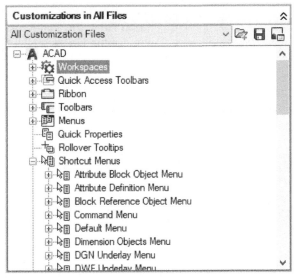

Figure 17–33

For example, in the **Dimension** shortcut menu, you might often use the **Move with leader** option. Instead of having this in a sub-category in the menu under **Dim Text position**, you can move it up to the top of the menu. Select the command in the list and drag it to the location in which you want it to display in the menu.

- You can create custom shortcut menus to work with custom commands created with AutoLISP or VBA.

- Shortcut menus are the same in all of the workspaces.

Hint: Migrating Existing Menus

If you have custom menus from previous releases of the software, you can easily migrate them to the current release. In the Customize User Interface dialog box, select the *Transfer* tab, as shown in Figure 17–34. Click 📂 (Open Customization File) in either pane. When the Open dialog box opens, set *Files of type:* to **Legacy menu files (*.mns, *.mnu)** and find your menu file in the folder list. When you click **Open**, it creates a copy of the file as a CUI file.

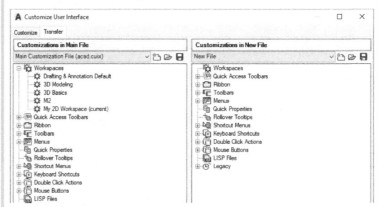

Figure 17–34

You can then add items to an existing file that has been specified in the other pane by dragging and dropping them to the appropriate area.

You can also use the new file as a partial CUI file. To do so, select the *Customize* tab, and in the *Customizations in All Files* pane, click 📂 (Load partial customization file) as shown in Figure 17–35.

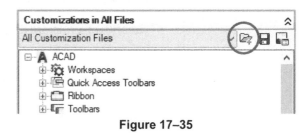

Figure 17–35

17.5 Keyboard Shortcuts

Two types of keyboard shortcuts can be customized: Shortcut Keys and Temporary Override Keys, as shown in Figure 17–36.

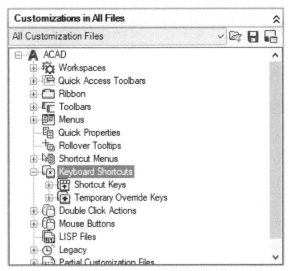

Figure 17–36

How To: Add a Shortcut Key

1. In the CUI dialog box, in the *Command List* pane, select the command that you want to use and drag it to the **Shortcut Keys** node in the *Customizations in All Files* pane.
2. In the *Properties* pane, in the *Access* area, next to **Key(s)**, click . The Shortcut Keys dialog box opens, as shown in Figure 17–37.

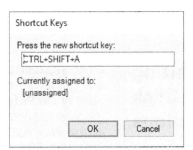

Figure 17–37

3. In the *Press the new shortcut key* field, type the shortcut key that you want to use.
4. Click **OK** to assign the shortcut key and click **OK** again to close the CUI dialog box.

- To add a Temporary Override, you need to create a new one by right-clicking on Temporary Override Keys in the *Customizations in All Files* pane and selecting **New Temporary Override**. You can then use the *Properties* pane to create the shortcut key.

Mouse Buttons

If you have a multi-button mouse or want to change the standard button defaults, you can do so in the **Mouse Buttons** node in the CUI, as shown in Figure 17–38. Select the option that you want to modify in the *Customizations in All Files* pane on the left side and make the changes in the *Properties* pane on the right side.

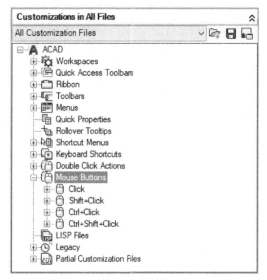

Figure 17–38

Customizing Double-Click Actions

When you double-click on objects in the software a command or action always starts. For example, the Properties palette might open or the **Polyline Edit** command might start, depending on the selected object. You can customize how you want the double-click action to function for each object type, as shown in Figure 17–39.

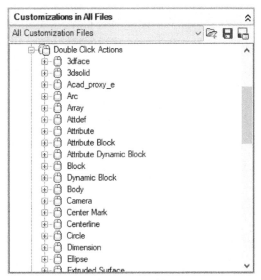

Figure 17–39

How To: Customize a Double-Click Action

1. Open the CUI dialog box.
2. In the *Customizations in All Files* pane, expand the **Double-Click Actions** node to display the various object types that can be modified.
3. Select the object type and the action that you want to modify.
4. In the *Properties* pane, you can type a macro that expresses the actions that you want the double-click action to take. You can also drag and drop a command from the *Command List* pane to the **Double-Click Actions** node.
5. When you have finished making changes to your customization file, click **OK**.

Other CUI Features

- *Partial CUI files* are loaded on top of the main CUI file without becoming part of the main file. Use the **cuiload** command (or click ⬚ (Load partial customization file) in the CUI dialog box) to load the partial CUI files. This works with legacy MNU and MNS menu files and CUI files. You can add items from partial .CUI files to workspaces. Use **cuiunload** to unload them.

- The **LISP files** node holds the names of the LISP or MNL files that are loaded with the customized menu. Right-click and select **Load LISP** to connect the LISP file to the menu. The LISP file is then loaded when the menu is loaded and is available for use in other menu options.

- Legacy interface objects include: Tablet Menus, Tablet Buttons, Screen Menus, and Image Tile Menus.

- Enterprise CUI files are copies of the Main CUI file that are customized by the CAD Manager, and then placed on a drive to be accessible to everyone in the office. This location is specified in the Options dialog box, in the *Files* tab, under **Customization Files>Enterprise Customization File**.

- The interface can be set back to its previous state or to the original state. In the Customize User Interface dialog box, right-click on the **ACAD** node and select **Restore ACAD.CUIX** or **Reset ACAD.CUIX**, as shown in Figure 17–40. **Restore ACAD.CUIX** returns the interface to the previous state before the immediate changes were made. **Reset ACAD.CUIX** returns the interface to its original state.

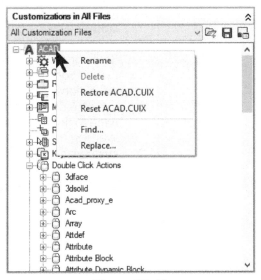

Figure 17–40

- When a command is selected in the *Command List* pane in the Customize User Interface dialog box, its information is displayed in the *Properties* pane.The Tags property is used when a search is performed in the Menu Browser. User-defined tags can be added to this field so that the selected command is included in different searches, as shown in Figure 17–41.

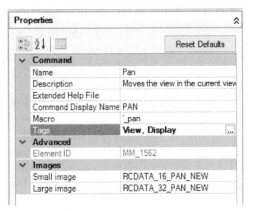

Figure 17–41

Practice 17a

Customizing AutoCAD

Practice Objective

- Using the Customize User Interface dialog box, create a new and custom tab and panel for the ribbon, a drop-down menu, a toolbar, and a shortcut key assignment.

In this practice, you will customize the ribbon, create a custom drop-down menu, create a custom toolbar, and create a custom shortcut key assignment. You will then reset the interface to the default configuration.

Customizing the Ribbon

In the following tasks, you will customize the ribbon. First, you will create a new ribbon panel to which you will add buttons. Then, you will create a new ribbon tab to which you will add panels. Finally, you will add commands to the Quick Access Toolbar. The customized tab is shown in Figure 17–42.

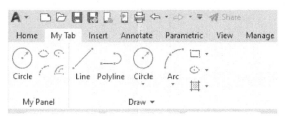

Figure 17–42

Task 1 - Create a ribbon panel.

1. Create a new drawing based on **acad.dwt**.

2. In the *Manage* tab>Customization Panel, click (User Interface) to open the Customize User Interface dialog box.

If an AutoCAD message displays, click OK.

3. In the *Customizations in All Files* pane, expand the **Ribbon** node, right-click on the **Panels** node, and select **New Panel**. Type **My Panel** as the panel name.

4. In the *Command List* pane, click in the *Search command list* field and type **Circle**. Drag the **Circle** command and drop it onto **Row 1**, located in My Panel in the *Customizations in All Files* list.

5. Right-click on **Row 1** and select **New Sub-Panel**.

6. In the *Command List* pane, click in the *Search command list* field and type **Ellipse**. Drag **Ellipse** and **Ellipse Arc** to the row under **Sub-Panel 1**.

7. Right-click on **Sub-Panel 1** and select **New Row**.

8. Search for **Arc** in the Command List. Drag **Arc** and **Arc, Center, Start, Angle** to the new row in **Sub-Panel 1**.

9. The Customize User Interface dialog box should display as shown in Figure 17–43.

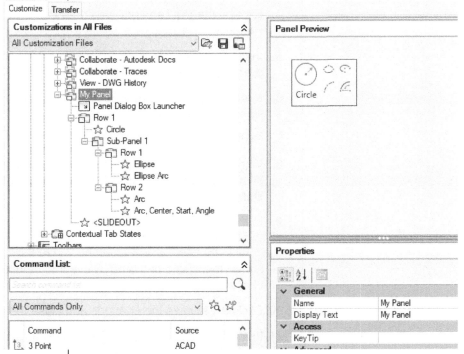

Figure 17–43

10. In **Row 1**, select **Circle**.

11. In the *Properties* pane, in the *Appearance* area, change the *Button Style* to **Large with Text (Vertical)**.

12. Click **Apply** to save the changes.

On the right side of the CUI dialog box, click the Button Image header to collapse its area if you need to create more space in which to display the Properties pane.

Task 2 - Create a ribbon tab.

1. In the *Customizations in All Files* pane, scroll up to the **Ribbon** node. Right-click on the **Tabs** node and select **New Tab**. Type **My Tab** as the name and press <Enter>.

2. Scroll down to the **Panels** node, right-click on the **My Panel** node, and select **Copy**.

3. Scroll up to the **Tabs** node, right-click on the **My Tab** node, and select **Paste**.

4. Expand the **My Tab** node and note that it now contains My Panel.

5. In the **Panels** node, select the **Home 2D - Draw** node and drag it to the **My Tab** node.

6. If required, drag the panels in the **My Tab** node so that My Panel is listed first.

7. Click **Apply** to save the changes.

8. In the *Customizations in All Files* pane, expand the **Workspaces** node and select **Drafting and Annotation Default (current)**.

9. In the *Workspace Contents* pane, expand **Ribbon Tabs**. In the *Customizations in All Files* pane, drag **My Tab** to Ribbon Tabs in the *Workspace Contents* pane. It is automatically added to the end of the list. Move it to be directly under Home - 2D.

10. Click **OK** to save the changes and close the CUI dialog box.

11. In the ribbon, select **My Tab** to display the tab you have created, as shown in Figure 17–44.

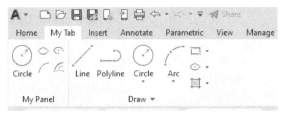

Figure 17–44

Customizing Menus

In the following tasks, you will create a custom pull-down menu, (as shown in Figure 17–45) and modify the shortcut menu for dimensions.

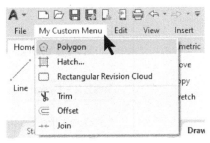

Figure 17–45

Task 1 - Create a custom workspace.

1. Expand the Customize Quick Access Toolbar drop-down list and select **Show Menu Bar**, as shown in Figure 17–46.

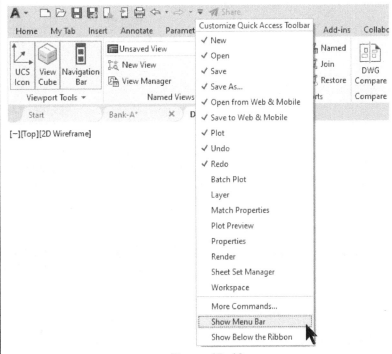

Figure 17–46

2. Open Properties and the Layer Properties Manager. Dock them to one side of the screen.

3. In the Status Bar, expand ⚙ ˅ and select **Save Current As...**

4. Save the workspace as **My 2D Workspace**.

5. Switch between workspaces and note the differences. Set **My 2D Workspace** to be the current workspace.

Task 2 - Create a custom menu.

---

1. Open the Customize User Interface dialog box.

2. In the *Customizations in All Files* pane, right-click on Menus and select **New Menu**. A new menu is added to the list. Type the name **My Custom Menu** and press <Enter>.

3. In the *Command List* pane, using the Filter drop-down list (All Commands only), select the *Draw* category, as shown in Figure 17–47.

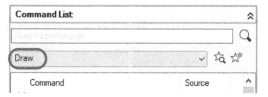

Figure 17–47

4. Select several drawing tools, such as **Polygon**, **Hatch**, and **Rectangular Revision Cloud**, and drag each one to the new menu called My Custom Menu in the *Customizations in All Files* pane.

5. Switch to the *Modify* category and drag several modification tools to the new menu.

6. In the new menu, drag and drop the commands to arrange them in the list so that all of the drawing tools are displayed first. Right-click on the last drawing tool in the list and select **Insert Separator**.

New menus are automatically inserted in all of the workspaces. You will need to select each workspace and remove the new menu from each of them except for your custom workspace.

7. In the *Customizations in All Files* pane, expand the **Workspaces** node and select a workspace other than My 2D Workspace. In the *Workspace Contents* pane, expand Menus. The new *My Custom Menu* is displayed at the end of the list. Right-click on *My Custom Menu* and select **Remove from Workspace**.

8. Repeat Step 7 to remove the new menu from all of the workspaces except **My 2D Workspace**.

9. Select your custom workspace. In the *Workspace Contents* pane, move the new menu to a new location in the menu list.

10. Click **OK** to save the menu file and close the CUI dialog box. In the drawing window, check that your new menu is working correctly.

11. Switch to the Drafting & Annotation workspace and verify that the new menu is not included there.

12. Switch back to your custom workspace.

Creating Keyboard Shortcuts

In the following tasks, you will create a custom shortcut key assignment, as shown in Figure 17–48. You will then reset the interface to the default configuration.

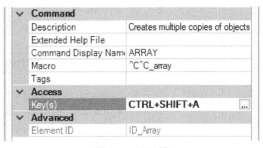

Figure 17–48

Task 1 - Create keyboard shortcuts.

---

1. Open the Customize User Interface dialog box.

2. In the *Customizations in All Files* pane, expand the **Keyboard Shortcuts** node and expand the **Shortcut Keys** node. Note that many shortcut keys are already assigned.

3. In the *Command List* pane, locate the **Array** command. Drag and drop it to the **Shortcut Keys** node in the *Customizations in All Files* pane.

4. Select the **Array** command where you added it to the shortcuts list. In the *Properties* pane, click in **Key(s)** edit box and click  (Browse).

5. In the Shortcut Keys dialog box, press <Ctrl>+<Shift>+<A> to automatically enter the shortcut into the field, as shown in Figure 17–49.

Shortcut Keys

Press the new shortcut key:

CTRL+SHIFT+A

Currently assigned to:
[unassigned]

OK   Cancel

Figure 17–49

6. Click **OK** to assign the shortcut.

7. Click **OK** to save the changes and close the CUI dialog box.

8. Press <Ctrl>+<Shift>+<A> to verify that it starts the **Array** command. Press <Esc> to close the command.

Task 2 - Modify a shortcut menu.

1. Draw a rectangle in the drawing window. Select the rectangle, right-click and expand Draw Order. Note that **Send to Back** is a sub-item under this command, as shown on the left in Figure 17–50. Press <Esc> to cancel.

2. Open the Customize User Interface dialog box.

3. In the *Customizations in All Files* pane, expand the Shortcut Menus.

4. Find the **Edit Menu** and expand it.

5. Expand Draw Order.

6. Drag **Send to Back** to the main **Edit Menu**. It should now be displayed in the list.

7. Drag it above the **Draw Order** option.

8. Click **OK**.

9. In the drawing window, select the rectangle again, right-click, and note the new configuration of the shortcut menu, as shown on the right in Figure 17–50.

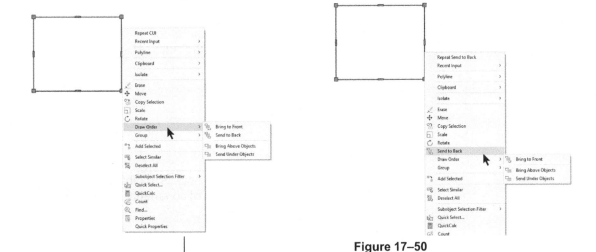

Figure 17–50

Task 3 - Reset the CUI file.

1. Open the Customize User Interface dialog box.

2. In the *Customizations in All Files* pane, select **Drafting and Annotation Default** to be active in the **Workspaces** node.

3. In the *Customizations in All Files* pane, right-click on ACAD and select **Reset ACAD.CUIX**. In the alert box, click **Continue**.

4. Click **OK** to save the changes and close the CUI dialog box.

5. In the Status Bar, expand ⚙ ˅ and select **Drafting & Annotation** to set it as the current workspace.

Chapter Review Questions

1. By default, any changes made to the CUI are made to the customization file that you have imported.

   a. True

   b. False

2. Which of the following automatically resize horizontally to fit into the available space when the AutoCAD window is resized?

   a. Ribbon buttons

   b. Ribbon fold panels

   c. Floating panels

   d. Ribbon tabs

3. You can create multiple Quick Access Toolbars, each containing different collections of commands. How many can be current in a workspace?

   a. None

   b. One

   c. Two

   d. Unlimited

4. In the CUI, which pane displays the list of commands when you do a search?

   a. Preview pane

   b. Button Image pane

   c. Command List pane

   d. Properties pane

5. When you are creating custom ribbon panels, you can display small, medium, or large panel buttons depending on the amount of screen space available. To do so, you need to create a custom _____.

   a. Row panel

   b. Drop-down panel

   c. Sub-panel

   d. Fold panel

6. To return the interface to its original state, _____.

    a. Right-click on the **ACAD** node in the Customize User Interface dialog box and select **Reset ACAD.CUIX**.

    b. Right-click on the **ACAD** node in the Customize User Interface dialog box and select **Restore ACAD.CUIX**.

    c. Reinstall the software.

    d. Right-click on the **ACAD** node in the Customize User Interface dialog box and select **Delete**.

Command Summary

Button	Command	Location
	Customize User Interface	• **Ribbon:** *Manage* tab>Customization panel

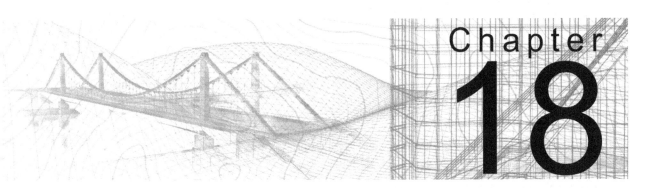

Macros and Custom Routines

Creating macros and custom routines helps you combine commands and automate repetitive routines. Several options are available to help you with these automations. In this chapter, you learn how to use macros to customize commands, run scripts, use the Action Recorder, and load and run AutoCAD® VBA routines.

Learning Objectives in This Chapter

- Create a new command with a new icon that is customized to suit a specific required action.
- Automate repetitive tasks by running scripts.
- Easily create macros to automate repetitive tasks by recording typical actions and playing them back in any drawing.
- Edit existing Action Macros using the Action Macro Manager.
- Load sophisticated programming routines into the AutoCAD software.

18.1 Custom Commands and Macros

Arranging existing commands of the AutoCAD software in custom ribbon tabs and panels is one step in customization. A further step is to create new commands that are customized to suit specific actions that are required for your work. You can do so at a basic level using command macros.

Creating a New Command

To create a custom command or modify an existing command, you can use the *Properties* pane in the Customize User Interface (CUI) dialog box. To create a new custom command, click

☆ (Create a new command) in the *Command List* pane and enter the properties in the *Properties* pane. For an existing command, select it in the *Command List* pane and change its properties in the *Properties* pane, as shown in Figure 18–1.

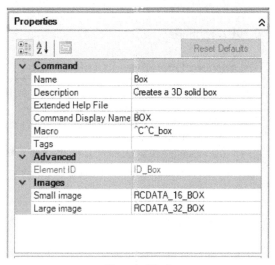

Figure 18–1

The properties of a command include its *Name* and *Description* (which display in the ribbon panel), its *Macro*, and the location of its *Images* (for commands that use icons).

- If you modify the properties of an existing command, you can click **Restore Defaults** in the *Properties* pane to restore the default properties.

Command Macro

Every AutoCAD command runs a *macro*, which is the action for that command. You can modify the macro of an existing command or create a new command to run a custom macro, as shown in Figure 18–2.

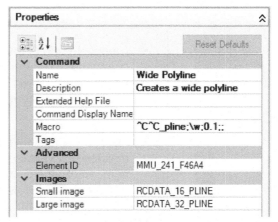

Figure 18–2

Macros are basically *bottled keystrokes*, so that anyone who knows how to type AutoCAD commands in the Command Line can create them. Macros can be used to issue commands with certain options selected automatically, such as inserting a specific block at a specific rotation angle. They can also be used to string together a sequence of commands that you initiate with a single pick.

When you prepare to write a macro, you should first work it out step-by-step in the Command Line. Use the actual command name. For example, **pline** is the command name (not **Polyline**), and **-insert** is the Command Line version of the **Insert** command. Count every keystroke that you make, especially when you press <Enter>.

When you have created a custom command with its macro, you can add it to any palette or menu.

Special Characters Used in Macros

- A semi-colon (;) represents <Enter>.

- A backslash (\) tells the software to pause for input. You can then pick a point, type a number, or select objects, after which the macro continues.

- ^C^C cancels the previous command.

- An apostrophe (') before the command name enables the command to run *transparently* in another command. For example, if you want to zoom without canceling the current command, use **'zoom**. Not all commands can run transparently.

- For commands that have both a Command Line version and a dialog box version, add a hyphen in front of the command name to run the Command Line version (for instance, **-layer**, **-insert**, **-xref**). However, you cannot select options in a dialog box using a macro.

- An asterisk (*) preceding the macro makes it a repeating macro.

Example:

The following macro sets the *current layer* to **Text** and then starts the **Mtext** command. In the **Mtext** command, three options are set: the *justification* (J) to **TC** (Top Center), the *style* (S) to **Title**, and the *height* (H) to **0.25**. Ensure that the **Height** option is last in any **Mtext** options in macros or it is not remembered.

-LAYER;S;TEXT;;MTEXT;\J;TC;S;TITLE;H;0.25;

An alternative to setting the layer is to use the system variable **clayer**, which sets the current layer.

CLAYER;TEXT;

- Macros can be included with commands in toolbars, ribbon panels, drop-down menus, and shortcut menus.

- It is better to use the full AutoCAD command in a macro than the one or two letter command alias. The alias is defined in the **ACAD.pgp** file, and that file can be different on different systems.

Button Image

To create a custom tool icon for the command, or to modify an existing one, click **Edit** in the *Button Image* area in the CUI dialog box. It displays when you have selected a command, as shown in Figure 18–3.

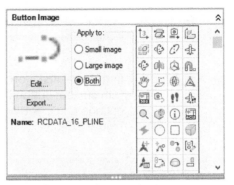

Figure 18–3

- The Button Editor dialog box is shown in Figure 18–4. To use the drawing tools, select a tool (**Pixel**, **Line**, **Circle**, or **Erase**) and select a color. To draw a line or circle, hold the pick button as you drag the pointer. **Pixel** and **Erase** change one pixel (dot) at a time.

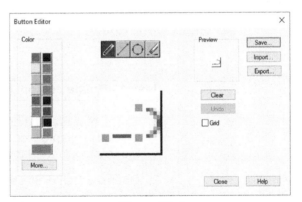

Figure 18–4

Use...	to...
Grid	display a grid to help you draw.
Clear	remove all of the colors from the icon.
Undo	undo the last command.
Import	open the Select Files dialog box in which you can select a .BMP, .RLE, or .DIB file, to load as the image for the button.
Export	save the icon to a BMP file. If the software cannot find the image file, it displays a question mark instead.
Save	save the current image in the CUI

Practice 18a | Custom Command Macros

Practice Objectives

- Create new custom command in the CUI, whose macros include a combination of other commands and some of their specific options.
- Add custom commands to a new tab and panel in the ribbon to test the custom macros.

In this practice, you will create a custom ribbon tab and panel with custom buttons and add simple macros to zoom with special options and insert text with specific formatting, as shown in Figure 18–5.

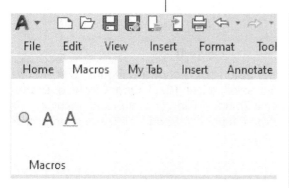
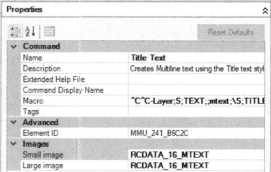

Figure 18–5

Task 1 - Create custom macros.

1. Start a new drawing based on **AEC-Imperial.dwt**, which is located in the practice files folder. (The text styles required for the macro are available in the template.)

2. Open the CUI dialog box.

3. In the *Command List* pane, click ✨ (Create a new command).

Delete any default text first.

4. In the *Properties* pane, add the following information, as shown in Figure 18–6:

   - *Name:* **Zoom Extents Plus**
   - *Description:* **Zoom Extents, then Zoom Out slightly**
   - *Macro:* **'zoom;e;'zoom;0.9x**

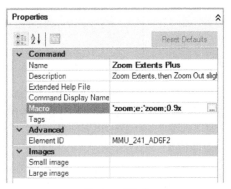

Figure 18–6

5. In the *Button Image* area, scroll through the set of available icons to find one of the zoom icons. Select it to use for this command. Select **Both** to set it for the small and large images.

6. In the *Command List* pane, click to create another new command and assign the following properties:

   • *Name:* **Title Text**
   • *Description:* **Creates Multiline text using the Title text style, center justified, and with a height of 0.25**
   • *Macro:*
     ^C^C-LAYER;S;TEXT;;mtext;\S;TITLE;J;MC;H;0.25;

7. In the *Button Image* area, select one of the text icons to use for this command. Select **Both** to set it for the small and large images.

8. Create another new command and assign the following properties:

   • Name: **Notes Text**
   • Description: **Creates Multiline text using the Hand text style, left justified, and with a height of 0.125**
   • Macro:
     ^C^C-LAYER;S;TEXT;;mtext;\S;HAND;J;TL;H;0.125;

9. In the *Button Image* area, select a different text icon to use for this command. Select **Both** to set it for the small and large images.

10. In the *Command List* area, change the *category* to **Custom Commands** to display the new commands.

11. In the ribbon, create a new panel named **Macros**. Drag the three custom commands to add them to the new panel.

12. Create a new tab named **Macros** and drag the Macros panel to add it to the new tab.

13. In the **Workspaces** node, select the **Drafting & Annotation Default (current)** workspace. Drag the new *Macros* tab and drop it in the **Ribbon Tabs** node in the *Workspace Contents* area. Drag it to a new location.

14. Note the new panel, tab, and tools in the ribbon.

15. Click **OK** to close the CUI dialog box.

Task 2 - Use custom macros.

1. Draw an object in Model Space and test the **Zoom Extents Plus** command.

2. Switch to the **A-sized** layout and test your new commands by creating text in the layout. If they do not work correctly, open the CUI dialog box and verify that the macros are correct.

3. If time permits, use the Button Editor to modify the text buttons to make them different to the standard text commands. Click **Save** and save the images with different names.

4. In the Customize User Interface dialog box, right-click on the **ACAD** node and select **Reset ACAD.CUIX**. Click **Apply** to revert back to the default interface.

5. Close the drawing. Do not save changes.

18.2 Running Scripts

A *script* is a text file that contains AutoCAD commands. When you run a script file in the software, the commands in the file are executed. The contents of a script file are similar to the contents of a macro, except that scripts do not permit pauses for input as macros do.

- To run a script, in the *Manage* tab>Applications panel, click

  (Run Script).

- Scripts can open and close files, while macros are only used for one drawing session.

- You can stop a script by pressing <Esc>.

- Continue a stopped script using the **Resume** command.

- Scripts can be used to automate repetitive tasks. For example, you could have a script to set drawing-based system variables the way you want them to be in a set of existing drawings, to add specific standard layers in existing drawings, etc.

Hint: Creating Scripts

You can create a script file using a text editor, such as Notepad. Create the text file as you would a command macro, but use <Enter> or <Spacebar> instead of the semicolon. Save the file with the extension SCR.

In a script file, any line that starts with a semicolon (;) contains a comment. Use a <Spacebar> or <Enter> in a script to indicate a return. The text **Rscript** at the end of a script causes it to repeat from the beginning.

Practice 18b | Running Scripts

Practice Objective

- Automate the process of several commands by running a script.

In this practice, you will run a script that automates the process of purging a drawing, creating several new layers, and setting the drawing units. The completed drawing is shown in Figure 18–7.

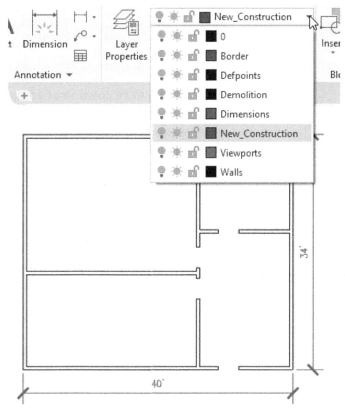

Figure 18–7

1. Open **Purge-Adv.dwg** from the practice files folder.

2. Expand the Layer Control to display the layers. There are several empty (unused) layers, several frozen layers, and note that there are no layers called **New Construction** or **Demolition**.

3. In the Application menu>**Drawing Utilities**, click **Units**. In the Drawing Units dialog box, note that the current *Precision* value for length is whole inches. Set the units for the *Insertion scale* to **Feet**. Click **OK** to save and close the Drawing Units dialog box. Click **OK** to update the values.

4. In the *Manage* tab>Applications panel, click ⌐>_ (Run Script). Select **Sample.scr** in the practice files folder and click **Open** to run it.

5. Expand the Layer Control. Several unused layers have been purged, one layer is thawed, two new layers have been added, and the current layer is set to **New_Construction**.

6. Open the Drawing Units dialog box. The precision is now **0'-0 1/8"** and the *Insertion scale* is set to **Inches**.

7. Open the text window (press <F2>) and scroll back to display the commands run by the script. The text of the script is shown in Figure 18–8.

```
LOck/Unlock/stAte/Description/rEconcile/Xref]: c
New color [Truecolor/COlorbook] : 5
Enter name list of layer(s) for color 5 (blue) <Walls>: New_Construction
Enter an option [?/Make/Set/New/Rename/ON/OFF/Color/Ltype/LWeight/TRansparency/MATerial/Plot/Freeze/Thaw/
LOck/Unlock/stAte/Description/rEconcile/Xref]: c
New color [Truecolor/COlorbook] : 1
Enter name list of layer(s) for color 1 (red) <Walls>: Demo
No matching layer names found.
Enter an option [?/Make/Set/New/Rename/ON/OFF/Color/Ltype/LWeight/TRansparency/MATerial/Plot/Freeze/Thaw/
LOck/Unlock/stAte/Description/rEconcile/Xref]: t
Enter name list of layer(s) to thaw: *
Enter an option [?/Make/Set/New/Rename/ON/OFF/Color/Ltype/LWeight/TRansparency/MATerial/Plot/Freeze/Thaw/
LOck/Unlock/stAte/Description/rEconcile/Xref]:
Command: clayer
Enter new value for CLAYER <"Walls">: New_Construction
Command: insunits
Enter new value for INSUNITS <2>: 1
Command: luprec
Enter new value for LUPREC <0>: 3
```

Figure 18–8

8. Close the drawing. Do not save changes.

18.3 Action Recorder

The Action Recorder makes it easy to create macros to automate repetitive tasks. A macro consists of a series of recorded commands that can be reused by playing back the macro. To create a macro, start the Action Recorder, perform the tasks, and then assign a name to the macro.

The Action Recorder can record typical actions from the Command Line, ribbon panels, Properties palette, Layer Properties Manager, Tool Palette, toolbars, and menus. You can replay the macro to repeat the procedure in any drawing file.

- Action Recorder tools are located in the *Manage* tab>Action Recorder panel, as shown in Figure 18–9.

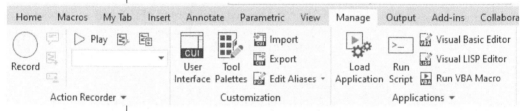

Figure 18–9

How To: Record a Macro

1. In the *Manage* tab>Action Recorder panel, click ◯ (Record).
2. Perform the tasks required to complete the macro (the Action Tree displays the process).
3. Click ☐ (Stop) to stop recording.
4. In the Action Macro dialog box, enter a name and description.
5. Click **OK** to save the Action Macro.

- Action Macros do not store the values for drawing settings. If the value for a drawing setting is critical to a macro, record the value with the system variable name or with the **setvar** command.

- Some commands cannot be recorded by an Action Macro. See the AutoCAD Help System for a list of these commands.

- If a command opens a dialog box while recording a macro, that dialog box also opens when the macro is played back. If you do not want the dialog box to display during playback, use the Command Line version of the command ("-" preceding the command name).

- Action Macros cannot have the same name as an existing AutoCAD command.

Adding a User Message

While recording a macro, click 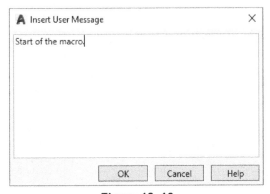 (Insert Message) to insert a user message in the Insert User Message dialog box, as shown in Figure 18–10. The message displays in the User Message dialog box when the macro is played, which gives you the option of continuing or ending the macro.

Figure 18–10

- There is a maximum of 256 characters in the message.

Requesting User Input

While recording a macro, click (Pause for User Input) to prompt the user for input instead of using the recorded value. For example, while recording the **Line** command, before you select the first point, click (Pause for User Input), and then input the first point. When the macro is played, the user is prompted to input a point or to use the recorded value.

Action Recorder Preferences

Click 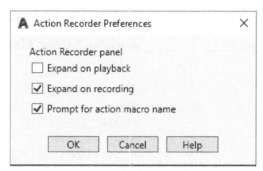 (Preferences) to open the Action Recorder Preferences dialog box (shown in Figure 18–11), which controls the behavior of the Action Recorder panel.

Figure 18–11

Expand on playback	Action Recorder panel expands when macro is played. It is **Off** by default.
Expand on recording	Action Recorder panel expands while recording macro. It is **On** by default.
Prompt for action macro name	When recording is stopped, the Action Macro dialog box opens, enabling you to input a name and description for the macro. If this option is not selected, the macro is automatically named **ActMacro\<num\>** where \<num\> is a sequential three digit number. It is **On** by default.

Playing Back Action Macros

After recording a macro, it is listed in the Action Recorder panel. You can play back the macro in any drawing file.

How To: Play a Macro

1. In the *Manage* tab>Action Recorder panel, click ▷ (Play).
2. Enter any required input.
3. When the macro is complete, the Action Macro – Playback Complete dialog box opens. Click **Close** to close the dialog box and end the macro.

- The Action Recorder panel flashes green while a macro is playing.

- When playing a macro that opens a dialog box, the macro pauses until the dialog box is closed. If the dialog box is canceled, the macro continues without the information from the dialog box. This can cause unexpected results from the macro.

- The results of an Action Macro played in different drawings can vary due to differences in drawing settings.

- Several alert boxes open the first time you run a macro, including *Action Macro - Playback complete* and *Action Macro - Input Request*. You usually do not need this input once you understand the process of using the macro. There is also an option enabling you to dismiss the alert permanently.

18.4 Editing Action Macros

Working with the Action Macro Manager

After an Action Macro has been recorded, it can be renamed, copied, or deleted. Action Macros can also be modified to remove actions, insert user messages or requests for user input, or to edit the behavior of an action.

The Action Macro Manager is where you can manage all of your saved Action Macro files. You can copy, rename, modify, and delete macros, as shown in Figure 18–12.

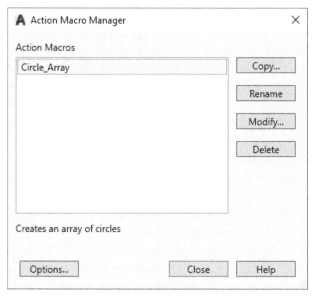

Figure 18–12

- Select an Action Macro in the list and click **Modify** to access the name and description, and some settings.

Select the Action Macro in the drop-down menu in the Manage tab>Action Recorder panel, and expand the Action Recorder flyout to open the Action Tree.

- To modify the contents of the Action Macro, you need to make changes to the Action Tree, including deleting or inserting a user message for the **View Change** command, as shown in Figure 18–13.

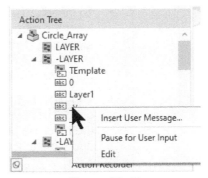

Figure 18–13

The Action Tree lists the recorded actions and input. The top node in the Action Tree displays the Action Macro name and is used to manage the macro file. Right-click on the **Action Macro** name node to display a list of commands, as shown in Figure 18–14.

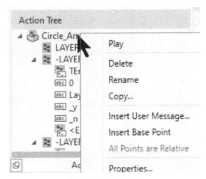

Figure 18–14

Play	Plays the Action Macro.
Delete	Deletes the macro file from the disk.
Rename	Enables you to change the name of the macro file.
Copy...	Creates a copy of the macro file.
Insert User Message...	Inserts a User Message, enabling you to add comments or instructions to the Action Macro.
Insert Base Point	Inserts a base point in the Action Macro.
All Points are Relative	All points entered in the Action Macro are relative to the base point.
Properties	Opens the Action Macro dialog box in which you can change the name, description, and playback options.

- To insert a user message, right-click on the node that you want the message to precede and select **Insert User Message**. The Insert User Message dialog box opens, in which you can enter the message to be displayed during playback of the macro.

- You can change any value node (point, text string, number, option, or object selection) to a request for user input. When the macro is played back, the user is prompted for the data and can input a new value or use the recorded value.

- When a value is set to **Pause for User Input**, a silhouette

  displays in the lower right corner of the icon ( ).

- Values can also be edited by right-clicking on the value node and selecting **Edit**. This enables you to change the current value of the node.

- Click **Options** in the Action Macro Manager to open the Options dialog box with the *Files* tab and Action Recorder Settings highlighted, as shown in Figure 18–15. You can specify the file locations here.

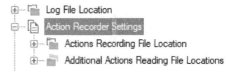

Figure 18–15

The **Actions Recording File Location** is where Action Macros are saved and where the software searches for existing macros.

You can share Action Macros using the **Additional Actions Reading File Locations**. You can also add multiple directories here. Any macros in this directory are listed in the Action Recorder panel and are available for playback.

- Action Macros have an .ACTM file extension.

Establishing a Base Point

When you modify an Action Macro, you can specify an absolute coordinate point that becomes the base point from which all other coordinates work. This can be very useful if you create a group of objects with the macro, and then want to insert it relative to a specific point in the group.

How To: Establish a Base Point

1. Create an Action Macro and expand the Action Tree.
2. Right-click on the title of the macro and select **Insert Base Point**, as shown in Figure 18–16.
3. Specify a base point. Type the coordinates or select a base point in the drawing window. The coordinate point is added, as shown in Figure 18–17.

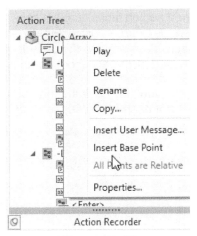

Figure 18–16

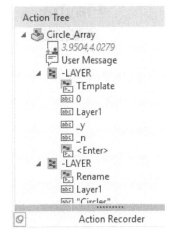

Figure 18–17

4. When you play back the macro, you are prompted for a new coordinate point. The remaining macro objects are then drawn from that point.

• By default, the macro prompts the user for a coordinate. If you want the coordinate to always remain the same, right-click on the new coordinate and clear the **Pause for User Input** option. The coordinate point displays in the Action Tree, as shown in Figure 18–18.

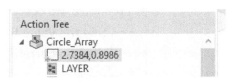

Figure 18–18

How To: Edit a Macro

1. In the *Manage* tab>Action Recorder panel, expand the drop-down list and select an Action Macro.
2. If the Action Tree is not displayed, expand the Action Recorder panel to display it and pin it open.

3. Right-click on a node and select the required command.
4. Modify the actions as required.

- Be careful when editing an Action Macro, because all of the changes affect the macro immediately and do not require a save.

Specifying Playback Values

When you create a macro, you often use default input values without considering how they impact macro use. For example, when setting limits, you typically press <Enter> at the *Specify lower left corner:* prompt to accept the default 0,0. However, a macro does not see the default information. It records that you pressed <Enter> without entering any information.

When you play back the macro, an alert box opens when a value has not been recorded, as shown in Figure 18–19.

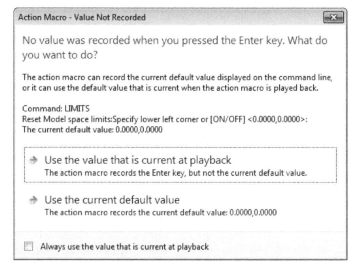

Figure 18–19

You have two options:

- **Use the value that is current at playback**
- **Use the current default value**.

If you select **Always use the value that is current at playback**, the alert box does not open.

Practice 18c | Action Recorder

Practice Objectives

- Record an Action Macro and play it back in another drawing to perform its functions automatically.
- Edit a macro to remove some actions and add other actions.

In this practice, you will record an Action Macro that creates a layer, creates a circle on that layer, and then creates an array from that circle. You will then play the macro in a new drawing to create the objects automatically. Finally, you will edit the macro to remove the display of the Layer Properties Manager, add a user message, and request user input. The result of the macro and its Action Tree are shown in Figure 18–20.

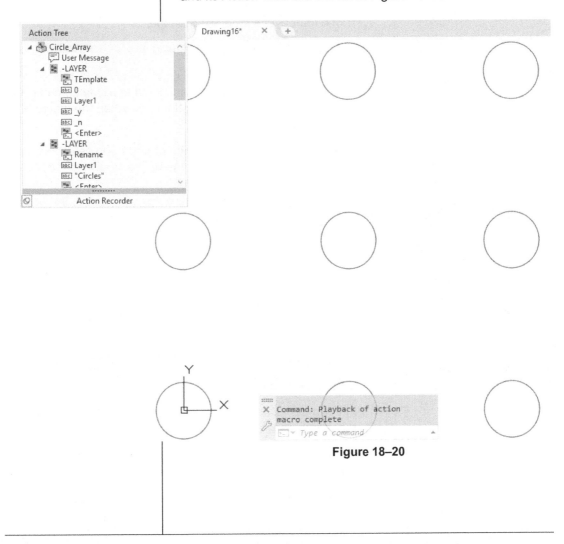

Figure 18–20

Task 1 - Create an Action Macro.

1. Create a new drawing using **acad.dwt** (provided with the software).

2. In the *Manage* tab>Action Recorder panel, click
   ◯ (Record) to start recording an Action Macro.

3. Open the Layer Properties Manager.

4. Create a new layer called **Circles**.

5. Change its color to **Red**.

6. Set the layer **Circles** to be the active layer.

7. Close the Layer Properties Manager.

8. Draw a circle at **0,0** with a radius of **1**.

9. Enter **-array** at the Command Line and press <Enter>. (You will use the Command Line version of the **Array** command so that the Array dialog box is not opened when the macro is played back.)

10. Type **L** and press <Enter> when prompted to select objects. This selects the last object created. Press <Enter> to continue with the **Array** command.

11. Select **Rectangular** as the type of array.

*You can also type **R** to select **Rectangular**.*

12. Enter **2** for the number of rows.

If the Action Macro dialog box opens, press <Esc> to exit the dialog box and continue with the Array command.

13. Enter **3** for the number of columns.

14. Enter **4** for the distance between rows.

15. Enter **4** for the distance between columns.

16. Enter **Z** at the Command Line to start the **Zoom** command.

17. Enter **E** to **Zoom Extents**.

18. In the Action Recorder panel, click ☐ (Stop) to stop the recording. The Action Macro dialog box opens.

19. In the *Action Macro Command Name* field, enter **Circle_Array**.

20. In the *Description* field, enter **Creates an array of circles** and click **OK** to save the file.

Task 2 - Play the Action Macro.

1. Create a new drawing using the **acad.dwt** template.

2. Ensure that **Circle_Array** is selected in the Action Recorder panel, as shown in Figure 18–21.

Figure 18–21

3. In the *Manage* tab>Action Recorder panel, click

   (Preferences) to open the Action Recorder Preferences dialog box. Select **Expand on playback** to display the *Action Tree* panel. Click **OK**.

4. Click ▷ (Play) to start the macro.

5. The Action Macro - Playback Complete dialog box opens, click **Close**. The layer, circles, and array are created exactly as they were when recording the macro. The Layer Properties Manager remains open because it was opened during the creation of the macro.

6. The *Action Tree* is displayed and remains open.

7. Close the Layer Properties Manager.

Task 3 - Edit the Action Macro.

1. Scroll in the Action Tree and note the list of recorded actions for **Circle_Array**.

2. Select **LAYER** (the first action in the list), right-click, and select **Delete** to remove this action from the macro. This action was the command that opened the Layer Properties Manager, which is not required.

3. In the Action Macro - Confirm Deletion of Action Node dialog box, click **Delete**.

4. In the *Action Tree*, select **Circle_Array**, right-click and select **Insert User Message**.

5. In the Insert User Message dialog box, enter **This macro creates a layer, a circle, and then an array of the circle** and click **OK**. A **User Message** node is added to the *Action Tree*.

6. Scroll down to the **Array** node.

7. Right-click on 2 and select **Pause for User Input**. The icon for this node changes (as shown in Figure 18–22) to indicate that the user is to be prompted for information at this point in the macro.

8. Repeat the previous step for nodes **3**, **4**, and **4.0000** for the **Array** command, as shown in Figure 18–22. This enables the user to control the number of rows and columns, and the distance for the array.

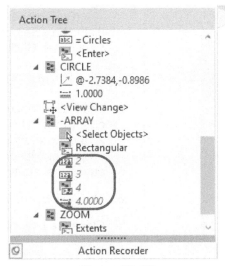

Figure 18–22

9. Click (Pinned) to unpin the Action Recorder panel.

Task 4 - Play the Action Macro.

---

1. Create a new drawing using the **acad.dwt** template.

2. Verify that the **Circle_Array** macro is selected in the Action Recorder panel and click ▷ (Play).

3. Read the User Message dialog box and click **Close**. This is the message you inserted when editing the macro.

---

*If the Action Macro - Input Request dialog box opens, select **Always pause playback for input** and select **Provide Input**. This hides this dialog box when you are prompted for input in the future.*

4. Enter **3** for the number of rows.

5. Enter **3** for the number of columns.

6. Enter **6** for the distance between rows.

7. Enter **6** for the distance between columns.

8. If the Action Macro - Playback Complete dialog box opens, click **Close**.

9. Close all files without saving changes.

18.5 Loading Custom Routines

The toolbar macros and scripts discussed earlier are a kind of programming, but are rather limited. More sophisticated programming in the AutoCAD software can be accomplished with AutoLISP, ActiveX Automation, AutoCAD VBA, ObjectARX, and .NET. These programming languages, known as Application Programming Interfaces (APIs), can create entirely new routines and commands for the AutoCAD software. While the details of these languages are beyond the scope of this course, you learn to load routines and see examples of what they can do.

- **AutoLISP:** Closely related to the LISP programming language, but specifically tailored for the AutoCAD software. Simple AutoLISP routines can be typed directly in the Command Line or included in menu macros. However, longer routines are generally typed in a text editor and saved as a .LSP file (a text file) or created using the Visual LISP editor. These routines must be loaded into the AutoCAD software before they can be used. LISP routines can also have the extensions FAS (a binary, compiled version of one LSP program) or VLX (a binary, compiled version of one or more LSP files).

- **Visual Basic (VBA):** Uses the AutoCAD ActiveX Automation Interface to modify AutoCAD objects or to communicate with other applications. VBA routines, called macros, are created in the Visual Basic editor, which can be opened directly from the AutoCAD software. VBA files have the extension .DVB.

- **ObjectARX (AutoCAD Runtime Extension):** Creates new commands using a compiled programming language. The commands operate as AutoCAD commands do. The **.NET** framework works in conjunction with Object ARX and enables developers to use other programming languages, such as VB, .NET, and C# to develop processes that run in the AutoCAD software.

Loading Routines

Before you can use an advanced customization routine, you must load it into the software, as shown in Figure 18–23. You can load an routine using the *Manage* tab>Applications panel by clicking 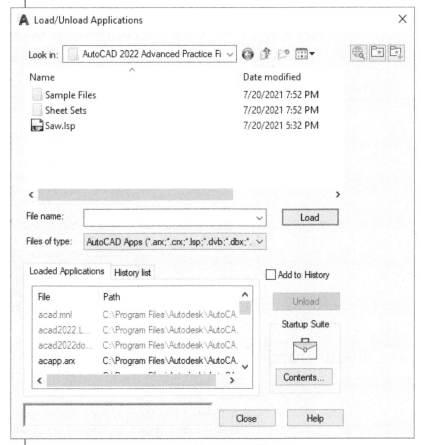 (Load Application) (**APPLOAD** command), Once the routine has been loaded, typing its name in the Command Line can start most routines, similar to starting an AutoCAD command.

Figure 18–23

- To load an AutoLISP routine in the Command Line, type the following: **(LOAD "file")**, where *file* is the name of the LSP file.

- To load an AutoLISP routine from a dialog box, use the **Load Application** command.

APPLOAD Options

The Load Applications options are as follows.

Look in	Specify which file to load.
File name	Name of selected file.
File of type	Control the types of files that display in the *File* area.
Load	Loads the selected file into the AutoCAD software.
***Loaded Applications* tab**	Contains a list of files that are currently loaded in the software. AutoLISP routines only display here if they were loaded with the **appload** command.
***History List* tab**	Contains a list of files that were loaded when **Add to History** was selected.
Add to History	When selected, all of the files that are loaded are listed in the *History List* tab.
Unload/Remove	Depending on the selected tab, the button **Unloads** the selected application or **Removes** it from the History List. LISP routines and some ObjectARX routines cannot be unloaded. When a file is removed from the History List, it is not unloaded, and when a file is unloaded, it is not removed from the History List.
Startup Suite	Contains a list of applications that are loaded when the software is started. You can drag files to the Startup Suite from the *File* area or from the Windows Explorer, or you can use the shortcut menu to copy files from the History List to the Startup Suite. Applications loaded with the Web Browser cannot be added to the Startup Suite.

Secureload

Controls are provided for software security to help prevent loading and running of unauthorized or malicious AutoLISP and VBA applications.

A Trusted File Search Path is included in the *Files* tab of the Options dialog box, as shown in Figure 18–24. It can also be accessed using the **TRUSTEDPATHS** and **TRUSTEDDOMAINS** system variables.

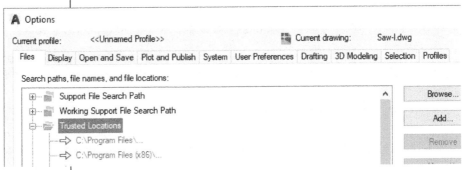

Figure 18–24

To restrict the locations from where executable files are loaded, click **Security Options** in the *Security* area of the *System* tab in the Options dialog box, as shown in Figure 18–25.

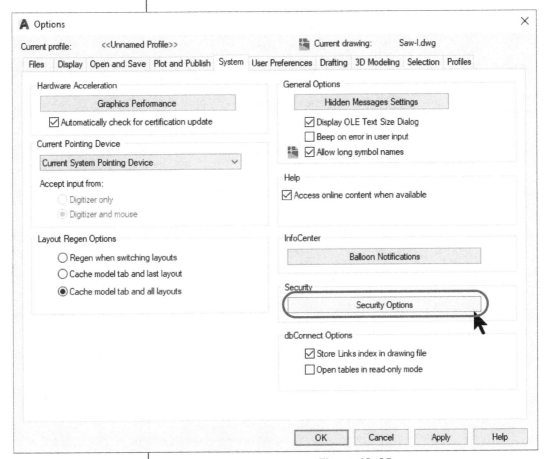

Figure 18–25

The Security Options dialog box (shown in Figure 18–26), enables you to set the various security levels.

- If you set the *Security Level* to **High**, the executable files are loaded only from trusted locations that were specified in the Options dialog box in the *Files* tab.

- Setting the *Security Level* to **Medium** enables you to load from trusted locations and displays a warning before loading executable files from outside these trusted locations.

- The **Off** setting loads the executables from all of the search paths and is generally not recommended.

- These options are applied to the **SECURELOAD** system variable and can also be set during the Deployment Wizard for network deployments.

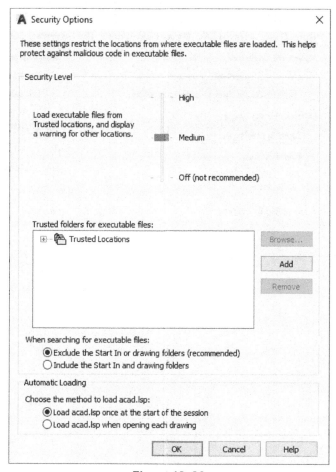

Figure 18–26

Practice 18d | Loading and Running an AutoLISP Routine

Practice Objective

- Load a custom AutoLISP routine and then initiate it.

In this practice, you will load a custom AutoLISP routine that defines a new AutoCAD command and then try the command, as shown in Figure 18–27.

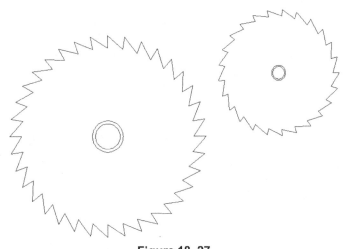

Figure 18–27

1. Open **Saw-I.dwg** from the practice files folder.

2. Type **Saw** and press <Enter>. The AutoCAD software returns an *Unknown command* prompt as it does not recognize this as a command. The routine must be loaded first.

*Depending on your **Secureload** settings (Security Level options (High/Medium/Off) in the System tab>Options dialog box), you might be required to accept to load the file in the File Loading - Security Concern dialog box.*

3. In the *Manage* tab>Applications panel, click 🔧 (Load Application). In the Load/Unload Applications dialog box, browse to your practice files folder, select **Saw.lsp**, and click **Load**. Once loaded, the routine defines the new **Saw** command. Close the Load/Unload Applications dialog box.

4. Use the **Saw** command to create two circular saw blades. Type **Saw** and press <Enter>.

5. Respond to the prompts using the following answers:

- *Center Point:* **16,5**
- *Outer Radius:* **8**
- *Inner Radius:* **7**
- *Number of teeth:* **36**
- *Hole Radius:* **1**
- *Hub Thickness:* **.25**

6. Type **Saw** again and respond to the prompts using the following answers:

- *Center Point:* **30,10**
- *Outer Radius:* **5**
- *Inner Radius:* **4.5**
- *Number of teeth:* **25**
- *Hole Radius:* **.5**
- *Hub Thickness:* **.1**

7. If time permits, find **Saw.lsp** in the practice files folder and open it in a text editor to display the code that runs the routine.

Chapter Review Questions

1. Which macro sets a layer named RED as the current layer?

   a. CLAYER/RED/

   b. CLAYER;RED;

   c. RED, LAYER, S

   d. S, LAYER, RED

2. What is the difference between the **Layer** command and the **-Layer** command?

   a. **Layer** runs in a dialog box and **-Layer** runs at the Command Prompt.

   b. **-Layer** does not have a layer delete option.

   c. **Layer** uses a dialog window and **-Layer** opens the Layer Control.

   d. There is no difference.

3. How do you create an Action Macro using the Action Recorder?

   a. Copy the geometry in a drawing and paste it into an Action Macro file.

   b. Copy the information from the Command Line, paste it into a text file, and save the text file as an Action Macro.

   c. Save the drawing file as an Action Macro file.

   d. Click **Record** in the Action Recorder, perform the actions, and click **Stop**.

4. Name two programming languages that can be used with the AutoCAD software.

   a. Visual Basic and Fortran

   b. AutoLISP and Script

   c. AutoLISP and Object ARX

   d. CAD-plus-plus and Object ARX

5. How do you make an advanced AutoLISP routine available for use in the AutoCAD software?

a. Save the AutoLISP routine in the *Program Files\AutoCAD* directory.

b. All AutoLISP commands load when the AutoCAD software is restarted.

c. Use the **Appload** command.

d. *Insert* tab>**AutoLISP** command

Command Summary

Button	Command	Location
	Load Application	• **Ribbon:** *Manage* tab>Applications panel • **Command Line:** APPLOAD
	Play	• **Ribbon:** *Manage* tab>Action Recorder panel
	Preference (Recorder)	• **Ribbon:** *Manage* tab>Action Recorder panel
	Record	• **Ribbon:** *Manage* tab>Action Recorder panel
	Run Script	• **Ribbon:** *Manage* tab>Applications panel
	Stop	• **Ribbon:** *Manage* tab>Action Recorder panel
	User Input (Recorder)	• **Ribbon:** *Manage* tab>Action Recorder panel

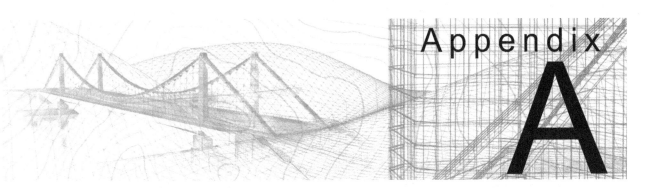

Cloud Collaboration and 2D Automation

The direct connection to the Autodesk Cloud environment enables teams to work together and share information, and it provides knowledge on how to display and edit a DWG drawing. In this appendix, you learn how to share drawing files so that they can be viewed, reviewed, marked up, and edited in the Autodesk® AutoCAD® web app. You also learn how to use the Trace tool to mark up the shared drawing in the Autodesk AutoCAD web app. Additionally, this appendix provides knowledge on how to automatically create 2D documentation of existing 3D models and to use building information modeling to coordinate models and collaborate with others on the project design team.

Learning Objectives in This Chapter

- Connect to Autodesk Account and social networking sites to improve productivity.
- Save drawings to the web and mobile devices.
- Share drawings on the cloud.
- Open, review, mark up, and edit the shared drawing in the Autodesk AutoCAD web app.
- Mark up the shared drawing using the Trace tool in the Autodesk AutoCAD web app.
- Attach Navisworks files.

A.1 Connecting to the Cloud

The AutoCAD software helps make collaboration easier and more effective. Using a Cloud environment, Autodesk 360 enables you to connect and share files directly from the AutoCAD software. In addition, you can connect directly to Autodesk social networks from the software.

Stay Connected Menu

In the InfoCenter, you can use the 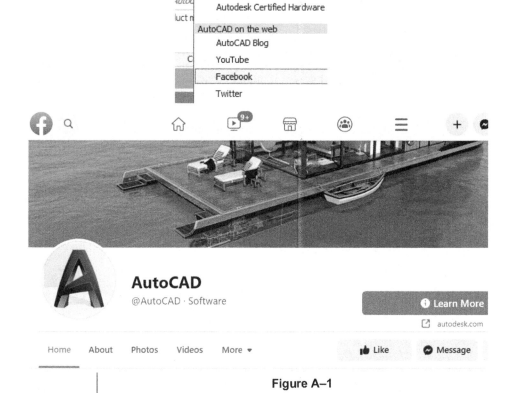 (Stay Connected) drop-down list to access the Autodesk Account, Autodesk Certified Hardware, and various social networking sites, as shown in Figure A–1. In the *AutoCAD on the web* area, select **AutoCAD Blog**, **YouTube**, **Facebook** (shown in Figure A–1), or **Twitter** to follow the latest news and get the latest tips and tricks on Autodesk software. You are required to have a working internet connection to access the options.

Figure A–1

© 2021, ASCENT - Center for Technical Knowledge®

Autodesk Account Log In

When you want to work with Autodesk on the cloud, you might need to log in to your Autodesk Account. If you do not have an existing account, you are required to create an account. Doing so is free and provides you with 25 GB of free space for storing drawings. Expand the Sign In drop-down list in the InfoCenter (as shown in Figure A–2) and select **Sign In to Autodesk account**. In the Autodesk - Sign in dialog box, you are prompted to log in using your Autodesk ID, or you can create an ID by selecting **Create Account**.

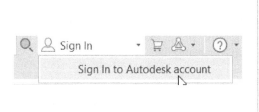

Figure A–2

- Once you have logged in, your user name displays in the in the InfoCenter. Expand the Sign In drop-down list to display the various cloud options, as shown in Figure A–3.

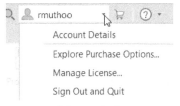

Figure A–3

Autodesk App Store

To connect to the Autodesk App Store, in the InfoCenter, click ⬚ (Autodesk App Store) or in the *Featured Apps* tab>App Store panel, click ⬚ (Connect to App Store). In the App Store, various plug-ins and standalone applications are available for you. Some of the popular apps are also listed in the *Featured Apps* tab, as shown in Figure A–4.

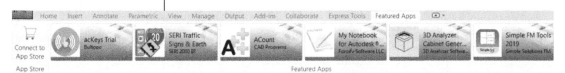

Figure A–4

Share Drawings

A.2 Share Drawings

With the **Share Drawing** tool you can collaborate with others through a virtual link to a drawing hosted online with Autodesk AutoCAD. The **Share Drawing** command functions very similar to the **ETRANSMIT** command. With the **Share Drawing** tool, you can share drawings containing any relevant referenced files such as XREFs as well as other type face and font file types.

The link to drawing file can be shared and then can be reviewed, marked up, and edited in the Autodesk AutoCAD web app. Through the Autodesk AutoCAD web app, collaboration can take place with any member of the team who has access to the share drawing link for the drawing file.

There are two levels of permission for recipients of a Share Drawing:

View only: Anyone with access to this link can view the drawing, including all XREFs. Recipients cannot make changes to the drawing and cannot save or download a copy.

Edit and save a copy: Anyone with access to this link can edit the drawing and save the drawing and all its XREFs as a copy. Recipients cannot make changes to the original drawing file that is owned by the sharer.

The ⬩ Share (Share Drawing) is available:

- In the Quick Access Toolbar, as shown in Figure A–5.

- In the *Collaborate* tab>Share panel, as shown in Figure A–5.

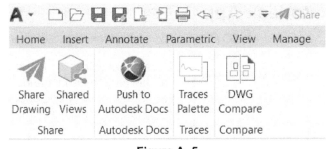

Figure A–5

- As a safety feature, the shared link automatically expires after seven days from when it was created.

- Main drawing file and/or each individual referenced drawing file must be less than 50MB.

- Complete project files including all documents must be less than 200MB.

- After saving a drawing file being shared to you, all attached external references are stored in the same location as the current drawing file.

How To: Share Drawings

1. Sign in to your Autodesk account, if you are not already signed in.
2. Open the saved drawing to share.
3. In the Quick Access Toolbar or in the *Collaborate* tab>Share panel, click  (Share Drawing).
4. In the Share a link to this drawing dialog box (as shown in Figure A–6), select the permission option. Note that a link has been created.
5. Select **Copy link** and send it to a recipient that you want to share the link with (when the recipient clicks the link, it opens the shared drawing in the Autodesk AutoCAD web app).

   or

6. Select **Preview** to open the link directly in the Autodesk AutoCAD web app.

×

Share a link to this drawing

Share a copy of the current version of this drawing, including xrefs. Link expires in seven days.
Learn more

👁 View only	✐ Edit and save a copy
Anyone with a link can view the drawing, but can't modify or save a copy	Anyone with a link can edit and save a new version of the drawing

https://web.autocad.com/acad/me/sid/shares/drawings/f1bc4688-13bf-482a-...

Preview	Copy link

Figure A–6

Autodesk AutoCAD Web App

Any user with access to the link can review the document through the Autodesk AutoCAD web app. This requires a free account through Autodesk to access the link information, as shown in Figure A–7. Once you are signed in with your free Autodesk account, you can review and do some light editing to the shared drawing through a completely interactive web interface.

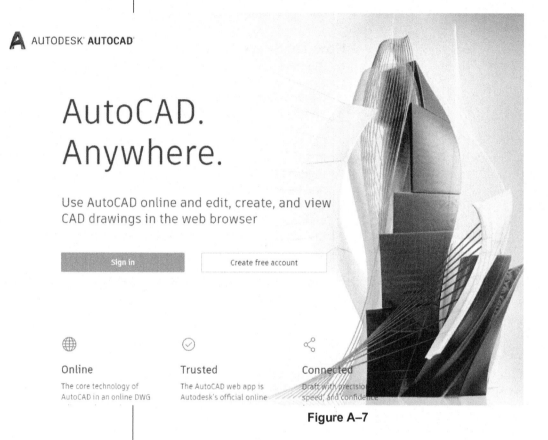

Figure A–7

It is the same account that you sign in to while starting the AutoCAD software.

How To: Open Drawing in AutoCAD Web App

1. Click on the link that was sent to you or click **Preview** in the Share a link to this drawing dialog box.
2. The AutoCAD web app screen displays (as shown in Figure A–7 above). Sign in to the AutoCAD web app by signing in to your free Autodesk account.

3. It opens the shared drawing in the Autodesk AutoCAD web app, as shown in Figure A–8.
   - Note that the Interface color has been changed to **Light** in

     ![settings gear icon] (Settings)>Preferences>Theme.

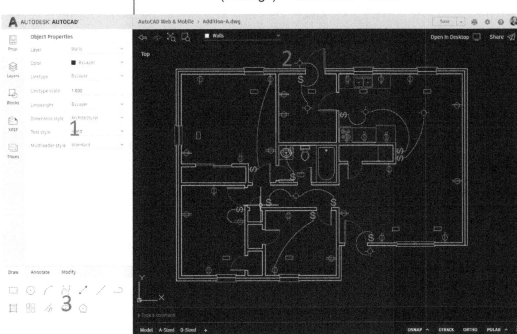

Figure A–8

AutoCAD Web App Interface

The Autodesk AutoCAD web app opens the temporary view link in a browser on your desktop. This enables you to share the drawing with stakeholders who do not have the AutoCAD software, without having to email files back and forth or install other viewing software. Using any internet browser software, they can review and mark up the design for better communication. Figure A–8 shows the Autodesk AutoCAD web app interface.

1. Palettes Bar

Multiple palettes are available to help analyze and review the drawing. Palettes include:

- **Properties**: Lists the properties of the currently selected object in the active view, as shown in Figure A–9. Properties can include color, layer, linetype, material, length, and more.

- **Layers**: Lists all layers in the Share Drawing.

- **Blocks**: Lists all blocks in the Share Drawing.

- **XREF**: Lists all XREF files in the Share Drawing.

- **Traces**: Allows reviewer to add overlay markups onto the drawing to share with the drafter.

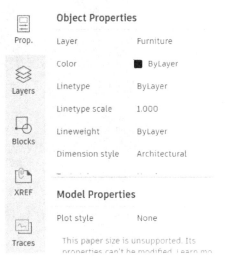

Figure A–9

2. Active View

The active view displays the model or sheet shared from AutoCAD. In the upper left corner of the active view, you have access to the **Undo**, **Redo**, **Zoom Extents**, and **Zoom Window** tools (shown in Figure A–10) to help you quickly work with the active view. It also displays the layers list, where you can select a layer to make it current.

Figure A–10

3. Toolbar

There are various tools provided in the AutoCAD web app that enable you to make minor modifications and add markups to the drawing, which helps to better communicate your input with other team members. The tools are grouped in three tabs: *Draw, Annotate,* and *Modify.*

- **Draw Tab**: The *Draw* tab contains tools (as shown in Figure A–11) for adding new information to the design. It includes typical AutoCAD draw tools, such as line, polyline, rectangle, circle, arc, spline, hatch, array, ellipse, polygon, and divide. The Draw tools can also be used with the Trace overlay function.

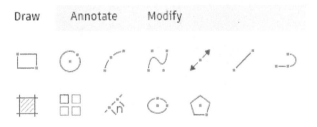

Figure A–11

- **Annotate Tab**: The *Annotate* tab contains tools (as shown in Figure A–12) for measuring existing content in the drawing. It also contains the Revcloud tool for adding markups to areas that require change. In addition, the tab contains tools for adding dimensions, text, and multileaders to tag notations in the drawing.

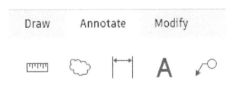

Figure A–12

- **Modify Tab**: The *Modify* tab contains tools (as shown in Figure A–13) for modifying the drawing. The tab contains the basic AutoCAD modification tools, such as move, copy, erase, rotate, scale, chamfer, trim, extend, and others.

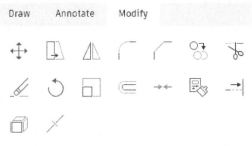

Figure A–13

Settings

You can set various drawing settings using the ⚙ (Settings) in the upper right corner of the AutoCAD web app screen. Clicking

⚙ (Settings) opens the Settings dialog box, where you can set the Preferences, such as setting the **Light** or **Dark Theme** for the Palettes area; select the **Object snaps** to be used (as shown in Figure A–14); and set the **Units** to be used in the drawing. Click **Done** once you have the required settings in place.

Settings

Preferences		
	☑ Endpoint	☐ Apparent Intersection
Tracking	☐ Midpoint	☑ Extension
Object Snap	☑ Intersection	
Units	☐ Geometric Center	☐ Tangent
Navigation	☑ Center	☐ Quadrant
	☐ Perpendicular	☐ Parallel
	☐ Node	☐ Insertion
	☐ Nearest	

Done

Figure A–14

Open in Desktop

Once all the feedback and the markups have been applied to the shared drawing, save the drawing in the AutoCAD web app. Open the shared drawing in the AutoCAD desktop software to review the feedback and make changes are required. In the

AutoCAD web app, click **Open in Desktop** 🖥. It opens the active drawing in the AutoCAD desktop software along with all the feedback and markups, as shown in Figure A–15. You can review the feedback and make the modifications to the drawing, as required.

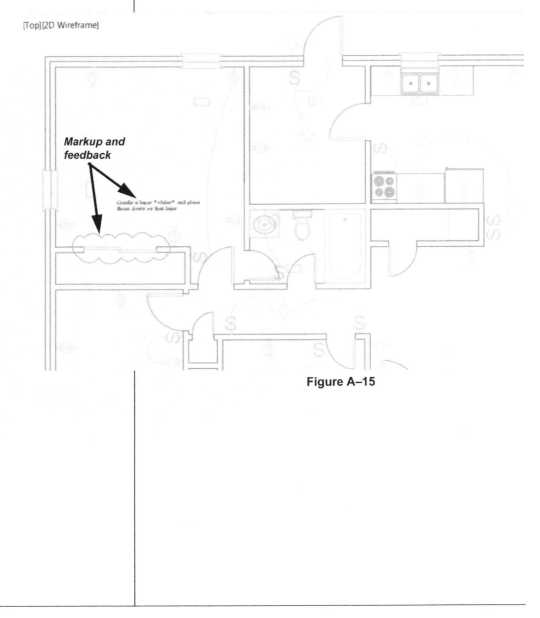

Figure A–15

Practice A1 | Shared Drawings

Practice Objectives

- Create a shared drawing and inspect it in the Autodesk AutoCAD web app.
- Mark up and modify some objects in the shared drawing.

In this practice, you will share a drawing and inspect it in the Autodesk AutoCAD web app. You will also make some markups and modify some objects in the drawing, as shown in Figure A–16.

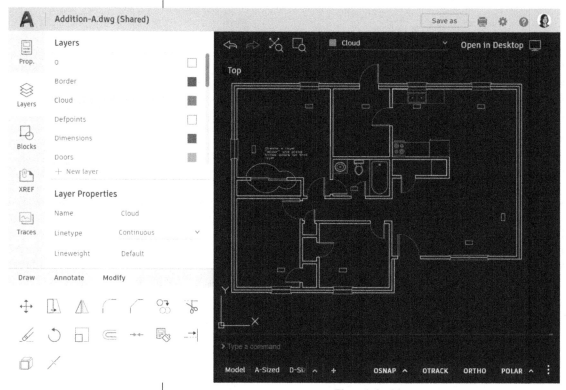

Figure A–16

Task 1 - Create a shared drawing.

1. Open **Addition-A.dwg** from your practice files folder.

2. In the Quick Access Toolbar or in the *Collaborate* tab>Share panel, click 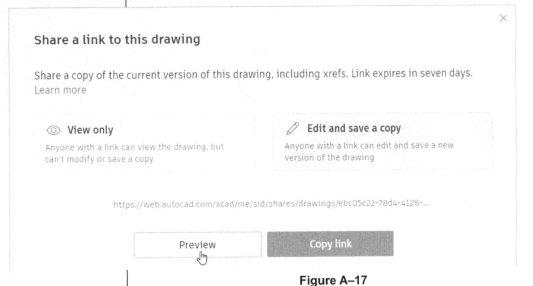 (Share Drawing).

3. In the Share a link to this drawing dialog box, select **Edit and save a copy** (as shown in Figure A–17). Note that a link is created.

4. Select **Preview** to open the link directly in the Autodesk AutoCAD web app.

You can select Copy link and send it to a recipient that you want to share the link with.

Share a link to this drawing

Share a copy of the current version of this drawing, including xrefs. Link expires in seven days. Learn more

◎ **View only**
Anyone with a link can view the drawing, but can't modify or save a copy

✎ **Edit and save a copy**
Anyone with a link can edit and save a new version of the drawing

https://web.autocad.com/acad/me/sid/shares/drawings/ebc05c22-78d4-4128-...

Preview   Copy link

Figure A–17

If you are already signed in to the web app, you might not get the Sign in screen.

5. The AutoCAD web app screen displays. Sign in to the AutoCAD web app by signing in to your free Autodesk account.

6. The shared drawing opens in the Autodesk AutoCAD web app, as shown in Figure A–18. Close the *Fonts are displayed as Simplex.shx* information box.

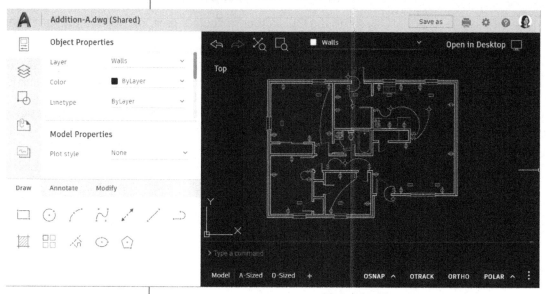

Figure A–18

Task 2 - Set the units and object snaps.

1. In the upper right corner of the AutoCAD web app screen, click ⚙ (Settings) to open the Settings dialog box.

2. Select **Units** and change the *Linear Format* to **Architectural** and *Precision* to **0'-0 1/8"**, as shown in Figure A–19.

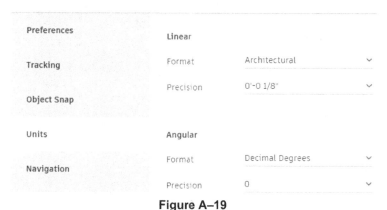

Figure A–19

3. In the Settings dialog box, select **Object Snap** and verify that the **Endpoint** object snap is selected.

4. Click **Done** to close the dialog box.

Task 3 - Measure objects.

1. In the toolbars area, in the *Annotate* tab, click 🖚 (Measure).

2. In the Measure Command line, select **Distance**, as shown in Figure A–20.

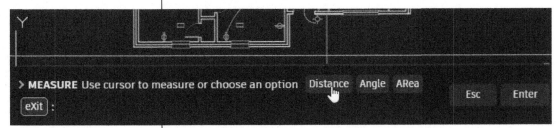

Figure A–20

3. Click a few different points to measure various rooms and objects to get an idea of how they relate to one another.

4. Click the points similar to that shown in Figure A–21. Press <Esc> to exit the command.

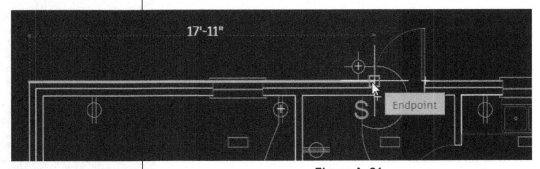

Figure A–21

Task 4 - Analyze the model using palettes.

1. In the Palettes bar, click 🗇 (Layers).

2. In the Layers palette, toggle off the layer **Electrical**, as shown in Figure A–22. Note that all the electrical elements are not displayed in the drawing.

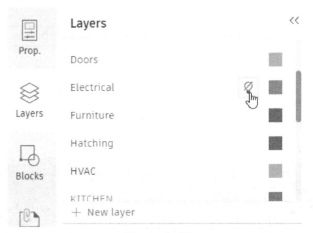

Figure A–22

3. In the Palettes bar, click 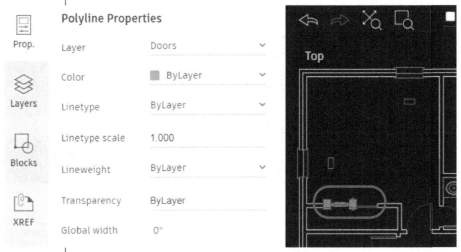 (Properties).

4. In the drawing window, click on one of the sliding doors of a closet, as shown in Figure A–23. Review its properties, and then press <ESC> to exit the selection.

Figure A–23

Task 5 - Create a markup.

1. In the Palettes bar, click ⬙ (Layers).

2. Below the Layers list, select **New Layer.** Change the name to **Cloud**. Select its color block and select the color **Magenta**, as shown in Figure A–24.

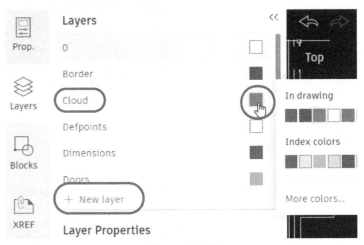

Figure A–24

To make a layer current, you can also select it directly in the Layer list.

3. Select the layer Cloud to make it current. Note that it is displayed in the Layer list near the top of the drawing window, as shown in Figure A–25.

Figure A–25

4. In the drawing window, zoom in to the area of the closet with sliding doors.

5. In the toolbars area, in the *Annotate* tab, click

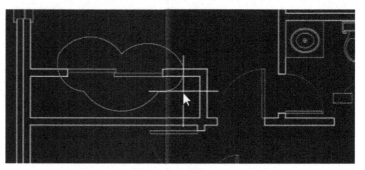 (Revcloud). Click and drag to place a cloud around the sliding doors, as shown in Figure A–26.

Figure A–26

6. In the toolbars area, in the *Annotate* tab, click **A** (Mtext).

7. In the drawing window, click two points near the cloud to create a text box. For the *height*, enter a value of **3.0** and, in the text box, enter the text **Create a layer "slider" and place those doors on that layer**, as shown in Figure A–27. Click

✓ to place the text.

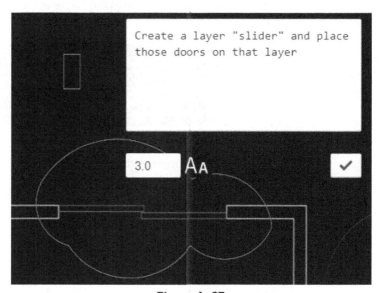

Figure A–27

Task 6 - Modify the drawing.

1. In the upper right corner of the AutoCAD web app screen, click ⚙ (Settings) to open the Settings dialog box.

2. Select **Object Snap** and select the **Midpoint** object snap, as shown in Figure A–28.

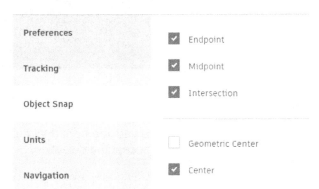

Figure A–28

3. Click **Done** to close the Settings dialog box.

4. Zoom in to the lower right corner of the living room (the room with the kitchen), as shown in Figure A–29. Note the two HVAC ducts near the window.

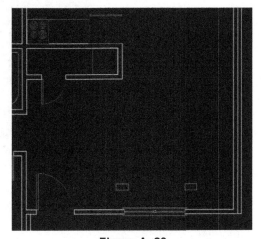

Figure A–29

5. In the toolbars area, in the *Modify* tab, click ⤢ (Move).

6. Select the left duct near the window. Press <Enter> to accept the selection.

7. Select the midpoint as the basepoint and move it straight to the right along the midpoint of the window, as shown in Figure A–30.

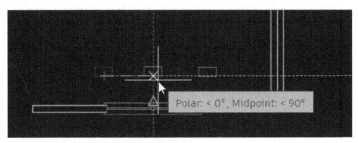

Figure A–30

8. In the toolbars area, in the *Modify* tab, click ↺ (Rotate).

9. Select the right duct near the window. Press <Enter> to accept the selection.

10. Using the lower right corner as the basepoint, rotate it 90° so that it is vertically oriented.

11. Using ✛ (Move), move it along the right wall, similar to that shown in Figure A–31.

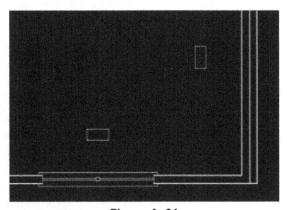

Figure A–31

You will continue working in the AutoCAD web app for the next practice.

12. Keep the shared drawing open in the Autodesk AutoCAD web app.

13. In your AutoCAD desktop software, close the Share a link to this drawing dialog box, then close Addition-A.dwg without saving.

A.3 Trace

Trace provides a safe space to add changes to a drawing in the web and mobile apps without altering the existing drawing. Trace behaves like using a tracing paper on top of an existing drawing to collaborate new ideas, plans, and feedback.

Traces are created in the web and mobile app interface, and then the drawing is shared with other collaborators on the team. They can review the trace changes and feedback in the desktop version of AutoCAD and make the requested changes there. In the web and mobile apps, you can use all the regular Draw, Annotate, and Modify tools that you used to add feedback and changes to shared drawing. The only difference is that the feedback that you add while in the Trace is associated with Trace only.

How To: Create a Trace

1. In the Autodesk AutoCAD web app, in the Palettes bar, click
    (Traces).
2. If this is your first time using this command, there is no trace available in the list. Click **New Trace**.
3. A trace overlay (light shading) window is added on top of the drawing, and information about the Trace is displayed in the Trace panel, as shown in Figure A–32.

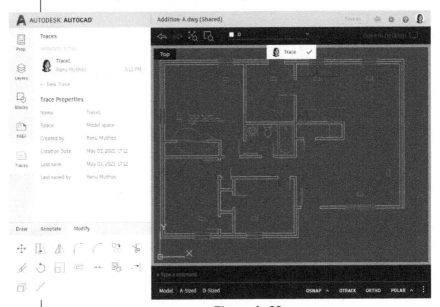

Figure A–32

4. Add your trace markups and modifications using the tools in the Draw, Annotate, and Modify toolbars.

5. After adding your changes, click ✓ in the

   🧑 Trace ✓ Trace bar near the top of the trace window. The trace window is closed along with all the trace markups.

• In this mode, you can add multiple Draw and Annotate items that will only exist in the current Trace overlay.

• Multiple separate Traces can be created in various areas of the drawing to show various updates to the drawing, as shown in Figure A–33.

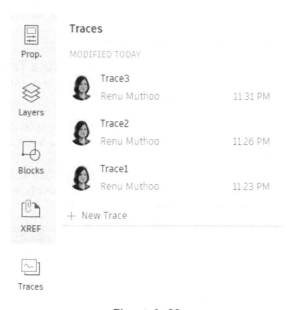

Figure A–33

Trace Mode

Once the Traces are created in the web and mobile app, save them and then you can open the shared drawing (where the traces are saved) in the AutoCAD desktop software to review the feedback and make changes are required.

• In the AutoCAD web app, click **Open in Desktop** 🖥️. It opens the active drawing in the AutoCAD desktop software. The drawing opens without the traces being displayed in the drawing window.

- A list of all the available Traces in that drawing are displayed in the Traces palette, as shown in Figure A–34. In the *Collaborate* tab>Traces panel, click 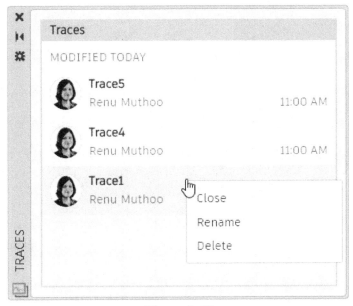 (Traces Palette) to display the Traces palette.

- In the Traces palette, you can right-click on a trace and **Rename** it to better indicate what the trace is about. When you have completed incorporating the changes requested, right-click on the trace and select **Delete** to remove it from the list.

Figure A–34

- In the Traces palette, select the trace you want to open. The drawing displays in Trace mode, with the trace overlay (light shading) and the associated trace feedback and markups added on top of the drawing, as shown in Figure A–35.

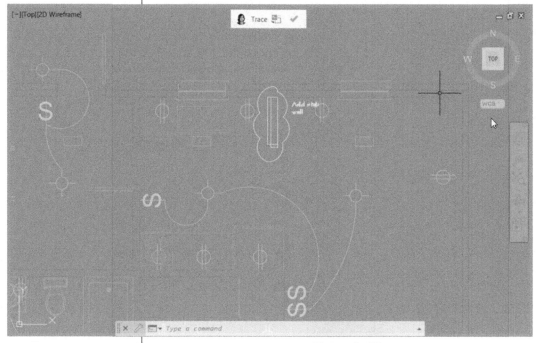

Figure A–35

- In the Trace toolbar, click ⬛ to make the drawing geometry switch to the front, and you can review the location of the trace markup with respect to the drawing geometry.

- You can use the system variable **TRACEFADECTL** to change the fade of the Trace overlay. Increasing the value makes the fade more prominent whereas reducing the value of the variable makes the fade lighter.

Practice A2

Create Trace in Share Drawing

Practice Objectives

- Create an overlay trace.
- Mark up the shared drawing using the Trace tool.

In this practice, you will use a shared drawing and create an overlay **Trace**. You will use the **Trace** tool within the Autodesk AutoCAD web app to make multiple markups, as shown in Figure A–36. Finally, you will display the shared drawing trace markups in the AutoCAD software where you can respond to any changes from the Trace.

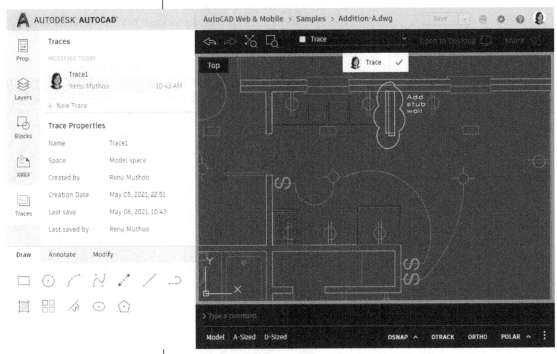

Figure A–36

Task 1 - Create a Trace overlay.

You have the shared drawing (**Addition-A.dwg**) already open in the Autodesk AutoCAD web app. Note that there are markups already added to the drawing from *Practice A1 Shared Drawings*.

1. In the Autodesk AutoCAD web app, in the Palettes bar, click (Layers).

2. Below the Layers list, select **New Layer**. Change the name to **Trace**. Select its color block and select the color **Yellow.**

3. Zoom in to the area of the kitchen.

4. In the Palettes bar, click 🔲 (Traces).

5. If this is your first time using this command, there is no trace available in the list. Click **New Trace**.

6. Your drawing window displays in the Trace mode with a trace overlay (light shading) window added on top of the drawing, and a new trace with its information displayed in the Trace panel, as shown in Figure A–37.

Figure A–37

Task 2 - Add trace markups.

1. Near the top of the drawing window, expand the Layers drop-down list and select the layer **Trace** to make it the current layer, as shown in Figure A–38.

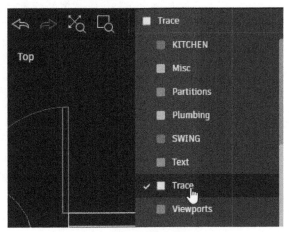

Figure A–38

2. In the toolbars area, in the *Annotate* tab, click ⊞ (Measure).

3. In the Measure Command line, select **Distance**, as shown in Figure A–39.

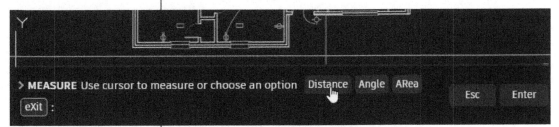

Figure A–39

4. Measure and note the length of the wall along the left side of the sink kitchen counter, as shown in Figure A–40.

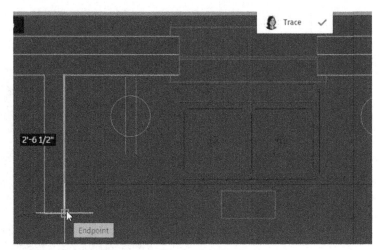

Figure A–40

5. Similarly, measure and note the width of this wall.

6. In the toolbars area, in the *Draw* tab, click (Rectangle).

7. Along the right side of the sink kitchen counter, draw a rectangle of width and length that were noted for the left side wall (**4-1/2"** and **2'-6-1/2"**; enter the width value and then use <Tab> to enter the length value), as shown in Figure A–41.

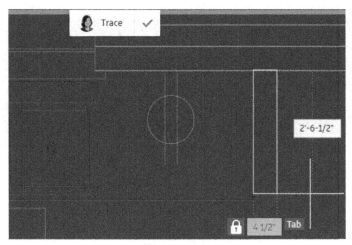

Figure A–41

8. In the toolbars area, in the *Annotate* tab, click  (Revcloud).

9. In the Command line, select the **Rectangular** option.

10. Click and drag to place a cloud around the stub wall, as shown in Figure A–42.

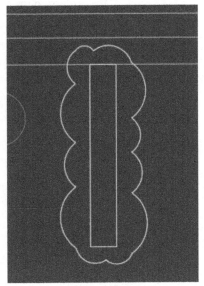

Figure A–42

11. In the toolbars area, in the *Annotate* tab, click A (Mtext).

12. In the drawing window, click two points near the cloud to create a text box. For the *height,* enter a value of **3** and, in the text box, enter the text **Add stub wall,** as shown in

   Figure A–43. Click ✓ to place the text.

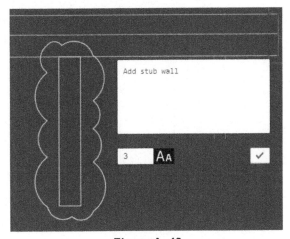

Figure A–43

13. In the toolbars area, in the *Annotate* tab, click

(Dimension).

14. Add the dimensions as shown in Figure A–44.

Figure A–44

15. Click ✓ in the 🧑 Trace ✓ Trace bar near the top of the trace window. Note that you are not in Trace mode and all the trace markups are not displayed. Your trace is saved as **Trace1** and listed in the Traces palette, as shown in Figure A–45.

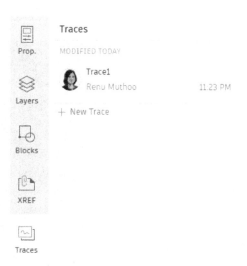

Figure A–45

16. In the Traces palette, click on **Trace1** in the list. Note that you are in the Trace mode with your trace markups displayed in the drawing window.

17. Click 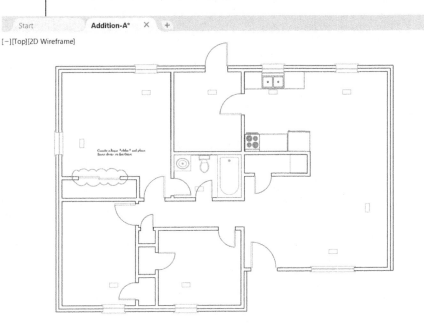 to exit Trace mode.

18. In the upper right corner of the AutoCAD web app window, click Save as .

19. In the Save As dialog box, create a new folder and save **Addition-A** on the cloud.

Task 3 - Review the trace in the AutoCAD desktop software.

1. In your AutoCAD desktop software, in the Quick Access Toolbar, click (Open from Web & Mobile).

2. Open **Addition-A.dwg** from the cloud, as shown in Figure A–46. Note that the changes/markups that were created in the shared drawing (magenta cloud and text and rotated ducts) are displayed.

Figure A–46

3. In the *Collaborate* tab>Traces panel, click 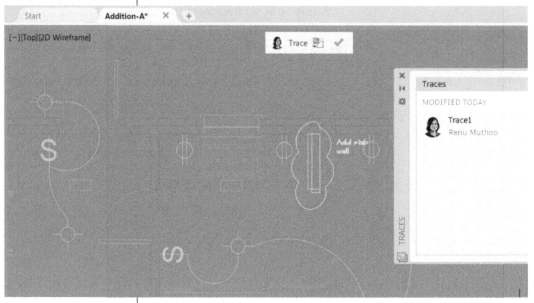 (Traces Palette). It opens the Traces palette with **Trace1** displayed in the list.

4. In the Traces palette, click on **Trace1** and note that the drawing window is in Trace mode, with the Trace displayed (yellow color markups), as shown in Figure A–47.

Note that the background color of the drawing window is changed to gray for yellow markups to become visible.

Figure A–47

5. Review the markup that asks you to add the stub wall. Also zoom in and check the dimensions and note them down.

6. In the Trace toolbar, click 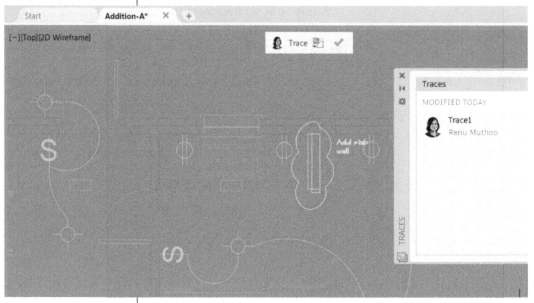 to make the drawing geometry switch to front (as shown in Figure A–48) to check clearly the location to draw this stub wall.

7. At the Command line, enter **TRACEFADECTL** system variable and reduce the fade to **10** to see the drawing geometry more clearly (as shown in Figure A–48).

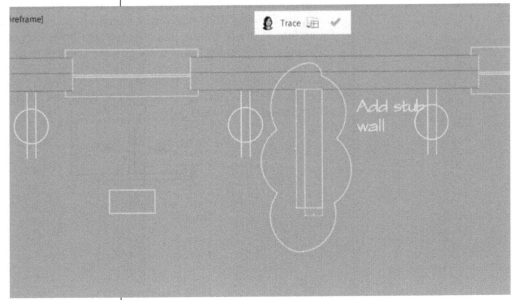

Figure A–48

8. Once done reviewing, in the Trace toolbar, click ✔ (Close Trace).

9. Save and close the drawing.

A.4 Save to Web and Mobile

As cloud services continue to improve, the ability to communicate plan changes increases. Saving files to the cloud using the **Save to Web & Mobile** command enables you to open those files in the field from any internet-connected device. This enables anyone to review and edit the models from any location.

- You can open files that have been saved to your mobile device and review the comments and red-lines applied there, as shown in Figure A–49.

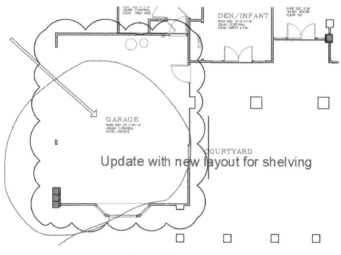

Figure A–49

How To: Save to Web and Mobile

1. In AutoCAD, in the Quick Access Toolbar, click (Save to Web & Mobile).
2. In the Save to AutoCAD Web & Mobile dialog box (shown in Figure A–50), navigate to the folder where you want to save the file, and then click **Save**.

Figure A–50

How To: Open a File Modified on Web and Mobile

1. In AutoCAD, in the Quick Access Toolbar, click ⬚ (Open from Web & Mobile).
2. In the Open from AutoCAD Web & Mobile dialog box, navigate to the folder where the file you want to open is located and select it.
3. Click **Open**

Open on a Mobile Device

The AutoCAD mobile apps enable you to create accurate lines or shapes and add markups to models to better communicate with others working on the project. The AutoCAD - DWG Viewer & Editor mobile app can be installed on most Apple or Android devices.

The following figures are shown on a iPhone. The Android and iOS applications may vary.

How To: Review a Drawing in AutoCAD Mobile

1. On your mobile device, open the AutoCAD - DWG Viewer & Editor app.
2. Sign in to your Autodesk account, as required.
3. Navigate to the folder location to display the list of drawings available in your account, as shown in Figure A–51.
4. Click on a drawing name to open the drawing, as shown in Figure A–52.

Figure A–51

Figure A–52

Creating Markups

The tools for creating markups vary according to the app you are using, but they generally follow the same basic layout as shown using an iPhone in Figure A–53.

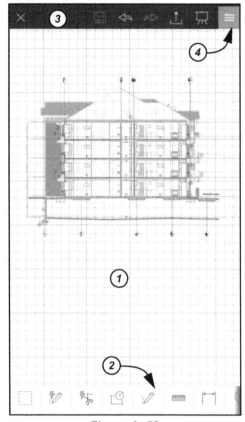

Figure A–53

1. Active View

This is the area where you can view and manipulate the model.

2. Toolbar

At the bottom of the screen, you can access tools to select, annotate, and measure objects in the drawing. The exact choices vary according to the mobile app you are using.

3. Quick Access Toolbar

Includes tools for saving the drawing (if it is not automatically saved), Undo/Redo, export, and clean screen.

4. Palettes

Click  to access the palettes for Layers, Views, Properties, Blocks, the External References Manager, and Drawing Settings, as shown in Figure A–54.

Layers

2D, 3D Wireframe, and 3D Solid options are not available on iOS

Views (iOS)

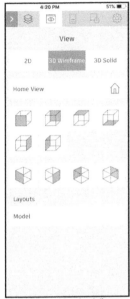

View (Android)

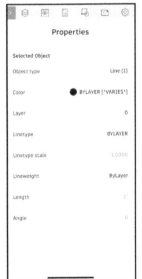

Properties

Blocks

External References Manager

Drawing Settings

Figure A–54

Navigate the Model on a Mobile App

Navigating AutoCAD models on a mobile device is very intuitive. A combination of gesture-based and on-screen tools enable you to pan and zoom models with ease. Navigation commands include the following:

Gesture / Icon	Command	Description
	Zoom in	• Start with fingers close together, then spread them apart.
	Zoom out	• Start with fingers apart, then pinch them together.
	Pan	• Swipe two fingers across screen. (If you are in a 2D view, using one finger to swipe works.)
	Orbit	• Swipe the screen with a single finger (3D views only - available on Android app only).

A.5 Rendering in the Cloud

In the 3D Modeling workspace, the *Visualize* tab>Render panel provides options that enable you to render drawings in the cloud while you continue to work on other drawings. To render up to four drawing views at a time and using Cloud space to process your work, click (Render in Cloud). In the Autodesk Rendering dialog box, you can select the model views that you want to render in the cloud, as shown in Figure A–55. You are prompted in the software when the renderings are complete and you can also be notified by email.

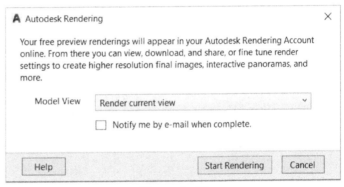

Figure A–55

- To browse your online render gallery, in the *Visualize* tab> Render panel, click (Render Gallery).

Practice A3

Working in the Cloud

Practice Objectives

- Render a drawing without using your computer's processor by using the Render in the Cloud command.
- Upload drawings and other files to A360 to easily share them with others.

In this practice, you will upload drawings to A360 and render a view in the cloud while continuing to work on your computer. A working internet connection is required.

Task 1 - Render in the cloud.

1. In the InfoCenter, select **Sign In to Autodesk Account** and enter your Autodesk ID and password in the Sign In dialog box, as shown in Figure A–56.

    - If you do not have an Autodesk ID, select **Create Account** and create one.

Figure A–56

2. Open **Kitchen-Materials.dwg** from the practice files folder.

3. Change to the **3D Modeling** workspace.

4. In the *Visualize* tab>Named Views panel, select the **Dining Area** view.

*If you get a message about the images not being loaded, select **Install the Medium Images Library**.*

5. In the *Visualize* tab>Render panel, set *Render Preset* to **High**, as shown in Figure A–57.

Render to Size

Figure A–57

6. Save the drawing.

7. In the *Visualize* tab>Render panel, click 🫖 (Render in Cloud).

*If the Render Online - Save Changes warning box opens, click **OK** to save the drawing.*

8. In the Autodesk Rendering dialog box, expand the Model View drop-down list and select **Render current view**. Clear the **Notify me by e-mail when complete** option and click **Start Rendering**.

9. The rendering is processed in the background as you work. You can check the status of the rendering by expanding your Autodesk Account name in the InfoCenter. If the drawing is still being rendered, **Rendering in Progress** displays at the bottom of the drop-down list, as shown in Figure A–58. A rotating circle is also displayed next to your name.

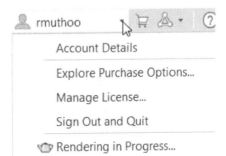

Figure A–58

10. Once the rendering is finished, expand the drop-down list and select **View Completed Rendering**.

11. The default browser will open to the Autodesk Rendering site>*My Renderings* tab.

12. Hover the cursor over the thumbnail of the rendering and click **View Project** to see the full rendering, as shown in Figure A–59.

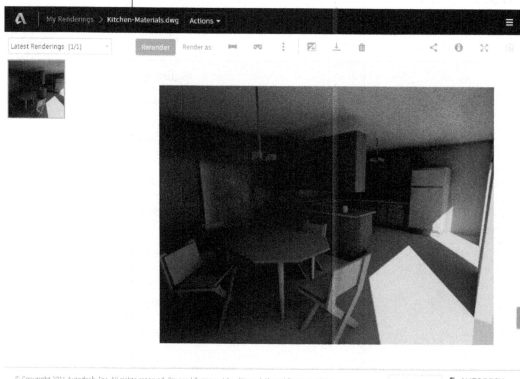

Figure A–59

13. Close the browser.

Task 2 - Save to web and mobile.

1. In the Quick Access Toolbar, click (Save to Web & Mobile).

2. In the Save to AutoCAD Web & Mobile dialog box, double-click on the folder where you want to save the file and type **Kitchen-Materials** for the file name. Click **Save**.

3. Close the drawing.

4. Open AutoCAD on your mobile device and log in to your Autodesk Account.

5. Open **Kitchen-Materials.dwg** by tapping on it in the list of drawings.

This figure is shown on an iPad.

6. The drawing opens, as shown in Figure A–60.

Figure A–60

7. Expand the Palettes area and click  (Layers) to display the list of layers.

8. Toggle off **CEILING_DINING** and **CEILING_KITCHEN**.

9. In the *Palettes* area, click (View) to open the View palette.

Note: Steps 10 to 12 can only be completed using the Android version of the app.

10. In the View palette, tap **3D Solid**.

11. Close the palette if needed and then use your finger to orbit around the model, as shown in Figure A–61.

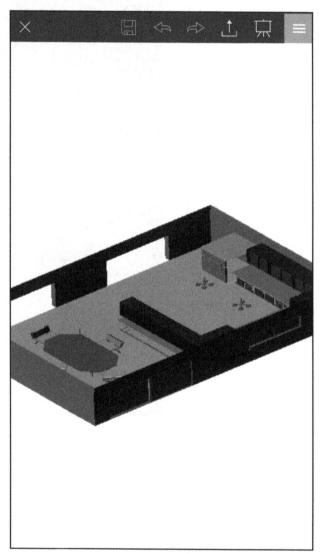

Figure A–61

12. If you have time, return to a 2D view and add some markups to the file.

13. Close the mobile app.

A.6 Attach Navisworks Files

The Navisworks software enables architecture, engineering, and construction professionals to integrate models from multiple software origins. Integrating models into one model ensures better communication to resolve conflicts, coordinate disciplines, and plan projects before construction begins. The AutoCAD software now has the capability to attach Navisworks (NWD or NWC) files for project coordination purposes. The **2D Endpoint** and **Center** object snap commands work on coordination models. The same tools used to attach external reference files are used to attach Navisworks files.

> **Hint: Supported Systems**
>
> Navisworks files can only be attached using 64-bit systems with hardware acceleration toggled on.

How To: Attach Navisworks Files

1. Open the External Reference palette. Expand the Attach drop-down list and select **Attach Coordination Model**, as shown in Figure A–62.

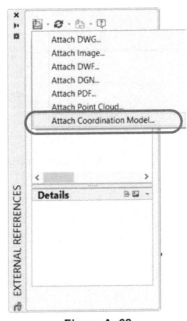

Figure A–62

Alternatively, in the *Insert* tab>Reference panel, click (Attach).

2. In the Select Reference File dialog box, in the Files of type drop-down list, select **Navisworks files**, as shown in Figure A–63.

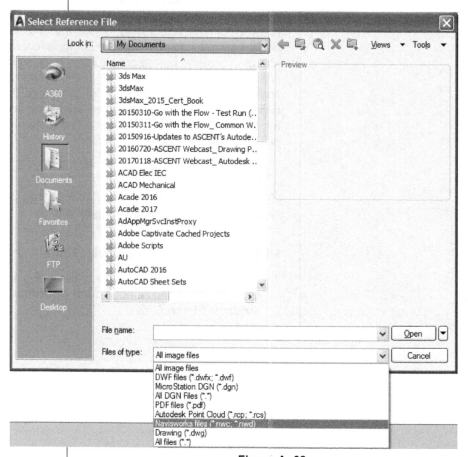

Figure A–63

3. Select the required file and click **Open**.

4. In the Attach Coordination Model dialog box (shown in Figure A–64), set the following:

- *Path type*
- *Insertion point*
- *Scale*
- *Rotation*
- *Display options*

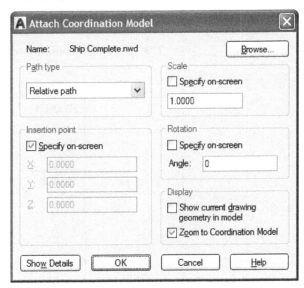

Figure A–64

5. Click **OK** to attach the file and complete the command.

> **Hint: Avoid Geometry Duplication**
>
> If the active drawing is part of the Navisworks model, you can hide that part of the model during the attach process. Simply uncheck the option **Show current drawing geometry in model** in the Attach Coordination Model dialog box.

Coordination Model Contextual Tab

The *Coordination Model* contextual tab provides a number of tools to help you navigate and correctly display any attached Navisworks models, as shown in Figure A–65.

Figure A–65

The tools are described as follows:

Button	Command	Description
	3D Orbit	Orbits the view around a 3D model.
	3D Swivel	Simulates the effect of turning a camera to change the view.
	3D Walk	Changes the 3D view interactively to create the appearance of walking through the model. Use the following keys to help you navigate: • W (forward) • A (left) • S (back) • D (right) OR Use the mouse to specify the view direction.
	Color Fading	Controls the amount of black blended geometry and attached coordination models.
	Opacity Fading	Controls the amount of dimming through transparency.
	Perspective	Changes the active view from an orthogonal view to a perspective view.

Practice A4 | Attach a Navisworks File

Practice Objective

- Attach an Autodesk Navisworks file.

In this practice, you will attach and view an Autodesk Navisworks model to an AutoCAD drawing file. Figure A–66 shows the completed practice.

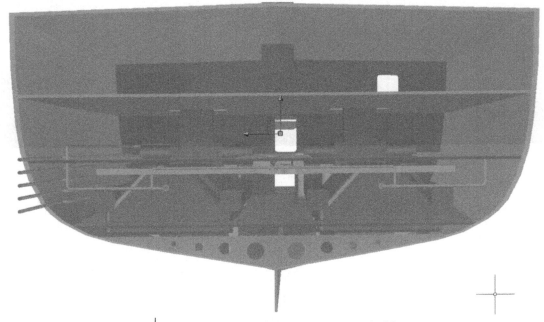

Figure A–66

Task 1 - Attach a Navisworks file.

1. Start a new drawing file from the default AutoCAD template.

2. In the *Insert* tab>Reference panel, click (Attach).

3. In the Select Reference File dialog box, select **Navisworks files** from the Files of type drop-down list, as shown in Figure A–67.

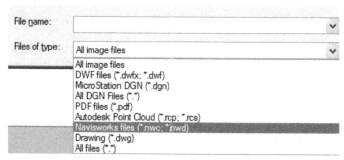

Figure A–67

4. Select **Ship Complete.nwd** from the practice files folder and click **Open**.

5. In the Attach Coordination Model dialog box, accept all the defaults, as shown in Figure A–68.

Figure A–68

6. Click **OK** to attach the file

7. For the insertion point, type **0,0,0** and click <Enter> to complete the command.

Task 2 - View the coordination model.

*If the background of the Drawing window for **3D parallel projection** is a dark color, change it to white in the Options dialog box>Display tab>**Colors**.*

1. In the drawing space, select the attached coordination model.

2. In the *Coordination Model* contextual tab>Display panel, click
   (3D Orbit).

3. In the model, click and drag a point with the cursor to view the model from other angles. Press <Esc> when done.

4. In the ViewCube, click **Back** to view the back side of the coordination model.

The model should be selected for the contextual tab to display.

5. In the *Coordination Model* contextual tab>Display panel, click
   (Perspective).

6. In the *Coordination Model* contextual tab>Display panel, click
   (3D Walk). Using the keyboard:

Press and hold a letter to see movement.

   - Press <W> to move forward.
   - Press <A> to move left.
   - Press <S> to move back.
   - Press <D> to move right.

7. Press <Esc> when done.

8. Close the file without saving.

Chapter Review Questions

1. How much storage space is provided by default in A360 when you create an account?

    a. 1 GB

    b. 10 GB

    c. 25 GB

    d. 250 GB

2. What does the **Stay Connected** menu ( ) enable you to access?

    a. Autodesk Account

    b. My computer

    c. Online Help

    d. Recent CAD files

3. You can save a file directly to the Cloud.

    a. True

    b. False

4. What limitations are important to consider when creating a Share Drawing? (Select all that apply.)

    a. The main drawing file and/or each individual referenced drawing file must be less than 50MB.

    b. The complete project files including all documents must be less than 200MB.

    c. There are no size restrictions.

    d. The sharer needs to save the original file at a different location to avoid unwanted modifications by the recipient.

5. In the AutoCAD web app interface, what are the three tabs where all the tools are grouped together?

    a. Draw, Insert, Manage

    b. Annotate, Modify, Manage

    c. Draw, Insert, Modify

    d. Draw, Annotate, Modify

6. Attaching a coordination model is supported on 32-bit systems.

   a. True

   b. False

Command Summary

Button	Command	Location
	3D Orbit	• **Ribbon:** *Coordination Model* contextual tab>Display panel
	3D Swivel	• **Ribbon:** *Coordination Model* contextual tab>Display panel
	3D Walk	• **Ribbon:** *Coordination Model* contextual tab>Display panel
	Attach	• **Ribbon:** *Insert* tab>Reference panel • **Palette:** External References
	Autodesk App Store	• **InfoCenter** • **Ribbon:** *Featured Apps* tab>Autodesk App Store panel
N/A	**Color Fading**	• **Ribbon:** *Coordination Model* contextual tab>Display panel
N/A	**Opacity Fading**	• **Ribbon:** *Coordination Model* contextual tab>Display panel
	Perspective	• **Ribbon:** *Coordination Model* contextual tab>Display panel
	Stay Connected	• **InfoCenter**

Mobile Commands

Button	Command	Location
	Orbit	• Gesture in model view
	Pan	• Gesture in model view
	Zoom in	• Gesture in model view
	Zoom out	• Gesture in model view

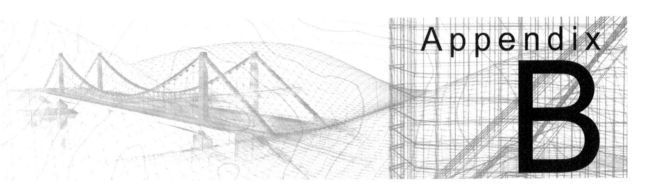

Skills Assessment

The following assessment has been provided to test your skills and understanding of the topics covered in this training guide. Select the best answer for each question.

1. Which of the following are annotation objects? (Select all that apply.)

    a. Multiline Text

    b. External References

    c. Tables

    d. Hatches

2. Text objects that automatically update in a drawing when the base information changes, such as a date or filename, are _____.

    a. Blocks

    b. Fields

    c. Dynamic Text

    d. Reference Text

3. If you add a new attribute to a block after it has been created, which command do you use to update the existing blocks in a drawing?

    a. **Update Block**

    b. **Edit Attributes**

    c. **Data Extraction**

    d. **Synchronize Attributes**

---

4. What command would you use to create a multi-sheet DWFx or PDF file that can be viewed in the Autodesk® Design Review software?

a. **Plot**

b. **Batch Plot/Publish**

c. **DWF Plot**

d. **3DDWF**

5. Which of the following components are parts of sheet sets? (Select all that apply.)

a. Views

b. Sheets

c. Properties

d. Model views

6. When you are setting up the CAD Standards tools in the AutoCAD software, what type of file do you create to hold the standards?

a. DWG

b. DWS

c. DWT

d. DWF

7. Which actions are available in the dynamic block shown in Figure B–1?

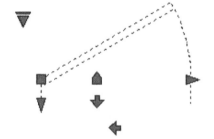

Figure B–1

a. Rotate, Align, Flip, and Stretch

b. Rotate, Flip, Move, and Stretch

c. List, Align, Flip, and Stretch

d. List, Flip, Move, and Rotate

8. Which of the following user interface objects can be customized in the CUI? (Select all that apply.)

   a. Toolbars

   b. Menus

   c. Ribbon Panels

   d. Keyboard Shortcuts

9. Which layer filter tool can be used to create a group of all the layers that are frozen in a drawing file?

   a. New Group Filter

   b. Isolate Group

   c. New Property Filter

   d. Invert Filter

10. You want to create a dynamic block that stretches in one direction. Which block authoring tools are required?

    a. **Stretch Action** only

    b. **Linear Parameter** only

    c. **Stretch Action** and **Linear Parameter**

    d. **Point Parameter** and **Polar Parameter**

11. Which command do you use to create hard copies of all of the sheets in a sheet set?

    a. **Batch Plot/Publish**

    b. **Options**

    c. **eTransmit**

    d. **Page Setup**

12. Plot Styles are used to _____.

    a. Save a plotter configuration.

    b. Control plotted properties of objects.

    c. Save the settings of a layout.

    d. Ensure uniform dimensions, text height, etc., in the plotted output.

13. When inserted as part of a block, some attributes can be visible while some are not. When do you specify the visibility of an attribute?

   a. At the time of inserting a block with attributes.

   b. When the attribute is created, before it is associated with a block.

   c. After the block has been inserted.

   d. The visibility of attributes cannot be controlled.

14. What is a Workspace?

   a. Defines the default file locations for your drawing files.

   b. Controls the arrangement of toolbars and palettes.

   c. Controls settings in a drawing.

   d. Sets up the default color scheme for the interface.

15. If a shared view seems to have the correct proportions but not the correct measurements, what can you do to fix it?

   a. Calibrate the measurements.

   b. Scale the shared view.

   c. Start the drawing from scratch.

   d. Set the correct units in the Setting dialog box.

16. How many drawings can be compared at the same time using the **DWG Compare** command?

   a. 1

   b. 2

   c. 3

   d. An infinite amount.

17. Only Android devices can open drawings shared to the web.

   a. True

   b. False

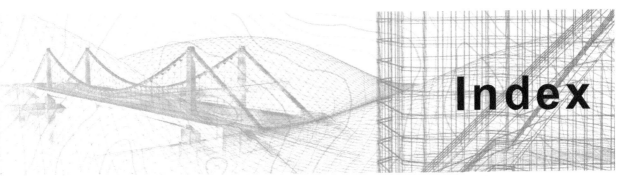

Index

Made in the USA
Coppell, TX
15 December 2021